THE WAR AGAINST THE GREENS

THE
WAR
AGAINST
THE
GREENS

The "Wise-Use" Movement, the New Right,
and the Browning of America

David Helvarg

JOHNSON BOOKS
AN IMPRINT OF BOWER HOUSE
DENVER

Cover Design by Margaret McCullough

Library of Congress Cataloging-in-Publication Data
Helvarg, David, 1951–
    The war against the greens: the "Wise-Use" movement, the New Right, and the browning of America / David Helvarg. – Rev. and updated.
        p. cm.
    ISBN 978-1-55566-328-5
1. Wise Use movement – United States. 2. Environmentalists – Untied States – Political activity. 3. Anti-environmentalism – United States 4. Right of property – United States I. Title.
GE197.H45 2004
333.72'0973–dc22

10 9 8 7 6 5 4 3 2

IN MEMORY OF:

My Parents,
Max Helvarg & Eva Lee, Refugees to Freedom

My Good Friends John Hoagland & Richard Cross,
Who Died in Other Wars

And My Life's Love, Nancy Ledansky,
Who Wondered about the Environmental Link to Breast Cancer

Contents

Preface

WHEN *The War Against the Greens* first appeared in the spring of 1994, there was a widespread media perception that the environmental movement had pretty much peaked with the mass rallies of Earth Day 1990, and that environmental regulation was now hurting the American economy.

Despite polls showing that 76 percent of Americans considered themselves green, the *New York Times* environmental reporter was promoting the Wise Use/Property Rights backlash as "the third wave" of environmentalism.

"I think that the [Wise Use] movement is maybe one of the most important and interesting movements to arise in environmentalism in a long time," he claimed, "because they are prying into the environmental issues that we've all grappled with for two decades. Is there really global warming? Is there really an ozone problem? Does toxic waste cleanup really represent the best use of public financing?" He went on to portray the anti-enviro backlash as a bottom-up citizen movement. "The Property Rights groups I know have no corporate funding at all. They're mom-and-pop community environmental groups," he claimed, and, because he was from the *New York Times*, other reporters believed him.

ABC's *Nightline* reported, "For a lot of people in this country, the environmental movement has gone too far. What's more, they're organizing into a powerful nationwide coalition (called Wise Use), and their battle cry is, 'The environmental movement has become an environmental disaster.'"

In going for the counterintuitive story of a citizen uprising against what then Texas pest exterminator—now House majority leader—Tom DeLay called "the jackbooted EPA Gestapo," the mainstream media failed to do their own investigative reporting. Rather they acted as a transmission belt for more conservative media outlets.

Following the Earth Day rallies of 1990 in which some twenty million Americans participated, a series of semihysterical stories and reports on "eco-terrorism" were issued by the Heritage Foundation, the *National Review*, *Human Events*, Rush Limbaugh, the *Washington Times*, and the right-wing editorial page of the *Wall Street Journal*. Their consistent theme was the threat posed by environmentalism and its "anti-human agenda." With the collapse of communism then taking place, the Republican Right and its captive media had, for the first time in forty-five years, lost a single unifying enemy to keep religious conservatives, gun advocates, antigovernment conspiracy buffs, and free-market advocates marching to the same beat. Replacing the red menace with the green menace and embracing a pro-industry backlash disguised as a citizen army seemed like sound strategy. Eventually the cachet that the Wise Use movement brought to this historic juncture would be folded into a larger "culture war" targeting not only "environmental extremists" but "feminazis"; gay rights; liberal Democrats; and, after 1992, all things associated with the name Clinton.

Shortly after my book came out, the Republican Party won a narrow off-year election victory, retaking the House of Representatives under the leadership of Georgia congressman Newt Gingrich. Interpreting their victory as a mandate for radical change, they began an effort to dismantle what they saw as the "New Deal regulatory state" established under Franklin Delano Roosevelt.

Although Gingrich's Contract with America never explicitly mentioned the environment, many of his followers had by then created a kind of white-sound feedback loop. They held public hearings at which industry fed them a stream of Wise Use mom-and-pop victims of environmental regulatory abuse, until they began to believe their own rhetoric. They assumed the public would now tolerate the dismantling of a generation of broadly popular environmental legislation. And so they were blindsided by the widespread public outrage over their attempts to gut the Clean Air, Clean Water, and Endangered Species Acts.

President Clinton was able to exploit their weakness in a series of showdowns with Gingrich leading to a partial government shutdown that the public blamed on Gingrich and which came to be symbolized by TV images of closed and padlocked gates at America's national parks.

My book, covering how public-lands industries and right-wing activists helped organize and covertly fund the often-violent backlash, was read by green activists, fellow reporters, and top decision-makers in the administration including President Clinton, the administrator of the Environmental Protection Agency, and the secretary of the interior. By the 1996 election, Vice President Al Gore was slamming Republicans for their ties to "extremist anti-environmental groups financed by large polluters."

Wise Use links to militia groups that I and other journalists documented before and after the deadly 1995 bombing of the federal building in Oklahoma City may also have contributed to the decline of Wise Use as its industry sponsors withdrew their support.

But by the turn of the century, Wise Use no longer needed to maintain an active constituency on the ground, since its rhetoric and ideology had been fully incorporated into the dominant wing of the Republican Party and their media cheerleaders on Fox News and talk radio.

Ten years after my book first came out I've seen some of the changes I predicted come true, including the emergence of a larger anti-green backlash linked to the fossil fuel industry, a backlash that has now been able to place one of its own in the Oval Office.

At the same time I've gone through some personal changes I could not have predicted. I moved from the California coast to Washington, D.C., where I've reported on the erosion of our democracy with the rise of a campaign finance system and special-interest culture that undermine the very spirit of public service. I've also been privileged to travel and report on climate change and eco-conflicts around the globe, from mud-hut barrios to tropical reefs to polar glaciers. I've conducted training sessions on environmental journalism and learned from brave and committed colleagues in Poland and the former Soviet bloc, Turkey, and the Middle East. In discussing journalistic ethics with them I often quote my late friend, *Newsweek* photographer John Hoagland, who was shot to death during the war in El Salvador. "There's no such thing as objectivity," he told me. "We all have a point of view. What I say is I won't be a propagandist for anyone. If you do something right, I'll take your picture. If you do something wrong, I'll take your picture also." Using John's example I've always strived to present an honest picture of reality in my reporting while also identifying my own point of view for the audience to evaluate and do with as it pleases.

I also got to write a book about my first love, the oceans. And in 2003, with support from consumer activist Ralph Nader and other good-hearted types, I decided to move from a thirty-year career in frontline journalism to a new one as a writer/activist and advocate for ocean protection.

I also lost a loving partner who remained my partner even when we thought we no longer were. Nancy Ledansky was a graphic artist, outdoorswoman, master photographer of nature, and irresistible natural force in her own right. She died of highly aggressive breast cancer in June 2002, aware, alert, and in control of her life until the end, which is how she wanted it. She was also no friend of the new crowd in Washington and urged me to update my reporting on the backlash even before I was approached by Johnson Books. So when Steve Topping, editor of this small but important western imprint, asked me to update my book, I was more than willing to oblige, despite the clarion demands of the everlasting sea.

I've cut out some dated and redundant chapters while updating much of the rest of the book. And despite all the documented tales of waste, fraud, and abuse you're about to read, I remain guardedly optimistic. While not underestimating the machinations of what President Teddy Roosevelt referred to as "the great special interests," I believe America's political class can still be reformed.

This belief is based in part on the reemergence of grassroots activism I've witnessed in the last several years as people both young and young in spirit rediscover the power and confidence that come from playing their part as active citizens of a democracy. Stolen elections, stateless terrorism, unilateral wars, climate change, and other challenges of the new century may at first seem too daunting for individuals to affect. But if small groups of individuals don't come together and begin the process, who will? I'm reminded of a long-ago night at the Rio Earth Summit, where I was reporting as thousands of social and environmental activists from across the city and the globe took to the streets. They loudly and joyfully marched behind a group of Buddhist monks with cell phones and a large banner that read, "When the people lead, the leaders will follow." I hope you find the following of use.

D. H.
January 2004

Acknowledgments

MANY PEOPLE HELPED make this book possible. I'm hoping that a significant number of them won't regret it. Although some may not agree with my analysis or conclusions, I appreciate the cooperation I received from the approximately five hundred people I interviewed over the course of a year. Less than a dozen people whom I asked refused to be interviewed—several for political reasons and about an equal number out of fear. A number of others would only speak off the record, although I generally tried to discourage this practice. I found that most people—including many anti-enviro activists—who were suspicious of the "liberal" and "preservationist" media—were nonetheless anxious to tell their sides of the various conflicts reported in this book. I have attempted not only to convey their statements and positions accurately but also to describe fairly the settings and contexts in which their stories unfolded.

Many journalists were willing to share with me tapes, articles, and information they had developed over long periods of time, disproving much of what is said about the cynical and cutthroat nature of our profession (at least the cutthroat part).

Several congressional staffers and government agency research officials in Washington proved both intelligent and instructive in helping me secure documents and figure out the byzantine pathways and the political bludgeons and barters by which various bills become the laws of our land. Given their disparate feelings about public recognition, I will keep my thanks to them generic.

While the FBI passed on several interview requests, other law enforcement professionals proved more than willing to take time out from their pursuits to share their knowledge, experience, and opinions with me.

If I've failed to acknowledge other people who were essential to the writing of this book, I hope their contributions are well reflected in the following pages. I salute the courage of some and remind others that it is a crime to use the U.S. postal system or telephonic communications for purposes of making a terrorist threat.

D. H.
January 2, 1997

First Encounters, 1990

"ARE YOU AN ENVIRONMENTALIST or do you work for a living?" reads the bumper sticker on the jacked-up four-by-four flatbed crawling down Main Street. With a plastic yellow ribbon flying from its radio antenna, it's one of a dozen pickups in a block-long procession going nowhere fast before making three-point turns at the end of town and heading back up Main Street toward the lumber mill. A couple of hometown patriots waving Old Glory and a portly family of five done up in yellow tee shirts, bill caps, and hair ribbons cheer from the sidewalk. A spirited young woman in a tank top and teased hair streaked an unnatural shade of yellow holds up a hand-printed sign reading "God Bless America."

You'd think Terry Anderson and the other American hostages still being held in Beirut had been freed or that U.S. troops were homebound from some CNN simulcast war. While the yellow ribbon, a symbol appropriated from a Tony Orlando and Dawn song about a felon returning home from prison, has come to be identified with people trapped in places they don't want to be, this is an entirely different use of the yellow cloth (or polypropylene, as the case may be). These ribbon wavers want to be right where they are, doing what they and theirs do best, which is cutting down trees and turning them into lumber for the Georgia-Pacific mill that blocks their view of the ocean right here in the small coastal town of Fort Bragg, California.

"Fuck you, faggots," shouts a high school kid with a buzz top as a van full of counterculture longhairs pulls into the empty dirt lot just north of the timber mill. Ben and Jerry's people are passing out free samples of Rainforest Crunch ice cream to some fifteen hundred demonstrators gathered here for an Earth First! "Redwood Summer" logging protest.

Across town, at Green Memorial Field, between a thousand and fifteen hundred people, many decked out in tee shirts reading "Timber Families

... An Endangered Species," are attending a community-solidarity rally organized by the anti-environmentalist Yellow Ribbon Coalition. Here they can buy beer, soda pop, hamburgers, or "fried spotted owl" (southern fried chicken, actually) at a dollar a body part. On nearby Harold Street, the airhorns of mammoth logging trucks bellow like cattle in the slaughter chute.

Between the two opposing rallies, 425 riot-clad police, sheriff's deputies, and highway patrolmen from throughout northern California keep a wary eye out for any trouble not of their own making.[1]

At the environmentalists' rally, speakers talk about preserving the state's last 5 percent of old-growth redwood, attack the timber corporations for cut-and-run logging (Louisiana Pacific has opened mills in Mexico and Venezuela while closing mills in California), play fair to middling acoustic music, and read some bad poetry.

At the Yellow Ribbon rally, the talk is of jobs and how those who work in the woods are best able to manage them sensibly. Congressman Doug Bosco, a Democrat who thinks he has a keen sense of the political wind drift, plays the crowd like a pro, smirking that the young enviros should go back where they came from, to New York or New Jersey, to clean up their own messes. "We need wood products, not another Woodstock," he thunders to enthusiastic applause. Bosco will go down to defeat at the next election, in large measure because he's alienated local environmental supporters, who see him as too close to the timber industry.

It's July 21, 1990, and I've driven north from San Francisco for four hours to cover these protests and any confrontation that might develop. Tension has been running high in Mendocino, Humboldt, and other northern counties for some time now as environmentalists move to protect California's ancient forest remnants and timber companies such as Georgia-Pacific, Louisiana Pacific, and Pacific Lumber—which has recently fallen into the hands of corporate raider Charles Hurwitz—respond by accelerating their timber cuts on public and private reserves well beyond what state foresters consider sustainable yield levels. There are competing initiatives on the upcoming November ballot (both will go down to defeat). The environmentalists' "Forests Forever" proposal would limit clear-cutting while allocating millions of dollars of state funds to buying up privately held redwood forests for parkland. The industry-backed "Californians for New Forestry—Global Warming

Initiative" would leave the timber companies free to operate as they have been. Supporters of this initiative justify its enviro-sounding title by arguing that since young trees absorb more carbon dioxide than "decadent" old trees, clear-cutting ancient redwood forests and replacing them with new tree farms will reduce global warming.

But the timber wars are not limited to ballot fights and protest marches. On May 24, 1990, organizer Judi Bari, the main force behind the Redwood Summer campaign, was maimed when a pipe bomb exploded below the driver's seat of her Subaru station wagon as she drove down a busy street in Oakland, California, with fellow Earth First! activist Daryl Cherney. They were driving through the Bay Area to recruit college students for these protests. Firefighters arriving on the scene had to use the Jaws of Life to cut the badly mutilated but still-conscious Bari from her crumpled car, where it had crashed into a guardrail in front of an elementary school. Cherney, who had been riding in the passenger seat, suffered injuries to one eye and his face. Within minutes, the FBI's domestic terrorism squad was on the scene, waving off the Alcohol, Tobacco and Firearms (ATF) agents who are normally responsible for investigating criminal bombings. Two months later, Bari, still in the hospital and recovering from her near-fatal injuries, faces FBI-inspired charges accusing her of knowingly transporting the pipe bomb.

Many of the Yellow Ribbon supporters in Fort Bragg, including some loggers who had been holding secret negotiations with Bari to try to prevent violence, believe the bomb was in fact hers, part of a terrorist plot aimed at their worksites, families, and communities. This belief is strongly reinforced when Hill and Knowlton, the PR firm hired by Pacific Lumber to counter the environmentalists, passes out photocopies of faked Earth First! flyers calling for violence during Redwood Summer, "to fuck up the workings of the Megamachine." (An internal memo later released as part of a lawsuit reveals that the timber company was aware that the flyers were probably fakes at the time that they were distributed to the media).[2]

At 2 P.M., Redwood Summer protestors begin marching down Main Street toward the front gate of the century-old lumber mill. By now several hundred angry men and teenage boys, spillovers from the solidarity rally, have gathered at the corner of Main and Redwood directly across from the gate. Some are slamming six-packs. Others have been drinking throughout the afternoon. One run-down fellow wears a tee shirt reading "Save a Logger, Eat an Owl."

"A lot of these guys are the same troublemakers we pick up every Saturday night," a local cop confides.

As they head toward the gate, the marchers, accompanied by motor-cycle and riot police, are heckled by a couple of leather-vested bikers. ("The only good tree is stumps" is an example of the bikers' poster prose.) As the first line of marchers, twelve across and filling the width of the street, approaches the corner of Main and Redwood, a throaty chorus of boos goes up from the sidewalk followed by a booming chant of "Go home! Go home!"

"We are home! We are home!" the protest crowd counterchants. As the marchers' sound truck comes to a halt in the middle of the intersec-tion, people start milling, unsure of what to do next. A line of the pro-testors carrying a fifty-foot-long banner reading "We support the timber workers, not the timber industry" try to attach their politically correct logo to G-P's padlocked security gate. Private guards hired by Georgia-Pacific videotape them from inside the yard. Fort Bragg po-lice chief Tom Bickle later confides that he had to talk G-P out of bring-ing in "goons from Georgia" to help out with crowd control.

"Trees grow back, trees grow back," the yellow-shirted crowd starts to chant.

A number of young men at the front of the crowd think this is a wussy chant. "Fuck you! Fuck you!" they shout, getting red in the face, flashing the bird at the enviros, and trying to psyche each other up to move out onto the street despite a riot cop's repeated warning for them to keep back. A second cop comes up beside the first. They give each other worried looks. A few more cops move in. A California Highway Patrol motorcycle officer drives slowly into position along the side-walk. There's some name-calling directed at the police. The officers push the Yellow Shirts back, holding their long riot batons in two-handed grips and thrusting them out at chest level. Before there's time for any of the local toughs to recover or regain their balance, a line of motorcycle cops, sirens wailing, rolls up the street cavalry fashion. They're followed by dozens of quick-stepping cops in blue jumpsuits and helmets who form a defensive line facing the Yellow Shirt crowd, riot sticks ready. Four men in the still-rowdy crowd are arrested, in-cluding one guy waving a billy club at the enviros. After that, nobody seriously challenges the cops' authority. A few moments later, a second line of CHP officers marches into position, turns to face the larger but more peaceable enviro crowd, and gradually opens up a corridor between the two opposing factions.

A woman climbs up on the sound truck and tries to address both crowds. "Lesbian, lesbian," come cries from the sidewalk as she begins to talk about the biosphere, one of those eco-buzzwords that seems to set off the pro-timber crowd.

The timber crowd begins another chorus of "trees grow back." Someone on the sound truck starts singing "America the Beautiful." As the environmentalists join in the chorus, the Yellow Shirt chant falters and fades into confused silence.

An Earth Firster gets on the mike and offers it to anyone who wants to speak from the other side. Despite some razzing from his friends, a young man of about nineteen with longish light brown hair peeking out from under his bill cap steps through the police lines. He climbs up onto the sound truck and looks around for a moment.

"We want to work. We don't want to go on welfare. And we don't need you people coming up here and telling us what to do. Why don't you just go home?" he asks the enviros.

"We *are* home," several voices shout back.

"How many of you are from Fort Bragg?" he asks skeptically.

Only a few hands go up. "How many of you are from Mendocino County?" he asks more confidently. About two-thirds of the crowd raise their hands. He looks dismayed, confused. "This is just bizarre!" he says after a moment's hesitation. The crowd responds with a heart-felt round of applause.

Only two years earlier, Fort Bragg had been the scene of a larger unified protest of some two thousand Mendocino residents, including fishermen, loggers, shopkeepers, homeowners, and local politicians, along with old-time hippies, rednecks, and hipnecks (the product of two generations of crossbreeding). They were united in their opposition to a federal plan to lease the area's salmon-rich offshore waters for oil and gas drilling. Now this same community is split into warring factions.

The Yellow Ribbon loggers and mill workers and their white-collar bosses are part of a new campaign, a self-styled "movement" whose members call themselves either Wise Use or Property Rights activists and support not only unrestricted timber cutting on public lands but also offshore "energy development." They support mining and drilling in national parks and wilderness areas; abolition of the Endangered Species Act; a rollback of clean-air, water-quality, and pesticide legislation; and cost-plus compensation from the taxpayer whenever a property owner or corporation is prevented from filling in a wetland, mining a river bottom, or grazing cattle on public rangeland. With deep roots in the political Right, the anti-environmentalists aim to undermine and destroy the "radical preservationists" and "pagans" of Earth First!, the Sierra Club, The Nature Conservancy, the National Wildlife Federation, and Greenpeace as well as small, community-based protest groups and their perceived cohorts in the National Park Service, Bureau of Land Management, Environmental Protection Agency, Army Corps of Engineers, Hollywood, the liberal media, universities, Congress, and the Democratic Party.

This is my first encounter with the anti-environmentalists, and although ignorant of their history, aims, and ambitions, I am impressed by their ability to mobilize grassroots power on the side of industry. The polarization of the community, open hostility, riot troopers on the streets, and general atmosphere of violence remind me of "Marching Days" in Northern Ireland. There I'd covered Protestant "Orangemen" and "green" Catholic nationalists clashing on the streets of Belfast over conflicts almost as ancient as the California redwoods, while the British army, with their Saracan tanks, rubber bullets, and CS gas, got to play peacekeeper for a week.

Of course, that was during wartime, and even with the violence around Redwood Summer (a Labor Day protest greeted with a hail of eggs and rocks, the beating of several activists on local back roads, and the head shaving in jail of four longhairs who had sat down to block a logging truck), it is hard for me to imagine that environmental conflict in the United States will ever begin to resemble some of the haunting scenes of violence and hatred I had come to know as a war correspondent in Northern Ireland and Central America. But today, years later, having seen the bomb and arson damage firsthand, and having met and talked to people who have been beaten or shot at, had their dogs mutilated, their cars run off the road, or their homes burned to the ground, I'm not so certain.

"When I say we have to pick up a sword and shield and kill the bastards, I mean politically, not physically," explains Ron Arnold, a founder and leader of the anti-environmentalist movement. "I'll tell you one thing, though. There are people out there today who are ready to pick up guns and form their own armies. I've told them, 'Look, we already fought one civil war and lost. This isn't the way to go.'" He is trying to reassure me minutes into our initial phone conversation.[3] It's the winter of 1993 and Ron, who prides himself on his understanding of social movements (he's a big fan of Lenin, having read the old Communist's forty-five-volume collected works), is aware that his movement has taken some serious hits in the media because of the simultaneous development of vigilante violence directed against environmental activists.

His rhetorical style—"We're out to kill the fuckers. We're simply trying to eliminate them. Our goal is to destroy environmentalism once and for all"[4]—hasn't helped his cause much lately. So he's reinventing himself, trying to create a new, slightly more centrist image. He's excited about an "inter-movement anti-violence treaty" he's planning to sign with Scott Trimingham, a dropout from the Sea Shepherd Society, a small, radical, direct-action environmental group known for ramming pirate whaling ships on the high seas.

"Philosophically, Scott and I are both followers of Gandhi," claims Ron.

Chuck Cushman, another Wise Use leader and close ally of Arnold's whose organizing style has earned him the nickname Rent-a-Riot, agrees. "The violence issue is just something the preservationists use to try and get at us by implying we want to advocate or promote violence. I've never advocated or called for violence," he insists. "Personally, we've always advocated nonviolence like Martin Luther King or that guy from India, what's his name?"[5]

Most Americans have probably never encountered the Wise Use/Property Rights philosophy except in the rhetorical prose of a Rush Limbaugh or the stump speeches of certain politicians like Senators Larry Craig of Idaho, James Inhofe of Oklahoma, and House Majority Leader Tom DeLay of Texas. Nevertheless, the movement has developed its own social base, idiomatic language, ideological alliances on the Right, and support network, which reaches from unemployed loggers, off-road motorcyclists, and rural county commissioners to the top levels of industry and government. On the political spectrum, the Wise Use/Property Rights movement appears larger than today's white separatist and armed "patriot" militias but far smaller than the Christian Right or pro-gun campaigns of the National Rifle Association (NRA) and Citizens Committee to Keep and Bear Arms (whose founder, Alan Gottlieb, is also Ron Arnold's boss).

While many Wise Use/Property Rights leaders claim the participation of millions of people (by adding up constituent memberships from anti-green groups such as the American Farm Bureau Federation, timber, mining, and other resource industry associations), people who pay individual dues or actively participate in ongoing Wise Use efforts numbered far fewer than a hundred thousand at the height of their movement. The strength of anti-environmentalism is not in its membership rolls but in its ability to mobilize a network of core activists to intervene in and politicize local conflicts, creating a perception of power that they hope can be used as a springboard for further expansion. Whenever a local election is turned in favor of a pro-development Republican, or an e-mail campaign skews a Sunday newspaper poll to suggest that a majority of readers think environmentalism has gone too far, or public land-use hearings are disrupted by hundreds of angry protestors, or the *New York Times* seeks out policy responses from "leaders of environmental, industrial, and property rights groups,"[6] anti-enviro leaders such as Arnold and Cushman score it as a victory for their "guerrilla warfare tactics."

At the same time, they and other key members of the leadership cadre find themselves fighting a constant battle against narrow-focus activists who "can't get beyond their own issues." They also view themselves as under the threat of localized agreements between labor and environmentalists or farmers and government resource agencies that might undermine the fever of indignation and outrage needed to fuel a national movement's growth.

At its core, Wise Use/Property Rights is a counterrevolutionary movement, defining itself in response to the environmental revolution of the past thirty-five years. It aims to create and mold disaffection over environmental regulations, big government, and the media into a cohesive social force that can win respectability for centrist arguments seeking to "protect jobs, private property and the economy by finding a balance between human and environmental needs." Simultaneously the movement pushes a more radical core agenda of "free-market environmentalism," "privatization," and the deregulation of industry.

Despite their insistence that they are not fronting for industry, many anti-enviro groups with green-sounding names, such as the Alliance for

Environment and Resources (AER), Environmental Conservation Organization (ECO), National Wetlands Coalition, and Greening Earth Society, have the same relationship to timber, oil companies, and developers that the smokers' rights movement has to the tobacco industry. In fact the logging industry's Wise Use rallies in the Northwest were later used as a template by the tobacco industry when it shut down its North Carolina mills and warehouses, paying some fifteen thousand of its workers to march on Washington, providing them with free buses, box lunches, and banners for a protest against a proposed health tax on cigarettes.

Other anti-environmentalist organizations, such as the Alliance for America, which Ron Arnold defines as "a bizarre hybrid of industry groups and grassroots," have grown beyond their corporate sponsorship to take on a fragile life of their own, complete with an internally self-validating protest culture. This culture includes Wise Use scientists who argue that there are no real environmental threats facing the world today, Wise Use "Political Prisoners" who have done short jail terms for filling in wetlands and dumping garbage, and conspiracy theorists who see "environmental hysteria" as part of an "anti-human" agenda to reduce world population through mass starvation (a charge that will later be adopted by biotechnology advocates who claim their critics want to "starve Africans"). With direct-mail contact lists, fax and e-mail campaigns, meetings, demonstrations, "battle books," lawsuits, and legislation aimed at the destruction of the "environmental establishment," they hope to win acceptance from the media and the public as a mainstream citizens' movement.

While there is much overlap in both leadership and membership among the hundreds of anti-environmentalist groups scattered around the United States, some broad generalities can be made. In the West, Wise Use has been primarily about protecting industrial and agricultural access to public lands and waters at below-market costs, with the primary emphasis on timber, mining, and grazing. Although hoping to broaden their appeal to off-track motorcyclists, ATV users, snowmobilers, and hunters out of touch with their sport's conservation ethic, the core constituency in the West has consisted of workers and middle management in limited-resource industries such as timber and mining. These are people whose livelihoods are threatened by industry cutbacks and who are open to the argument that environmental protection means lost jobs (an argument reinforced by the disinterest conservation organizations have historically shown to the social consequences of wilderness protection).

Wise Use also appeals to western ranchers, corporate farmers, and businesspeople whose margin of profit is directly threatened by any fee increases on grazing, water reclamation, and other uses of public resources. As a general rule, however, people in these categories are more likely to express themselves through established anti-green organizations such as the Farm Bureau and the Cattlemen's Beef Association.

East of the Mississippi (and in some western suburbs), the movement is more oriented toward property rights, appealing to a constituency of landowners, developers, and developer wannabes whose opportunities for subdividing land and building commercial equity are limited or restricted by regulations governing wetlands, endangered species, wild and scenic rivers, and other environmental protections broadly favored by the American public. Although the key players in the Property Rights movement are upscale conservatives, more likely to own a second home than a second mortgage, they try to portray their interests as compatible with those of rural, low-income property owners. On several occasions in Connecticut, Nebraska, and elsewhere, they have won broad community support, only to see it erode when the scenic river designations they were opposing were shown to enhance rather than undermine property values. This reflects another key truism about the anti-enviro movement: at its core it is not about differing conservation philosophies or ecological worldviews, religion, or politics, but about basic economic interests.

"People are losing their jobs, rural communities are becoming ghost towns, education for our children is suffering, social services are being starved of income. There's a lot of real pain out there," says Bill Grannell, founder of the anti-enviro group People for the West! It's a refrain that has resonance in the recession of the early 1990s, a time of massive layoffs by industry giants such as General Motors (GM), IBM, Bank of America, and Boeing; of wrenching structural dislocations as defense industries try to retool for the post–Cold War global market; and of massive government debt slowing economic recovery. A decade later, things seem remarkably unchanged with the prosperity and surpluses of the Clinton years now a fading memory, high unemployment again stalking the land, and unprecedented federal deficits linked to massive tax cuts that mainly favor the affluent.

The Wise Use/Property Rights response to crises like this has been to argue that environmental protection is costing jobs and undermining the economy, an argument also embraced by the oil-heavy administration of George Walker Bush Jr.

This appealingly simple argument doesn't always hold up in the face of complex economic realities. But for out-of-work loggers in dying timber towns, workers in polluting factories being challenged by vocal community activists, or struggling farmers unable to fill in or sell off wetland acreage, it answers the question of why the American dream seems to be slipping from their grasp. For people in desperate circumstances whose needs are not being met by the system, Wise Use has provided an identifiable enemy, "the preservationist," on which to focus anger and vent rage. If, as Ron Arnold has put it, Wise Use is engaged in a "holy war against the new pagans who worship trees and sacrifice people," it's the pagans who have suffered most of the casualties.

"We were told if we killed any of them there was $40,000 that was there to defend us in court or to help us get away," says Ed Knight, an ex-logger and Hell's Angel describing how he was hired to lie in ambush with an Uzi, waiting to shoot Earth Firsters in the California woods.[7]

"I was driving home from a concert and saw a glow in the mist. By the time I got to my house a mile and a half in from the highway it was burned to the ground," recalls Greenpeace USA's toxics coordinator Pat Costner of the arson fire that destroyed her Arkansas home of almost twenty years.[8]

Maine anti-logging activist Michael Vernon recalls another arson fire, which destroyed his house and almost cost him his life. "I'm not sure if it was the smoke alarm that woke me up or if it was just light in the house," says Vernon, "but I jumped in my boots and threw my coveralls on and I opened the door and the flames were starting to come up the stairs. There was a porch right outside the door, so I ran out and jumped off the porch into the snow."[9]

"After they cut my throat they poured water in it from the river and said, 'Now you'll have something to sue about,'" says Stephanie McGuire, a local activist who was raped and tortured by three men in camouflage clothing after she protested water pollution on the Fenholloway River in Taylor County, Florida.[10]

"We think it was murder," says a friend of Leroy Jackson, a Native American environmentalist whose body was found by the side of a

New Mexico highway several days before he was scheduled to fly to Washington to testify against clear-cut logging on the Navajo reservation.[11] A coroner's report found that Jackson had died of a methadone overdose, although those who knew him described him as a healthy man who never drank alcohol or took drugs.

Along with the growth of Wise Use/Property Rights, the last decade saw a startling increase in intimidation, vandalism, and violence directed against grassroots environmental activists. Observers of this trend have documented hundreds of acts of violence, ranging from vandalism, assaults, arsons, and shootings to torture, rape, and possibly murder, much of it occurring in rural and low-income communities. Simple acts of intimidation—phone harassment, anonymous letters, and verbal threats of violence—may number in the thousands. "Death threats come with the territory these days," admits Andy Kerr, conservation director of the Oregon Natural Resources Council, who was told he'd be killed at a public meeting.[12] Lois Gibbs, executive director of the Citizens Clearinghouse for Hazardous Wastes, a coalition of eight thousand local groups, adds, "People have been followed in their cars, investigated by private detectives, had their homes broken into. I'd say 40 percent of people protesting toxic waste sites and incinerators around the country have been intimidated."[13] And while only a small part of this violence can be directly linked to organized anti-enviro groups (Yellow Ribbon, the Sahara Club, People for the West!, Adirondack Solidarity Alliance), much of the rhetoric and anger springs from a common fount of explosive rage that blames greens for everything from the contracting of resource industries to the closure of the American frontier.

The anti-environmental backlash represents both a danger and a challenge—not only to conservationists and anti-pollution activists but to all citizens concerned about their right to speak out and protest without fear and intimidation. Unfortunately the anti-enviro ranks have grown from resource users protecting their federal subsidies and property owners unhappy with land-use regulations to the fringes of America's dangerous underbelly of militia violence and homegrown terror, where social causes become excuses for sociopaths motivated by fear, greed, and hatred, or private security agents working on behalf of outlaw industries.

As issues of sustainability and survival become more critical in the early years of the new century, affecting the things people hold most dear, including their families, health, and property, the urge to heap blame and deny reality will inevitably increase. If people don't begin finding ways to live well on an increasingly crowded planet without destroying the carrying capacity of their natural resource base—if they let short-term special interests define their long-term strategies for maintaining clean air, clean water, and nature's diversity—they may end up deceiving themselves and denying their children's future. Unfortunately, killing the messenger has become a favorite sport for far too many Americans, who have begun to act like disoriented coal miners, crawling around at the bottom of a poisoned mine shaft in their "Save a Miner, Eat a Canary" tee shirts.

one

Masters and Possessors of Nature

We do not inherit the earth from our fathers. We borrow it from our children.
                        —David Brower

I do not believe that there is either a moral or any other claim upon me to postpone the use of what nature has given me, so that the next generation or generations yet unborn may have an opportunity to get what I myself ought to get.
     —Senator Henry M. Keller, Colorado, February 26, 1909

IF THE WISE USE PERSPECTIVE—that there's too much wilderness protection and environmental hysteria and not enough logging, pesticide spraying, and mini-mall construction—seems a bit strange by today's societal standards—it might help to remember that the environmental ethic, the idea that the earth's resources are limited and must be managed in a sustainable manner, is a new and still-fragile construct within our culture. In contrast, appeals to unrestricted property rights and the promise of unlimited frontiers hold a deep and abiding place in our nation's social history going back more than half a millennium. The first major conflict between environmental sustainability and advocates of property rights in America was fought along racial lines: whites versus Native Americans.

When Columbus arrived on the island of San Salvador in 1492 in search of a trade route to India, he reported of the New World that his eyes "would never tire beholding so much beauty, and the songs of the birds large and small."[1] Other early European explorers would describe the Florida countryside as "the fairest, fruitfullest and pleasantest of all the world," and the outer banks of the Carolinas as "a land full of deere, conies, hares and fowle in incredible abundance." Having recorded their first impressions of North America's natural beauty, the discoverers quickly set about in search of gold and other objects of value.

These explorers and the settlers who followed them also encountered American Indians, as Columbus misnamed the indigenous people. These folks had been occupying the continent for upwards of twenty thousand years, ever since their ancestors first crossed the Bering Strait land bridge from Asia to kill and displace the woolly mammoths. Although initially skeptical, the Indians tried to make the newcomers from Europe feel welcome by, among other gracious acts, saving the Plymouth settlement from winter starvation.

The estimated four million Indian residents of North America, despite cultural differences among their tribal groups that often led to intercommunal raids, wars, and other common human (male) activities, were as a whole qualitatively different from these new settlers. While they practiced slash-and-burn agriculture along with fishing, hunting, and the gathering of wild edibles, they hadn't experienced the surplus-generating, plow-based agricultural revolution that had shaped the European landscape with its overcrowded cities, cleared forests, and indentured peasantry. As essentially nomadic peoples with low-density populations, these indigenous groups had far less of an impact on the natural terrain and wildlife that supported them than did the Europeans.

The Italian explorer Amerigo Vespucci (for whom America is named) found the natives "barbarous" and "shameless" even if they did show themselves to be "desirous of copulating with us Christians." He was most shocked, however, by their communal habits. "They neither buy nor sell. In short, they live and are contented with what nature gives them," he wrote. "The wealth which we affect in this our Europe and elsewhere, such as gold, jewels, pearls and other riches, they hold of no value at all."

In both the avaricious Christianity that characterized the Age of Discovery and the scientific empiricism that marked the Enlightenment, human beings were seen as being apart from and having hegemony over nature, "the masters and possessors of nature" in the words of René Descartes. North American Indian cultures and religions, by contrast, were nature-based, seeing humans as integral players in a larger cosmology of the spirits and seasons of Mother Earth. Today's Wise Use advocates like to portray environmental radicals (indeed all environmentalists) as "druids and Pagans" or else as "Marxist watermelons" ("green on the outside, red on the inside"), but these descriptions, when not used in a purely cynical fashion, tend to reflect their own Eurocentric bias. Those of today's environmentalists who have the time or feel the need for some new paradigm of faith are far more likely to identify with Native American spirituality than with the religions and philosophies of the Old World.

The key rationale used by the white settler culture to justify the expropriation of natives' lands and displacement of their cultures was the concept of private property rights as applied to landownership. This justification was even articulated as official policy in the report of the Interior secretary for 1851: "To tame a savage *you* must tie him down to the soil. You must make him understand the value of property, and the benefits of its separate ownership. You must appeal to those selfish principles implanted by Divine Providence in the nature of man for the wisest of purposes, and make them minister to civilization and refinement."[2]

By contrast, the indigenous view of the land and of the white European settlers' relation to it was best summarized by Sitting Bull in 1877, the year after the Battle of Greasy Grass (Little Bighorn):

> Behold my brothers, the spring has come: the earth has received the embraces of the sun and we shall soon see the results of that love!
>
> Every seed is awakened and so has all animal life. It is through this mysterious power that we too have our being, and we therefore yield to our neighbors, even our animal neighbors, the same right as ourselves, to inhabit this land.
>
> Yet, hear me, people, we have now to deal with another race small and feeble when our fathers first met them but now great and overbearing. Strangely enough they have a mind to till the soil and the love of possession is a disease with them.
>
> They claim this Mother of ours, the earth, for their own and fence their neighbors away: they deface her with their buildings and their refuse. That nation is like a spring freshet that overruns its banks and destroys all who are in its path.[3]

With such diametrically opposing views, conflict was inevitable. Between 1600 and 1890 (the year Sitting Bull was murdered by Indian police sent to arrest him), more than two hundred major battles would be fought between indigenous groups and settlers, some four hundred treaties signed and broken, and three-quarters of the Native American population destroyed. Along with their technological edge in metallurgy, guns, and gunpowder, the Europeans' utilitarian approach to nature provided them with a range of combat strategies inconceivable to the Native Americans. These included germ warfare (General Jeffrey Amherst handing out smallpox-infected blankets to the tribes around Fort Pitts) and resource denial ("Kill a buffalo, starve an Indian" was a motto favored by General George Crook's cavalry forces in the West). The near elimination of the buffalo as part of a strategic plan to "civilize" the western plains stands as a prime example in U.S. history of this utilitarian approach to nature.

IN THE WAKE OF THE American Civil War, the railroad companies, army, and Texas stockmen found common cause in the eradication of the buffalo. In 1867 the Union Pacific shipped the first twenty-box carloads of cattle from the dusty Chisholm Trail town of Abilene, Kansas, to Illinois for slaughter. By 1871 it was shipping 700,000 longhorn a year. The growth of a national beef industry was limited only by the competition for wild grass forage from the great herds of migratory bison. In 1869, completion of the Union Pacific Railroad divided the plains buffalo into a northern and a southern herd estimated at approximately forty million and twenty million, respectively. With rail towns such as Dodge City for the shipping of hides, and rail-company employees and army garrisons willing to pay for the provisioning of meat, thousands of hunters, including Buffalo Bill Cody, Charlie Rath, and Frank Mayer, spread across the plains with their .55-caliber Sharps rifles, turning what had been selective hunting into industrial slaughter. The railroads joined in the carnage, advertising special excursions where passengers could shoot buffalo from the windows of passing trains. British royalty and other wealthy Europeans traveled out west for elegant weeklong trophy hunts. By 1874 the southern herd had been eliminated.

General Phil Sheridan, commander of the armies of the West, whose famous quote was, "The only good Indians I ever saw were dead," appreciated the strategic value of the bison killing. Addressing a group of Texas legislators (many of them cattlemen), he admitted that buffalo hunters were "doing more to settle the vexed Indian question than the

entire regular army has done in the last thirty years. They are destroying the Indians' commissary."4 General George Crook, newly arrived
on the plains from the Apache wars in the Southwest, gave standing orders to his cavalry patrols to shoot buffalo on sight.

When the hunters went out in search of northern buffalo in the
spring of 1881, they couldn't find any left alive. In place of the great
thundering herds were swarms of carrion-engorged blackflies. The
decade of slaughter complete, a number of unemployed hunters became
bonepickers, spreading out across the plains in buckboard wagons to
collect the "white harvest" of skeletal remains, which, shipped back east
by railcar, sold for five to eight dollars a ton as phosphorus fertilizer.

THE NOMADIC PLAINS INDIANS never recovered from the loss of the
buffalo and were soon driven by hunger onto government reservations,
where they could be controlled and "civilized." In order to feed them,
government agencies contracted millions of dollars of beef cattle from
western ranchers and then cheated the tribes out of much of the meat by
never delivering it. In Washington the stockmen's Beef Ring became no-
torious for feeding at the public trough. The Cherokee Strip Livestock
Association, the predecessor of today's Cattlemen's Association, fought
for white ranchers' access to reservation grazing lands. However, not all
the tribes were starved into submission by the loss of the plains buffalo.

Three tribal nations—the Sioux, Cheyenne, and Arapaho—had, in
the fertile Black Hills of South Dakota, plenty of elk, deer, antelope,
and other game to sustain them on what they considered their sacred
lands. In 1870 the army, enforcing the two-year-old treaty that had
ended the Bozeman Trail war (during which the Sioux and Northern
Cheyenne managed to shut down one of the four major settlement
routes west), turned back a gold-mining expedition headed into the
Black Hills. This led to a riot by thousands of angry miners in Sioux
City and the establishment of a Black Hills lobby in Washington to
open up the area to "advancing civilization." Charles Collins, a color-
ful and bombastic Sioux City promoter, argued that the "Indian monopoly" on the Black Hills, which the U.S. government had promised
to honor "as long as the grass shall grow and the rivers flow," was no
different than the railroad monopoly in the rest of the nation: designed
to keep honest white men from earning a productive living.

In 1872, Congress passed a mining law that would allow hardrock miners to take title to public lands for $2.50 an acre. The following year, the army began doing armed mineral surveys in the Black Hills while holding private discussions with railroad magnate Jay Cooke about opening new lines through the treaty lands. Among the military commanders who sought to provoke a conflict with the Indians was survey commander George Armstrong Custer, who took several reporters along with him on his patrols. A subsequent dispatch in the *New York World* reported, "Custer's Expedition Reaches Its Destination—A Region of Gold and Silver Mines and Lovely Valleys Discovered." The gold rush that followed led to skirmishes with the Indians and increased army activity leading to war. Custer's ill-fated decision to try to take on a vastly superior (and better-led) Indian army in the summer of 1876 resulted in his death, along with that of 212 of his men, at the Battle of Little Bighorn. Over the next year, General George Crook was able to overcome Indian resistance in a hard-fought campaign using thousands of army troops, rapid-fire Gatling guns, and artillery. Companies such as Homestake Mining (later to become a financial backer of the anti-enviro People for the West!) got their start digging gold in the Black Hills while the Indians were pushed onto increasingly smaller and less productive reservation lands.

On their return east in 1877, elements of Custer's Seventh Cavalry were mobilized for riot duty in Chicago as popular resentment and worker dissatisfaction over wage cuts led to a nationwide railroad strike. Thousands of locomotives and railcars were burned amidst urban street fighting that spread to dozens of towns and cities. Unlike the Indian monopoly of the Black Hills, the railroad monopoly was not broken.

The rapid growth of cities and their smokestack industries also led to bacterial diseases and epidemic outbreaks from decaying garbage piles, inadequate sewage systems, bad water, and soot smoke. Anti-smoke leagues were formed in New York, Pittsburgh, and other cities. In San Diego, debate over whether to industrialize raged between self-described "Smokestacks" and "Geraniums." Late nineteenth-century urban industrialization also meant increased demand for coal, iron, lead, and copper (used for telegraph and electrical wiring). Mine workers suffered from black and brown lung disease as well as lead and mercury poisoning. Mill workers and goldleafers lost their breath to silicosis. Tuberculosis and pneumonia were the common diseases of the meat-packing industry. Class conflicts raged in the eastern cities, taking on the appearance of industrial warfare in the intermountain West, where thousands of armed miners clashed with state militias and federal troops. Still, most people failed to link the causes of urban squalor and occupational death with the depredations of nature being practiced as part of their culture's industrial resource expansion.

The late nineteenth century was also marked by militant agricultural movements. Expanded production and industrial depressions resulted in low farm prices and a revolt amongst the farmers against industrialism and corporate power. The Populist movement demanded democratic reforms, including direct elections to the Senate, graduated income taxes, and inflationary money policies that would favor the farm producer. William Jennings Bryan, the fiery Populist candidate for president in 1892 and 1896, declared, "The great cities rest upon our broad and fertile Prairies. Burn down your cities and leave our farms, and your cities will spring up again as if by magic: but destroy our farms, and grass will grow in the streets of every city in the country."[5]

IN 1890 THE U.S. Census declared the frontier officially closed, but wealthy stockmen and timber thieves, used to having their way on both the open range and the mountain range, were having none of it. The Forest Reserve Act of 1891, which set aside the first thirteen million acres of what was to become the national forest system, was angrily denounced by stockraisers, loggers, and western land developers, collectively known as "boomers." Where it was inconvenient to systematically steal timber from these new reserves, arson was employed as a tool of protest.

According to Mike Weiss in *Mother Jones* magazine, a similar pattern of arson fires appeared on U.S. forest lands in the 1990s. Major forest fires, including the 1992 Fountain Fire in California, appear to have been deliberately set in order to promote salvage logging, which allows for commercial timber sales on burned-over U.S. forest lands that would otherwise be off limits to logging.[6] Similar plans for commercial forest thinning and salvage logging were being promoted by President George W. Bush a decade later, this time in the name of forest fire prevention.

THE COMING OF THE twentieth century, celebrated with millennialist fervor from Maine to California, saw a dramatic change in the government's commitment to conservation, largely as a result of three men's work: naturalist John Muir, forester Gifford Pinchot, and President Theodore Roosevelt.

Like Henry David Thoreau before him, Scots immigrant John Muir was a romanticizer of nature. His wanderings through California's Sierra Nevada and his writings about his wilderness encounters, popularized in books and magazines, led to the creation of Yosemite National Park in 1890. An advocate of wilderness preservation, he also founded the Sierra Club in order to "be able to do something for wildness and make the mountains glad."

Pinchot, an avid outdoorsman, was one of the first Americans to be trained in European forest management, which sought to create a sustainable yield in wood products. Convinced that government control of the forests was the only way to stop the destructive practices of the big logging companies, he became head of the Agriculture Department's forestry division under President McKinley.

Teddy Roosevelt, big-game hunter, adventurer, and politician, helped found one of the first conservation organizations in the United States, the Boone & Crockett Club (named after Daniel Boone and Davy Crockett), to protect big-game animals and their habitat (for hunting). He fought to save Yellowstone Park from development and for passage of the 1891 Forest Reserve Act. Vice president of the United States when McKinley was assassinated in 1901 and elected to a second term in 1904, Roosevelt was the first chief executive to actively work on behalf of wilderness and conservation, developing close friendships with both Muir and Pinchot. He promoted the latter to chief forester of the nation.

In expanding or creating the nation's system of parks and national forests, reclamation projects, reservoirs, and wildlife sanctuaries, Roosevelt came into direct conflict with the western boomers—the "landgrabbers and great special interests," as he called them. "The rights of the public to the [nation's] natural resources outweigh private rights and must be given its first consideration," he argued. In 1906 he imposed the first fees for cattle and sheep grazing in national forests. "Whoever takes public property for private profit should pay for what he gets," he insisted to howls of protest from western resource industries and the congressmen and senators they controlled. One western newspaper called him a dictator, editorializing that if he "continued to create reserves there would be little ground left to bury folks on." The boomers also claimed that forest reserves hurt small homesteaders.

"Our policies favored the settler as against the large stockholder," Roosevelt countered in his autobiography, "although in places their ignorance was played upon by demagogues to influence them against policy that was primarily for their own interest."[7]

In many of these resource battles, Pinchot and Muir worked as a team—Pinchot as the consummate Washington bureaucrat, fighting in the halls of power while Muir beat the band to raise public support. But Muir and Pinchot, who introduced the term *conservationist*, also had strong philosophical differences. Muir believed in wilderness preservation for its own sake, while Pinchot advocated the "wise use" of resources, believing they should be carefully utilized to meet people's needs. During his presidency, Roosevelt often refereed their conflicts, supporting Muir in turning down a proposal for mining in the Grand Canyon in 1906 but reluctantly siding with Pinchot over Hetch Hetchy, the issue that would turn the two friends against each other. The city of San Francisco wanted to dam Hetch Hetchy, a spectacular valley inside Yosemite National Park, for water and electric power. Pinchot backed the city's plan and branded Muir and his valley supporters "unreasonable nature lovers." In 1913 the dam was built. A year later, Muir died, his heart and spirit broken.

Today's Wise Use activists like to claim that they are following in Pinchot's conservationist footsteps, although philosophically (and often genealogically) they are direct descendants of the western boomers whom Pinchot, Muir, and Roosevelt all fought to defeat. Even Ron Arnold's use of the term *Wise Use* has more to do with marketing psychology than with any deep philosophical reflection on Pinchot's legacy. "*Wise Use* was catchy," Arnold told a reporter for *Outside* magazine, "and it took up only nine [sic] spaces in a newspaper headline, just about as short as *ecology*."[8]

THE FIRST TWO DECADES of the twentieth century saw increased urbanization and demand for food that led to a level of farm prosperity not seen before or since. Fearing a resurgence of the farmer-based Populist movement of the 1890s, agro-oriented companies such as John

Deere, International Harvester, and the Rock Island Railroad joined with the U.S. Chamber of Commerce to help promote the Farm Bureau Federation, a conservative outgrowth of the U.S. Department of Agriculture's farm extension program. Initially advocating mechanization of agriculture, over time the Farm Bureau would become a major promoter of agricultural subsidies, chemical fertilizers and pesticides, corporate farming, biotechnology, and low-priced agro exports. The bureau's indifference to the plight of the family farmer and to organic crop production, and its open hostility to farm laborers, wetlands, wilderness legislation, and wildlife, would make it a major anti-environmental player over the next three-quarters of a century.

The era of farm prosperity ended on October 24, 1929, with the crash of the stock market. America quickly sank into the Great Depression: the country's gross national product declined 25 percent in three years; Wall Street traders jumped to their deaths from high-rise buildings, whose windows still opened; breadlines formed outside Red Cross and Salvation Army soup kitchens while militant "unemployed councils" broke into supermarkets to feed the hungry. In 1931, Governor Franklin D. Roosevelt of New York established the first state relief organization in the country to try to feed the urban unemployed. Conditions in rural America were even worse. One-third of farmers lost their land to foreclosures and evictions even as an extended drought created a vast dust bowl that stretched across the middle part of the country from Kansas to Oklahoma. "Okie" dust bowl refugees who tried to find work as migrant farm laborers in California were turned back at the border by armed state troopers.

In 1932, Franklin Roosevelt easily defeated incumbent Herbert Hoover in the presidential election, initiating a "New Deal" policy of government intervention to "pump-prime" the economy. Roosevelt's basic economic theory, that unlimited growth and expansion had to be replaced with well-regulated management to assure every American a comfortable living, soon found expression in his approach to natural resources. Like his distant cousin Teddy Roosevelt, FDR considered himself an ardent conservationist. Of the many New Deal programs he established in the early 1930s, his favorite was the Civilian Conservation Corps. Employing almost three million urban youths during its lifetime, the CCC planted trees and built trails, watchtowers, and ranger stations in national parks and forests. It ran soil-conservation projects, dug irrigation ditches and reservoirs on the plains, and created greenbelt parks around many towns and cities.

Other New Deal efforts to help America's earth and people recover from recent abuses were establishment of the Soil Conservation Service, a program of farm-price supports and rural electrification that included the formation of the Tennessee Valley Authority. The TVA was the first major effort to restore an ecologically and economically devastated region through programs of soil and water conservation. But its network of publicly owned power dams was condemned by the major utility corporations as socialistic. These companies, along with the U.S. Chamber of Commerce, National Association of Manufacturers, and DuPont Chemical Company, formed the American Liberty League, a right-wing organization of wealthy industrialists who considered Roosevelt "a traitor to his class." FDR also faced challenges from the radical Left and organized labor, particularly the Congress of Industrial Organizations, whose sit-ins, rallies, and strikes were often met by violence from police and company guards. Isolationists and "America Firsters," who believed that the nation had gained little from its participation in World War I, were also suspicious of Roosevelt's "internationalism." Roosevelt tried to steer a middle course between the isolationists and America's overseas allies. But the military expansionism of Nazi Germany in Europe and of imperial Japan in Asia soon put the United States under tremendous pressure to come to the aid of its battered friends. FDR's lend-lease program to Britain and the Soviet Union in 1940–1941 jump-started America's industrial capacity for war production while also eliminating the last economic downturn of the Depression era.

With its entry into World War II following the December 7, 1941, Japanese air attack on Pearl Harbor, the United States emerged as a major world power. The nation's remarkable war mobilization of industrial and scientific resources expanded its productive capacity as nothing else before or since. America tapped its natural resource base for the production of steel, aluminum, gasoline, aviation fuel, glass, lead, magnesium, wool, fiber, and myriad other components that went into the making of airplanes, ships, and tanks. The petrochemical industry was given a boost by the demand for synthetic rubber in 1942, rubber trees being one of the few natural resources not available on the North American continent.

The war effort also spurred scientific research in a number of specialized fields such as physical oceanography, with its focus on acoustics, water temperature, waves, currents, and other things that might affect submarine and ship operations (and would later help the U.S. oil and gas industry expand its offshore drilling operations). The most extensive top-secret research was directed toward the development of the atomic bomb, which scientists feared the Germans might get first. However, by the time the Manhattan Project had a working test bomb, Berlin had fallen and the war in Europe was over. Watching the first mushroom cloud rise over the New Mexico desert test site in July 1945, project director J. Robert Oppenheimer was reminded of a quote from Hindu scripture: "Now I am become death, the destroyer of worlds."

The end of World War II, marked by the atomic bombing of Hiroshima and Nagasaki in Japan, also heralded America's emergence as the planet's preeminent power and the beginning of a forty-five-year-long Cold War with the Soviet Union. Ironically, the only post–World War II victims of America's nuclear arsenal would be the thousands of military troops, Native American uranium miners, downwind ranchers, bomb factory workers, and Pacific islanders exposed to radiation from weapons development, construction, and atmospheric testing. By the late 1950s, radioactive strontium 90 from bomb testing would be detectable in human bones and mothers' milk. Other Americans would be exposed to military toxins ranging from organic solvents to heavy metals to dioxin in Agent Orange defoliant as the national security state exempted the military from the environmental safeguards gradually adopted by the rest of society.

U.S. government agencies such as the Atomic Energy Commission downplayed the risks of ionizing radiation by promoting the "friendly atom" for commercial power generation. New agricultural and petrochemical products were broadly welcomed by postwar society, which saw unregulated scientific and commercial innovation as the road to prosperity. The use of chemical farm pesticides increased thirty-threefold between 1945 and 1985. Ironically, the percentage of crops lost to insect pests also rose slightly during this same period.[9]

An affluent culture of consumer-driven conformity emerged in the 1950s. There was the postwar baby boom, the creation of single-family suburbs such as New York's Levittown, and broadcast television, which replaced radio as the dominant medium of communications. The American landscape was dramatically altered by a postwar construction boom that spread with the interstate highway system, soon accounting for 80 percent of everything built since the arrival of the Pilgrims. The optimistic pro-business boosterism of the 1950s was also reflected in Washington's natural resource policies. President Eisenhower referred to the New Deal legacy of public power projects as "creeping socialism," while his secretary of Interior, a former Chevrolet salesman named Douglas McKay, was so anxious to transfer federal lands to states and private industry that he became known as "Giveaway McKay." One of the major resource fights of the era was over plans by the federal Bureau of Reclamation to build a series of power dams and reservoirs on the upper Colorado River, including one at Echo Park inside Dinosaur National Monument. Conservationists, fearing a new Hetch Hetchy that would open the national park system to commercial exploitation, launched a major campaign to stop the dam. Ex-mountaineer and Sierra Club executive director David Brower led a coalition of groups who flooded Congress with letters and testimonials protesting the plan on both aesthetic and practical grounds. Brower's successful effort to stop the Echo Park dam would be followed by similar efforts to prevent the damming of the Grand Canyon and to designate a number of now-famous wilderness reserves. Still, Brower's early victory at Echo Park would prove bittersweet. As part of the final settlement, he agreed not to protest construction of the Glen Canyon Dam in Arizona, only later discovering the hidden wonders of the soon-to-be-flooded canyonlands below Rainbow Bridge, the highest rock arch in the world. Floyd Dominy, the U.S. commissioner of reclamation appointed under Eisenhower, considered the Lake Powell reservoir that grew up behind the dam a great improvement on nature's hidden canyons, even penning a poem in honor of his work:

> To have a deep blue lake
> Where no lake was before
> Seems to bring man
> A little closer to God.[10]

"About seven hundred feet closer," Dave Brower responded with tongue firmly in cheek. Brower, like John Muir before him, would later prove uncompromising in his wilderness campaigns, helping to found a number of environmental organizations along the way, including

Friends of the Earth, the League of Conservation Voters, and the Earth
Island Institute.

Ron Arnold traces present-day Wise Use rhetoric that brands environmentalists as "pagans who worship trees and sacrifice people" to
Encounters with the Archdruid, a 1971 book by author John McPhee
in which Hilton Head developer Charles Frasier is quoted as saying of
Brower, "Ancient druids used to sacrifice human beings under oak
trees. Modern druids worship trees and sacrifice human beings to those
trees." Replied Brower at age eighty-two, "Really, I've just always
loved people who loved trees."[11]

The election of President John F. Kennedy in 1960 marked a dramatic
change in America's cultural attitudes. The youthful president's call for
a "new frontier" of freedom and social involvement found resonance in
the writings of Supreme Court Justice William O. Douglas, whose rulings helped establish the legal framework for the field of environmental law. Newly named secretary of Interior Stewart Udall was among
the first in government to challenge "uncritical acceptance of conventional notions of progress" and to identify links among unchecked population growth, pollution, urban decay, and wilderness protection.
"The history of America," John Kennedy agreed, "has been the story
of Americans seizing, using, squandering, and, belatedly, protecting
their rich heritage."[12] In 1961, Kennedy, in an address to Congress,
called for a wilderness bill, surveys for new national parks, and the establishment of national seashores. Governor George D. Clyde of Utah,
speaking on behalf of western economic interests — the oil and gas, mining, timber, and cattle industries — warned that the new administration
was threatening to "bottle up enormous quantities of natural resources." Kennedy, the wry, aristocratic easterner already condemned
by the hard Right for not launching a full-scale invasion of Cuba during the Bay of Pigs fiasco, now became the subject of deep distrust
among the cowboy capitalists of the West.

By the early 1960s, America's burgeoning urban population was
growing increasingly alarmed by the visible by-products of unrestrained
economic growth. Smog and air pollution were choking cities from
Pittsburgh to Los Angeles. Industrial and municipal waste was poisoning the Great Lakes, seashores, and rivers. Cleveland's Cauyahoga River,
covered with oil and industrial sludge, caught fire, burning two overhead bridges, as it seeped its way into phosphate-choked Lake Erie.

Along with Michael Harrington's *The Other America* and Ralph Nader's *Unsafe at Any Speed,* the 1962 publication of Rachel Carson's book *Silent Spring* gave voice to the nation's growing concerns over poverty, consumer fraud, and environmental degradation. In an impassioned, fact-filled attack on the use of DDT and other synthetic chemicals, Carson demonstrated how human-made insecticides killed tens of thousands of birds and other nontarget species, posing grave danger to the soil, food chain, and human health. The impact of *Silent Spring* would prove so seminal to the development of a new ecological awareness that even today few anti-enviro conferences or seminars take place where the late author is not excoriated for her "preservationist hysteria" and "bad science."

With the assassination of John F. Kennedy in Dallas, Texas, on November 22, 1963, America suffered a political trauma that many would later come to identify as a historical turning point for the nation. The promise of government-sponsored political reform to ease the burdens of racism and injustice was quickly forgotten as Lyndon Baines Johnson sacrificed his War on Poverty in order to pursue the Great Frontier's war in Vietnam.

The devastation of Vietnam's people and landscape from massive U.S. bombing and "resource-denial" strategies—using the air cavalry to push "hostiles" out of "Indian territory"—recalled America's earlier white-settler wars. The clearing of jungles, helicopter attacks on elephant herds (suspected Viet Cong transport), and defoliation of rainforest canopy using dioxin-based herbicides in a program called Operation Ranch-hand led to charges of ecocide. Black humor grew among the troops spraying the poisons. They shortened the U.S. Forest Service slogan "Only you can prevent forest fires" to "Only you can prevent forests."

Disillusionment over America's role in Vietnam became widespread among civil rights activists, college students, and the working poor at home. "If we are to get on the right side of the world revolution, we as a nation must undergo a radical revolution of values. We must rapidly begin the shift from a 'thing-oriented' society to a 'person-oriented society,'" said Dr. Martin Luther King in a 1967 anti–Vietnam War speech condemned by the major media.[13] In California, Cesar Chavez and the United Farm Workers began a unionization drive among migrant laborers demanding an end to stoop labor and the spraying of fieldworkers with toxic pesticides. Countercultural hippies sought social transformation through a back-to-the-land move to rural communes and organic living profiled in the 1970 book *The Greening of America.*

On April 22, 1970, twenty million citizens, including a strong representation of the antiwar youth culture, demonstrated across America on Earth Day, a protest/celebration that marked the beginning of the contemporary environmental movement. Organized by Senator Gaylord Nelson of Wisconsin and Denis Hayes, a Harvard student, the event included local beach cleanups, tree plantings, horseback rides down interstate highways, parades of gas-masked marchers in urban centers, open-air campus teach-ins on ecology, and a thousand other innovations on a theme. The John Birch Society denounced Earth Day as a veiled attempt to celebrate Lenin's birthday, while some leftists argued that it was an establishment plot to co-opt the youth movement. In fact it was a near-spontaneous reaction by a growing cross section of Americans worried over the health effects of pollution, an issue not being addressed by traditional wilderness-oriented conservation groups. Even Richard Nixon, who had a paranoid fear of any form of political opposition, was an astute enough politician to realize that public concern over the environment was a cause better embraced than challenged. "The 1970s absolutely must be the years when America pays its debt to the past by reclaiming the purity of its air, its waters and our living environment. It is literally now or never," he told Congress in his 1970 State of the Union message shortly before ordering the invasion of Cambodia.

The Nixon, Ford, and Carter administrations would pass almost all the landmark environmental legislation that exists today and, in the process, help clean up some of the most visible and dangerous forms of pollution, including sulfur dioxide, lead, DDT, asbestos, mercury, industrial sludge, and untreated municipal sewage. In 1970, Nixon signed the National Environmental Policy Act (NEPA), which requires the government to estimate in advance the ecological impacts of its various projects and activities. This would prove so effective a piece of legislation that today's anti-environmental "property rights" bills mimic its language. Nixon also established the Environmental Protection Agency (EPA) and the White House Council on Environmental Quality. The Marine Mammal Protection Act was passed in 1972, the Endangered Species Act in 1973, and the Safe Drinking Water Act in 1974, the year

Nixon, facing impeachment for his involvement in the Watergate break-in and cover-up, was forced to resign. Clean Air and Clean Water Acts passed in the early 1970s were strengthened, reauthorized by Congress, and signed into law by President Jimmy Carter in 1977.

The 1970s also saw the emergence of a new kind of environmentalism, which mixed the militant advocacy of the 1960s with grassroots community organizing efforts. Direct-action outfits such as Greenpeace, which mounted maritime blockades of whalers and nuclear test sites, and neighborhood-based groups such as the Love Canal Homeowners Association, which rebelled against the toxic poisoning of communities where young children were being raised, created a powerful demand on society to restructure its industrial processes and reduce waste production. The oil embargo of 1973 and energy crisis of 1979 generated new demands for the development of renewable energy sources such as wind, solar, and biomass. President Carter called the energy problem "the moral equivalent of war" and offered a program of energy conservation and renewables (along with oil and gas deregulation) that, had it been pursued, would have seen 25 percent of U.S. energy being generated by non-carbon-based power sources by the year 2000. The oil industry went along with the plan once it had effectively lobbied against a proposed windfall profits tax (the renewables program was eliminated in the early days of the Reagan administration).

At the same time, attempts by the utility industry to offer a radical expansion of commercial nuclear power as an energy alternative generated widespread opposition among the new environmentalists. Antinuclear groups such as New Hampshire's Clamshell Alliance and California's Abalone Alliance led militant nonviolent blockades of nuclear power plants under construction. Industry responded by hiring private security firms to spy on and infiltrate the groups while right-wing law firms such as the Pacific Legal Foundation, established in 1973, filed nuisance suits against the protestors.

In 1974, Karen Silkwood, a twenty-eight-year-old worker and union organizer at the Kerr-McGee plutonium plant in Crescent, Oklahoma, died in a single-car accident while on her way to meet a union official and a *New York Times* reporter with documents and photos she claimed would prove unsafe handling of nuclear materials at the plant. No documents were found in the wreckage of her car, but dents on the left rear fender and body panel suggested she was forced off the road.

The possibility that Silkwood had been murdered sent a chill through the anti-nuclear movement.[14] Nonetheless, by the time of Pennsylvania's Three Mile Island nuclear accident in 1979, issues of safety, waste storage, and widespread public hostility had effectively blocked expansion of the nuclear industry in the United States.

The realization that environmentalism was now in a position to cripple a major industry led to some serious reflection among the leaders of corporate America. A handful of companies, recognizing the long-term benefits of pollution prevention, began to reevaluate their management systems and develop less harmful, more efficient means of production, packaging, and distribution. A much larger number of companies saw popular environmental concerns as a public relations issue and responded with a series of "greener" ad campaigns. Still others, primarily in resource extraction industries such as oil, coal, timber, and beef, decided it was time to fight back against the environmentalists. Thirty years earlier writer Bernard De Voto had predicted where these corporate resource giants might go to find their battle champions. "The West does not want to be liberated from the system of exploitation that it has always violently resented," he wrote in 1955. "It only wants to buy into it."[15]

two

Rebels and Reaganites

*You chaps who are in favor of this conservation program are all wrong.
You are hindering the development of the West. In my opinion, the proper
course to take with regard to this [public lands] is to divide it up among
the big corporations and the people who know how to make money out
of it and let the people at large get the benefits of the circulation of
the money.* —Secretary of Interior Richard Ballinger, 1909

We will mine more, drill more, cut more timber.
—James Watt, Secretary of Interior, 1981

MILES AND MILES of nothing but miles and miles may be an apt description of Nevada's bone-dry, mineral-rich landscape. Eighty-six percent
owned by the U.S. government, it is both the most federalized and (surprisingly) the third most urban state in the country, with more than 80
percent of its population living in either Las Vegas or the Reno–Carson
City area. Yet Nevada perhaps more than any other state retains the
wide-open spirit of the Old West, with legalized gambling and prostitution, easy access to guns and liquor, and lots of cheap land for
transnational mining companies and government-subsidized ranchers
under a system described by *The Economist* as having "tempered
rugged individualism with socialist infrastructure."[1]

Still, the cowboy ranchers and rural land barons of Nevada have
never been comfortable with even minimal restrictions on "their" land
and water rights, often treating U.S. range managers from the Bureau
of Land Management (BLM) and the U.S. Forest Service as if they were
disrespectful ranch hands in need of a whipping. So it isn't surprising
that a quarter century ago, Nevada was the birthplace of what came to
be known as the Sagebrush Rebellion, a much-ballyhooed and yippie-

yi-yo-ed attempt (actually the fourth of the twentieth century) to transfer control of western lands from the federal government to state authorities. Statute 633, a bill introduced into the Nevada legislature in
1979 by State Representative Deane Rhodes, claimed all BLM land in
the state, some forty-eight million acres, in the name of the people of
Nevada. The next day, *Washington Post* reporter Lou Cannon picked
up on the story, giving it its handle as the "Sagebrush Rebellion." The
idea of state takeovers of federal land quickly spread to Utah, Idaho,
Wyoming, Arizona, and Alaska (where it became known as the "Tundra
Rebellion"), gaining the support of the Cattlemen's Association, Farm
Bureau Federation, oil and gas industry, coal industry, NRA, and western sports groups. In Oregon, Bill Grannell, a Democratic state representative who would later found People for the West! teamed up with
Republican Denny Jones to introduce Sagebrush legislation calling for
a commission to study federal land transfers.

The Sagebrush Rebellion, with its image of tobacco-chewing cowboys versus pencil-pushing bureaucrats, was a natural for the media,
getting wide regional and national play. Congressman James Santini of
Nevada went on network television to complain that since passage of
the mildly environmental Federal Land Policy and Management Act, it
had become impossible for ranchers to work with the BLM (forgetting
to mention that he had voted in favor of the act). Idaho senator Jim
McClure, a sheep rancher, sponsored an amendment to an appropriations bill to limit the BLM's power to regulate grazing for environmental purposes. Utah senator Orrin Hatch, sponsor of a federal
land-transfer bill, referred to Sagebrush as "the second American Revolution" and claimed that the United States was "waging war on the
West," encouraged by "environmental extremists and toadstool wor-
shippers" whom he also branded as "land embalmers."

Some westerners didn't buy into that argument. Arizona governor
(later secretary of Interior) Bruce Babbitt called the rebellion "a land
grab in thin disguise." But when Bernard Shanks, an associate professor at Utah State University, labeled Sagebrush "the new McCarthy-
ism" (after Senator Joe McCarthy, the famously ill-informed red-baiter
of the 1950s), the Woolgrowers Association, Cattlemen's Association,
and Utah Farm Bureau wrote to the university president threatening to
block new building funds if Shanks wasn't fired. The university assured
them that Shanks was on his way out.[2]

Acts of vandalism and intimidation were also associated with the Sagebrush Rebellion, although mostly of the phone threat and tire-slashing variety, not the dog-killing, shooting, and house-burning type of violence later associated with Wise Use and the militia movement. Ironically, elected officials often acted as vigilante cheerleaders, encouraging a sense of militancy among the "rebels." Utah county commissioner Calvin Black warned BLM employees to travel in pairs or groups along back roads to avoid being shot at by local people, and Congressman James Santini asked a group of angry miners for "solutions to the Bureau of Land Management short of assassination." (At a 1992 meeting in Goshen, Washington, Wise Use leader Chuck Cushman, responding to a suggestion that environmentalists be shot, cautioned, "The idea is to participate in the public process before you have to get that excited.")³

"The fact that 1980 was an election year had a lot of impact on the Sagebrush Rebellion," Deane Rhodes later recalled. "Right after the election, President Reagan sent me a telegram saying he was a Sagebrush Rebel and supporter. We had a major meeting in Salt Lake, where I read that telegram. Later he called me up and invited me to Washington. That meeting at the White House lasted about forty minutes. It included Reagan and [Attorney General] Ed Meese and [Nevada senator] Paul Laxalt. He didn't come right out and say he supported us that time, but he did say we should keep up our efforts and that he would also direct the [federal land] agencies to be more responsive to us."⁴

Ronald Reagan's 1980 election victory was a triumph for the conservative wing of the Republican Party and its supporters on the religious Right. Many of the central players in today's anti-enviro movement won their spurs in the "Reagan revolution." Colorado brewer Joseph Coors, a close friend of the new president and member of his "kitchen cabinet," established both the Mountain States Legal Foundation (MSLF), dedicated to fighting "bureaucrats and no-growth advocates," and the Heritage Foundation, the conservative think tank that would emerge from relative obscurity to set much of the policy agenda for the new administration. New Right leader Paul Weyrich, who helped Coors set up Heritage and encouraged Jerry Falwell to form the Moral Majority, hired Ron Arnold to write a subsidized biography of James Watt after Watt left Mountain States to become Reagan's first secretary of Interior.

Direct-mail fundraisers Richard Viguerie and Alan Gottlieb raised hundreds of millions of dollars for various right-wing causes. Gottlieb alone raised tens of millions for the 1980 and 1984 Reagan campaigns. A former head of Youth Against McGovern and board member of Young Americans for Freedom and the American Conservative Union (which led the fight against the Panama Canal Treaty), Gottlieb would take credit for being the first Republican to identify "Reagan Democrats" through selective mailings in six states. Floyd Brown, director of Gottlieb's Center for the Defense of Free Enterprise (CDFE), would go on to produce the infamous race-baiting Willie Horton TV ad in the 1988 presidential campaign along with the less successful 1-800-Gennifer Flowers anti-Clinton ad in 1992. Ron Arnold would take over Brown's responsibilities at CDFE while Gottlieb was serving jail time for tax evasion.

John McLaughery of Vermont, a Reagan national campaign staffer and speechwriter, would move to the White House as senior policy advisor, where he'd help ensure Chuck Cushman's appointment to the National Parks System Advisory Board. Roger Marzulla was assistant attorney general under Ed Meese in the Reagan Justice Department. Today he and his wife, also a former Justice Department official, run the Washington-based Defenders of Property Rights, part of a network of right-wing legal foundations that function as the litigating arm of anti-environmentalism.

Mark Pollot, Marzulla's special assistant on land and natural resources, went on to become a key player in efforts to push anti-enviro "takings" cases through the federal court system. Steve Symms, who for a time would be the voice of the anti-environmental movement on Capitol Hill, was first elected Republican senator from Idaho in the 1980 Reagan landslide. The NRA; the Farm Bureau; and oil, cattle, forestry, and other resource associations that play important roles in today's anti-environmental campaigns were all strong backers of Reagan. The NRA broke its own 109-year tradition of presidential nonpartisanship in order to endorse the former cowboy actor turned politician.

After its founding in 1982, the *Washington Times,* a daily newspaper owned and controlled by the Reverend Sun Myung Moon's Unification Church, would act as media cheerleader for the Reagan revolution. With more than a billion dollars in U.S. investments, the self-styled Korean messiah was a major financial backer of various right-wing and conservative causes. His church-affiliated efforts have included fundraising for Ollie North and the Contras, bailing Richard Viguerie out of a financial tailspin in 1987, and establishing the American Freedom Coalition, which played a key role in early Wise Use organizing drives. Today the *Washington Times* continues to provide comprehensive and sympathetic coverage to the anti-environmental cause (along with Rupert Murdoch's Fox News and other conservative media).

Despite its seminal role in the formation of much of today's anti-green infrastructure, the Reagan revolution would prove a disappointment to many of its most faithful believers. They felt it failed to bring about the kind of long-term institutional changes they desired: reduction of the size of government, creation of an unrestricted free-market economy, silencing of the demands of women and minorities, and elimination of environmental roadblocks to growth and development. A prime example of this disappointment can be found among the West's former Sagebrush rebels. With President Reagan's endorsement of the Sagebrush Rebellion, western resource users believed a massive federal-to-state land transfer was about to take place, but all too quickly they found themselves blindsided by the more radical New Right ideologues gathered around the Heritage Foundation.

"What happened that really lost the momentum of the rebellion is people from Heritage didn't want state control, they wanted privatization," recalled Deane Rhodes. "I remember we had a meeting in Reno where someone from the Heritage Foundation started talking about this privatization angle and things quickly went downhill from there. The sportsmen's groups were the first to drop out, because they all imagined losing access to their favorite fishing holes and hunting areas. Our intent had been, you know, there might be some privatization, but the states would make those decisions."

"We just felt that state governments would prove even more corrupt land managers than the federal bureaucrats," recalls R. J. Smith, who was a consultant to Reagan's Council on Environmental Quality.

Western business interests listened to these warnings of state corruption, smiled, and nodded encouragingly, but the New Right eggheads didn't seem to get it. The last thing western miners, ranchers, and logging companies wanted was to pay full market value for the public lands they were already operating on at little or no cost.

Meanwhile, Reagan advisor Senator Paul Laxalt of Nevada had been given the nod to choose a secretary of Interior. He picked former Wyoming senator Clifford Hansen, but Hansen was unwilling to submit financial disclosure statements. So Laxalt turned to a little-known public-interest lawyer from Denver admired by Attorney General Ed Meese. James Watt, president of the Mountain States Legal Foundation, was an outspoken advocate of the conservative cause who liked to classify people as "liberals" or "Americans."⁵ A Christian fundamentalist, he favored unlimited development of natural resources. Though personal faith should not be a factor in evaluating political appointees, Watt seemed to take pleasure in aggressively arguing his messianic faith as justification for his policy decisions. Asked in a congressional hearing why he was so determined to see public lands rapidly developed, he responded that there was no point in long-term conservation because "I do not know how many future generations we can count on before the Lord returns."⁶ His statement was an early example of what the Christian Right and Wise Use advocates refer to as "dominion theology," a literal reading of Genesis 1:28: "And God blessed them and said to them, Be fruitful and multiply, and replenish the earth and subdue it."

Lanky, bald, and funereal in appearance, Watt was not above questioning the patriotism of those with whom he disagreed. "What is the real nature of the extreme environmentalists, who appear to be determined to accomplish their objectives at whatever cost to society? Is it to delay and deny energy development? Is it to weaken America?" he asked after his first run-in with the militantly moderate conservationists at the National Wildlife Federation.

Watt brought William Perry Pendley, one of his supporters from Mountain States, into the Interior Department as assistant secretary for energy and minerals. He also lobbied for Anne Gorsuch to head up the EPA. Among Gorsuch's qualifications was that she was a leader of the self-styled Republican "crazies" in the Colorado statehouse, where she had opposed hazardous-waste control laws. Her appointment was assured after she agreed with Budget Director David Stockman that the agency could easily get along with a 50 percent cut in funding, a hoop an earlier candidate for the job had refused to jump through. Her chief counsel at the EPA would be a lawyer from Exxon, her chief of enforcement a lawyer from General Motors. She later married Bob Burford, a millionaire Colorado rancher also heavily invested in banks, trailer parks, and oil wells who had been named to head the Bureau of Land Management.

Often identified as a Sagebrush leader, Secretary of Interior Watt was in fact quite happy to see the Sagebrush Rebellion go under in order to get on with the more radical business of selling off the public lands or else leasing them out at what the General Accounting Office (GAO) later termed "fire sale prices."

Privatization of public lands, a bold idea in free-market theory, proved a nonstarter in the real world, with few congresspeople or senators willing to tell the folks back home that their favorite fishing lake or campground had just been sold to Donald Trump, Ted Turner, or some OPEC oil sheik. Nor were most developers spinning cartwheels at the thought of a totally unpredictable nineteenth-century-style land rush. When Watt proposed putting an initial thirty million acres out for bid, environmental lobbyists heading to the Hill to protest found themselves trampled underfoot by real estate lobbyists fearful of the consequences of that much property suddenly being dumped on the open market.

Determined to find some way to transfer all that wealth to the private sector where it could "be put to work," Watt announced that he would open up a billion acres of the outer continental shelf, along with 100 million acres of Alaskan land, to offshore oil leasing and drilling. He leased out millions of acres of western lands for shale-oil and geothermal drilling, pushed for energy development in wilderness areas, tried to block congressional funding for the National Park Service, and held the largest public coal sale in history in the Powder River Basin of Montana and Wyoming north of Teapot Dome.

According to a GAO investigation, the final $67 million coal sale was underpriced by $100 million.[7] After the Mineral Management Service in Wyoming gave its estimate of the market value (an estimate later determined to be too low), two of Watt's deputies in Washington decided the field estimates should be lowered further. These new minimum bids were then illegally leaked to the coal companies (the Reagan Justice Department declined to prosecute). At a meeting on March 19, 1982, three of Watt's men, including William Perry Pendley, decided that the new minimum-bid system should be replaced with an "entry-level" bid, which in practice meant cutting the lowest asking price another 40 percent. Having burned a lot of calories coming up with this formula, Pendley and a fellow bureaucrat went off to dinner with a couple of coal industry attorneys, who picked up the $494.45 meal tab. When Congress decided to investigate the coal-lease system at Interior and depositions started to be taken, Pendley resigned and headed back to Colorado, where several years later he was named president of the MSLF.

Watt—whose confrontational style was rapidly losing him points across the political spectrum, including with Nancy Reagan, who didn't like any shadows crossing her husband's untroubled visage—made several gaffs that would prove fatal to his career. First, he tried to have the Beach Boys banned from performing on the Washington Mall on the Fourth of July, believing they lacked the moral wholesomeness of Wayne Newton, another performer scheduled to appear. That attempt at eccentric moral censorship was publicly laughed off by the southern Californians at 1600 Pennsylvania Avenue. Not so easy to laugh off was his comment following a Senate vote to stop any new coal sales until a special commission reviewed his policies. In extolling the commission, Watt bragged that "we have every kind of mix you can have. I have a black, I have a woman, two Jews and a cripple."[8] Shortly thereafter, having embarrassed the Teflon president, Watt was driven out of town on a rail (with a stake driven through his heart by Nancy Reagan). Among those saddened by his departure was Carl Bagge, president of the Coal Association, who in explaining Watt's leasing policies from industry's point of view told Congress, "We're working for coal, God, and America. All we want is to make a buck and develop coal resources and bring fuel to America."

Meanwhile, another congressional investigation would find that under Anne Gorsuch the EPA was failing to protect the environment. Illegal private meetings with regulated companies, deals for reduced fines to polluters, suspension of safety rules on waste disposal, and new appointees continuing to represent old clients in conflict with the agency became the agency's new standards. With industry favors flying fast and furious, the morale of professional civil servants at the EPA plummeted. One middle manager hung up a hand-lettered sign in his office reading "No good deed goes unpunished."[9]

Typical of the deals going down was a Gorsuch meeting with the Thriftway Company, a small southwestern gasoline refiner that complained about the cost of conversion to unleaded gas. She told them it didn't make sense to enforce EPA regulations on removing lead from gas, since changes were being proposed. After the meeting she talked briefly with a Senate aide who caught up with the Thriftway reps and relayed the message that, although she couldn't tell them directly to break the law, she hoped they'd gotten the point.[10]

In the fall of 1982, the House Energy Committee began requesting EPA documents on hazardous waste dumps and questionable Super-fund enforcement decisions. The White House ordered Gorsuch to withhold the documents under executive privilege, a position even a conservative Republican member of the committee called "bizarre, at best." Rita Lavelle, in charge of the hazardous waste program, took this delay as a sign to begin shredding scores of subpoenaed documents. In the middle of this oversight conflict, flooding in the Midwest spread dioxin contamination throughout the town of Times Beach, Missouri, leading to the emergency evacuation of more than two thousand residents. With the media focus this brought to the congressional hearings, the administration decided it was time to cut its losses. In a move engineered by the White House, the just-married Anne Gorsuch, now Anne Burford, was forced to resign along with some twenty other appointees. Rita Lavelle would eventually serve six months in jail for perjury and obstruction of justice. While later scandals (the savings-and-loan bailout, Iran-Contra) would receive greater media play, the early goings-on at Interior and the EPA would set the tone for the Reagan administration's approach to environmental issues.

Vice President George Bush would also make a fair stab at gutting environmental protections through his oversight of the Task Force on Regulatory Relief. Responding to what the U.S. Chamber of Commerce called the "terrible twenty"[11] business regulations, the Bush task force tried to eliminate or weaken rules for classifying hazardous waste and potential carcinogens, protecting water quality, and licensing nuclear power plants.

As the Reagan era came to a close, Bush, despite his faithful eight years of service, found that he had few friends among the Reagan revolution's true believers, who had never forgiven him for his 1980 primary campaign description of Ronald Reagan's trickle-down, supply-side tax program as "voodoo economics." Bush was seen as a pragmatic preppy in the Nelson Rockefeller mold, and his planned ascension to power in 1988 stirred a deep sense of dread among the party's New Rightists,

Christian fundamentalists, and radical conservatives, a brooding distrust hard to fathom for people outside the hothouse atmosphere of Republican power politics.

Certainly right-wing ideologues such as CDFE's Alan Gottlieb questioned his loyalty to their cause. "My impression of him is that he tries to make you think he supports your position no matter what it is. He's a bit phony and it comes across," Gottlieb claimed, recounting a cocktail-party meeting he and other leaders of the American Conservative Union had with Bush in the spring of 1986. "He's not a very warm person. He doesn't want you to get to know him, was how I felt. I spent most of the evening with Barbara, who I liked very much."[12]

Bush's 1988 campaign rhetoric about being "the environmental president," viewed as an election ploy by seasoned political observers, was taken as a cause for worry by resource industry leaders. Opinion polls were showing interest in the environment crossing traditional political boundaries between Democrats, Republicans, and independents, and anti-enviros feared that George Bush would not let his personal beliefs, whatever they might be, stand in the way of what was popular or expedient.

"No question, we were not greatly enamored of Bush," says Grant Gerber of the Wilderness Impact Research Foundation (WIRF), a nonprofit outfit founded in 1986 with help from the Farm Bureau Federation to oppose federal wilderness designations. "It was pretty scary when Bush came in. Bush was definitely perceived as a danger," agrees Ron Arnold of CDFE. "Bush would suck up to the environmentalists while going to the country club with the corporate types. We were afraid he was going to give the shop away."

Once he was elected to office, Bush's appointment of establishment Republican environmentalists such as Bill Reilly to head the EPA and John Turner as director of the U.S. Fish and Wildlife Service gave the anti-enviros a real case of nerves.

"My boss told me to spend a week getting everything I could on William K. Reilly and what I found out scared the hell out of me," recalls Trent Clarke, legislative aide to former senator Steve Symms (Republican, Idaho). "I went back and told my boss, this guy's a hardcore preservationist, very anti-property. Steve talked to John Sununu. John agreed we couldn't trust him but said his boss wanted the guy, so please let him be nominated."[13]

The anti-environmentalists were reassured by the presence of trusted friends such as White House Chief of Staff John Sununu, who as governor of New Hampshire had pushed hard for the Seabrook nuclear power plant, and Vice President Dan Quayle, whose White House Council on Competitiveness blocked or weakened a number of environmental initiatives. They also liked Office of Management and Budget (OMB) director Richard Darman, who in a speech at Harvard proclaimed, "Americans did not fight and win the wars of the twentieth century to make the world safe for green vegetables." Future president George Bush Jr. would manage to top this inane remark by referring to environmentalists as "Green, Green, Lima Beans."

While resource industries and special-interest lobbies like the Farm Bureau, the American Petroleum Institute, and the American Mining Congress contributed heavily to the Bush election effort, they also hedged their bets in a small but significant way by encouraging and participating in a couple of meetings designed to coordinate anti-environmental campaigns aimed at the creation of pro-industry grass roots.

"Beginning in 1985 we'd held a series of ad hoc meetings with major players from the Farm Bureau, Mountain States Legal Foundation, and Pacific Legal Foundation [PLF], a changing group of eight to twenty people, mostly meeting in Salt Lake City, Utah," recalls Grant Gerber.[14]

In June 1988, Gerber's Wilderness Impact Research Foundation (WIRF), along with the MSLF and the PLF, staged a two-day National Wilderness Conference at the Hilton Hotel in Las Vegas, a large smoke-free casino resort that would later gain notoriety as the site of the navy's sexually predatory Tailhook convention. Announced as "a gathering of groups and individuals concerned about the impact of federal wilderness policy on wildlife, recreation, cities, and industry," it drew some two to three hundred people from sixty industrial, resource, hunting, and motorized-recreation groups to respond to the "threat" of expanded federal wilderness.

"People equate preservationists with socialism, and they're right to do that because the preservationists believe government is the answer to all their problems," explains Gerber, an attorney who runs WIRF out of his single-story graystone law office in Elko, Nevada. "People don't understand that the rancher is the best range manager there is, that when you designate wilderness and take man out of the equation you actually begin to destroy habitat.

"When the first white man came to the Ruby Mountains [outside of Elko] in the 1820s, there were virtually no deer," says the stolid, blond, fourth-generation Nevadan. "Now it's a cornucopia of wildlife. The reason is the cowboys created habitat. The cattle grazed off the grasslands, and shrubs and weeds came up that provided forage for the deer population to grow. Shepherds killed off the predators, the coyotes and bobcats. In the twenties they started using poisons for predator control, and then the deer population exploded. In 1910 there were forty deer in the Rubies. By the 1970s there were forty thousand."

These and similar arguments favoring multiple use of public lands were heard at the conference's nine official sessions. And between the panels, people from various industry associations and state and regional groupings began to network, something relatively new for conferees used to doing their political lobbying from a single-issue or industry perspective. "The meeting included all the majors," Gerber recalls, "the American Petroleum Institute, American Mining Congress, Richard DeChambaugh from NRA, the Farm Bureau. Don Rollins of the Farm Bureau chaired the meeting. Clark Collins from the Blue Ribbon Coalition was there. Ron Arnold and Chuck Cushman were also there. Later, Arnold took all the credit for the movement's founding. But at this meeting, we'd already selected a national steering committee and planned a series of follow-up meetings that took place in eighty-nine, ninety, ninety-one."

"The word *movement* never occurred at Grant's meeting. We went to his conference and thought it was not sufficiently broad enough, that it was still just about wilderness with industry talking to itself," responds Ron Arnold. "Chuck and I were knocked off the program, or only given fifteen minutes each instead of the thirty we'd been promised. We did our Ron and Chuck dog-and-pony show but really we thought it was time to try another tack."[15]

Two months later, in August 1988, CDFE sponsored a three-day Multiple-Use Strategy Conference at John Ascuagga's Nugget Hotel in Reno. This meeting also drew some two to three hundred people. In addition to the $10,000 put up by CDFE, funding and in-kind services were provided by five other groups, including Cushman's National Inholders Association and the Moon-affiliated American Freedom Coalition.

"Essentially this was a militant, very grassroots base. We invited panels of lawyers and citizens groups like Consumer Alert [criticized as anti-consumer by Ralph Nader and Consumers Union]. It was a very spirited conference," Arnold recalls.

Despite its activist tone and commitment to "destroy" the environmentalist enemy, the Reno conference included many of the same players who'd attended Gerber's Las Vegas meeting: the NRA, Farm Bureau, MSLF, PLF, mining and timber associations, some big corporations such as Exxon and DuPont, and small motorized-recreation groups such as the Sourdough Snowmobile Club and Alaska Motorcycle Racing Association.

"The difference between our meeting and Grant's was we weren't going for any of that industry self-pity, that hand-wringing stuff," Arnold claims. "We had this three-hundred pound guy we called the Cuddler, and anytime someone would start hand-wringing in a session he'd go up to them and wrap his arms around them and pat them on the shoulder going, 'There, there.'"

What really set the Reno conference apart, however, was the follow-up publication of a paperback book titled *The Wise Use Agenda,* put out by the Free Enterprise Press, a CDFE subsidiary. By soliciting suggestions from conference participants and then assembling them into a twenty-five-point agenda for a "movement" whose name he'd invented, Ron Arnold was able to advance the process of anti-environmental consolidation he'd been promoting since 1979. That was when he'd first argued that "industry can't stand alone; it needs a grassroots movement to fight for its goals."

Arnold claims that Wise Use, a term appropriated from Gifford Pinchot, is powerful "because it taps a psychological need for symbolic ambiguity," but a reading of "The Top Twenty-Five Goals of the 'Wise Use Agenda'" suggests a complete lack of ambiguity. The goals, drawn from the written suggestions of the American Freedom Coalition, NRA, MSLF, Blue Ribbon, and other conference participants, include the following:

- Immediate development of the petroleum resources of the Arctic National Wildlife Refuge in Alaska.
- Logging three million acres of the Tongass National Forest in Alaska.
- Conversion of "all decaying and oxygen-using forest growth on [sic] the National Forests into young stands of oxygen-

producing carbon dioxide–absorbing trees to help ameliorate the rate of global warming" [cutting down old-growth trees to solve a problem anti-enviros deny exists].

- A foreign policy that "takes steps to insure raw material supplies for global commodity industries on a permanent basis."
- Exempting from the Endangered Species Act, "non-adaptive species such as the California Condor, and endemic (locally based species) lacking the biological vigor to spread in range. ..."
- The right of pro-development groups "to sue on behalf of industries threatened or harmed by environmentalists."
- Opening up seventy million acres of federal wilderness to commercial development and motorized recreational use.
- Opening all public lands "including wilderness and national parks" to mining and energy development.
- Expanding national park concessions under the management of private firms, "with expertise in people-moving such as Walt Disney."[16]

The book was given a bit of symbolic weight by the reprinting of a generic telegram of greeting from President Bush not to the Reno conference but to a meeting of another "member organization of the Wise Use movement," and by a back-cover photo of Bush with Alan Gottlieb. The photo was taken at the 1986 American Conservative Union cocktail party Gottlieb attended with then Vice President George Bush. When Arnold and a small delegation traveled to Washington and tried to personally present their Wise Use agenda to President Bush, they were directed to "some low-ranking, low-echelon official in the back of the executive office building," he recalls with some bitterness.

Nonetheless, as could be predicted, a number of follow-up newspaper and magazine articles would refer to President Bush's telegram of support "to the Wise Use Conference" and appearance with "Wise Use leader" Alan Gottlieb. It was the kind of subtle media ploy that Arnold and Gottlieb would become renowned for.

Anti-environmental organizing efforts, in abeyance during the Reagan administration, began to increase in the wake of the Reno conference, gaining momentum as the economy went into recession. Rising unemployment and the threat of layoffs opened a significant segment of the public to arguments that blamed the breakdown of the traditional family, women in the workforce, immigrants, and environmentalists for their increasingly desperate financial straits. Within a few years of the Las Vegas and Reno conferences, the anti-enviros would be able to claim their first significant victories, won with the quiet assistance and encouragement of key Bush administration insiders.

"There were seven hundred people there. You can't imagine the virulence of the outcry. I was Saddam Hussein, a Communist, a fascist, everything else you could think of. One lady got up there, jaw quivering, used her time to say the Pledge of Allegiance, then looked at me and called me a Nazi. They loaded the hall," recalls former Yellowstone National Park superintendent Robert Barbee of his January 24, 1991, encounter with anti-enviros at a public hearing on the Yellowstone vision document in Bozeman, Montana.[17]

The Yellowstone vision document was a sixty-page plan that grew out of congressional hearings in the mid-1980s. It was designed to chart a long-term course of protection for the vast natural ecosystem surrounding Yellowstone National Park, a twenty million–acre expanse of lightly settled lands that extends through parts of Montana, Wyoming, and Idaho, including Grand Teton National Park and six national forests. Coordinating the effort for the Park Service was Lorraine Mintzmyer, the only woman to serve as a National Park Service regional director.

The Yellowstone vision draft, released in July 1990, stated that the first consideration in land management should be its environmental impact—that though logging, grazing, mining, and drilling would continue in the national forests, they should in the future be done in ways "sensitive to other resource values and uses of the land." The vision plan, although modest in its aims, would limit activities such as geothermal drilling on the northern park boundary that might impact Old Faithful and that was then being planned by the Church Universal and Triumphant, a wealthy religious cult in Park County, Montana. More significantly, it could restrict plans for a massive open-pit gold-mining operation being planned by Crown Butte, a subsidiary of Canada's Noranda, near the tiny mountain settlement of Cooke City on the park's northern border.

Opposition to the vision plan soon coalesced within the mining, logging, and cattle industries. Wise Use, working with these groups, began to organize grassroots resistance, focusing on three public hearings scheduled for Montana. Thousands of letters went out to local residents from the mine industry–financed People for the West, Chuck Cushman's National Inholders Association, and a local resource users coalition. A typical People for the West! letter warned, "What is being proposed is a national park 8.5 times the size of Yellowstone."

"You will lose many of your existing rights," Cushman warned in another letter. "The plan will govern your life."

"We mailed out in the neighborhood of twenty thousand letters, and the trade associations probably did another ten thousand," Cushman recalls. "We included a little postcard saying, 'Please send us a copy of the vision document.' Can you imagine what happened to the people in the vision document headquarters when they got something like ten thousand requests for copies of this? They had no money for it. They literally couldn't pay themselves, because they had to do printing after printing after printing to keep up with it. This gave us more time to organize.

"In Bozeman, a college town that's always been pro-environment, we had 600 out of 750 people on our side," Cushman continues. "We had yellow armbands and the politicians literally looked out on a sea of yellow. ... It wasn't just us. We were in a team play with People for the West, the Western Environmental Trade Association, the Cattlemen, the Farm Bureau from three states. We crushed them in this process."[18]

People for the West! dominated the Montana meetings with prehearing rallies and bus caravans bringing in angry citizen protestors from Wyoming and Idaho. They were given yellow armbands as they got off the buses and told they were fighting for nothing less than their lives and their land. Also helping to organize the protests were staff members from Montana Republican congressman Ron Marlenee's office (Marlenee would go down to defeat in the next election).

After the Bozeman hearing where Park Superintendent Barbee was shouted down, the Department of Interior cancelled planned additional hearings and released a shortened ten-page vision document eliminating any reference to ecosystems management or environmental priorities. Shortly thereafter, National Park Regional Director Lorraine Mintzmyer was reassigned to Philadelphia.

Wise Use activists trumpeted their "Victory at Yellowstone," and soon even environmentalists were repeating their claim. The vision document had been gutted, because Wise Use "out-organized and out-shouted both bureaucrats and environmentalists at public hearings," according to the January/February 1993 issue of *National Parks* magazine.

But a congressional report released in July 1993 showed that a plan had already been under way to destroy the vision document for political reasons and then claim it was done in response to negative public opinion. The 461-page report put out by the House Committee on Post Office and Civil Service and titled "Interference in Environmental Programs by Political Appointees" revealed "an improper concerted activity by powerful commodity and special interest groups and the Bush Administration to eviscerate the Draft Vision document because the commodity and special interest groups perceived it as a threat." The Department of Interior and special-interest groups first destroyed the sixty-page scientific document, turning it into a ten-page "brochure," the report said. "They then developed a story that would explain the revisions and keep their actions a secret. Finally, to protect their acts and in apparent retaliation against Ms. Mintzmyer, the Department of Interior effectuated a directed reassignment which moved Ms. Mintzmyer out of the Rocky Mountain Region and away from the Vision document process."

The fifteen-month investigation of civil service abuses directed against Lorraine Mintzmyer, who resigned after her reassignment when bureaucratic retaliations against her continued, included interviews with forty-five witnesses and reviews of six thousand documents. The report traced the initial plan to destroy the vision document to a series of letters and meetings in the summer and fall of 1990. These included a letter from David Rovig, president of Crown Butte Mining, to Secretary of Interior Manuel Lujan, and meetings among Department of Interior and Agriculture officials, Republican senators Simpson and Wallop of Wyoming, and representatives of commodity groups, including the Wyoming Farm Bureau. There was also a conversation between White House Chief of Staff John Sununu and Deputy Assistant Secretary of Interior for Fish and Wildlife Scott Sewell, in which Sununu told Sewell that from a political perspective the existing draft of the vision document "was a disaster and would have to be rewritten."

In one of the congressional report's chapters, "Keeping the Concerted Activity Secret," the report explains how in the winter of 1991:

1. The individuals and groups involved in the concerted activity
   artificially manufactured the appearance of negative public
   opinion at a few select, local public meetings.
2. Mr. Sewell closed down previously scheduled national hearings
   to avoid anticipated positive comment.
3. The scientific interdisciplinary (ID) team was maneuvered out
   of the revision process.
4. The participants used the manufactured, negative public
   comment to explain why the revisions were allegedly necessary.

Ironically, the congressional report on these abuses was itself subject
to political censorship. The original draft report, dated December 30,
1992, refers to a "conspiracy" between the Bush administration and
commodity and special-interest groups. In the final report, the word
conspiracy has been replaced with the milder *concerted activity*.[19]

On December 18, 1991, President Bush also signed a new multibillion-
dollar highway bill. The bill included a rider, the Symms National
Recreational Trails Act, that allocated $30 million a year for back-
country trail construction, to be paid for out of federal gas taxes. A
minimum of 30 percent and possibly as much as 70 percent of that
money would go for off-road motorized vehicle trails. The act was
named for retiring Republican senator Steve Symms of Idaho and is
likely to be remembered as his outstanding legislative achievement during twelve years in office. Clark Collins, an Idaho trail-bike racer and
founder of the anti-enviro Blue Ribbon Coalition, coordinated much
of the lobbying effort for the act, considered the prime (and only) example of federal Wise Use legislation to be enacted into law. "This is
the first time the preservationists had to accept legislation they opposed
as vigorously as they opposed this bill," says Collins, a mild-mannered
former electrician who refers to environmental organizations such as
the Sierra Club and the Wilderness Society as "hate groups."

"We mobilized recreational users. We drove a tiny wedge between
hiking societies and the hate groups," he claims. "Mountain bikers are
one of the fastest growing groups in the country. We think we can reach
them. We say they're already riding on two wheels, they just haven't
figured how to attach a motor yet."[20]

Millions of Americans, continuing a seventy-five-year-old love affair
with the internal combustion engine, own and use recreational vehicles,

ranging from two-stroke dirt bikes to snowmobiles, dune buggies, and Jet Skis. The off-road vehicle (ORV) industry, aside from providing smelly, high-speed fun and excitement, contributes billions of dollars a year to the balance-of-trade deficit, since most of these small-engine vehicles are manufactured in Japan.

Clark Collins raised his family working as a construction electrician in Pocatello, Idaho, but like tens of thousands of other guys with rangy frames and a good sense of balance, he found religion on any Sunday there was a motocross or cross-country trail-bike race. "I was Eastern Idaho 1972 Overall Motorcycle Association champion, rode a Hodaka, a Japanese bike," he recalled proudly. As he got into the politics of racing and motorcycle associations, his whole family became involved in ORV sports. At sixty, his mother cracked her shoulder falling off a trail bike. Today she rides a four-wheel ATV.

As a member of the International Brotherhood of Electrical Workers (IBEW), Collins fought against a right-to-work law championed by right-wing Idaho senator Steve Symms. But when a wilderness bill threatened to close down one of his favorite dirt-bike trails, he ended up working with Symms to block the Sierra Club proposal and later mobilized "motorized recreationists" for Symms's 1986 reelection campaign.

In 1987, Collins established the Blue Ribbon Coalition with Darryl Harris, publisher of several Idaho-based specialty magazines, including *Potato Grower*, *The Sugar Producer*, and *Snowmobile West*. Their aim was to unite motorized recreationists and resource users from around the country under the tagline "Preserving our natural resources for the public instead of from the public." Early supporters included the American Petroleum Institute, Suzuki, Yamaha, and Kawasaki. In 1988, Collins began meeting with the Washington, D.C.–based American Recreation Coalition (ARC), the Motorcycle Industry Council (MIC), and other small-engine producers and aficionados to develop off-road trails legislation. He also received a grant from the Honda Motor Company that allowed him to work full-time as Blue Ribbon's executive director, attending anti-enviro conferences, contributing his trails proposal to the Wise Use agenda, and lobbying in Washington for adoption of the trails act.[21] Japanese manufacturers of motorcycles and snowmobiles also took out full-page ads in his *Blue Ribbon* magazine (actually a tabloid newspaper), reasoning that any new U.S. wilderness trails for ORVs would quickly translate into new sales for them.

As an act of Wise Use solidarity, the pro-logging Oregon Lands Coalition (OLC) campaigned for the trails bill during its 1991 "Fly-In for Freedom" lobbying trip to Washington. Despite opposition from such groups as the National Wildlife Federation and American Hiking Society, the bill gained momentum. The ARC, MIC, American Motorcyclist Association (AMA), International Snowmobile Industry Association (ISIA), and other off-road vehicle lobbies set up a working task force to push for the bill's passage. ARC's Derrick Crandall ran their day-to-day lobbying operations on the Hill.

"I made a lot of trips to D.C. in ninety-one when it got real intense, when it got down to the short strokes on the final passage and they were trying to sidetrack it," Collins recalls of the last-minute maneuvering that went on around the bill.[22] Finally, on Sunday, November 24, 1991, just before a House/Senate conference committee voted in favor of the Trails Act, Senator John Warner of Virginia suggested the bill be named in Symms's honor. Three weeks later, President Bush signed off on the highway-transportation bill including the Symms rider.

After passage of the Symms Act, the Blue Ribbon Coalition fought budget cutbacks while continuing to try to promote other anti-enviro causes among ORV enthusiasts. The cover story of their winter 1993 issue of *Blue Ribbon* magazine was titled "Crown Butte Mines Assist Snowmobilers," a long paean to the mining company's efforts to help snowmobilers by rerouting them around a mine construction road. This was near Cooke City on the border of Yellowstone, where Crown Butte planned its huge open-pit mining operation. Blue Ribbon also argued that Forest Service construction of logging roads was not really a timber industry subsidy, since they could later be used as motorcycle and ATV recreational trails once the trees had been removed. Clark says his preservationist opponents "want all our roadless areas to be designated 'Wilderness,'" but under the Symms Act several new trails were built in the mountains outside of Pocatello, Idaho, trails that Clark takes great pleasure in riding on his Honda XR-250, which he calls "a nice quiet bike."

At the end of the September 1991 Fly-In for Freedom, the second D.C. lobbying trip organized by the OLC participants from around the country met in a room at the Marriott Hotel in Crystal City, Virginia, where they decided to hold a follow-up meeting in St. Louis on November 8. There, "where the wagon trains formed up to head West," they formed the Alliance for America, an anti-enviro network of local activists and resource associations that modestly described itself as "the most powerful grassroots organization this country has ever seen."

They set up a steering committee that included the Oregon Land Coalition's Tom Hirons; WIRF's Grant Gerber; June Christle, a tugboat company operator from Alaska; Joan Smith, a rancher's wife from California; and Tee John Mialjevich, a commercial shrimper from Gretna, Louisiana, who'd been leading Gulf of Mexico fishing boat blockades in protest of TEDs, turtle excluder devices, which reduce the death rate of endangered sea turtles caught and drowned in shrimpers' trawl nets. In 1989, George Bush's secretary of commerce Robert Mossbacher had been widely criticized after he tried to lift TED requirements in response to the "volatile situation" Mialjevich had created in the Gulf. Among Secretary Mossbacher's critics were the writers and illustrators of the *Teenage Mutant Ninja Turtles* comics, who introduced into their strip a new anti-turtle villain, the evil "Captain Mossback."[23]

David Howard, a Property Rights activist and resident of New York's Adirondack Park, was named chairman of the newly formed Alliance for America. Alliance funding came from the Moon-affiliated American Freedom Coalition, the American Farm Bureau Federation, Cattlemen's Association, American Mining Congress, Chemical Manufacturers Association, Petroleum Institute, and several other industry groups.

The third Fly-In for Freedom, and the first sponsored under the alliance banner, was held in September 1992 and drew some 350 people from across the country, including loggers, lobbyists, lawyers, miners, a couple of farmers from Wisconsin, Property Rights activists from New Hampshire and the Adirondacks, and Tee John's shrimpers from Louisiana and Texas. They lobbied against the Clean Water and Endangered Species Acts, argued about the need "to put people back in the environmental equation," and picketed CBS, claiming that Dan Rather was an environmentalist. Their lobbying efforts and much of their access to various government agencies were facilitated by members of the Bush reelection campaign. In the wake of the Rio Earth Summit that June, the administration had staked out a hard line anti-environmental position. But not all the Bush officials they met with proved themselves loyal to their commander in chief.

Joan Smith recalls how she and Nadine Bailey, an unemployed logger's wife from Hayfork, California, had, during an earlier scout trip with Federated Women in Timber, met David McIntosh, the policy director for Vice President Quayle's Council on Competitiveness. "He was very nice and cut to the essence and told us we needed someone to carry our banner, and I don't remember how we were then put in touch with Pat Buchanan [who was running against Bush in the Republican primaries at the time] but we were. Pat and his wife and aides later flew into Redding Municipal Airport, and we had cars there to meet him and led a caravan to Hayfork. He mentioned that visit to Hayfork during his speech to the Republican convention."[24]

While anti-enviro groups such as People for the West!, Blue Ribbon, and the Alliance for America were gaining strength during the Bush years by attacking the Washington political establishment that was quietly using and supporting them, the spotted owl controversy exploded in the Pacific Northwest. The administration's refusal to enforce the Endangered Species Act after years of government-subsidized overcutting of old-growth forests and a subsequent federal court order suspending all logging in spotted owl habitat on the region's public lands set off a broad-based, well-organized environmental backlash. By the spring of 1993, the growing conflict had begun to poison the region's reputation for social tolerance. Stories in the newspapers and on TV showed spotted owls shot and nailed to Forest Service signposts, long-haired protestors being dragged off logging trucks, and angry mill workers marching through the streets of dying timber towns. But it was still difficult to get a sense of who all the players were. On the environmental side there were some familiar names like Earth First!, the Oregon Natural Resources Council, and the Sierra Club Legal Defense Fund joined by several new players, including commercial salmon fishermen and Native American tribal councils worried about declining fish runs and dying rivers resulting in part from clear-cut logging. But to the national media it was all "owls versus loggers," or, for the factoid-oriented press like *USA Today*, "4,600 Owls vs. 32,100 Jobs."[25]

If environmentalists' arguments got lost in the media coverage, the timber industry's political forces were reduced to an insulting caricature of a wide-suspendered logger wearing a "Spotted Owl Tastes Like Chicken" tee shirt. Perhaps, as many suspected, the urban-based media were simply unfamiliar with who was doing the ground-level organizing to turn out industry's troops.

Who were timber's frontline political warriors and how effective a force did they really have to combat the environmental revolution's advancing agenda? The only way to find that out would be to travel to the scene of the conflict and let the counterrevolutionaries speak for themselves.

three

The Forest for the Trees, 1993

The working class and the employing class have nothing in common.
                              —Preamble to the Constitution of the
                                        Industrial Workers of the World

Hungry and out of work? Eat an environmentalist.
     —Bumper Sticker Seen at an Industry-Sponsored Logging Rally

THE OREGON STATE CAPITOL in Salem was built in 1938 in what might be described as a World's Fair Neo-Greco-with-turret style of architecture. Two Vermont marble frescoes, of Lewis and Clark and a covered wagon, bracket the main entrance. Atop the giant thimble-shaped turret stands a twenty-three-foot-high goldleaf statue of a bare-chested pioneer logger holding a single-bladed ax. Just inside the building, beyond the rotunda, is a Georgia-Pacific display case filled with old saws, axes, and logging photos. You'd never guess that timber represents less than 5 percent of Oregon's modern workforce, although admittedly a twenty-three-foot-tall goldleaf statue of a bare-chested software designer might create its own set of problems.

I enter a meeting room on the third floor of the four-story building where sixty people have gathered from the Oregon Lands Coalition (OLC), the state's anti-enviro umbrella group. The OLC was established in 1989 by log company operator Tom Hirons along with Valerie Johnson, sister of State Senator Rod Johnson. Financial support has come from Weyerhauser, Boise Cascade, the Oregon Farm Bureau, and the NRA among others.[1] An outgrowth of the 1988 Oregon Project run by Bill and Barbara Grannell (now of People for the West!), OLC has organized anti–spotted owl and anti–endangered species rallies. It has led a boycott of a Turner Broadcasting Audubon special on logging, and has helped establish the Alliance for America, which sponsors annual Fly-In for Freedom lobbying trips to Washington.[2] OLC spokeswoman Jackie Lang introduces me to Marlin Aerni and three of his union brothers who have joined eastern Oregon ranchers, their rural community supporters, and logging association employees for today's state lobbying effort.

Aerni is a bluff, gregarious guy with a quick, wide smile who looks like he might be hiding a medicine ball under his black-striped engineer's shirt. His thinning blond bangs frame a squared-off, sun-weathered face. His penetrating blue-gray eyes have an edge of hardness that doesn't always match his ready smile. Aerni is president of Local 1189, the Halsey, Oregon, pulp mill chapter of the 250,000-member United Paperworkers International. Over the last five years, he has helped mobilize his 130 workers for yellow-ribbon and OLC rallies against Forest Service restrictions on logging and against endangered species protection of the spotted owl, an indicator species for the forest's health.

"Last year our local spent $9,000 on timber issues. Just this month, with the timber summit coming up and all, we're spending $6,000 on newspaper ads," he tells me. "I lobby here in Salem and also fight environmental overregulation. And the company doesn't put any restrictions on me. When they foot the bill to send me to D.C. to lobby on resource issues, they know I also lobby on the striker bill [which bars employers from hiring permanent replacements for workers on strike]. They don't mind. They know we're not going to strike, because we've got the best contract in the industry."

In 1988, companies such as Pope & Talbot, Simpson Timber, James River, Boise Cascade, and Georgia-Pacific began working closely with a number of their employees to provide paid days off and free transportation and meals for those attending anti-environmentalist yellow-ribbon rallies.[3] Some companies even paid their workers' membership dues in anti-enviro organizations. The companies also provided their unions with industry-funded research on the impact of the Endangered Species Act, log exports, and other forest issues the unions couldn't afford to research on their own (having recently been forced to accept pay cuts by many of these same companies).

Marlin Aerni was raised in Albany, Oregon, close to the Pope & Talbot mill, where he now works. His father and uncle also worked the mills. His grandfather, a dairy farmer in the Trout Lake area, used to float his cheese downriver by raft to Portland. "There were twenty-five mills in the area when I was growing up. Now there are maybe six left. The first time the company approached our local about helping them, in eighty-eight, we said we couldn't work with them. They were jerks back then," Aerni laughs. "But then the expansion they'd been planning didn't come, and we saw 100 to 150 new union jobs go down the tube because of this dioxin talk. So I got a week off from the company and they gave me some names, some retired university people, and I began to research this dioxin thing. I went to the environmentalists and even the Centers for Disease Control and all them other agencies. I asked this environmentalist lady, 'What is it you want?' She said, 'We don't want you on our river.' After I almost strangled the bitch, I realized very few of these people are credible or interested in the facts. It's more like a religion for them."

So Aerni got active in the OLC. "The first time I met Charlie Janz [the outgoing president of OLC], well, he's an anti-union gyppo [independent] logger, and we just glared at each other. Finally I got in his face and said, 'Are your guys unionized?' and he said, 'Hell, no.' And I said, 'Well, you must treat your workers well, 'cause none of them have called me up.'"

I ask Aerni and the other union men how they feel about working in coalition with gyppo loggers, industry lobbyists, and Republicans. Paul Sullivan, a bald, mustachioed official with the Association of Western Pulp and Paper Workers, shakes his head morosely. "You have to understand. When I'm down here lobbying and feel depressed, I go visit a Republican, because they're the ones with us on these resource issues."

Aerni cuts off his friend. "The thing is, see, we have to get the Democrats off this liberal green, save-the-world kick and back to doing what's right for the workers here," he explains. "We had this Jim Jontz of Indiana who was going after our jobs out here, who wanted to lock away the resource, and so we took fifteen union people out to his district to canvass door-to-door. The way I was going to do it was to hit up local industries here for the money, but it turned out that was illegal. So Mike Drapper [head of the Western Council of Industrial Workers] said, 'Let me set up a PAC,' and we went back there and our brothers in the United Auto Workers [UAW] didn't like us at all and were fairly hostile because Jontz was their man. So we agreed not to come around their factories or union halls, but we were out there in the malls and on the local talk radio and stuff and we beat him. He lost the election."

Jim Jontz, a four-term Democratic congressman from Indiana, was defeated in the 1992 elections by a combination of factors, including large oil, timber, and mining donations to his Republican opponent, Gulf War veteran Steve Buyer, who campaigned in his chocolate-chip camouflage utilities. Jontz was also targeted by the Farm Bureau because of his support for protection of the Indiana dunes area along Lake Michigan.

"Those fifteen union guys had a very marginal impact. They were a sideshow at best," says the ex-congressman, who, when interviewed in late 1993, was back in Washington lobbying against the North American Free Trade Agreement (NAFTA). "They set up a $30,000 PAC, a P.O. box in Indiana, to fly themselves in and put themselves up for two weeks at the nicest motel in Kokomo, but labor wouldn't let them do anything once they got there. What had a greater impact, I think, was the $50,000 in direct donations the timber industry provided my opponent."

Jack Williams, of UAW Local 685 in Kokomo, is less sanguine in his assessment. "I hope to hell those guys come back to visit us now," he says, following with an anatomically improbable suggestion involving his union brothers and a spotted owl. "They call themselves labor but they weren't brave enough to come see us, to sit down and talk things over. Instead they were off with the Republicans, doing their dirty work. We have over 10,000 UAW members in the Fifth District, and any time we had a problem with plant closings or anything like that we could count on Jim for help and support. He had something like a 100 percent voting record for labor. Now we have a quite anti-union congressman, partly because of those guys. And the funny thing to me is they're fighting to kill their own jobs, which is what will happen in a few years if they cut down all the forests. What they should be fighting is that cheap labor overseas with those log exports and runaway shops."

I go along with Aerni and six others from the OLC lobbying group to a 3 P.M. meeting with State Representative Greg Walden, the Republican majority leader in the Oregon House. Our group is left waiting in a small conference room for fifteen minutes while Walden finishes off talks with lobbying seniors, health care providers, and sheriffs. He finally enters the room wearing the small yellow flower and lapel ribbon the OLC passed out earlier. Walden's a tall, bland-looking man with a high forehead and the flat brown eyes of a predator fish. He tells us how he remembers the first big yellow-ribbon demonstrations outside the statehouse back in 1988 and how he'd told the organizers they should do a similar march on Washington. He then turns to Aerni. "I heard how you guys helped get rid of Jim Jontz. You really made the difference. That was a great job you did."

Aerni flashes his wide smile. "We understand you're thinking of running for governor," says Aerni, "and we're not happy with Barbara [Roberts, the Democratic governor]. We know where you're at and we'd like to support you if certain union things could be resolved. We should talk about union issues sometime."

"Absolutely," Walden agrees.

Aerni leans back, crossing his hands across his gut, a satisfied man.

"We need to do something about this salmon business," complains a rancher from eastern Oregon. "You know, most of those fish are disappearing at sea or behind the dams. There's no reason to be blaming the cattleman."

"That's federal," Walden commiserates. "I don't think there's a lot we can do about that, but I think what we can do at the state level is move back to minimal federal standards on things like the Clean Air Act. We don't need to punish ourselves by being more stringent than we have to be."[4] Although solidly Republican/Wise Use, the eastern Oregon ranch vote has about as much real impact as the Portland grunge rocker vote. To put it another way, if elk could vote, most politicians east of the Cascades would have antlers and wet noses.

At the end of the day, Aerni invites me to visit his pulp mill anytime I want. A week later I take him up on his offer.

ON MY WAY to the Halsey, Oregon, mill I stop in Centralia, Washington, a onetime railroad and logging center. On the walls of the old brick-fronted downtown along Tower Avenue are historic murals of an 1860s farmyard, the railroad station, even Buffalo Bill's Wild West Show, commemorating its visit to town in 1910. Only the gunfight and lynching of 1919 are missing. I stop by the *Centralia Daily Chronicle*, where I'm guided to a framed copy of the newspaper dated Tuesday, November 11, 1919. I'm surprised at the main headline: "Coal Miner Strike Ends, Indianapolis, U.M.W." Only below that is the local banner:

"McElfresh, Grimm and Casagranda killed by IWW. Five more Centralians wounded by Wobblies, murderers are nearly lynched. Soldiers who defended our country shot down on streets by IWWs as they marched down Tower Avenue. Boys had no chance to defend themselves. Town scoured for skunks." As I'm copying this down, two young reporters are teasing a third who doesn't want to go hunting with them. "I just don't like guns," he smiles, shaking his head no.

I drive down to the Skookumchuck, a brown, slow-moving river that runs past the freeway. Where the old trestle bridge once stood is a green steel-frame span rebuilt in 1959 near a Seventh-Day Adventist church. It was here on the night of November 11, 1919, that they lynched Wesley Everest, a World War I veteran. This was just one more incident in the ongoing labor wars then convulsing the northwestern timber industry, as lumberjacks and mill workers attempted to organize for an eighthour day, wages they could live on, and clean camps. In Seattle a hundred thousand workers staged a five-day general strike followed by police raids and hundreds of arrests. In Spokane the Industrial Workers of the World—the Wobblies mentioned in the *Chronicle* article— led a free-speech fight, filling the jails in protest after their street meetings were banned. Beaten and starved, several men died in their cells before the ban was finally lifted. In Everett, Washington, vigilantes and police opened fire on two steamboats carrying three hundred IWW members to a picnic and rally. Five Wobblies were killed along with two vigilantes, more than fifty people were injured, and seven were reported missing. And in lumber camps all across the north woods there were strikes, bedroll burnings, double bunks axed down to singles, and tree spikings when the industry tried to break the strikes using the Loyal Legion of Loggers and Lumbermen. In Centralia the Lumber Trust worked with the American Legion to destroy the local IWW: Legionnaires raided the union hall and beat up Wobblies with gas pipes and rubber hoses. When the Legionnaires returned a few weeks later, marching past the union hall on Armistice Day, gunfire broke out. It was never established who fired first, but as Legionnaires charged the hall, Wesley Everest, wearing his army uniform, was heard to tell a union brother, "I fought for democracy in France and I'll fight for it here. The first man through that door is gonna get it." He was as good as his word and shot a man, but then his rifle jammed and he headed for the river, a pistol in his hand, chased by an angry mob. Halfway across the river he turned and, firing from the hip, killed a second man, Dale Hubbard, the nephew of the timber boss who had organized the anti-IWW raids. As he was beaten, Everest taunted the mob, "You haven't the guts to hang a man in the daytime." He was right. That night he was taken from the town jail, castrated, and hung from the Skookumchuck River bridge, his body riddled with rifle fire. "Tell the boys I died for my class," he'd told his cellmates just before he was taken away.

No one was ever arrested for Wesley Everest's lynching, but according to a later state inquiry, six Wobblies were wrongfully convicted for the Tower Avenue shootings and served fifteen years in prison before being pardoned in the 1930s.[5]

Unlike the coal trusts in Appalachia, whose industrial wars with the United Mine Workers (UMW) ended in an armed truce, the northwestern timber industry succeeded in destroying the Wobblies and those who followed them in attempting to organize the region's widely dispersed loggers and mill hands. The resulting weakness of organized labor in the Northwest was reflected as recently as the 1980s when, under the anti-labor policies of the Reagan administration, a number of unions were forced to downsize and take $2-an-hour wage cuts at a time when the timber industry was posting record profits.[6]

Ninety minutes after crossing into Oregon, I leave Interstate 5 on my way to the Halsey mill and drive past flat green fields of grazing sheep toward white plumes of smoke rising in the distance. Several chimneys come into view, the largest, at more than three hundred feet, a red and white vapor stack. I turn off at a fenced drive with a large wooden sign reading "Pope & Talbot, Inc." to admire a thick log segment in front of the company's administration building. A plaque tells me that the log is 87.5 inches in diameter and was taken from a 434-year-old Douglas fir cut down on federal land back in 1970. The plaque doesn't say how tall the tree was, only that it produced sixty thousand board feet of lumber.

The guard at the main gate directs me through a complex of giant industrial cookers, silos, and overhanging pipes to a four-story concrete-block building. Opposite the concrete building are 150-foot-high cinnamon-brown mounds of woodchips and sawdust. Clanking around on top of these chip dunes are a pair of big yellow bulldozers, pushing the stuff into drifts and piles—the kind of work every child in America wants to grow up to do. Aerni, wearing a purple union jacket, comes out to meet me and leads me upstairs to a cafeteria area where the snack machines are located. We're joined there by Robert Sherwood, the company's environmental manager. Through the fourth-floor windows, I watch a dozer climb past us on its way to the top of a chip mound. Aerni and Sherwood begin to talk about their problems with the nearby city of Corvallis, population 4,300.

"Our discharge pipe is upriver from the city water treatment," Bob Sherwood tells me. "We have to purify 90 to 95 percent of our waste, just like they do, but our wastes are stronger."

"The city of Corvallis doesn't want to spend money on sewage treatment. They want to ratchet down on our permits, and they think if they can squeeze us down they won't have to spend the money," Aerni claims. "The people I've met are raising hysteria. It's all bullshit lies. Tannin releases are more visible is all. We used to bleach out the tannin with chlorine so our effluent wasn't visible and nobody complained, but since 1987 we stopped doing that and the color went visible."

When you stand on the bank of the Willamette downstream from the plant's outfall pipe, you can see what Aerni's talking about. There's a line in the river where the water turns from green-blue to a brown-tea color. The brown color comes from lignin (or tannin), the glue that holds wood fibers together. It looks weird, froths the surface, and stains boat hulls but is considered relatively harmless by the state Department of Environmental Quality, at least compared with the chlorine compounds the company once used to bleach its effluent. In fact, it's the chlorine bleaching of white paper and the dioxin that process creates that have raised concern about human health and environmental impacts in recent years. The Halsey mill is now in the process of building an oxygen delignification cooker to reduce its dependence on chlorine.

"We'll meet our requirements to be chlorine-free, or almost totally chlorine-free, by 1997," Sherwood promises. "The technology's coming online. We can solve the dioxin problem, but wood supply and this vocal public comment is another problem. One of Corvallis's big concerns is they don't want us expanding, no matter what."

"They have this 'I got mine and I don't care' attitude," Aerni says of the plant's numerous critics in town. "A good share of them are retired and have nothing to do but keep track of us." His brow furrows as he prepares to make the most onerous charge one can hurl in Oregon. "A lot of them are from California," he claims. "The first thing I ask is where they're from, and it's either California or back east somewhere."

Aerni takes me through the shop area to his Oldsmobile Royale parked outside. We climb in and drive around to the back side of the chip pile, where we watch a big semi-trailer detach from its cab, rise up on a hydraulic lift like a Patriot missile launcher box ready to fire, and spill a load of chips from its bottom doors. With some five hundred tons of pulp processed here every day, the mound receives about a hundred truckloads of Douglas fir chips and sawdust daily. Aerni takes a pinch of wintermint-flavored Kodiak Smokeless Tobacco and puts it inside his mouth up against his cheek. Soon he opens the door and spits the first of a series of brown wads onto the ground.

We pass under a pipe bridge connecting the pulp silos and the James River paper mill across the road. There's a white lime buildup on the ground and a blistery refrigerant odor in the air. As we climb a ladder above the water intake tanks, Aerni explains the pulping process to me. "We take the chips and run 'em through the digester that cooks out the lignin, the glue that holds the tree together. Then we take the fiber — the cellulose — and wash out the chemicals from the digester using lye and other caustics. We bleach the fiber with chlorine and take it to the paper-making machines across the road."

From the roof of the recycling plant, we have a sweeping vista. Sixty acres of scummy brown settling ponds are being aerated by giant blue fiberglass eggbeaters. Frank Perry, who was also in Salem for the OLC lobby day, joins us here. He's a jolly-seeming guy with full white hair, a sandy mustache, and a respectable beer belly, although nothing to compare with Aerni's. He's brought along a yellow hard hat and safety glasses for me. Perry is IBEW political director for the mill as well as the union's environmental lobbyist. Aerni and Perry explain that in the days when the plant's effluent was chlorine-bleached, the clarified wastewater would be run through a fish tank to test it for toxicity.

"Those fish grew pretty big," Perry says. "Wonder what happened to them?"

"They were some good-looking fish. I wouldn't be surprised if someone didn't take them home for a barbecue dinner," Aerni smiles.

We go inside and up to the ninth floor of the roaring recovery unit, past small glass ports that look into the flaming heart of the furnace where the green and white chemical "liquors" used to process the cellulose are recycled. "The caustic cooks the chips ... lime and calcium carbonate are used in the cellulose-washing system," Perry shouts to me over the thundering din of machinery. We enter a control room where three men are watching banks of switches. Perry points to a pair of black and white monitors showing the burning heart of the pressure vessel. "We put the green liquor through the evaporators and run it off," he continues, still shouting. "It's extremely volatile at this stage, the controlled green liquor." I nod like I understand what the hell he's talking about.

Back outside, we walk past railroad boxcars used for taking out pulp and black chemical tanker cars that bring in the chlorine, caustic soda, and limestone used in processing the chips. We stop at the union trailer where Aerni has his office.

"Last strike we had was in eighty-eight," he recalls. "Over contract language. It lasted fifteen days. We were out there on the line and they had to operate with their own management people, so we knew that couldn't go on too long."

"Jesse Jackson was here," Perry volunteers. "Yeah, Jesse Jackson came out and spoke on the picket line, got everyone fired up. It was a great scene. Don't know who's gone off with his picture though," Aerni says, pivoting around on his chair as if to search it out. He points to a plaque hanging over his desk. "I'm kind of proud of that one."

It's a bronze and wood plaque reading "1991 APA Activist of the Year," given by the American Pulpwood Association, the industry lobby. "It's the first time they ever gave one to a union person," he grins. "We're all learning we've got to work together, because if this industry goes down our jobs go down with it."

Frank Perry motions for me to follow him out of the trailer and over to the washing unit. On the ground floor is a continuous vertical belt about eighteen inches wide, made of hard rubber segments connected with metal teeth. Small pop-up metal platforms with handholds are part of the belt coming out of the floor. I watch Perry step onto one and rise toward a hole in the ceiling above us. I follow. The belt pulls us up through concrete holes a little wider than shoulder width through the floors of the building. Looking up, I can see Perry step off the moving belt on the fourth-floor ledge above me. I step off after him. We're standing near a wide corridor flanked by big metal cookers that look like brewpub tanks lying on their sides. The first one has open side panels, and we can see yellow pulp cooking away in a goopy corn-colored mix. Down the central aisle on the other side we can see blackish pulp churning away. From the last cooker on the left, we pull out some bleached white pulp that looks and smells like wet paper towels. When this pulp crosses the pipe bridge over the road to the James River Company, the wire paper machines will turn it into "rough product" such as paper towels and toilet paper. We wave to the men and women in the computerized control room before climbing back onto the belt loop.

Outside I pause to talk with Perry. I've noticed that when Aerni's around, Perry tends to keep his peace, the volume of available air in any given space being what it is. It turns out that Perry is an ex–Green Beret and seventh Dan blackbelt, but very laid back about it.

"I was in Vietnam in the early sixties doing preparation work for what was to follow. You know JFK was preparing to withdraw [from Vietnam] within eighteen months of his reelection. I think JFK was killed by the military-industrial complex. I know *they* had no intention of getting out of there." I ask him if he's seen the Oliver Stone movie based on the same premise, but he hasn't. He begins talking about the oxygenation system they're installing at the mill and mentions that they've just avoided a nine-month shutdown.

"Because of the logging restrictions?" I ask.

"No. Because Sweden devalued the Kroner. That's allowed the Scandinavians to flood the European market, which means that Pope & Talbot lost its niche there. Pope & Talbot sells pulp at $330 a ton, versus the $243 a ton the Swedes can now offer. So instead of a $3 million loss this year from increased chip costs, they began looking at a $15 million loss. They thought that with a nine-month shutdown here they could save $10 million, but then after considering the loss of continuity and what their absence from the market might do, they decided against it. It was strictly an economic decision on their part."

"So what do you make of that?"

"I take my karate students to Japan every year and so maybe that gives me a different perspective from outside the area, but I can see that it's all a part of a world economy now. These adjustments will take place, there'll be a new standard established for a sustainable yield, and some of the smaller companies probably won't make it. But that's what happens. I just hope Oregon stays affordable so that the people who were born here will be able to keep on living here. Right now, the way it's going, I think the state will be unaffordable in my kids' lifetime."

I ask him about the anti-enviro rally the unions are organizing with the OLC and Wise Use for the upcoming Forest Summit in Portland. The summit, promised by Bill Clinton during his 1992 election campaign, will bring together all the players in the northwest timber wars to try to resolve their conflicts.

"It will be kind of a last hurrah for the timber issue," he says, surprising me. "Things are never going back to the way they were. And the thing is, I don't really blame it on the spotted owl or marbled murrelet [another endangered bird]. We let the government get away with fifty years of mismanagement and that makes me angrier than spotted owls or any of that stuff. They just did the bidding of the special interests and let things go until they reached the state they're in now."

GOOD FORESTRY is a matter of perspective. For two days before the April 1993 Forest Summit in Portland, Oregon, local television is inundated with thirty- and sixty-second spots from OLC, Weyerhauser, and other industry reps showing lush ridgelines full of luxuriant second-growth Douglas firs. Shot from about five hundred feet above the ground, the ads carry the message that the region's trees are a bountiful and renewable resource for today and tomorrow. This message is visually confirmed by the vast-seeming forests passing majestically in the foreground as well as the second green ridgeline visible in the middle distance. What the ads fail to show is the third ridgeline or the valley in between.

On the day after we arrive in Portland to cover the Forest Summit, Nancy and I take a flight at twenty-five hundred feet above Gifford Pinchot National Forest in a yellow and white Cessna Cardinal. From here the mountain range resembles an old retriever dog suffering from a terminal case of mange. In any direction you look you see a patchwork landscape of broken wood lots and tan-colored earth. We pass a four thousand–foot mountain that's been stripped bare and cut up from summit to base by logging roads making cross-hatchings in the late spring snow. Banking, we fly along a ravine too steep for easy logging, passing a ragged fragment of mixed 200- to 300-year-old Douglas fir, cedar, and hemlock that looms above and protects a narrow blue-line stream looking like it might harbor some good-sized fish. Over the next ridgeline we spot a red front-loader and some yellow trucks parked near a raw exposed bog in the middle of yet another clear-cut, a cut that goes downslope to a river without the required protective buffer of trees. I click on my headset mike and ask Jay Noyes, our pilot, "Isn't that illegal?" "Probably," he answers, sounding as if he's seen worse.

Noyes thinks the yellow trucks might be there for replanting. The companies like to replant 80 percent Douglas fir to 20 percent hemlock. Alders will also sneak in to colonize cutover areas. Alders are good trees for replacing nitrogen in the soil but lousy for lumber. The companies don't like them and, where they can, spray them with herbicide.

We fly over a serpentine hillside where forty- to sixty-year-old second-growth fir is coming back as evenly and luxuriantly as the fur on a ranch-bred pelt. As we approach its southern boundary, I wonder what forester Gifford Pinchot would think of this half-cleared national tree farm. Looking down, we can see a razor-straight line of trees that marks the end of the patchy U.S. forest and the beginning of Weyerhauser's private lands, a vast denuded moonscape running down to the Swift Reservoir. The bad/worse dividing line stretches in either direction as far as the eye can see. It's a depressing example of free-market environmentalism, or at least the export tax incentive program that inspired the lumber companies to ship one out of four logs to Asia during the record cuts of the 1980s.[7] Heading back toward Portland, we fly along the Columbia River, passing over rafts of logs floating below the huge Weyerhauser pulp plant at Kelso/Longview. We cross over the Cowlitz River where it feeds into the Columbia, its waters still gray from ash more than a decade after the eruption of Mount St. Helen's, which rises, cloud-shrouded, in the distance.

Thirty thousand feet up is another perspective worth having. If the weather cooperates, any commercial airline flight between San Francisco and Seattle will provide the opportunity. Looking down at Mount St. Helens from that height, seeing the gray landscape, the debris-filled lake, the altered rivers, and the ravages from the 1980 volcanic eruption gives one momentary pause, restoring a sense of wonder and awe at the overwhelming power of nature to mark the land. At six hundred miles an hour, you've left the volcano behind in a few moments. What you haven't left behind, what is so subtly imprinted on your mind that it takes an act of will to realize, is the much greater imprint on the landscape produced by years of clear-cut logging and development. Although we still speak of the great northwestern forests, what we really see during hours of overflight is not a forest at all, but a strained ecosystem patchwork no wilder than grandma's quilt.

"Twenty Niner One, you're cleared for landing," the control tower tells us as our Cessna bumps down through turbulence over suburban Portland. We land on a secondary runway and taxi to the commercial airport's civil aviation area. Noyes, at the controls of the small single-engine plane, is an aerial photographer who works out of Hood River, Oregon. He's tall and slim with gray-blond hair. "When I moved out here from Colorado," he tells me as Nancy and his other passenger climb out from under the wing, "I figured I'd rather have a plane and a small house than a large house and no plane." He admits that he bought his Cardinal "half thinking of what would be the best plane for Lighthawk."

Lighthawk labels itself the environmental air force. It's made up of volunteer pilots from around the country who provide overflights of threatened habitats for activists, politicians, and the media from Canada to Costa Rica. On the day before the Forest Summit, they've assembled five prop planes and a helicopter for media overflights of some of the disputed logging areas. As we enter the terminal, a CNN crew is gearing up, hoping to beat out the storm front now gathering over the mountains. They'll be flying with George Atiyeh of Mill City, Oregon, in his blue and white twin Comanche.

A youthful-looking forty-five with dark brown hair pulled back in a ponytail, a cavalry man's mustache, and lively gray eyes behind thin gold glasses, Atiyeh is an eminent member of a long-established local clan. But even his deep familial roots in Oregon's timber and mining culture—his family filed its first claims in 1859, one of his grandfathers ran Pacific Lumber, his uncle was the state's governor in the 1980s— haven't kept Atiyeh from being targeted in the ongoing timber wars.

"In the late seventies and early eighties, I was flying back and forth to our sawmill in eastern Oregon, and from the air I could see how overcut the forests were," he explains. "After a few years of this, I was having trouble reconciling my own rhetoric about sustainable yields with what my eyes were seeing."

In 1981, Atiyeh sold his logging interests and began speaking out for better forestry practices. In 1983 he testified at the statehouse in favor of a wilderness bill and scenic-river protections his uncle, the governor, opposed. He also spent much of the 1980s battling the U.S. Forest Service. He had an underground silver mine in the Opal Creek area, forty miles east of Salem, amidst a three thousand–acre stand of old-growth forest, including eight hundred–year–old Douglas firs. Early in the decade, he decided he was going to protect Opal Creek. Since it was inside the Willamette National Forest, he expanded his "Shiny Rock" mining claims, using the 1872 mining law to block the Forest Service from logging in the area. "We had to go to court and spend hundreds of thousands of dollars fighting them, because they knew that what we really intended to do was save those trees," Atiyeh explains, an involuntary grin creeping across his face. In 1989 he got a bill introduced in the statehouse to try to turn Opal Creek into a state park.

"This was around the time the spotted owl was designated an endangered species. Mills closed throughout the southern part of the state and the mill workers were paid to go to the state capital to demonstrate that day. They surrounded the capitol with logging trucks, and some of the people I saw outside demonstrating had been sending out flyers for Friends of Opal Creek, this nonprofit we'd set up the day before. I went out to the rally to ask them what was going on and they said, 'When we got to work this morning they told us this was our work today.'

"Right after that I became the focus of a lot of this anti-environmentalist anger and started getting two or three death threats a day. They slashed the tires on my wife's car. A log truck tried to run my seventeen-year-old son off the road when he was out driving my car, and they held my twelve-year-old daughter down in the schoolyard and tied her up with yellow ribbons. I heard that some guys joked about shooting my plane out of the sky."

I ask him about the phone threats. "The phone threats were like, 'You're a dead son of a bitch' and 'Get out of the canyon.' I said, 'Listen, my family's been in the state from before the turn of the century, a lot longer than you, asshole, so we're not going anywhere.' Finally it got so I just left a tape on my machine. It said, 'Please leave a message or, if this is a death threat, just calm down and take a deep breath, because you're probably nervous, and then leave your name and address and I absolutely will get back to you.' Well, there were still a few threats, but none of them had the balls to leave their names. Finally I called up the mill owner, who I figured was behind most of it. This is a guy who was born with a silver log in his mouth. I said, 'You better stop this or be damn sure the first shot counts, because if it doesn't I'm coming after you and I know where you live.' Right after that the threats stopped."

Atiyeh was particularly angry that his family was being targeted. "After they tied my daughter up with the yellow ribbons, I called the school authorities and said, 'Cut it out, it's like putting a swastika on a Jewish kid.' And they did stop it after that. But it went so far that they killed a music program in the high school and instituted a forestry program instead, to teach the kids how to be loggers. A bunch of kids wanted to come to Opal Creek to visit the preserve and the school board wouldn't let them go. They came anyway, and that became a big story. Of course, I was still a social pariah in my town. No one would sit next to me at the high school football games. Friends were afraid to visit my house. Merchants who tried to stay neutral, who didn't go along with the yellow-ribbon stuff, were threatened with boycotts, so they'd hang up 'We support the timber industry' banners and tie yellow ribbons around their stores. They'd also give money to Friends of Opal Creek on condition we didn't publicize their names. Eventually things calmed down. I think my standing up made a difference. Plus, most of the people in my town are good people. It's just that a few have too much power. It's still a kind of feudal economy in many of these lumber towns."

In 1992, Atiyeh arranged to donate the three thousand–acre Opal Creek forest area to Friends of Opal Creek for eventual transfer to The Nature Conservancy as a permanent preserve.[8] He sees this original old-growth forest he's helped to save as compensation for some of the vigilante harassment he and his family suffered through.

"My middle son got the most shit," he says. "Other families wouldn't let their kids associate with him. He got flak from the other guys at school. He decided he was going to move to Portland to stay with my sister and finish high school up there. I agreed that was okay if that's what he wanted. Then a few nights before he was going to leave, he was watching MTV and saw this Grateful Dead video 'You Can Run but You Can't Hide'—and there were two pictures of him, clips from this Audubon documentary, 'Rage over Trees.'[9] And that's when he decided to stay. He turned to me grinning and said, 'To hell with them. None of *them* have been on MTV.'"

"STUMPS DON'T LIE" reads the stage banner at the Ancient Forest Concert held on Portland's Willamette River the night before President

Clinton's Forest Summit conference gets under way. Fifty thousand people have turned out in the rain to hear the music and support the cause. "What right do we have to tell other countries to stop cutting their forests when we haven't stopped cutting ours?" asks Kenny Loggins before his set. "My daddy grew up in Butte, Montana, the [mining] hole that wouldn't stop. It's a ghost town today, 'cause no one would say stop."

Black rap group U-Krew plays as a white signer for the deaf tries to keep his hand movements flipping and rolling as fast as the song. It becomes a game between them, ending with bear hugs and a big round of applause. David Crosby, still alive despite his sybaritic ways, sings "Long Time Gone." Carole King, down from her home in Idaho, does "Smackwater Jack" and a new song she calls "No More Welfare Timber." Ninety-five-year-old Pacific Northwest activist Hazel Wolfe totters to the microphone. "I couldn't believe as a young girl that the limitless forests I knew would be almost gone someday, but I'm confident now that in my life they'll be saved." Ann and Nancy Wilson of Heart sing "Dreamboat Annie." Nat Bingham, a salmon fisherman out of Fort Bragg, California, talks about how salmon are disappearing because the clear-cuts are stripping away shade and putting silt in the rivers.

"Clinton and Gore, cut no more!" chants the crowd. By now the sun has set and the rain is coming down in sheets. Neil Young squints out over the rain-slickered crowd as stagehands set up his pipe organ. "Nice weather ... for trees," he deadpans before reeling into a final set that includes "Comes a Time" and "After the Gold Rush." The last speaker is Native American activist Winona LaDuke, who comes up onstage with her two children. "Our lands, our forests are our sacred places. Our forests are about our survival. We all have to reduce our levels of consumption. We need to get back in order with the natural law," she tells the crowd, which responds with sustained applause before dispersing into the night.

––––––––––

"ENVIRO-ELITISTS rock 'n' roll while timber families starve" reads the sign carried by Christy Britt, the wife of a contract logger at the next morning's OLC's Wise Use rally. Their Family Forest Summit is taking place as the official conference is getting under way across the river. "There's a lot of timber workers' suicides, a lot of broken families, there are people losing their homes," Britt tells a reporter from the *Oregonian,* Portland's daily paper.[10] "I read about that concert last night. I was struck by the difference between the people there and the people struggling to survive. From what I could see, the people who were doing the singing and playing sounded very smug and self-righteous."

Several boats cruise the river with banners. One reads "Mr. Babbitt, where did your hardwood floors come from?" The rain is pouring down even harder than the night before. Up to half the sodden crowd of ten thousand industry supporters and their families manage to squeeze under the large white tent that OLC has erected for the event. Inside they listen to a country-and-western band and various speakers from Montana, Oregon, and Washington, but seem most interested in what's being said on the television monitors carrying a live feed from the convention center. A number of the men wear their safety helmets or company bill caps. One humorist carries a placard that reads "Hug a logger, you'll never go back to a tree." There's also a story hour for the kids featuring an original narrative about "the old-growth tree that wanted to be cut down rather than left to die in the forest so it could help supply forest products for people."

But most of the people here, like their fellow blue-collar workers facing shutdowns at military bases across the country, seem to realize that things are not going to go back to the way they were before. They're desperately concerned about their jobs and their futures. "I'm too old to retrain. I've had back surgery. If I went somewhere else, they wouldn't even look at me," says fifty-eight-year-old Dave Field, a Boise Cascade mill worker. "They talk about training you on computers." He holds up his hand to show the stub of a finger lost in the mill. "I can't type. It ain't gonna work."

The rally ends with the adoption of a "vision statement" for resource management that would open up more public lands to logging. This document was written by a grassroots committee that includes OLC's Tom Hirons, Valerie Johnson, and Charlie Janz.

The official daylong Forest Summit takes place across the Steel Bridge at the spacious, green glass–spired Portland convention center. Participants include President Clinton, Vice President Gore, half the Cabinet, invited guests and panelists, and just about every cop within a five hundred–mile radius. The summit is to consist of three panels to examine the human, environmental, and economic aspects of the timber crisis. I'm

expecting a lot of talk of conciliation and compromise, along with competing claims over who loves the forest most and who's been hurt the worst.

I join the six hundred other journalists covering the event as we're
searched and shuttled into a large, dry basement hall wired with phone
lines, Minicams, radio feeds, and television monitors. Only a handful
of pool reporters and photographers are allowed upstairs into the conference hall (my camera-laden partner Nancy smiles her way into the
pool). The rest of us, like the demonstrators down by the river, follow
the event on TV, exchanging gossip and snacks with old friends and
young competitors.

Four or five hours into the summit, Clinton and Gore are still fully
engaged in the discussions, questioning panelists about the relative
merits of various fiberboard-compression techniques, value-added tax
credit structures, and other minutiae that are, to policy wonks like
themselves, what good poker hands are to normal men. I can't help
thinking that Ronald Reagan would be three hours into his nap by now,
George Bush Sr. would be bored silly, and—a decade later—George
Bush Jr. wouldn't need a summit. He has appointed longtime timber industry lobbyists (and Wise Use champions) like Mark Rey of the
American Forest and Paper Association to oversee his forest policy.

After summit participants have their say, they come downstairs to
talk to the press. There's Nadine Bailey, the dynamic six-foot three-inch
unemployed logger's wife from Hayfork, California, who's been traveling the Wise Use talk circuit for the last two years. She's walking
down the hall doing establishment shots with her husband and daughter
for a camera crew from ABC while strategically praising Bill Clinton
to Barry Serafin.

Western Industrial Workers Council union boss Mike Draper, bald-
ing, bearded, and built like the proverbial brick outhouse, makes an appearance downstairs. Testifying before the president, he expresses the
hope that "together we can find a solution that protects the forests of
God and the families of man." To the press he claims he's always been
a strong union Democrat (Jim Jontz might disagree) and resents the way
Rush Limbaugh is attacking Clinton on the radio. Local reporters more
interested in bear-baiting than PR statements try to draw Draper and
his equally swarthy enviro nemesis, Andy Kerr of the Oregon Natural
Resources Council, into pawing range of each other, but the two manage to avoid taking notice of each other.

A reporter suggests to Kerr that he looks like a spotted owl. "That really ruffles my feathers," Kerr responds. He tells a group of reporters that he thinks it's okay if the summit results in increased lumber prices owing to old-growth logging restrictions. "Right now the number one product in landfills is paper. Number two is wood. If you get rid of the Forest Service subsidy for logging, the market price is going to go up. The free market is fine, allowing for greed with some social restraints. The problem is that the old guard of the forest industry are dinosaurs who just don't want any change or innovation."

Draper is talking to another group of reporters. "I think, for the most part, we're hearing a change in the rhetoric here today because this administration has brought a sense of optimism. This is the first time the *human* element has been brought into the debate. I'm ecstatic with the outcome. You could see he [Clinton] was captivated by the process." President Clinton finishes the eight-hour conference with a plea to the participants: "I ask you to stay at the table and keep talking and keep trying to find common ground," he says. "I don't want this situation to go back to the posturing, to positioning, to the politics of division that have characterized this difficult issue in the past."

Bill Clinton, with his hands-on approach, seems to have established a de facto cease-fire in the timber wars that will hold for three months, until release of his Option Nine Forest Plan on July 1, 1993. The plan dramatically reduces logging on U.S. federal forest lands but does not protect all old growth, results in some job loss but also provides relief aid, and protects salmon and rivers but allows some cutting in owl and murrelet habitat. In all these ways it succeeds in creating the common ground Clinton has spoken of. Both the timber industry and environmentalists condemn it for not giving them what they want.

Before leaving Portland, I arrange to meet ex–mill worker Gene Lawhorn at a Chinese restaurant on the east side of town. Gene is about five-foot-seven, thin and wiry, with light gray eyes, silvery blond hair, and a jutting beard. He has a tattoo of a flaming skull on his right forearm and the remnants of an Appalachian accent. He's wearing jeans, a jean jacket, and, incongruously, a green Earth First! tee shirt.

Lawhorn is a relative newcomer to the Northwest and relatively poor. Looking for work, he moved to Oregon from Ohio in 1985 with his wife and two young daughters. He'd seen his town of Mansfield, Ohio, shut down after Westinghouse closed its plant and moved overseas. The

Empire Steel Works, where his father and grandfather worked, had laid off most of its employees. "We were just hillbillies, just working people from the little Tennessee section of town," he smiles, stroking his beard. "There wasn't much we could do but leave." He got his first mill work in Westbrook, Oregon, working on the cleanup crew as a log head spotter and tail spotter for $5.80 an hour. "We had logs blow up on us when they didn't feed right. I was pinned against the wall by a board that would have killed me if my friend hadn't hit the stop button they'd just put on the line. As it was, I was knocked unconscious."

It was at the Westbrook mill that Lawhorn first heard about the spotted owl. "They'd call a shift meeting and give us all coffee and donuts and bring in speakers, foresters from the lumber companies, and other outside speakers and tell us about the spotted owl and the preservationists. They'd have these postcards for us to sign with a collection box to drop them in—these spotted owl protests to Congress. I signed them along with everyone else. They'd scare you into thinking you'd lose your job if you didn't."

He was laid off anyway but found new work at the International Paper sawmill in Gardner, a union shop. "I was impressed with the better conditions I found there, plus I was making $8.00 an hour now, so I decided to get involved with Local 3127 of the International Woodworkers of America. I became a shop steward, but when people asked me, 'What's the union done for me?' I was bothered that I couldn't answer, so I went to the library and got out a book, *Labor's Untold Story*. And that book was like an awakening for me. I began reading labor history and understanding how history can help you find out the truth about what's going on today."

In early 1987, Lawhorn had a tee shirt printed up with "Just Wait till '88," which was when their union contract was set to expire. His whole crew began wearing the shirt, and it spread throughout the mill. "There were some guys, they'd wear that shirt all week long, and management started getting nervous. Two weeks before Christmas the company announced it had sold the mill and laid us all off."

He heard that Roseburg Forest Products was hiring and was able to get another union job at their Dixonville veneer mill. He became shop steward again and began writing history articles for the Western Council of Industrial Workers newspaper. "But they stopped running them because I wrote that the way labor had been treated in the past was like what was being done to the human rights of people in El Salvador and South Africa, and Mike Draper said you can't write that. That's un-American.

"But that didn't bother me too much, because by then we were on strike. We were out from January through May of eighty-nine, out for five months." He smiles strangely. "What I saw on the picket line, it was like that science fiction movie *They Live*, where you could see who were the aliens when you put on these sunglasses. It was like putting on those glasses. A lot of people in the union were wearing yellow ribbons at the time to protest the environmentalists, only I began to notice this thing and I said to the other people on line, 'What does every vehicle crossing our line have in common? The cars and pickups of the scabs, the strikebreakers, the log trucks, the managers' cars?' They all flew yellow ribbons. So on the picket line the yellow ribbons started disappearing."

Visiting another mill on strike, Lawhorn was surprised to find Earth First! activists picketing with the workers. "I began to see that they were human, not the ogres we'd been told about. They were reaching out and talking to me and actually blocking the cars of scabs. I went to Portland and debated them on the radio and started seeing that they had a point of view too. But I didn't become that vocal until shortly after the strike ended, when the timber/labor coalition was formed to protest against the spotted owl and they announced this big September rally in Salem, where they would shut down the mills and go protest. So me and a couple of other guys had a press conference to denounce the rally, not liking this whole yellow ribbon business anymore. Only about four of us showed up, but because the press likes controversy we still got a lot of play on TV and in the papers, and the union president threatened to kick my ass. Anyway, that rally was a flop. The company rented five buses for the day and bought a bunch of box lunches, but only about forty people went on the buses of the four or five hundred who took the day off. Most of the others went fishing, I guess.

"Some time after that, Roseburg Forest Products held one of these meetings after lunch where we got an extra paid hour to listen to these OLC people. They had this Wise Use group called TREES, Timber Resources Equals Economic Stability, and another called WOOD, Workers Of Oregon Development, but nobody was joining them. So they came and talked and all you had to do was sign up and the company would pay your $12 membership fee so they could then go to lobby and say, 'Look, we have three thousand dues-paying members or whatever.' It was a scam."

By this time Lawhorn was beginning to identify himself openly as an environmentalist. The only thing he couldn't tolerate about the Earth Firsters he was meeting was their advocacy and use of tree spiking, with its potential to injure or kill forest industry workers.

"In March of 1990 I'd talked a bunch on the phone with Judi Bari, trying to get her to renounce tree spiking. And then I got a tape of her folk music singing 'Spike a Tree for Jesus' and got real pissed off. So at this University of Oregon conference I attended, I challenged her face-to-face, and she immediately agreed to renounce it, which caused a big stir with some of the other Earth Firsters. But most of the environmentalists who were there thought tree spiking was wrong anyway and gave her a big round of applause.

"I thought this was a big thing, that an Earth First! leader would promise never to tree-spike again, but Mike Draper called it 'just another preservationist tactic,' and the timber industry denounced it as some kind of plot. It was like they didn't want tree spiking to end, 'cause it made it easier for them to talk about ecoterrorists."

Soon, like hundreds of other grassroots environmentalists across America, Lawhorn and his family began to encounter their own form of terrorism. "I was put back in the Dixonville plant, which was in a real rural area. There were about 125 people working there. And there was this real pro-industry millwright guy who drove up to me on a forklift my first day there and said, 'Are you that environmentalist, Lawhorn?' And I said, 'Yeah, I'm that environmentalist, Lawhorn.' And he said, 'If you don't quit this plant we're going to cut your nuts off.' Well, I knew you have to come back at a threat like that, hopefully in some creative but direct way, so shortly thereafter I walked up to the guy and I handed him a small knife. I had a larger knife in my back pocket just in case. And I said, 'Here, you want to cut my balls off,' and he kind of backed down. He said he didn't mean he was going to do it, he meant someone else might. Not long after that Judi Bari was bombed and things got kind of scary. Then this guy started bad-mouthing me when I wasn't around, and someone put my name and number on the bulletin boards at different mills saying, 'This is a spotted-owl-loving son of a bitch. Call him up and tell him what you think.'

So then we started getting all the calls, hang-up calls, death threats, calls telling my wife she was an owl-loving bitch. We changed our number half a dozen times, but that didn't help. Somebody broke the windshield of my Nissan pickup. People would drive up to the house in the middle of the night, break beer bottles in the driveway, and then peel out. Then they started driving by the house firing off guns. Angel and Terra, our two little girls, were five and eight at the time. I started sleeping with a loaded thirty-thirty rifle by the bed to defend my wife and family. The local cops came out a few times but didn't do much. Lisa, my wife, was at a yard sale when one cop told her, 'You people should get out of here, move somewhere else.' She came home really mad, feeling like the cops were on the side of whoever was doing this. She had this big Dodge truck with a bumper sticker reading 'Justice for Judi Bari' and she was twice driven off the road, off of Route 42, by log trucks. The kids were with her at the time and they were shaken up, pretty scared, you know.

"Lisa was also harassed at the Pentecostal church she attended because of these environmental letters I was writing to the editor of the town paper there in Sutherlin, and she couldn't get work. The manager at the Kentucky Fried Chicken where she applied for a job told her, 'We don't want you troublemakers here.'"

Lawhorn was laid off at the mill in late 1990 and soon realized he wasn't going to be rehired. He moved his family to Portland in 1991, where he now works as a warehouse supervisor.

"One of the things that really changed my way of thinking," he reflects, "was going deer hunting, going after blacktail, in the Siuslaw National Forest back in eighty-six. I came to this bog with a family of beaver working in the water and I just sat down and watched those beavers for about three hours. It was just fascinating watching the way they worked together. And at some point I stretched my legs and popped my knee or something and one of those beavers heard it, slapped his tail on the water, and, boom, they were all gone, just like that. I came back to that place two years later and it was gone, nothing but clear-cut, bulldozed, scarred-over land. So you wonder about where the beaver are going, and the salmon that are threatened now, and you realize this country was once the promised land, once had everything, but now it's all polluted, its working people are living on the edge, and cutting the last ancient forests just won't get us back on our feet."

four

Grass Roots for Sale

Alarmed by the success of the environmental movement, industries such as mining, logging and ranching are trying to duplicate it: they are forming grass-roots groups in a loose-knit coalition dedicated to the "wise use" of natural resources. —Washington Post

Because they were new organizations and active and well-funded, I think they really had an impact on the Western Senators and congressional delegations.
—Jim Baca, Former Director, Bureau of Land Management

WITH THE TIMBER COMPANIES clear-cutting ancient forests, the coal companies strip-mining Appalachia and the western plains, and the plastic and petrochemical processors cracking hydrocarbons along the Gulf Coast, traditional resource-based industries find themselves under tremendous pressure to change or die as the United States engages a new world market. Here, on the global scale, America is unable to compete in nails, ceramic tile, or wood products, but leads the way in fiber optics, wind turbines, and computer drives. Those companies that can meet the new century's requirements for more energy-efficient, environmentally clean means of production will survive to play on a vastly expanded field. Those that are unable to make the transition are fated for economic obsolescence. Simultaneous to and paralleling this change is a demographic shift that is dramatically altering the American West. Expanding city- and town-based populations are putting new multiple-use demands on our public lands—for recreation, scenery, and watershed and wildlife protection—and threatening the monopoly long held by government-subsidized users in mining, logging, and grazing. Agriculture also faces a serious choice: whether to move toward low-input, labor-intensive forms of family-based farming (including organic) or to continue chemically mining the soil and expanding factory-farm production methods to every last river, dell, wetland, and low-lying depression that hasn't already been developed for real estate.

A handful of rearview visionaries have staked out a consistent position on these and other natural resource issues. They choose to defend the conventional against the unknown, the extractive against the regenerative, and promise industry that with a little financial support they can stem the tidal changes now occurring in the New West and across America.

Ron Arnold likes to warn and cajole; Chuck Cushman entertains and alarms; Bill Grannell plays the friend of the worker; Grant Gerber drones and deals; Clark Collins is the patient negotiator; William Perry Pendley is the supercilious lecturer. What all six of these men have had in common are distinct, often competing claims to leadership in the anti-environmentalist movement. They are driven, fiercely self-assured individuals, suspicious of each other's motives and interests, and anxious to prove themselves the largest, most brightly colored fish in their small pond. They are, in Chuck Cushman's words, "the old dogs" of a radical but influential movement whose scars and bite marks are as likely to have come from each other as from their "preservationist" enemy.

"Chuck Cushman isn't a real organizer. Chuck is a forager," Bill Grannell claims. "He goes into battle where the fights are under way but doesn't leave much infrastructure behind. Arnold and [his sponsor Alan] Gottlieb are on the extreme Right. They don't represent anyone but themselves."[1]

"Grannell's just a profiteer," countercharges Chuck Cushman. "He doesn't believe in reaching out to others. Mostly his work is about money, and so I think he views us as a threat. He and his wife are skilled organizers and could do a lot, but they're not willing to make economic sacrifices for the cause, and that turns off the grassroots."[2]

"Please don't try to tar the property rights movement with Mr. Arnold. Ron's not everything he makes out to be," Grant Gerber warns. "Most of the major players in the property rights movement— the Farm Bureau, the NRA, the Cattlemen's Association—will have nothing to do with Ron or his friend Alan Gottlieb. They're profiteers and they have some very unsavory connections."[3]

"Everyone who's ever worked with Grant Gerber knows he's a back stabber," Ron Arnold responds. "We know all the bullshit and libels you spread about us and we love you, Grant. Every time you say those things you send the media to us and get a hair up your ass."[4]

"Splintering multiplies a movement's power," Arnold adds a few moments later, going on to argue that movements are by nature "segmentary, polycephalous, ideological networks." He's attempting to find a sociological rationale for the personality-driven divisions that mark the often contentious network of anti-enviro activists who are leading the fight against the greening of America.

Environmentalists and liberal politicians have accused the Wise Use/Property Rights groups of being little more than a front for greedy corporations and public lands profiteers. "These organizations are not grassroots. They are Astroturf laid down with big corporate money," claimed Jay Hair, former president of the National Wildlife Federation.[5] Congressman George Miller, who chaired the House Committee on Natural Resources, warned, "All of these people have their hands and their noses and their snouts deep into the taxpayer's pocket."[6]

It's a charge that infuriates ranchers, loggers, small-business people, and frustrated developers such as Peggy Reigle of Dorchester, Maryland. In the early 1980s, Reigle, a former vice president for finance at the *New York Daily News*, along with her husband, Charles Jowaiszas, purchased an eighteenth-century house in rural Dorchester County on the state's scenic Eastern Shore. They also bought a nearby 138-acre abandoned farm for $400,000, hoping to subdivide it into fourteen home sites as well as a site for their own dream house. When the area was classified as a wetland, Reigle and her husband watched their investment sink like a cinderblock in wet sand.[7] In July 1990, a frustrated Reigle founded the Fairness to Land Owners Committee (FLOC) to oppose President Bush's "no net loss of wetlands" pledge along with what she calls "the ecofascist movement." Over the next four years the group grew, by her count, to twelve thousand members (only five hundred paying dues). She and other second-tier organizers around the country — cattleman's wife Joan Smith in Yreka, California; former log company operator Bruce Vincent in Libby, Montana; Maine second-home owner Eric Veyhl in Concord, Massachusetts — working for little more than their own self-interest, feel deeply insulted when they're accused of being corporate shills. They believe they're creating a genuine broad-based grassroots movement to oppose the preservationists, a feeling reinforced by at least some of the coverage they've received.

ABC's *Nightline*, in a setup piece to a debate between Al Gore and Rush Limbaugh in February 1992, described Wise Use as a movement "ranging from ... Exxon, which would like to use the land for oil drilling, to ordinary citizens like Peggy Reigle, who simply want to use the land to build their dream house."

In an interview for a *New York Times* article titled "When the Bad Guy Is Seen as the One in the Green Hat," published that same month, Reigle explained to reporter Keith Schneider how "landowners, and I mean moms and pops, not oil companies and miners, are being abused by restrictions that no longer make sense. Their lives have been devastated and their land is being held hostage by these [environmental] laws."[8]

"Committee leader Reigle does not pay herself a salary, answers her own phone and counts on an array of volunteers, including public interest lawyers and former regulators, for assistance," reported a May 1993 *Insight* magazine article on Reigle's efforts to pass Property Rights legislation in Maryland. This Moon publication piece described "a classic David and Goliath duel" between FLOC and the Chesapeake Bay Foundation, with annual assets of $6.6 million. "Land rights activists fielded no professional lobbyists, but the environmentalists pulled out all the stops ... accustomed to being seen as the underpaid underdog, they are taking on a small movement that receives virtually no support from major industry or large foundations."[9] The article failed to report on the intense statehouse lobbying efforts of the Homebuilders Association, Maryland Farm Bureau, Maryland Association of Realtors, and other corporate supporters of the property rights legislation, however.

Still, anti-enviro activists perceive themselves as working with, not for, resource industries, which they often disdain as being too willing to compromise with the enemy. In trying to organize among unemployed loggers, resource workers, small independent business people, and frustrated middle managers, they have even incorporated a thinly veiled "anti-capitalist" message. They use class resentment as a cudgel by portraying environmentalists as wealthy elitists, part of a "green establishment" with links to transnational corporations, the Rockefellers, and the United Nations. Bill and Barbara Grannell claim that environmentalists are "the elitists at the top, driving Mercedes and BMWs and telling average Americans what to do."

"The Nature Conservancy is a capitalist institution designed to promote socialism," insists Grant Gerber, referring to the huge nonprofit organization that buys up wild and undeveloped private land for preservation, often reselling it to the national park system. "Corporate executives ... direct seven out of every ten public affairs dollars from their firms and corporate foundations to organizations that act to destroy business and industry," claim Ron Arnold and Alan Gottlieb in their self-published book, *Trashing the Economy*, an exposé of the greens based on a classic far-right thesis that capitalism is surrendering itself to an alien force (in this case environmentalism) and needs a dynamic new movement (Wise Use) to rescue it from degeneracy.

As part of their anti-elitist rhetoric, the Center for Defense of Free Enterprise (CDFE) and People for the West! disseminate figures indicating that the environmental "establishment" generates an annual gross income in the neighborhood of $3 billion (*Money* magazine placed it at $2.5 billion, *Outside* magazine at $0.5 billion). Impressive a figure as $3 billion is, what it really indicates, if accurate, is that organized environmentalism in the United States has the same economic clout as the (pre-eBay) television home-shopping industry. In other words, if all the environmental groups in the United States agreed to pool their resources, Green, Inc., would still only be about one-eighteenth as big as Wal-Mart, ranking well down on the Fortune 500 list of top companies. Of course, it *would* be the only member of the Fortune 500 trying to change the resource utilization, production methods, and long-term strategies of the other 499.

The anti-Greens claim to be doing their nationwide organizing work on a gross income of between $10 million and $100 million a year, a far smaller amount than the (far larger) environmental movement has to work with.[10] Reviews of 1990s IRS filings confirmed that most of the established anti-enviro groups (Blue Ribbon, CDFE, WIRF, People for the West!) operated in the $50,000–$500,000–a–year range.[11] However, these figures can also mislead by failing to take into account in kind services provided by major institutional players from the corporate sector and the political Right, including the multibillion-dollar Farm Bureau Federation, NRA, American Legislative Exchange Council, pro-business nonprofit law firms, and numerous resource industry organizations such as the California Forestry Association.

CFA's communications manager, Kathy Kvarda, along with putting out the state industry association newsletter, is paid to coordinate the anti-enviro Alliance for Environment and Resources (AER) out of their office. "It would be nice if we could get a statewide grassroots umbrella group going that was more independent in terms of industry identification. But then again, we're a poor association," the cheerful blond publicist says brightly, explaining how AER was originally established in the mid-1980s "when people in the Forest Service told us we needed non-industry input to balance the preservationists in the forest planning process."[12] In 1993, Kvarda's job requirements included coordinating the Alliance for America's five-day "Fly-In for Freedom" lobbying trip to Washington.

In a few places, such as Alabama and Alaska, state governments have taken on a leadership role in creating and promoting the Wise Use backlash. In 1992, Alabama state forester Bill Moody set up his own anti-enviro group, Stewards of Family Farms, Ranches and Forests, funneling more than $7,000 in start-up funds into it from the state Forestry Commission, along with secretarial support. Moody put commission staffers to work producing videos and literature for the group. Before his activities were exposed in the *Montgomery Advertiser*, he held a secret commission meeting that voted to allow him to work for Stewards on state time (Alabama paid him $80,000 a year plus gave him the exclusive use of an airplane). He had also planned to send thirty commission staff members in state cars to the group's founding meeting in December 1992. Moody, the subject of an ethics investigation and a lawsuit, retired from the Forestry Commission in September 1993. Meanwhile, the Forestry Commission provided support for a second anti-enviro group, EAGLE—Alabamians: Guardians of our Land and Environment—whose spokesman, Colin Bagwell, equated environmentalists with Communists, "infiltrating all of the nation's institutions."[13]

Scattered in hundreds of small rural towns and suburbs across America; made up of ad hoc groups in need of constant resuscitation by paid professional organizers and right-wing legal foundations; kept in communication by fax, e-mail, flyers, and conferences whose attendance never exceeds the low three figures; and promoted by friends in industry, government, and the media, Wise Use/Property Rights may be neither "the most powerful grassroots organization this country has ever seen"—as reported in the Alliance for America newsletter, circulation 2,500—nor the "brutally destructive anti-environmental onslaught" portrayed in a Sierra Club fundraising mailer. Rather, Wise Use/Property Rights is a militant force on the political Right that has shown the power to impede and occasionally sidetrack attempts at environmental protection, intimidate politicians and local activists, and polarize or misdirect needed discussions over jobs, health, and natural resources.

"Their very heated attacks didn't significantly change the nature of the state's environmental goals, but it certainly makes it more difficult to have a large-scale debate when people come in with this strong ideology," says Jonathan Lash, former secretary of natural resources in Vermont. Chuck Clarke, the former director of Washington State's Department of Ecology who inherited Lash's old job as Vermont's secretary of natural resources, takes it a step further. "These extremists have injected fear into the political process. In Washington State they had a hard core of two hundred or so who would turn out for every meeting and protest. A few hundred people with a canned speech and canned concerns can have a tremendous impact, even if 85 percent of the public disagrees with the protestors."

Mark Smith, the legislative director for Democratic senator Max Baucus, claims that "they have their real impact on hard-pressed local communities like Libby, high unemployment areas in the northwest of Montana. They're not a statewide force. My boss, who has a good instinct for mainstream Montana, thinks these groups represent legitimate opinion but not mainstream opinion. Their strength is in packing meetings."

"Wise Use hasn't generated much sympathy or even awareness that it exists among the general population," adds Bob Langsencamp, deputy land commissioner for the state of New Mexico. "You see it mostly in rural southeast New Mexico and in the towns of Pecos and Cuba, small northern towns outside of Santa Fe. They've really tried to focus themselves on decision-makers in Washington. At the state level they haven't been terribly effective, even in coalition with the Cattlemen and the Farm Bureau."

What anti-enviro activists lack in numerical strength, however, they more than make up for in a moral certitude bordering on self-righteousness that finds kindred souls among anti-abortion militants, SUV-burning "ecoterrorists," and the militia movement with which many Wise Users have found common cause. Like other political true believers, they have little problem justifying intimidation tactics or rationalizing anti-environmentalist violence. Their potential and their limitations as a social force can best be evaluated by looking at the dif-

ferent organizing styles, habits, and histories of three of the movement's
scrappy, meat-eating "old dogs": Ron Arnold, Chuck Cushman, and
Bill Grannell.

IN TERMS OF media presence, Ron Arnold is to Wise Use/Property
Rights what Fox News is to journalism, or Ann Coulter is to reasoned
discourse. He has taken a personal bitterness against the environmental
movement, the organizing theories of Lenin, the collective-behavior
analysis of a couple of professors in the social movements field, and a
broad reading of Abraham Maslow, and synthesized them into an influential force on the political Right that sees environmental change as
an imminent threat to free enterprise and industrial civilization.

In 1979, Arnold began to develop a theory that industry could no
longer stand alone, that it needed a grassroots movement to fight for its
goals. When he joined up with New Right fundraiser Alan Gottlieb in
1984, he gained the means and wherewithal to begin mobilizing that constituency. Labeled one of the top ten "Enemies of the Earth" in a *People*
magazine poll of environmental organizers, Arnold bills himself as the
chief theorist and philosopher of Wise Use. If you leave downtown
Seattle heading east across Lake Washington's floating bridge, you
quickly come to Bellevue, an edge city with a recently constructed core
of ten- and twenty-story, copper-colored glass low-rises, upscale hotels,
and flippy neon shopping malls. On the edge of this edge city is a woodsy
business park containing a two-story, brown cedar complex called Liberty Park. The owner is New Right wunderkind Alan Gottlieb, a
diminutive, middle-aged businessman with the attentive, wet-eyed look
of an intelligent mole. Gottlieb took title to Liberty Park following a
series of creative real estate transactions in 1982 and 1987 involving himself, his wife, and the nonprofit foundations he runs (the foundations
paid over $700,000 for Liberty Park, but the Gottliebs ended up owning
it). The complex is home to the CDFE, Citizens Committee for the Right
to Keep and Bear Arms, the Second Amendment Foundation, and the
Co-op Service Bureau, which operates his computers and phone banks.
Other conservative groups, such as the American Freedom Coalition,
Accuracy in Media, and various county secessionists, tax rebels, and anti-
abortionists, used to rent space at Liberty Park but have since moved on.

Gottlieb is one of a handful of direct-mail fundraisers conservative columnist George Will once called "quasi-political entrepreneurs who have discovered commercial opportunities in merchandising discontent."[14] A number of his compatriots on the Right have accused him of personally profiting from his causes. One example: In 1991 his Second Amendment Foundation (SAF), which he calls the smaller, "intellectual" part of his program operations, paid him $35,000 as part-time director at large plus another $51,000 in rent. The *Seattle Times* reported that his nonprofits were paying him twice the fair market value for commercial rental space. The foundation also paid $474,512 to Gottlieb's for-profit Co-op Service Bureau for data processing and other services, and $327,760 to Merril Associates, his for-profit marketing and publishing company. More than half the $1.75 million raised by SAF that year went directly to Alan Gottlieb or the corporations he controls.[15] In addition to his fundraising and publishing operations, he maintains part interest in a couple of television stations, and a radio station in Portland, Oregon, which he purchased in partnership with his two gun foundations — although the foundations appear to have provided all the cash. They also invested in a radio syndicate. "We own the western airwaves at one A.M. in the morning," he brags.

Gottlieb, who was raised in a liberal New York Jewish family, traces his political conversion to his teenage reading of Barry Goldwater's *The Conscience of a Conservative* (as an adult he chose to make a religious conversion to Catholicism). Attending the University of Tennessee in the late 1960s, Gottlieb became involved in YAF, the Young Americans for Freedom, a pro–Vietnam War group with a reputation for attracting clean-cut white males who would rather attend a William Buckley speech than a Rolling Stones concert. "You didn't join YAF to meet a girl, that's for sure," Gottlieb admits with a laugh. "Most members, a lot of them anyway, were overweight and had acne."

Thin and smooth-skinned, Gottlieb quickly advanced to a leadership position in the group, becoming national head of Youth Against McGovern and the Student Committee to Keep and Bear Arms (which evolved into his Citizens Committee). Like George Bush Jr. and other Vietnam War supporters of a certain class and disposition, Gottlieb volunteered to serve his country in the National Guard. In 1970 he ran the conservative youth campaigns of Senate candidates Jim Buckley in New York and Bill Brock in Tennessee. Brock ran against and defeated Senator Al Gore Sr. "I did this radio spot with this ad agency. We used the voice of a good Tennessee dirt farmer," Gottlieb recalls, faking a southern drawl. "'Where was Al Gore when our boys were fighting in Vietnam? Was he in Tennessee fighting for us? Was he in Washington fighting for us? No. He was in New York City at an antiwar moratorium!' We played up New York, where I was from, knowing how all New Yorkers are hated in Tennessee. We played off patriotism for the war and Tennessee as the volunteer state. At the end the farmer says, 'I'm a lifelong Democrat but I can't vote for Albert Gore.' It was a devastating spot, real fun," he grins, unembarrassed by the memory.

After moving to Seattle, Gottlieb got involved in direct-mail marketing. "My first campaign was for a ballot measure for farmworkers' protection here in Washington. It was a very well-written measure. It protected farmworkers so they wouldn't be taken advantage of by farmers, but at the same time protected them from Cesar Chavez, from organized labor."

In 1977, working through his friend Richard Viguerie's mailing house, Gottlieb sent out half a million Citizens Committee fundraising letters reading "From Congressman ———" with local representatives' names in the blanks. The only problem was, many of these congressmen hadn't agreed to let their names be used.

"I cannot believe there is anyone in the Congress more opposed to gun-control legislation than I am," said Republican representative Robert Walker of Pennsylvania. "However, I cannot and will not condone this kind of irresponsible special-interest appeal for money." When Walker called Gottlieb to demand a retraction of the letter on which his name appeared, Gottlieb hung up on him. Congressman Bob Carr, a Michigan Democrat and gun-control advocate, was even more upset by the pro-gun solicitation that went out under his name. "It is gross and wanton fraud to use my name in a way that implied that I favor something that I actually oppose," he howled. Claiming that it was all a mistake on Viguerie's part, Gottlieb's nonprofit gun committee agreed to return the funds they'd collected.[16]

Once he had his gun foundations and private business ventures under way, Gottlieb decided to launch a new project, a pro-business bicentennial think tank called the Center for the Defense of Free Enterprise.

In a corner space on the second floor of Liberty Park, Ron Arnold has found a comfortable niche and platform as CDFE's executive vice president. He shares an outer office with Gottlieb's secretary. On the walls behind him and to the side are several kitschy pictures of cowboys, killer whales, and Karl Marx lighting his cigar with a dollar bill. Alan's larger inner office is decorated with original artwork of cowboys, neon guns, and bullets.

Since Ron Arnold came aboard in 1984, the center has distinguished itself from a plethora of other right-wing think tanks by focusing its attacks on environmentalism and producing seminars, conferences, "battle books," radio spots, and numerous direct-mail funding pitches aimed at spreading the anti-enviro Wise Use message. Alan has also led fundraising seminars for a number of other anti-enviro leaders, including Chuck Cushman, Clark Collins, and William Perry Pendley. Of the $12 million a year he brings in with his direct-mail operations, about $2 million goes to various anti-environmental clients.[17] The year Ron Arnold joined the center, 1984, was also the year Gottlieb served eight months of a one-year federal prison sentence for tax evasion. In 1978 he'd claimed an income of just over $17,000 but forgot to report some personal expenditures, including $10,000 he spent on his fiancée's engagement ring and $8,000 that went into his stamp collection. His parents refused to confirm his story that he'd borrowed the money from them. His lawyer then called the charges politically motivated, an accusation Gene Anderson, the Reagan-appointed U.S. attorney prosecuting the case, called "infantile."[18]

Still, a man like Alan Gottlieb, both personally pleasant and able to generate cash faster than an ATM, does not lose friends over small things like felony tax convictions. "I'm well aware of his classic battle with the Internal Revenue Service. I've seen him go through meat-grinder situations and come out stronger than ever," wrote then senator Steve Symms of Idaho in his introduction to Gottlieb's self-published book, *The Gun Grabbers*.[19] CDFE's later congressional supporters included Republican senators Alfonse D'Amato of New York, Ted Stevens of Alaska, and Jesse Helms of North Carolina. Its 1992 list of distinguished advisors included former secretary of defense, and now vice president of the United States, Dick Cheney.

CDFE claims a membership mailing list of 125,000, 52,000 of whom, according to Gottlieb, can be counted on to pay their dues. Of that group all but 8,000 are Wise Use members, he says. Ron Arnold claims that of these 44,000, about 14,000 are "hardcore activists," although it would be difficult to image anyone as hard-core as Arnold himself.

I ask ARNOLD about his distinctive beard. "I've worn it this way since I was twenty-three," he tells me, sounding oddly defensive. "Preservationist journalists have attacked me, claiming it's a Mennonite or an Amish beard." In a December 1991 article titled "Brown Fellas," *Outside* magazine described Arnold as "a dour man with a Mennonite beard."[20] For the sake of accuracy, it should be noted that the beard is a full, snowy-white facial adornment sans mustache, a classic patriarch's beard of nondenominational character. The only other person I've ever met with a beard like Ron Arnold's is C. Everett Koop, the AIDS- and cancer-fighting surgeon general under Ronald Reagan. Koop is a larger man than Arnold, with a broader face and lively blue eyes.

Arnold's slate-colored eyes are cool and wary behind a pair of metal-frame glasses. Fifty-six when we first meet, tall, trim, and trenchant, he is perhaps the most competent Wise Use leader when it comes to press relations. He understands the value of a good quote. During our eight-hour interview, he will periodically toss out little prepackaged sound bites as if chumming for media sharks. "King Bruce Babbitt will generate a genuine insurrection in this country," he'll say, referring to the mild-mannered secretary of Interior under Bill Clinton. Or, "The National Park Service is an empire designed to eliminate all private property in the United States."

I'm reminded of the Guatemalan army major who told me that the North American Jew Sol Linowitz was the main agent of the Communist International in the Carter White House. As a journalist you're not quite sure whether to be delighted (by the quote) or appalled (by its content). Arnold once told a reporter he was the Darth Vader of the capitalist revolution, but now prefers to quote Princess Leia, identifying Wise Use with the federation forces battling the evil empire of environmentalism. He has the original Star Wars trilogy in movie-screen letterbox format at home, a dark, tree-shaded, four-bedroom ranch set back from a pleasant residential street three minutes from the office. He understands the mythic power of the Skywalker cowboy archetype that George Lucas created three years before Ronald Reagan cantered into the White House. Arnold, however, seems closer in spirit to a postmodern riverboat gambler, calculating the odds as he ups the ante.

Born in Houston, Texas, in 1937 at the tail end of the Depression, he was abandoned by his father as a toddler. With his mother incapacitated by illness, he was adopted and raised by his grandparents, who moved to San Antonio when he was eight. His grandfather ran a hobby shop, where Arnold worked after school. He played French horn in the high school band. On Saturday nights the band would play on the river-banks of the Rio San Antonio.

The river has since evolved into a major tourist mecca of outdoor cafés, shops, and malls. Still, San Antonio remains best known for the Alamo, a surprisingly small stone and adobe fort where Davy Crockett, Jim Bowie, and other Anglo heroes of the West fell in the battle for Texas independence. The Alamo seems an appropriate symbol for Ron Arnold's coming-of-age. Today he must feel similarly besieged trying to build a counterforce to environmentalism, which, like the women's movement, has evolved from a social protest to a societal ethic.

After high school, Arnold attended the University of Texas for a year before drifting west in 1956 with a couple of buddies, ending up in Seattle. There he met a young woman, got married, and found work assembling B-52 bombers for Boeing. Eventually, after taking a few courses at the University of Washington, he became a production illustrator and computer graphics artist for Boeing. He worked on a range of government contracts, from the SST supersonic transport to the B-70 bomber. "We had some weird stuff going through there in the sixties, like the moon rover and all sorts of top-secret gear, including giant lathes for the Saturn booster O rings," he recalls. "I couldn't believe NASA found guys dumb enough to sit on top of rockets built by the lowest bidder, but they did."

Arnold went through a lot of turbulence in his personal life during those years. He's been married three times and has a schizophrenic adult daughter from his first marriage. He lost a son in infancy before his second wife, Phoebe, an opera singer, died of a brain tumor. "They misdiagnosed it as a nervous breakdown. She spent time with a shrink and when she got worse was put into an institution for six weeks. But when her motor functions began going, that indicated there was an organic cause. She was operated on and they removed a tumor the size of a tennis ball. The doctor told me she had nine months left to live. Her shrink suggested I not tell her or our daughter Andrea. He said, 'Why have death hanging over them when you could be helping them to live life to the fullest?' In a way I regret I listened to him, and I didn't tell them. I developed an ulcer instead. But we did have a wonderful time.

We got a mobile home, toured all over the country, went to Disneyland. When Phoebe went back into the hospital, I remember going to pick up my little daughter from the babysitter. I said, 'Mom is in the hospital again.' She said, 'Will she die?' I told her yes. Then she looked at me and said, 'If we're alone we'd better take good care of each other.' To hear this greatness of spirit coming from this six-year-old child is something I'll never forget."

He goes on to rhapsodize about his daughter, as many fathers will. Andrea's a Stanford graduate, plays cello with the Seattle Philharmonic, and has written a book, *Fear of Food: Environmentalist Scams, Media Mendacity, and the Law of Disparagement,* for the center's Free Enterprise Press. "She's brilliant," says Arnold. "She had an IQ of 176 last time we tested her. Mine's only 163."

In 1974, a year after his second wife died, Arnold married his current wife, Janet. "It was love at first sight," he says with a rare smile.

· Surprisingly, it was his recreational interests that would turn into an obsession and new career path. In 1960 he joined the Sierra Club, which he saw primarily as a hiking outfit. "I hiked all the trails in the Olympics, some seven hundred miles. It was great. I was young and fit and would keep running into these other backpackers, most of whom belonged to this group, so I joined." He took a Sierra Club mountain-climbing course but was terrified when he got up onto the rockface. "I thought they were really crazy. It seemed like a good way to kill yourself," he recalls. "After a while the club suggested I join their conservation group, and we began doing these industrial tours on the weekends, dog and pony shows put on by the timber companies and dam builders. Brock Evans was the Northwest lobbyist for Sierra back then. I did some slide shows for the club in sixty-five with two projectors synched to music and narration. It was a big thing at the time, similar to the work I was doing at Boeing for the SST."

But the defense plant design man soon began to feel out of place among the generally liberal, antiwar heirs of John Muir. "Sierra was getting very political in the sixties. I was familiar with how they exaggerated and stretched the truth in their conservation campaigns and I didn't mind that. Still, I could see how they were changing from a nature and hiking orientation to more rabid environmentalism," he claims.

In the late 1960s, Arnold began working with the Alpine Lakes Protection Society, which he says was funded by a small Sierra Club grant.

He recalls spending several years hiking and charting a proposed area for wilderness and multiple-use forest designation, drawing maps, and putting together a slide show of the backcountry's hidden wonders. "At the last minute the Sierra bigwigs came in and expanded the wilderness area. Our more moderate multiple-use proposal was sabotaged," he complains.

He then tells of his moment of apostasy, when the scales fell from his eyes and he saw environmentalists revealed for the power-hungry elitists they really are, a story he's repeated hundreds of times over the decades.

"We had this guy come into one of our meetings with some photos of a deck of logs that had fallen into a creek. I knew enough about the timber industry by that time to see that it was a mistake, that these were some valuable logs, that the couplings maybe broke on them without the yarding crew's knowledge. And I said to Brock, 'Look, I know Weyerhauser's cleanup guy. Why don't I call him?' And Brock looked at me and said, 'Our demographers tell us environmentalism only has two or three years of public popularity left. Why give that company a chance if we can smear them now?' It ended up as legislation by headline, with that picture of those downed logs running in the newspaper. That's when I realized they didn't give a damn about saving that creek or the forests or anything. They were only interested in their own political clout."

"That sounds like horseshit of the highest order," responded Brock Evans, while working as vice president in charge of national affairs at the Audubon Society. "Basically I remember Ron as a weird loner kind of guy. I don't think I ever spoke to him much at all. I remember he had a slide show he wanted to sell to us on Alpine Lakes, and we said, 'Look, we're a volunteer group. We don't really have the money for that.' He got disgruntled and quit a short time later. Some people thought he might have been a plant when he turned around right away and started attacking us at these forestry council meetings in 1970. You have to remember this was in the Nixon era, and that sort of thing, political spying, wasn't uncommon."

Dave Knibb, a Seattle-based attorney who was active in the Alpine Lakes Protection Society, also questions Arnold's reconstruction of events. "I think it helps Ron's cause to say he was betrayed in some dramatic way, but I just remember that he was never really in step with us philosophically. And as time went on he felt less and less comfortable and just kind of faded from the scene.

"I think Ron might have gotten involved with ALPS because it was a smaller group than Sierra and he could gain more recognition. We never got any grant money from Sierra. He's wrong about that. We got more closely aligned with them years later when we were getting the Alpine Lakes legislation through Congress, but nobody felt like we'd been sold out. We thought it was a great victory.

"Ron had a special talent for putting together these slide shows with sound and narration," Knibb continues. "And when he offered his services, we thought that was wonderful. The one he did for us was great, and we used it a lot but that was pretty much the extent of his role. I don't remember his making any maps or doing any surveys. I do remember he always asked questions that were different from the kinds of questions everyone else was asking at the time. Some people in the group were very suspicious of him, but I tried to give him the benefit of the doubt. He appeared to me to be very gullible. He'd already quit Boeing and was working for timber companies for his bread and butter and would say, 'My clients in the timber industry told me this, and isn't this the truth?' He was easily led astray, was my impression."

By 1971, Arnold had left Boeing and started his own graphics company. "The first business I got was the result of work I'd done in the Sierra Club," he says, going on to describe a $6,000 slide show he produced for Simpson Timber. He did thirty to forty films for Weyerhauser and a slide-show history of floor waxing for the GAO. "I was familiar with industrial processes. I had developed this vast knowledge of industry and of resources and of how fragile the whole system of economic interdependence was, and I understood our opponents wanted to destroy industry and transfer power into their own hands," he explains. He soon began giving anti-environmentalist lectures and became a contract writer for various industry publications, including *Coal Age* and *Agrochemical Age*. In 1977 he was hired by three lumber companies—Simpson, Arcada, and Louisiana Pacific—to fight the expansion of the Redwood National Park in California. "I told them, 'Look, you can't win. Redwoods are a sacred cow, but I can help you give away only half of what they want and make them pay you top dollar for that.'" As part of his anti-park campaign, he helped organize a convoy of twenty logging trucks from California to Washington, D.C., arranging for them to do three laps around the Indianapolis speedway en route.

In 1979, Arnold wrote a series of articles for *Logging Management Magazine*, warning industry against attempts at compromise with the environmental movement. For his hard-line advocacy, he was chosen by the Committee for a Free Congress, Paul Weyrich's New Right action group, to pen a subsidized biography of Reagan's first secretary of Interior, James Watt. Following the 1982 publication of *At the Eye of the Storm: James Watt and the Environmentalists*, Arnold gained popularity as a speaker for chemical manufacturers such as Dow and Union Carbide looking to counter the growing anti-pesticide movement in the Northwest and Canada. In a 1981 lecture to the Washington State Weed Control Association, he declared that "anti-chemical activists are the world's number one crop pest. Once you recognize that, you must treat them like a noxious weed or a pernicious disease that attacks public opinion and public policy. They are just another hostile organism that must be controlled."[21]

In another industry presentation, he suggested an effective fumigant. "We can't let motives go by without mentioning the fact that marijuana cultivators do not like pesticides at all because some of them kill their cash crop. I have found that the public has come to realize and accept this motive of anti-pesticide activists as a fact. If you find such a motive to be credible in your local situation, I would strongly suggest that you do everything possible to associate the word *anti-pesticide* with the word *marijuana*. Keep hammering at that one long enough and it may do more to win your ultimate battles than all the science you can ever get someone to listen to."[22]

In 1984, Alan Gottlieb, in the middle of raising $10 million for the Reagan reelection campaign, was browsing in a D.C. bookstore, looking at the flyleaf of James Watt's biography, when he saw that the author was based in Bellvue. Returning home, he gave Arnold a call and the two of them got together. "Reagan was killing us at the time," Gottlieb recalls without irony. Like other conservative fundraising outfits, the center was losing its base of support as the Reagan administration made everything else on the Right seem redundant. Arnold pitched Gottlieb his idea for building a movement that would target "runaway environmentalism."

"At the time, we picked it up and played with it only because we really didn't have a good issue for the center to sink its teeth into," Gottlieb admits ten years later. "It worked out far better than I would have predicted. I've never seen anything pay out as quickly as this whole Wise Use thing has done. What's really good about it is it touches the same kind of anger as the gun stuff, and not only generates a higher rate of return but also a higher average dollar donation. My gun stuff runs about $18. The Wise Use stuff breaks $40."

Once ensconced at CDFE, Arnold began turning out a series of books and working with fellow anti-enviros such as former insurance salesman and national parks nemesis Chuck Cushman. "Throughout the seventies, I'd known what the problem was but didn't have a solution to offer industry in my talks and seminars," Arnold recalls. "Then I read *People, Power, Change* by Luther Gerlach and Virginia Hine, and their analysis helped me to realize that in an activist society like ours the only way to defeat a social movement is with another social movement. So now we had a nonprofit mechanism to work with and told industry, let us help you to organize our constituencies."

People, Power, Change is a minor work in social movements theory that nonetheless reflects the progressive changes that overtook the field in the late 1960s and early 1970s. In the late nineteenth century, Gustave Le Bon, known as the father of social psychology, wrote *The Crowd*, in which democracy and popular social movements are seen as a pathological break with traditional (or "natural") hierarchies. At the beginning of the twentieth century, sociological theories tried to explain social movements through analogies with nature. Lyford Edwards, for example, thought revolutions were like elephants, slow-breeding but powerful creatures. Harvard's Talcott Parsons wrote *The Structure of Social Action*, introducing "unit acts" theory, which viewed societal goals as determined by the inputs of various social units in an almost mathematical formulation paralleling the mechanistic economic theories of Adam Smith.

In 1957, Parsons's student Neil Smeleser wrote *Theory of Collective Behavior*, a book that analyzed crowd psychology from a normative point of view. Crowds and disruptive social groups were compared to electrical "short circuits" in the smooth functioning of society. This theory of social aberrance made sense in the context of the 1950s, with its invisible underclass of Negro ghettos and rural sharecroppers. This was a time when only Beatniks and Communists were perceived as standing outside the dominant paradigm, and society's response to a perceived threat was to short-circuit Julius and Ethel Rosenberg, the so-called atom bomb spies, at Sing Sing prison.

However, with the emergence of the civil rights and antiwar movements of the 1960s, oppositional groupings were seen as having a rational
basis rather than simply being an irrational response to a rational society,
and sociologists turned from looking at crowds to analyzing organized,
long-term social movements. John McCarthy at Catholic University
and Meyer Zald at the University of Michigan developed a "resource
mobilization theory," arguing that social movements were as strong as the
resources—people, money, and media—they could mobilize. Anthony
Oberschall wrote about "rational calculation," suggesting that social
movements exist because people know they can gain more through
their participation. In 1971, responding to conservative social critics
such as Eric Hoffer and Bruno Bettelheim, Gerlach and Hines wrote
their book *People, Power, Change*. They closely followed the better-
known models established by McCarthy, Zald, and Oberschall in recognizing the catalytic role social movements can play in pluralistic
societies such as the United States and Canada. Exposed to collective
behavior theory through this relatively obscure work, Arnold adopted
a utilitarian/evangelical approach to social change, preaching the need
for industry to support anti-environmental groups. "Give them the
money. You stop defending yourselves, let them do it, and you get the
hell out of the way. Because citizens' groups have credibility and industries don't," he preached.[23]

Along with identifying the need to create pro-industry grassroots,
Arnold was among the first on the Right to link environmentalism with
communism. As real communism faded toward oblivion around 1990,
this trend became increasingly popular with right-wing think tankers,
magazines, and conservative pundits such as George Will and Pat
Buchanan.

In a 1984 talk to a pesticide trade group in Canada, Arnold explained
how "the Soviet Union would never allow such a thing as a wilderness
area in which valuable resources of petroleum or timber or non-fuel
minerals could never be extracted, yet they encourage the Free World to
voluntarily lock up more and more of their natural resources from economic production. ... Environmentalism is an already existing vehicle by
which the Soviet Union can encourage the Free World to voluntarily
cripple its own economy."[24]

The following year, Arnold speculated that the Union Carbide disaster in Bhopal, India, which killed twenty-five hundred people, might

not be his former client's fault. "Sabotage is not farfetched," he wrote. "The Soviets were certainly the propaganda beneficiaries. What really happened? We may never know. It may be another failure of human technology. But it could also be another Soviet mass murder."[25] He also wrote that Fernando Pereira, a photographer killed in 1985 when French secret agents bombed the Greenpeace ship *Rainbow Warrior*, was "reported to be" a contact agent for terrorists and the KGB.[26]

Arnold's ongoing travels in Canada, helping timber giants such as MacMillan Bloedel set up pro-industry groups, did not go unnoticed by that nation's media and politicians, whose fear of foreign meddling was not limited to the Soviet Union. A 1992 report by the Canadian Library of Parliament, entitled "Share Groups in British Columbia," states that "the forest companies have provided these 'local citizens coalitions' with much of their organizational impetus and financial backing. Their apparent objective has been to pit labour against environmentalists and environmentally oriented persons. Their effect has been to divide communities and create animosity in the very places where honest communication and consensus should be encouraged.

"While the rank and file membership of the Share movement may not be aware of its connection with the Wise Use movement," the government report continues, "the tactics and language of the two movements indicate a common source of counseling and training, namely Ron Arnold and his associates."[27]

Around this time Arnold began promoting a new threat: his own people's potential for violence and insurrection. In the course of one interview, he brings up this possibility eight times. "Things are so regulated and restricted that people are sensing themselves as an oppressed class, and that's how you get revolutions," he says. And, "Try telling a logger who's lost his job and house and whose neighbor is molesting his daughter because he has nothing else to do that he should remain nonviolent—that we'd rather see him work within the system. I've had calls in the middle of the night to talk to a guy who was armed and wanted to kill someone, an environmentalist or whoever. I've driven two hundred miles to tell him, 'Listen, you silly son of a bitch, this will just get you killed and the government will be in here with army regulars and cannons. There'll be nothing left of your town.'"

I ask Arnold why he thinks President Clinton held a Forest Summit in Portland, Oregon, rather than an Auto Summit in Detroit, where

GM has laid off more than a hundred thousand people, more workers than are employed in the entire northwest logging industry.

"There's not a civil war rising there," he claims unblinkingly. "There are not people there ready to march with guns." I must look somewhat skeptical, thinking that Arnold might never have been to Detroit. "Ask the FBI," he tells me. "They're very concerned and they should be. There's a war brewing."

A few years later, after the militia movement has won widespread support among Wise Use activists and Gulf War veteran Timothy McVeigh has blown up the federal building in Oklahoma City, killing 168 people, Arnold will backtrack furiously. He will insist Wise Use was never that militant or angry, and that I and other reporters are trying to smear the movement by associating it with violence.

WISE USE ORGANIZER Chuck "Rent-a- Riot" Cushman spends much of his time on the road.

"I try and get people to let go of their anger and have some fun," says Cushman to the crowd of sixty-five timber workers, ranchers, and lobbyists gathered in a conference room of the Sacramento Radisson Hotel for a meeting of the Alliance for Environment and Resources (AER). Cushman has turned down the offer of a dais and microphone. He's more comfortable pacing, getting close to his audience, taking off his jacket, putting it down, picking it up, moving around, laughing, letting them see what he's made of.

"How many of you have heard me talk before?" he asks. About half the people in the small audience raise their hands.

"What's your biggest problem right now? You think it's timber supply, but I think it's [Democratic senators] Boxer and Feinstein, because there's no balance left. So either we're going to have a second Boxer rebellion or have to do something to offset these guys. ... This desert [protection] bill is your first opportunity to fight. It's an opportunity for you to say to Dianne Feinstein, 'Your pollsters are all wet. I'm going to fight you on the desert and make this a statewide issue.' If that bill passes and they create a national park down there, you know the Sierras are next. I've always said wilderness is like aspirin. Two are good for you; one hundred will put you in the hospital."

While not as big as all outdoors, Chuck Cushman still cuts an impressive figure at six-foot-two and 260 pounds, with his wattle-hugging, white beard; lively blue eyes; and toothy, bad-boy grin. The most active anti-enviro field organizer in the United States, Cushman operates the National Inholders Association, League of Property Rights Voters, and other letterhead organizations out of a rambling farmhouse in Battle Ground, Washington. He figures he attends six to eight meetings a month, many with small local groups, providing them with needed resources and inspiration. Others he advises by e-mail, fax, and phone. His speech to the AER meeting follows the same broad outline, including many of the same anecdotes I'll hear repeated, live and on tape, at half a dozen meetings in California, Washington, Nevada, and Michigan.

"The preservationists have become like a new religion, a new paganism that worships trees and sacrifices people," he tells his listeners. "They say they want to be reasonable, they want 50 percent. So you agree and go on with your life. Five years later they're back. And what do they want? Fifty percent. Understand that these guys have a gun at your head and they want to take what you've got. So you're going to have to draw a line in the sand somewhere. The key to this is creating controversy because that opens people's minds. ... Our side always wants to fight with facts, with truth. The other side is fighting with perception. Congress operates on perception, not reality. It doesn't matter what's true. It's what people *believe* is true and what people contacting them believe is true. So we have two jobs to do: education and building public awareness. But we also have to drive up the front steps with people so that they get the perception that all hell is going to break loose if they don't allow some of our people to survive.

"What are the three most important words in political action?" he asks rhetorically. "*Lists, lists, lists.* If you don't have a list you're not in the game. We have a list on computer of every miner in the country, every rancher who has a grazing permit, every timber purchaser on federal land. Every special use permittee in a national forest. This is not rocket science to realize we have to stay competitive with the other side. The next most important words are *network, network, network.* So, okay. Let's talk solutions."

He has his audience paying attention now. Some are even leaning forward in their chairs.

"First of all, try and be nonpartisan, be team players," he tells them, moving around, smiling, working the room like the top-flight insurance salesman he once was. "Encourage entrepreneurship, encourage new groups to form. Bring in other multiple-use groups. Make it fun, share information. Put aside anger. ... Let me give you some examples of how we've helped people be creative. How many of you have heard of Jim Jontz? He was a congressman in Indiana, past tense. The timber industry played a big role getting him defeated in Indiana. This is the archenemy of the timber industry. Let me tell you a brief story—but if that tape recorder's on, could I get you to turn it off while I tell this story?" I turn my tape recorder off while continuing to take notes.

"We were going to picket Jim Jontz's office the day he announced the Ancient Forest bill. As a dig at Jim, Congressman Don Young [Republican from Alaska] had introduced a bill to declare Jontz's Indiana district an ancient forest. We asked Young to reintroduce it while we demonstrated, but he didn't have the time. We said, '*You* introduce it. We'll cover the PR.' So we put out nationwide press faxes from our office, changing the internal ID and time code on our nine machines to make it look like it was coming from Young's office in D.C. Next, we redid the machines and put out protest fax releases that looked like they were coming out of Indiana, saying, 'Why the hell is Jontz messing with this forest stuff instead of taking care of business here at home?' I had a list of the Indiana talk-radio stations, and we flooded them with calls from people in the Northwest saying they were calling from Jontz's district and why did this other congressman want to turn Kokomo into a national forest? It was a stealth operation. We had a lot of fun with it."

With the tape running again, Cushman tells a few of his other favorite war stories.

"We heard that Congressman Ron Wyden [now Democratic senator from Oregon] was going to have a hearing in Portland on retraining loggers. He hadn't done a thing to help loggers up to that point. I called up this friend of mine and said, 'I need to know the name of the biggest logger you know.' And he said, 'There's Nils Madson, about six-foot-six and 320.' I talked to Nils and said, 'Come dressed for work and bring the biggest chain saw you can find,' and he came down in front of Wyden's office with that chain saw on his back and we put a sign on him saying, 'Congressman Wyden, I want to be retrained. I want to be your brain surgeon.'"

He segues into his next story. "Last year the preservationists were going to propose a bill called the High Desert Preservation Act [sic] in eastern Oregon. They said they wanted to eliminate ranching and announced that they were going to have this conference at a place called the Malheur Field Station. So we were asked to come down and show these local folks, who had a lot of anger, how to do something that was nonviolent and fun. We did a silent protest. We got the ranchers prepared with signs at this place way out in the middle of the desert. And I had them walk inside this building where the preservationists were meeting and up each side of the aisles and just turn in towards these people and for the next two hours we didn't say a word. This preservationist guy was visibly nervous and stumbled over his speech. All their speeches were screwed up; they could hardly talk. And then, when the head guy gets up to talk, I had everyone move in about two feet. It made them feel like the building got smaller. Worked great. We had lots of press, lots of fun. That's 1991. In 1992 people called me up and said, 'They're doing it again.' Now, our people had had so much fun the previous year, we had lots of new folks. So visualize a mile-and-a-half-long line of cars, coming over this dusty hill just as the sun is rising. Imagine Butch Cassidy and the Sundance Kid. Who *are* those guys? If I was a preservationist waiting there looking out for us, like I know they were, I would have run for the head real fast. Anyway, we came up and they'd moved into this metal building maybe twenty feet from the road and we brought with us two logging trucks and two cattle trucks. And we pulled the cattle trucks on either side and we put the mama cows in one truck and the baby cows in the other truck and for the next three hours we had stereophonic cow." This gets a big laugh from his audience. "They couldn't hear themselves think. A national newspaper story said '... through the din of bawling cattle.' "

The "national newspaper" was the Portland *Oregonian*, which reported, "About seventy-five people picketed the conference at the Malheur Wildlife Refuge, thirty miles south of Burns, Saturday. Signs carried slogans such as 'Save the Desert, Plant a Preservationist,' and protestors marched to the accompanying din from bawling, stamping cattle in two huge metal stock trucks."[28] The article went on to reprint the poem that Scott Greacen, one of 170 people attending the environmentalist conference, recited to the 75 ranchers:

Thank you for coming and bringing the press.
A well-informed public will help us clean up your mess.
You'll give us some grief, but the conference is full.
'Cause we don't want your beef, and we don't need your bull.

The *Oregonian* also quoted "protest organizer" Chuck Cushman as accusing environmentalists of "systematic, cultural genocide of rural America."

Rural Clark County, Washington, across the river from Portland, is a reminder of why zoning has become popular over the last seventy years. Turning off the highway past the Volcano View Llama Ranch, you pass by beer delis, gas stations, and garden supply stores; drive through a quiet county park; and pass a few struggling truck farms and a large cluster development of identical tract homes looking out of place in a weedy green field. In several yards stand double-width trailers, old trucks, or satellite dishes. By an unpainted barn, a small herd of cows grazes, and next to new exurban ranchettes, several horses and ponies are corralled. Beyond the clutter of dying agriculture and new real estate construction is a stunning view of snowcapped Mount St. Helens.

I pull in at the fifteen-acre Cushbaum Farm. It's named for Chuck and his "spouse-like person," Christine Bauman. They are in the process of breaking up, even though the property is still in her name. As a property rights activist, Cushman seems to have an ambiguous relationship to real property. Aside from the farm bought in his girl-friend's name, he has two park inholdings (private lots within a public park, one in his son's name) and a string of tax liens, small claims, and civil losses totaling more than $20,000 in the California counties of Tulare and Sonoma. While living in Sonoma before moving to Battle Ground in 1991, he also twice defaulted on a $50,000 home mortgage.[29]

The front yard of the farmhouse is planted in decorative wooden pinwheels. Half a dozen cars and vans are pulled into the drive. In addition to the brown three-bedroom farmhouse there's a prefab garage, a flat-topped red building, and an old dairy barn where Christine keeps her Vietnamese potbellied pigs. A possum recently killed the chickens, but there are still some ducks and three Pinscur beef cattle on the small spread.

At the back of the main house is an extra door leading to the office for National Inholders. Inside are a couple of copiers, two free-standing fax machines, and fax boards attached to half a dozen IBM clones. A heavyset woman and two local teenage girls are busy at a long table doing Cushman's secretarial work. "Right now we have three ladies working here full-time. Well, one full-time, two part-time. But that's because technically, according to the state, I'm only allowed one woman here. The others work very full part-time jobs," Cushman will later tell me with a conspiratorial grin. With its mismatched furniture, boxes of paper, yellowed carpet, and general sense of clutter, the office has the feel of a small-town environmental center without the wildlife posters or wall hangings.

Cushman greets me dressed hobby-farm casual in jeans and a checked western-style shirt. His private office is a scene of impressive disorder, with piles of newspapers, reports, and open cardboard boxes on wall shelves labeled "mining law," "mailings," "land use," "receipts," and so forth.

"What I like is the combat, the excitement when the phones are all ringing and the faxes are going, and the office is full of people, and we're up all night, maybe contacting three or four thousand people. I just love it." He stops to take a phone call from Washington. Into the receiver he says, "I'm frustrated with [American Mining Congress attorney] Jack Gerard. Rome is burning and we're fiddling. What?" His brow furrows. "We're not going to lose on the mining law? All I can tell you is your perception and what's happening there don't jibe. We don't have team play. I can't get a call back from them unless I tell them it's an emergency. I can still get twenty to thirty thousand letters out, and I can get a few thousand comments on the record for the Senate hearings, but I don't have the resources right now. ... I'm not taking in a dime. We can turn this around if you have the resources to help. We're down to the short hairs now. I spent three months building a relationship with them, but now either they don't know how to work with the grass roots or they don't care to. Industry is not taking advantage of all the tools available to it to save itself."

Cushman is a natural player, simultaneously making his funding pitch and making sure I'm getting down his end of the argument, shifting blame away from Wise Use in case the 1872 mining law goes down the tubes. He once interrupted an interview with another reporter for a call from Washington, explaining that Congress was about to take a crucial vote. "And they need your permission?" the reporter wondered.

Cushman was born and raised in the suburbs of Los Angeles, attending North Hollywood High where he wrestled and played football. His father, Dwight, an L.A. teacher and former Boy Scout official, owned a cabin in Yosemite and worked there as a naturalist and interpreter during the summers (Chuck has told a number of rural audiences he was raised in Yosemite). In 1962, Dwight Cushman was forced to sell his cabin to the National Park Service or else lose his summer job. It was an injustice that would be long remembered and many times avenged by the oldest of his three sons.

Chuck's first brush with fame came in 1963, when, at the age of eighteen, he was profiled in the *Los Angeles Times* as Dodger Stadium's loudest, most successful peanut vendor. Within a few years he'd taken his sales abilities to a new level, becoming one of the top insurance salesmen in Los Angeles and Beverly Hills, for thirteen years in a row selling more than $1 million a year in coverage. He invested in property, including a private cabin inside the Yosemite park boundary (an inholding). In 1975 he divorced his first wife, with whom he'd had the first two of his four children, and in 1977, suffering from migraine headaches, he retired on full disability and moved to South Lake Tahoe. A man of boundless energy, Cushman bought a four-wheel-drive truck, had a brief second marriage, and looked for other ways to keep himself entertained. Then, on September 14, 1977, he received a letter from the National Park Service saying cabin owners in Yosemite were prohibited from modifying their homes or building on their property and that new laws and regulations were under consideration to limit development inside national parks. In Cushman's mind, this was a repeat of the abuse his father had suffered, although he claims not to have been immediately aroused to action. "I didn't pay much attention to it until January of seventy-eight," he recalls, "when a group of six or eight of us met in a room at the Holiday Inn in Sacramento and decided to form the Inholders Association. I had the time to work on it. Using Freedom of Information requests and threatening to sue one regional park superintendent a week until I got the names, I got lists of other inholders from the Park Service."

With those names, Cushman began a campaign of lawsuits and protests targeting the Park Service. The Inholders Association grew rapidly, forcing the Park Service bureaucracy to reform some of its more arbitrary activities: to open up hearings on land acquisitions and

limit the use of condemnations against unwilling sellers. But Cushman
also developed a reputation for shooting from the hip and the lip and
for creating conflicts where none had previously existed.

In 1979, after an insurance investigator took note of his hectic cross-
country organizing schedule, Cushman's former employer, Mutual of
New York, cut off his disability payments. Cushman briefly moved to
Washington, D.C., as an anti-parks lobbyist, but didn't last long. "In
Washington you dance together on Saturday and beat each other's
brains out on Monday," he tells anyone who will listen. "I was better
at the Monday part." Still, with Ronald Reagan's election, he found he
had a number of new friends in high places. John McClaughery, a
senior policy analyst in the White House, pressured James Watt to ap-
point Cushman to the National Parks System Advisory Board. "Chuck
is a loud force, and I figured he'd shake things up, which he did,"
McClaughery says.[30] Cushman recalls fondly the time he served alongside astronaut Wally Schirra, Lady Bird Johnson, and other distinguished board members. "I was the skunk at the lawn party," he says.
He also met and became fast friends with Watt biographer Ron Arnold.
"We're like brothers. I have absolute trust and faith in Ron," Cushman
says today. When Arnold hooked up with Alan Gottlieb, Cushman
began taking fundraising courses from the sweet-natured New Right
tax felon. He also developed contacts with the Farm Bureau and other
groups that were likely to support him in his organizing against the National Park Service and any other agencies that might attempt to establish new parks, wildlife sanctuaries, or wilderness areas.

In the 1960s the Army Corps of Engineers targeted the Middle
Delaware River valley of New York State for a series of dams to provide power and water to New York and other big cities. Before the
plans fell through, hundreds of rural residents had been forced from
their homes. When the Park Service took over administrative control
from the corps, it had houses bulldozed that had been occupied by
squatters. By the mid-1970s, the Upper Delaware River had become a
favorite recreational area for thousands of weekend canoeists from
New York City. The local population was divided between those who
favored the economic benefits of this new industry and those who disliked the impact of the mostly young, urban weekend partyers. In 1978,
when Congress declared the Upper Delaware valley "wild and scenic"
and ordered the Park Service to develop a land-use plan for it, the canoe

outfitters began to fear that they would become a regulated park concession. After years of debate and discussion over land use, the outfitters hired Cushman to fly in and mobilize the local populace against the Park Service. It was here on February 6, 1984, dressed in his buckskins, that he earned the moniker "Rent-a-Riot."

"They're going to come in and strangle you! You're going to lose your valley! The Park Service wants to get rid of you!" he shouted to the many valley people who had gathered that night at a local school gym. He warned that hunting and fishing would be restricted, farms and stores shut down, ancestral lands seized.[31] He still remembers the three-hour barn raiser of a presentation as something very special.

"I came to that meeting and it was a magic experience. There were nine hundred people in Eldred, New York, in this small brick schoolhouse gym. It wasn't far from where that big concert took place, Woodstock, and it had some of that electricity. People were standing there shoulder to shoulder in the middle of this snowstorm outside, and I showed a movie, *For All People for All Time*, that John McClaughery produced. And it showed the Park Service bulldozing thousands of homes, some not far from there, and these people were just stunned. That night someone slashed tires and painted a swastika on a Park Service vehicle, and that was the only thing that happened while I was there. It could have been some misguided person who was too upset to act effectively or it could have been something done to discredit us."

In the following weeks and months, a campaign of harassment against local environmental activists developed under the aegis of the Upper Delaware Alliance led by Don Rupp, a real estate agent later active with the Property Rights movement in New York and New England. When the *River Reporter*, the local newspaper, exposed numerous inaccuracies in Cushman's presentation, residents organized a boycott of the paper and threatened to burn down its office. By 1986, Rupp and his followers, having lost much of their local support, were disrupting public planning meetings and talking about tarring and feathering town officials and burning out or shooting "traitors" who participated in the land-use process.[32]

"Don Rupp wrote a letter to my paper saying he was in 'gorilla warfare' with the U.S." recalls Glenn Pontier, editor and publisher of the *River Reporter*. "So we did an editorial cartoon of him as a gorilla jumping up and down on a conference table. A short time later my house burned down." Despite police and FBI investigations, no one was ever arrested in connection with the suspicious fire.

"I'm no apologist for the Park Service, but you cannot come in here and tell people they'll lose their homes and sow dissension and tear the fabric of a community apart and then walk away as if nothing happened," said Pontier. "That's what Cushman did, and I can never forgive him for that."

"Unfortunately," recalls Cushman, "there were some extreme conservative folks out there, and I had to sever my relationship with them. And as a result I got killed financially. They never paid me what they owed me."

Since that time, Cushman has led dozens of other anti-enviro fights, helping to derail congressional funding for the National Heritage Trust and blocking a Tallgrass Prairie Reserve in Oklahoma and "Wild and Scenic River" listings in Washington and Oregon. "The only fight I ever lost was for the Columbia Gorge in Oregon," he claims.

The Niobrara River in northern Nebraska is a favorite recreation area for high plains hunters, fishermen, and canoeists. It is known for its whooping cranes, wild turkeys, bald eagles, cool flowing waters, dramatic river bows, and green-mantled bluffs. In 1989, Cushman was hired by backers of a proposed 180-foot-high Bureau of Reclamation dam to organize opposition to a "Wild and Scenic River" listing for the Niobrara, which was passed into law by Congress in 1991.[33]

"We had a good time in Nebraska. We had a big parade and demonstration with a mile-long line of tractors and combines and angry farmers. But the problem was with the group there," Cushman explains. "They weren't all working together. We gave them the tools for the plans but they didn't follow through. Also, the *Omaha Herald* was outrageously biased against us. Still, we won," he insists, although others might count the "wild and scenic" designation as a loss for the dam builders. "We felt good that we got an improved bill from Congress that builds a high wall of protection for property owners," he explains, taking credit for agreements negotiated into the bill by local farmers who were opposed to the dam.

In 1991 a friend at the NRA put Cushman in touch with vintners and developers in Sacramento who were opposing the creation, on one of the last undeveloped green spaces left in California's Central Valley, of a 25,000-acre Stone Lakes National Wildlife Refuge. "If you like the

IRS you'll love the Fish and Wildlife Service," Cushman warned a group of forty landowners he addressed in Walnut Grove, California, near the southern border of the proposed migratory waterfowl refuge. Shortly after his visit, opponents of the refuge formed the South Stone Lake Preservation Council.

Richard Spotts was the Sacramento representative of Defenders of Wildlife, one of the environmental groups supporting the refuge. "When Cushman came on the scene," he says, "it turned into what I'd call a borderline violent situation. I was incredibly heckled, and a couple of farmers came close to beating me up. Lots of environmentalists were so intimidated they left the hearings without testifying." A short time later, a nine-page letter went out to thousands of homes in the area signed by Marcie Spears, a "concerned mother and housewife," warning of the danger of killer mosquitoes. The letter explained that if the refuge was established, mosquito-borne encephalitis outbreaks could easily leave dead and brain-damaged children in its wake. "Don't get me wrong, I care very much about wildlife and the environment too," the letter read in part. "But this refuge just goes too far. If just one person dies or one child suffers permanent brain damage because of these extremists, I just couldn't live with myself if I didn't speak out."

The local Mosquito Control District, which favored the refuge, explained that the amount of water in the refuge during mosquito season would be smaller than what was already stagnating in the area's irrigation ditches. Contacted by reporter Glen Martin of the *San Francisco Chronicle*, Spears denied having written the letter, saying it was put together by several activists close to Cushman.[34] Cushman denies having had anything to do with the letter, but insists that killer mosquitoes are a legitimate issue of concern.

In 1992, he became active in his home state and county around land-use and growth-management issues, helping to form the Washington Private Property Coalition, which paid him just under $2,000 a month as a part-time consultant (his normal rate is $500 to $1,500 a day plus expenses). He first organized his semirural Clark County neighbors against a proposed wetlands protection law, sending them letters warning that the county intended to take away their property and raise their taxes. The letter predicted that future regulations would "strangle and curtail farming and home ownership," and asked them for donations to help lead the resistance.

Hundreds of people donated money and turned out for a series of public hearings, shouting down elected county officials and insisting on delays and revisions. With police standing by to maintain order, the county agreed not to pursue any wetlands protection or set up any long-term land-use planning programs. In May 1992 the *Columbian*, Clark County's main newspaper, located in Vancouver, Washington, ran an in-depth profile of Cushman titled "The High Priest of Property Rights." In the article, reporter Loretta Callahan quoted Robin Winkes, a Yale University history professor who had served with Cushman on the national parks advisory board.

"One of the things I always felt about his approach is, he starts with a grain of truth, then the sky is falling on your head," Winkes said. "The bottom line is, as a person, I kind of like Chuck. But I also think he's mischievous, dangerous, and often out of line."[35]

In 1993, Cushman and a Pacific Legal Foundation lawyer filed suit against Clark County for establishing a construction moratorium on cluster suburbs in rural areas. He also threatened to lead a secession movement in his semirural neighborhood. A *Columbian* editorial suggested he might want to name the new entity "Cushman County."

Cushman also continued to finance his hectic nationwide organizing efforts through fundraising. He claims he raises $300,000 a year and pays himself $35,000. Exact figures and parameters between his personal and organizational income are hard to come by, since the Inholders Association and his other groups are private, for-profit operations. "He was able to raise a great deal of money, but when it came in I didn't see him being responsible about how it got spent," Kathleen Rueve, one of his former bookkeepers, told the *Columbian*.[36]

Cushman claims that his National Inholders Association has sixteen thousand members who help finance its work. "Those names Chuck has are really more of a client list than a membership list," says Andy Neal, chief lobbyist for the California Farm Bureau. "We always get calls from Chuck and these other groups for money, and really all I see from Chuck is funding requests."

In trying to keep his accounts balanced, Cushman has borrowed large sums of money from several elderly members of the Inholders Association, failing to repay his debts until ordered to by a judge. In 1983, J. R. and Betty Tallackson, who owned land along a "Wild and Scenic River" near Oak Ridge, Tennessee, loaned the association $6,700 on agreement that Cushman would pay it back with 10 percent interest within the year. By 1987, when only $1,450 had been paid back, the Tallacksons got a Sonoma municipal judge to order him to make good the difference.

Daniel and Mary Defoe were lifelong California ranchers who had had a vacation cabin in the King's Canyon area of the Sierras since 1932. They met Cushman in the late 1970s when the Park Service was trying to buy their cabin from them. He helped them to hang on to it, and Daniel later loaned Cushman more than $7,000, interest-free.

"It was a verbal agreement that he'd borrow it for a certain amount of time. It was done on a handshake," Daniel Defoe recalls. "That agreed time passed, and I didn't feel he was doing everything he could do to repay his loan. We had to put a lien on his house. Eventually he paid it off when he sold the house. I still respect what he's doing, but I was discouraged that he didn't carry through on his promise. I'm not much of a sport for this Inholders stuff since that happened."[37]

On October 15, 1993, Clark County sheriff's deputies seized about $13,000 worth of antiques from Cushman's farm to settle another old debt. The widow of Bernard Vandewater of Oregon, who had loaned Cushman and National Inholders about $10,000, hadn't received the majority of payments Cushman had been ordered to make following a 1989 court case. According to the *Columbian*, Cushman said he believed Bernard Vandewater had made a contribution, not a loan, to the Inholders Association, but lawyers for Mrs. Vandewater said her deceased husband had won his case by producing a signed promissory note from Cushman.

The IRS has also filed a $22,379.87 tax lien against Cushman. In a December 1992 deposition, he complained that "they're on me like stink on a pig."[38]

His personal life seems as unstable as his financial status. "Every woman I know has a bone to pick with me," he jokes. "Christine is an environmentalist, you know. She does total recycling, no chemicals in the garden, doesn't believe in that stuff. ... She and I are just on two different pages. It makes a relationship more difficult. She doesn't share my interests; she doesn't go on political trips. I was married the first time for almost ten years," he continues. "My second marriage I wanted a mother for my kids. I had a housekeeper who was wonderful with kids but I had a hard time affording her economically, so I made a mistake, rushed into that marriage. We're still good friends, though. I'm good friends with all my wives," he laughs. He goes on to talk about what "a great gal" his former third wife is. "I've never had to have two lawyers in a divorce yet," he grins.

Bluff and engaging in a bearish sort of way, Cushman, when I meet him, is back into the singles lifestyle at the age of fifty-one. One woman recalls him hitting on her at a singles volleyball group, another spotting him at a *Columbian*-sponsored dance. And bar talk overheard after one of his Wise Use presentations reveals keen interest among forty-something country women in pearl-button blouses and acid-washed jeans.

"My problem is I don't have a committed partner. If you can do things together, if you can go on trips, it's much better," he muses. "Ron [Arnold] has that with his wife, Jan. She's a wonderful lady and real support for him, something I don't have right now."

So with little obvious control over his organizational, financial, or personal life, Chuck Cushman has been forced to go for the adrenaline rush: fighting new battles while raising funds to pay off his old ones, eating on the run, worrying about his health and weight, catching flak from the media. Almost by default, he has taken on the role of the anti-enviro movement's smoke jumper, flying from place to place across America looking for local brushfires to break out so he can add fuel to them.

The last time I hear Cushman give a speech is in 2000 at a Senate hearing on restoring full funding for the Land and Water Conservation Fund (LWCF). Created in 1965, LWCF set aside some $900 million a year from offshore drilling revenues for parks and wilderness. Beginning in 1980, however, Congress hijacked some $12 billion from the fund for other purposes. With record federal surpluses at the end of the Clinton administration and a looming presidential election, both parties now see an advantage in freeing up more money for the environment. Still, some westerners at the hearing, including Larry Craig of Idaho, aren't happy about the idea of any new wilderness parks. "I don't want the federal government owning one more acre in Idaho. I'm mainly concerned because federal lands become king's lands," Craig complains. I wonder when the United States became a constitutional monarchy and how I missed that vote.

After a first panel of witnesses testifying in favor of the funding, including the mayor of Knoxville (urban parks will also get new funding), and celebrity witness Terrell Davis of the Denver Broncos, a second panel opposed to funding is seated. This one includes Cushman, who asks me what I'm doing at the press table. Actually, I'm working on a book about the oceans, though he assumes I'm there to hear what he has to say. Larry Craig welcomes him, saying that "Chuck Cushman is an old friend." Cushman begins testifying about cultural genocide and rural cleansing, comparing the impact of national parks on rural Americans to Serbian ethnic cleansing, massacres, and atrocities then taking place in Kosovo. At this point I realize listening to his rants is no longer part of my job description, so I leave.

"WHEN [Clinton assistant secretary of Interior] George Frampton shuts down logging communities, it's really not that different from when the militia shot down all those miners in the [1914] Ludlow massacre [in which more than two dozen striking miners and their families were killed]," asserts Bill Grannell. "The only difference is the militia killed them outright while Frampton is leaving them to live in poverty with their kids unhealthy and uneducated. It's like what the coal companies created in Appalachia with their strip mines. Frampton and the Sierra Club are the new set of elitists ruling our country."

Pug-faced and tenacious, with a fringe of gray-brown hair, a jutting beard, and pointy cowboy boots, Bill Grannell, of People for the West! (PFW), talks with the pneumatic cadence of a John Wayne, and numbers radical labor leader Harry Bridges and 1960s organizer Saul Alinsky among his heroes. His vision is to apply the organizing techniques they used to mobilize dockworkers and the urban poor in building a rural, chapter-based anti-environmental movement.

Reeling from declining farm income, the depressed commodity prices of the 1980s, and unrelieved depopulation going back more than thirty years, small-town rural America has, by the 1990s, become disenfranchised in much the same way as the inner city. It's seeing a declining tax base, deteriorating schools, and increased dependence on social welfare programs. The members of the social elite of these rural ghettos—mine company operators, wealthy ranchers, and gyppo loggers—anxious to deflect their neighbors' anger and frustration away from themselves and their corporate sponsors, have become the local leaders and champions of PFW.

Like Charles Collins, the nineteenth-century Sioux City promoter who campaigned to open the Black Hills to white gold miners with arguments equating Native American "land monopolies" with the railroad trusts, Bill Grannell and his wife, Barbara, aim to convince the rural poor that their predicament is the result of a privileged elite. This elite, they argue, is typified not by Homestake, Phelps-Dodge, Energy Fuels, and other giant mining companies that have scarred their landscape, irradiated their families, and polluted their rivers, but by the West's new "preservationist" settlers, who are gentrifying towns like Boise, Bozeman, and Santa Fe.

PFW is a project of the Western States Public Lands Coalition, established by the Grannells in 1988. With more than twelve thousand dues-paying members and several full-time organizers, it is the largest of the anti-enviro groups, although careful to distinguish itself from Wise Use.

"The Western States Public Lands Coalition is not part of Wise Use. That's our official position," Grannell explains. "They're too far right, too shrill. The game of political extremism doesn't work."

But PFW's critics, such as former BLM director Jim Baca (who accuses PFW of fomenting violence and compares Grannell to ex-Ku Klux Klansman David Duke), point out that the group's 1992 budget of $1.7 million was almost wholly provided by mining companies looking to fight reform of the 1872 mining law. "These are the industry types who just don't want to get off the gravy train," he says.[39] It's a credible argument, given that twelve of the group's original thirteen board members were mining executives.

"Those who pay, play," Grannell shrugs, drinking a cold Budweiser to the plinging sound of slot machines at a casino bar in Reno. Having just finished promoting his group at an anti-enviro meeting, he's more than happy to kick back and reflect on what he sees as the seamless flow of his political evolution from Democratic union organizer to defender of corporate mining. "My grandfather was an IWW organizer in Terre Haute, Indiana, where [socialist party leader] Eugene Debs was from. My father was a labor organizer for the Carpenters Union. I organized for the National Education Association (NEA) for a couple of years.

"My father worked in construction, and we moved around the West and Midwest a good deal while I was growing up," he goes on. "I went to the University of Denver in sixty-three and one and a half years to the law school before deciding that wasn't what I wanted. I moved to Coos Bay, Oregon, in my early twenties, where I bought a boat and started fishing for salmon. I got involved with the Democratic Party and joined the county central committee. That's when I became friends with Senator Wayne Morse. Imagine. I'm twenty-two, twenty-three, sitting in a bar in Coos Bay drinking with Wayne Morse and [Longshoremen's leader] Harry Bridges. It was heady stuff."

"You were against the Vietnam War?" I ask, recalling that Morse was one of the earliest, most consistent critics of the war in the U.S. Senate.

"Pretty much," Grannell admits reluctantly. Among the constituency he is now trying to organize, Vietnam is still considered a winnable war lost by traitors in the media and Congress. It's also the bitter core of an anecdote repeated regularly at Wise Use/Property Rights events. The story may be apocryphal, combining as it does elements of hostility toward the rich, leftists, women, the media, and the West's new settlers. As it's told, Ted Turner and his then wife, Jane Fonda, try to cut in line at a popular steakhouse in Manhattan, Montana, not far from Turner's 100,000-acre ranch. Told that they have to wait their turn like everyone else, they go into the bar. The bartender, either a decorated Vietnam veteran or the brother of someone who'd been killed in Vietnam, depending on who's telling the story, looks Turner in the eye as he sidles up to the bar, shakes his head, and says, "I'll serve you, but the bitch has to go." This punch line is usually followed by appreciative laughter.

After working salmon for a few years, Bill Grannell sold his boat and became a union organizer with the NEA, attending Saul Alinsky's organizer training school in Chicago, where many of the most effective 1960s radicals honed their skills. "I find that what I learned there is still very useful," Grannell says. "It was everything from how to organize a strike to how to shut down a shop to how to make a peace. Saul said if you make a war be sure you can win it. Also be sure you know how to negotiate the peace that comes afterwards."

In 1972 Grannell was elected a Democratic state representative from Oregon's Fourth District. He would serve ten years in the Oregon statehouse before quitting in 1982. During that period he also published a weekly newspaper, the *Bay Reporter*, distributed up and down the south-central Oregon coast.

"I became chairman of the revenue committee in the Oregon House," he recalls. "The first bill I carried in seventy-three was for public employees' right to collective bargaining. ... Natural resource production was also vital for the state. It provided revenue for the schools and I fought hard to protect it."

"Bill was not a liberal," says Larry Campbell, the square-jawed Republican speaker of the Oregon House. "It was hard for Bill to move legislation that was favorable to the natural resources industries, because he was part of a very liberal caucus and at loggerheads with them. But Bill himself was not a liberal."[40]

Democratic Senate Majority Leader Dick Springer agrees. "He was a collective bargaining leader but was not known as an environmentalist, not coming from Coos Bay."[41]

White smoke billowing from the stack of a lumber mill marks the far end of Coos Bay, across the water from the oceanside fishing harbor and lighthouse park. The old, brown, ten-story Tioga Hotel, set back from Bayshore Boulevard's railroad tracks, is the largest building in this sleepy town of fifteen thousand, but the old flophouse is dwarfed by the white superstructure of the *Neptune Jacinth*, tied up at the waterfront. A massive log freighter out of Singapore, the *Jacinth* has four yellow deck cranes that are ready to pick up a new load of Douglas fir, fill its hull, and stack the surplus logs topside between the upright steel beams that picket the deck. Three of its Asian crew are leaning on a rail sharing a cigarette, looking out over the misty town and the green and brown checker-cut hills just beyond. For these sailors from Singapore, a high-tech city-state where it's against the law to own a car more than three years old, Coos Bay, Oregon, must seem a lot like Kompong Som, Cambodia, or any of the other Third World ports where they tie up to collect raw logs. For the people of Coos Bay, however, it's a nice place to call home, even if the cutthroat trout are disappearing from the Umpqua River because of siltation and shade loss resulting from the clear-cuts.[42] Coos Bay is also a nice place to visit if you want to try to understand the politics of resource-industry Democrats like Bill Grannell.

At the turn of the twentieth century, the O & C Railroad got involved in real estate speculation on public lands it had been given to build a rail line. As it became clear that no rail line would be built, the federal government decided to reclaim the property and provide 50 percent of future timber revenues to the local counties that had been cheated out of the promise of transportation and development. Coos County was one of eighteen O & C counties in western Oregon that would use this income to run their school systems, eliminating the need for local property taxes. Residents of O & C counties—like the residents of Alaska, where the state collects 90 percent of all federal oil, gas, and mineral revenues—quickly developed a sense of entitlement. They came to believe that they shouldn't have to pay the same taxes other Americans did because their areas created "new wealth" from the ground. That sense of entitlement would spread rapidly during the Reagan years, fueled by supply-side economic theory, which argued that tax cuts, particularly for the rich, would increase federal revenues by stimulating investment, creating "new wealth" that would trickle down from above.

After retiring from the statehouse with his ten-year severance in 1982, Grannell got a job as a lobbyist with the Association of County Governments. "They hired me to come up with an answer to the school-funding crisis. We put a sales-tax initiative together, but it failed. The voters weren't interested," he recalls. "This was at the time of the tax rebellion, Jarvis-Gann and Proposition 13 in California. Howard Jarvis even came up here to Oregon to campaign against our measure. I was also lobbying in Washington for the BLM and Forest Service budgets [in order to generate timber sales]. This was when the Gramm-Rudman balanced-budget deal was passed in 1984. The first mandated cuts would sequester 14 percent of shared revenues. The only amendment, the only exception that got passed, was sponsored by Senators James McClure [of Idaho] and Mark Hatfield [of Oregon]. It protected our natural resource revenues and I authored it.

"Groups like the Wilderness Society, Audubon, and Sierra were always against us," he continues. "They would argue that forest sales were below cost—saying, for example, that the roads the Forest Service constructed should be charged to the timber companies. But those aren't just logging roads, you know. They serve recreation and the Forest Service can use them to study wildlife or respond to fires. So it became obvious to me that they just wanted to stop timber harvesting in all public forests. At the local level, I was finding the same kind of groups—like the Oregon Natural Resources Council, Andy Kerr's group, which was appealing each and every timber sale. It wasn't just fiscal conservatives we were up against but this other agenda put out by the anti-harvesting, anti-cattle groups, and it didn't take a rocket scientist to figure out that these people were out to one-up themselves. They had had some successes in the past with environmental protection, and now they were into the realm of environmental extremism, of New Age religion. ... It was very frustrating. In the eighties, under Reagan, we had no revenue sharing, plus Gramm-Rudman, plus the environmentalists cutting out what revenue base we did have."

Given a choice of enemies to go after—the most popular president in the nation's history or owl-loving environmentalists—Bill Grannell, like a number of other rural Democrats, including then House Speaker Tom Foley, chose the easy target.

Grannell met his wife, Barbara, in 1982. She was a legislative staffer in Salem working against Oregon's tax-limitation initiative. They got married in 1984 while she was leading the school-tax-initiative campaign. For the next six months, she continued to work for the schools initiative in Oregon. Grannell went back to Washington to lobby for the counties. This would set a pattern of separation and reunion that still continues in their highly politicized, on-the-run marriage.

"Around that time my father died and my mother was pretty elderly, so we went back to Denver and I became the city's lobbyist," Grannell recalls. He campaigned for construction of the Two Forks Dam, an environmentally risky water project cancelled in the early days of the first Bush administration. "We also began publishing a newsletter, *Public Lands Report*, out of our home that went to county offices, the BLM, Congress. The environmentalist problem kept accelerating. All the timber, oil, and gas leases were being appealed. Industry folks asked me if I thought we could create a coalition to oppose them. Barb and I spent a year talking to corporations that were looking for support to organize a grassroots response. We talked to 220 corporations, but only four bit: Chevron, Medford Timber, Energy Fuels [a uranium-mining company in Colorado], and Homestake Mining [which got its start mining gold in the Black Hills following the battle of Little Bighorn].

"We incorporated Western States Public Lands as a nonprofit that allowed us to lobby. Our first issue was the spotted owl in Oregon. We put together the Oregon Project in eighty-eight, pulling together a coalition of sixty-two groups in ninety days. Barb and I were the main organizers. Later we added Joe Sand, the ex–AP bureau chief up there. He did the press for us. Joe died of a cerebral hemorrhage, driving back from a lands meeting last year. Joe was a dear friend of ours," he pauses. "We put the project together for $120,000, half from our four companies, half from the Counties Association. By the end we had fourteen timber companies involved. We got over 170,000 names on a timber harvest petition. We had Hatfield with us and turned Bob Packwood around. We got the Hatfield-Adams amendment that said all the lumber caught up in legal appeals shall be cut. In terms of separation of powers it probably wasn't legal, but it sure sent a message. ... The local groups we organized into the Oregon Coalition. The Oregon Coalition, along with the Yellow Ribbon to their right, later became the Oregon Lands Coalition [OLC], which helped form the Alliance for America."

People close to the OLC claim that the Grannells left Oregon when the timber companies wouldn't pay them an $80,000 fee to continue organizing. Grannell says the OLC got co-opted by the timber corporations and moved too far to the right.

"By ninety-one the timber companies had bailed on us. They put their money into the American Forest Resource Alliance (AFRA), a beltway operation where they hired a bunch of D.C.-based experts on 'grassroots' organizing. They also put money into the Oregon Lands Coalition. But Medford stayed with us, and Homestake and Energy and Chevron were still with us. We decided to move from Denver to Pueblo. A lot of our supporters think big cities like Denver are the problem. We also decided to apply the lessons of Oregon to the mining industry. We got a lot of response because of the success we'd had in Oregon. When the Society of Mining Engineers joined us, which included many middle-level managers and CEOs, that brought us the mining companies and industry support."

Mining supporters included Nerco Minerals, which donated $100,000; Cyprus Minerals, $100,000; Chevron, $45,000; Hecla Mining, $30,000; Bond Gold, $30,000; Pegasus Gold, $15,000; Homestake Mining, $15,000; Minerex Resources, $15,000; Energy Fuels, $15,000; and the American Mining Congress, $15,000.[43] Fifteen thousand dollars was the minimum price demanded for membership on the board of directors for Western States Public Lands, although this rule would later be amended to allow grassroots members from states with ten or more PFW chapters to be represented. The first grassroots member named to the board was Marvin Watts, a small-mine owner from New Mexico.

PFW spokesman Joe Sand told reporters that Western States had collected $1.7 million from the mining industry for their organizing work. But IRS records show that in 1991 they raised just over $500,000, a figure that increased to slightly over $625,000 in 1992.[44] Whichever figure is accurate, the investment would prove worthwhile to the mining industry, which was desperately looking for new means of defending the 1872 mining law. That law has given mining companies the right to extract hard-rock minerals such as gold and silver from millions of acres of public lands without paying the government any royalties. It's also allowed them to take title to land for as little as $2.50 an acre, a price originally set in 1872 to encourage development of "unsettled" Indian lands. With no modern-day provisions for cleanup and reclamation, the mining law contributed to environmental degradation associated with abandoned mines and runoff that has polluted streams and rivers throughout the West. It wasn't surprising, then, that a poll commissioned by the industry in 1991 found 82 percent of respondents thought mine companies should be forced to pay royalties and restore abandoned mining sites.[45] The pollsters cautioned the industry not to debate the mining law in public forums. However, the creation of PFW gave the industry a way of advancing its cause in the name of Populist empowerment. PFW's strategy would be to argue that any restriction on mining was a first step in a preservationist plot to limit multiple use of federal lands for logging, ranching, and recreation.

PFW's early campaigns targeted Montana and New Mexico, two states where mining proposals for test drillings and cyanide-leach gold processing were meeting stiff environmental opposition. When congressional hearings on the 1872 mining law were held in Santa Fe, PFW turned out five hundred protestors, many of them Phelps-Dodge and MolyCorp employees bused in by their companies. MolyCorp had earlier donated $10,000 to Western States. Ed Cordova, MolyCorp's head of security, was also chairman of the local PFW chapter in Questa, New Mexico, a boom-and-bust company mining town in the northern part of the state.[46]

"We started out looking at the mining law, which is the mining companies' major cause," Bill Grannell admits, "but in our organizing efforts we got a range of people involved, which necessitated a more moderate broad-based approach. ... You can't empower people and think you have a string attached to their back."

Still, PFW's efforts to organize people around nonmining issues—be they water rights, cattle grazing, off-road recreation, predator control, or Spanish land grants—always seem to circle back to protection of the mining industry.

PFW tried to organize the 130 or so residents of Cook City, Montana, around the issue of water rights. Not coincidentally, two miles outside Cook City, on the northern border of Yellowstone National Park, is where Noranda wanted to open its huge New World Gold Mine. Montana rancher Paul Hawks complained, "Mining is given preference over all other uses, but they don't tell you that at their [PFW] meetings. I have yet to see them lay out what the 1872 mining law does."[47]

Says Jim Baca, "I've never understood why a cowboy who's expected to be a steward of the land would want to go to bat for a miner who comes in, makes a mining claim, takes the land, pollutes the water, and leaves without paying anything for it."

PFW campaigns have also included efforts, beginning in 1993, to organize trail-bike riders and loggers in southern Missouri's Mark Twain National Forest, where test drilling by the Doe Run Lead Mining Company was going on. PFW's Missouri campaign was coordinated by the president of the state Mining Industry Council (with financial backing from the company).

At the same time, EPA worker Becky Horton was confronting toxic pollution from mines in poor rural areas of southern Missouri, documenting elevated levels of lead in children's blood. When in 1997 she spoke out in favor of protecting the region's water quality and health, she was assaulted, bound, and left tied in her truck overnight.

Death threats, a dead cat left in a mailbox, and other forms of intimidation had already been directed against local environmentalists. The Doe Run lead company denied any link to the violence even as local PFW leader William Jud told community meetings that UN troops enforcing environmental laws would soon drive Ozarks residents "into primitive concentration camps on the outskirts of large cities such as St. Louis."

Horton, who often gave interviews on water quality, reported that on July 31, 1997, in response to a phone request, she went to a riverfront campground to meet what she thought was a cable-TV news crew. Instead she was confronted by four drunks, two young men and two women, who called her a "commie" and a "greenie" who cost mining jobs in the Ozarks. When she tried to leave, one of the men beat her with a stick, trashed her EPA van, and left her duct-taped to the seatbelts. They then duct-taped a video, *Behind the Green Curtain*, to her arm and stuffed a Sierra Club pamphlet in her mouth. The video, featuring Wise Use founder Ron Arnold, argues that environmentalists are usurping people's property rights. Although Horton reported the incident to the EPA and the local sheriff, no arrests were ever made. Still, she returned to her community work. Horton, unlike her attackers and those who incited them, is no coward. Nor is she the first critic to be targeted in the long and bloody history of mining in America.

five

The Golden Rooster

Five men are known to be dead and 16 are already in the hospital: the Frisco mill on Canyon Creek is in ruins: the Gem mine has surrendered to the strikers, the arms of its employees have been captured, and the employees themselves have been ordered out of the country.
—Spokane Weekly Review, July 14, 1892, reporting on a typical labor/management dispute in U.S. mining

The biggest gold heist since the days of Butch Cassidy.
—Secretary of Interior Bruce Babbitt on the 1872 Mining Law

THERE'S A GOLDEN ROOSTER in a glass display case between the registration desk and the slot machines at John Ascuaga's Nugget Hotel/Casino in Reno. It's eighteen-karat gold, weighs more than fourteen pounds, and is insured for $140,000. Aesthetically, I'd rate it the equal of some of the nicer tin roosters I've seen for sale on the streets of Tijuana, although it's not really my place to be judging poultry art. It's the 206.3 troy ounces of gold in the statue, or more specifically how that gold was mined, that has brought me here today.[1]

"Mineral Information Network Exchange"—Mine Net to those in the know—is listed on the hotel's meetings board along with a wedding, the World Dreambuilders, an AA meeting, and a drumming workshop. About sixty people are attending this one-day conference, which was organized by Chuck Cushman. The event has been billed as an attempt to create "grassroots support" for the 1872 mining law, that legacy of the nineteenth-century Indian wars that allows mining companies to patent, or take title to, federal lands and mine the hardrock minerals they find there without paying fees. Today the law results in a loss to the Treasury estimated at half a billion dollars a year.

According to a GAO report, the law has also led to widespread real estate speculation on public lands. The report cites one example when mine patent holders bought 17,000 acres of public land for $42,500 and resold it a few weeks later for $37 million.[2] Under this patenting process, 3.2 million acres of public land, an area the size of Connecticut, have already been sold. Moreover, twelve thousand miles of western rivers have been contaminated by acid, arsenic, and heavy metals in mine runoff, and mine tailing piles have contaminated soil, lakes, watering holes, and drinking wells from Appalachia to the Rocky Mountains. Half a million acres of worked-over mine sites now lie abandoned, and forty-eight such sites have been deemed EPA Superfund cleanup sites. The Berkeley open-pit copper mine in Butte, Montana, is the largest hazardous waste site in the country.[3] Given its history and impact on the U.S. taxpayer and the environment, the 1872 mining law is about as likely to win broad popular grassroots support as is pedophilia for profit.

Among those in attendance at today's Mine Net conference are Cushman's co-chair, Steve Borell, from the Alaska Miners Association; Jim Burling, an attorney with the Pacific Legal Foundation; an exploration geologist for Amex Gold; a representative from the Independence Mining Company; a general manager for a Canadian-owned mine; someone from Kennecott; an Elko, Nevada, city council member; a couple of mining engineers; a couple of drill operators; some recreational miners; and three people from a group called Grassroots for Multiple Use.

Cushman paces in front of the room, flashing his big grin. Today he's wearing a western-cut sports jacket, blue shirt, grizzly bear belt buckle, brown slacks, and cowboy boots. "My role here is to pretend I'm Phil Donahue, to let people talk as much as possible and keep it informal," he explains. Then, as a group-dynamics exercise, he has everyone stand up and rearrange their tables into a U shape. Five minutes later, as if on cue, someone says, "Look, just getting us to reorganize the room is an example of the unity we have to solidify, to get things done."

Cushman points out that "since the press is here" there should be no attribution—that is, no speaker should be quoted by name, in order to keep the discussion "unrestrained and free-flowing." During the first break I get him to agree that people appearing on the panels can be quoted by name.

The key panel includes Duane Gibson, a sallow young assistant to Senator Ted Stevens of Alaska, and Jack Gerard, an amiable, round-faced lawyer in a red and white striped shirt from McClure, Gerard and Neuenschwander (McClure as in James A., former senator from Idaho). Gerard is representing the major transnational corporations of the American Mining Congress.

"Pegasus and the other majors are bailing on us," complains an un-attributed (or UA) conferee.

"Can we sue the majors for negligence? Because if they don't initiate [Property Rights] 'takings' suits, they're not doing right by their stock-holders," another UA suggests.

"It's true the judiciary now has more friendly Reagan-Bush appointees for life, but before we go the litigation route we have to fight our perception problem in Congress," Gerard points out. "The perception is you're buying land for $2.50 an acre, converting it to golf courses, and selling the minerals for your South African owners, and we have to alter that perception. We have to point out that 60 percent of western mining is U.S.-shareholder owned, so it's not all foreign owned."

"We just don't want the Mining Congress shooting us in the foot as they go around the back door," says a suspicious UA in a cowboy hat.

"Look, the AMC is not there to stick it to you," Jack Gerard tries to reassure the group. "But we're going to have to give something up. That's just realistic. So maybe we can't live with a royalty on gross, but maybe we can accept a royalty on net."

A militant from Idaho stands up to speak. "The majors in mining give us nothing. Maybe they kicked some money in for People for the West!, but they haven't done anything in Idaho. But I'll tell you if my little eight-man mining company goes down the shitter, I'm going to put logging roads all through the Frank Church Wilderness Area and trash it, 'cause I have the permits for logging [as part of his mining patent]. We should just tell George Miller [chairman of the House Committee on Natural Resources until Republican Don Young takes over and drops the word *Natural*] you're going to piss off a lot of people and we can trash your Endangered Species Act and anything else we choose, and maybe if you're lucky we'll let you keep something."

"That's not the perception they have in Congress," Cushman points out.

"How many people here work at actual mining operations right now?" asks Ivan Urnovitz from the Northwest Mining Association, one of the speakers on the next panel. About twenty out of sixty participants raise their hands. Discussion begins to shift to preservationist congresspeople and to (then vice president) Al Gore's plan to destroy all industry west of the Mississippi.

"We're dealing with religious zealots who want to turn the country into a national park. And when you're dealing with irrational people, you have to start acting irrationally too, so that's what I've started doing," says Dave Parkhurt, a panelist with Nevada Miners and Prospectors. Duane Gibson returns the focus of the discussion to the third planet from the sun, saying that his boss, Senator Stevens, believes that people in the mining industry should try to work to influence the Clinton administration through the Western Senate Coalition.

A month later, western Democrats led by Max Baucus of Montana will get Clinton to drop mining, grazing, and timber-sale reforms from his 1994 budget plan. The president agrees to their demands supposedly to gain support for his jobs bill, but since no western Republicans are asked to trade anything for these concessions, he ends up losing on both deals.

"These guys must have never played poker. It's like they're getting on-the-job training up there," complains Bob Langsencamp of the New Mexico Land Commissioner's office, expressing a widely held feeling among public land-reform advocates in the early days of the Clinton administration.[4]

Chuck Cushman and Bill Grannell (reluctantly attending Cushman's meeting as a personal favor to Steve Borell) each take time from the mining meeting to make pitches for their respective groups.

"National Inholders is essentially a phone company to facilitate all you people in Mine Net," Cushman explains, rubbing his beard with his knuckles. "We're a political guerrilla fighting outfit. That's what we do best. We have nine faxes and can reach three to four thousand people overnight. Ours is a grassroots, bottom-up operation, so please don't view us as competitive with your work."

"People for the West! has over one hundred chapters. We have organizers in Montana, Colorado, Arizona, New Mexico, and California," Grannell explains. "We've had hearings where we've shown up from Denver to Anchorage to Salt Lake City. We fax selectively. We try and reach out to labor. We realize that we gotta be moderate and mainstream. It may be therapeutic to say, 'Let's burn down the White House,' but it ain't gonna happen. We have to live in the world as it is."

Jack Gerard points out that money, waste, and reclamation remain the main perceptual issues that supporters of the 1872 mining law have to address.

A woman consultant in a red dress with short, stylishly feathered hair offers a suggestion. "After the Summitville incident in Colorado, it's important we be perceived as opposing bad actors. Rather than always saying how awful the existing environmental regulations are, we should say, 'We're very happy with them because they do what needs to be done to protect the environment, but we don't want things to go too far over in the other direction.'"

"So you're talking window dressing? Just restating what we're already doing?" asks another UA.

"Exactly."

Her reference is to the ongoing pollution that began in 1986 at the Summitville Gold Mine in southern Colorado's San Juan Mountains, where cyanide used in heap-leaching operations has poisoned seventeen miles of the Alamosa River, a tributary of the Rio Grande. Galactic Resources, Ltd., the Canadian company that opened the mine in 1986, declared bankruptcy in early 1993, leaving the state of Colorado stuck with the $20 million cleanup bill and a 170 million–gallon tailings pond built into a dammed-up valley that continues to leak cyanide.[5] A decade later, in 2003, the founder and fugitive CEO is working with the military dictatorship of Burma to set up a massive copper-mining operation in that country.

I head down to the casino lobby for a drink thinking I'm not half as cynical a reporter as I thought I was. Over a Cuervo and orange juice, I decide that while here in Nevada, I'll try to visit a working mine site.

Although best known for its gambling and irradiated sheep, Nevada really got its start with pickax mining. In 1859 the state was the empty quarter of the Utah territory also known as Zion, a vast forgotten desert basin considered, even by the Latter-day Saints of Salt Lake City, too barren to bother with. Then two Irish miners, Patrick McLaughlin and Peter O'Riley, digging on the eastern slope of the Sierra Nevada, unearthed the greatest silver strike since the Spanish conquistadors found their mountain of silver at Potosi. It was named the Comstock Lode, after Henry Comstock, the man who cheated McLaughlin and O'Riley out of their claim. Over the next five years, gold and silver strikes in the Great Basin would attract more than seventy thousand people to the area, including a number of forty-niners who'd failed to strike it rich in California's gold rush. Mining for gold, silver, quicksilver, gemstones, and copper would provide Nevada with the wealth and population it needed for statehood.[6] Nineteenth-century mining strikes throughout the West would also help fuel America's expanding Industrial Revolution, but at a terrible price. Within twenty years of the Sutter Creek gold rush, California's Indian population would decline from a hundred thousand to thirty thousand people as peaceful tribes were decimated by miners' guns, forced slavery, diseases, and liquor. More than any other industry, American mining has been marked by violent conflicts over territory and labor. These have left a bitter legacy still seen in the strip-mined and mountaintop-torn shotgun-shack poverty of Appalachia, the twelve thousand miles of poisoned rivers that crisscross the intermountain West, and the hospital wards of Arizona's Navajo nation, where former uranium miners are dying from an epidemic of lung cancer.

The history of the mining industry is probably best summed up in *Dave Barry Slept Here*. In this humorist's history of the United States, the author explains that labor unrest was "caused by coal miners emerging from the ground and making radical demands such as: (1) they should get paid; or, at least (2) they should not have the tunnels collapse on them so often. The coal companies generally responded by bringing in skilled labor negotiators to bargain with the miners' heads using clubs. This often resulted in violence, which forced the federal government, in its role as peacekeeper, to have federal troops shoot at the miners with guns. Eventually the miners realized that they were safer down in the collapsing tunnels, and there was a considerable decline in labor unrest."[7]

This style of labor negotiation was first practiced in the middle of the nineteenth century against Irish immigrant miners in the anthracite coalfields of Pennsylvania. Irish survivors of the potato famine, working for starvation wages in the mines, organized a clandestine group called the Molly Maguires, named after an Irish widow who took great pleasure in shooting British landlords and their agents back home.

In their "long strike" of 1874–1875, the Mollies dynamited mineshafts, shot a number of unpopular mine superintendents, and threatened to shoot any miner who went back to work. The Mollies' organization was eventually broken up after being infiltrated by a

Pinkerton detective named James McParland. In the summer of 1877, the state of Pennsylvania hanged nineteen miners named as Mollie gunmen by McParland. It was no secret that the mine owners, railroad tycoons, and other leading industrialists of the time hoped these mass executions would mark an end to American labor unrest. But it was not to be.[8] Just a month later a nationwide railroad strike broke out that rapidly reached insurrectionary levels of violence in major towns and cities, with hundreds killed by state militias. Where the state militias sided with the rioters, federal troops were brought in to open fire on the mobs. It was after the railroad strike of 1877 that National Guard armories were first constructed in major cities across America to guard against future uprisings.

The United Mine Workers (UMW) were next to field an army of labor. They tried to unionize the coal country of Pennsylvania, leading a hundred thousand miners out on strike in 1897. This was the first in a series of bitter strikes for union recognition, decent wages, and mine safety that would, over the decades, convulse the coalfields of Ohio, Indiana, Pennsylvania, Tennessee, Kentucky, and West Virginia.

But it was in the Rocky Mountain West that turn-of-the-century mining conflicts took on the appearance of industrial war, complete with major gun battles, broken treaties, and political assassinations.

In 1892, striking miners in the Coeur d'Alene region of Idaho began what would become a generation of deadly warfare with armed and deputized strikebreakers. By 1899, with the mine owners refusing to recognize the miners' unions, and mines and mills being dynamited by wildcat strikers, Governor Frank Steunenberg declared parts of Idaho "in a state of insurrection and rebellion." President McKinley sent in federal troops and martial law was declared. Thousands of miners were rounded up and held in specially erected "bullpens" until the strikes were broken. Governor Steunenberg, who when elected had been a man of modest means, left office a suspiciously wealthy individual. He didn't get much time to enjoy his prosperous retirement, however. In December 1905, someone tied some fishline to the front gate of his huge sheep ranch. When he opened the gate it set off a charge of dynamite that killed him instantly.[9]

In Colorado the Western Federation of Miners led the fight for the eight-hour workday. The WFM was headed up by William Dudley Haywood. A one-eyed giant of a man, "Big Bill" Haywood was a cowboy turned miner turned revolutionist with a penchant for packing a six-gun when he went out to the mining districts to organize his "boys."

In 1901 the gold and silver miners of Telluride went out on strike. After the first month, Arthur Collins, superintendent of the Smuggler-Union Mines, decided to reopen his operations using armed and deputized strikebreakers. The Telluride chapter of the WFM sent a purchase order to a Denver gun dealer for 250 Winchester rifles and fifty thousand rounds of ammunition. On July 3, with their consignment delivered, the local union miners ambushed the Smuggler "deputies" in a gun battle that lasted the better part of a day. Finally the strikebreakers raised a white flag, and the miners allowed them to take their dead and wounded and leave the area. Later the governor of Colorado sent a commission of inquiry, who reported, "Everything is quiet in Telluride: the miners are in peaceful possession of the mines," a conclusion that sent shudders through the national business community. The following year, somebody shot former mine superintendent Arthur Collins dead as he sat reading by a lighted window in his home.

In 1902 the Colorado Mine Owners Association blocked passage of state legislation for an eight-hour workday. Bundles of cash were reportedly passed out to lawmakers on the assembly floor of the statehouse. In 1903, Cripple Creek miners, frustrated with the legislative process, went on strike for the eight-hour day. Governor James Peabody, a banker and close friend of the Mine Owners Association, declared Cripple Creek and Telluride to be "in a state of insurrection and rebellion" and sent the Denver militia to take control. When a newspaper editorial declared the action unconstitutional, the state judge advocate replied, "To hell with the Constitution: we are not following the Constitution."[10]

Miners were seized on the streets and taken from their homes at gunpoint. Hundreds were held without charges, in barbed-wire bullpens for weeks on end. The editor of the *Victor Record* was arrested after his paper questioned the actions of the militia. When a civil judge tried to hold habeas corpus hearings, the military surrounded the courthouse and put a bayonet to his chest. Stores that sold provisions to miners were looted and burned. An ex-congressman was shot and wounded by soldiers. The Citizens Alliance, a mine owner–organized vigilante group, beat up and terrorized strike supporters with impunity. Big Bill Haywood and WFM president Charles Moyers snuck in and out of

The Golden Rooster 133

Cripple Creek armed and ready to shoot it out with militiamen if they
attempted to capture them. The WFM decided to spread the strike to
other mines around the state. The governor responded by putting those
districts under martial law. In 1904 a train bringing strikebreakers into
Cripple Creek was dynamited and derailed. The state retaliated by
forcibly deporting dozens of union officials to Kansas and New Mexico. With most of their leadership jailed, shot, or in exile, the strikes
eventually faltered and the miners returned to their ten-hour shifts in
the mines.[11]

In 1905, Bill Haywood and Charles Moyer journeyed to Chicago
where, along with Eugene Debs, Mother Jones, Emma Goldman,
Daniel DeLeon, and two hundred other militant labor leaders of their
day, they formed the IWW, the Industrial Workers of the World. The
Wobblies, as they came to be known, believed in "one big union" open
to all races and nationalities. In their vision, through general strikes and
without great violence, the union would put the mines, mills, and factories into the hands of their workers. This was a very western, shoot-
the-moon kind of idea, based more on organizers' personal strike
experiences than on the ideologies of European Marxists. Still, it was
the kind of class-based revolutionary proposal guaranteed to displease
America's industrial elite.[12]

Within months, Haywood, Moyer, and an associate, George Pettibone, were kidnapped by state marshals and taken to Idaho, where they
were charged with ordering the murder of former Idaho governor
Frank Steunenberg. They had been named by a sometime union member named Harry Orchard. During a three-day jailhouse interrogation
by James McParland, the same Pinkerton detective who had infiltrated
and condemned the Molly Maguires almost thirty years earlier, Orchard
himself admitted to the actual assassination by dynamite.

The arrest of the three raised a cry of "Frame up!" from the work-
ing-class movement as newspapers across America and Europe reported their arrest, trial, and possible execution. One hundred thousand
marchers in New York demanded their release. Nationally famous attorney and defender of lost causes Clarence Darrow traveled to Idaho
to represent them. In Terre Haute, Indiana, IWWs (including perhaps
Bill Grannell's grandfather) rallied around socialist party leader Eugene
Debs. Debs, until then a lifelong advocate of nonviolence, wrote to
Darrow to suggest that a worker militia be raised to march on Idaho

and free the prisoners from the gallows. In the newspaper *Appeal to Reason* he wrote, "If they attempt to murder Moyer, Haywood and their brothers a million revolutionists, at least, will meet them with guns. ... If the plutocrats begin the program, we will end it."

President Teddy Roosevelt, after reading these words, sent a copy of them to his attorney general with a note: "Is it possible to proceed against Debs and the proprietor of this paper criminally?" In another letter to a politician friend, Roosevelt referred to Haywood, Pettibone, and Debs as "undesirable citizens." Soon thousands of college students began wearing buttons reading "I am an undesirable citizen."

In May 1907 the Idaho trial began. Clarence Darrow, the consummate defense attorney, called Orchard "the most monumental liar that ever existed," tearing his testimony apart as the fabrication of Pinkerton's McParland. During his testimony McParland remained impassive as Darrow called him a paid professional liar and asked him how it had felt to befriend the Molly Maguires in order to send them to their hanging deaths. (McParland replied that he had just been doing his job.)

In his eleven-hour summation, Darrow, wearing a rumpled gray suit and clutching his eyeglasses in one hand, told the jury that they had the power to kill Haywood. "If you kill him, your act will be applauded by many: if you should decree Haywood's death, in the great railroad offices of our great cities men will sing your praises. If you decree his death, amongst the spiders and vultures of Wall Street will go up paeans of praise for those twelve men who killed Bill Haywood. ... But if you free him there are still those who will reverently bow their heads and thank you twelve men for the character you have saved. Out on the broad prairies, where men toil with their hands: out on the broad ocean, where men are sailing the ships: through our mills and factories: down deep under the earth, men who suffer, women and children weary with care and toil ... will kneel tonight and ask their God to guide your judgments ... to save Haywood's life."[13]

On July 28 the jury returned a verdict of not guilty. It would prove a sweet if short-lived victory for the defendants and their unions.[14]

With the horrific conditions that existed in the mining industry—thousands of miners dying from cave-ins, slate falls, coal dust, and gas and dynamite explosions, and living conditions in the aboveground mine camps not much better—labor unrest continued to expand. The most dramatic confrontation of the era grew out of a western coal strike organized by the UMW. In 1913, eleven thousand coal miners in southern Colorado, many of them Italian and Greek immigrants, went out on strike against the Rockefeller-controlled Colorado Fuel and Iron Corporation. Evicted from their shacks in isolated company towns, the miners set up tent cities in the hills. John D. Rockefeller hired gunmen from the Baldwin-Felts Detective Agency to help break the strike, but after a series of unprovoked shootings the miners began to collect arms to defend themselves. There followed a series of gun battles, during which the miners succeeded in driving back an armored train and disabling an armored truck known as the Death Special. The governor of Colorado responded to the shifting balance of forces by sending in the militia to help reopen the mines (Rockefeller agreed to pay their wages). The strikers, refusing to give in, held out in their tent cities throughout the cold winter of 1913–1914. In the spring the militia, including many company gunmen who had simply changed uniforms, set up machine-gun positions in the hills above the tent colony at Ludlow, where a thousand men, women, and children were encamped. On the morning of April 20, after a miner and a guard got into a fight, the militia opened fire with their machine guns. When strike leader Lou Tikas approached to ask for a cease-fire, he was shot dead. A number of people, unable to find shelter in the shallow trenches the miners had dug for protection, were cut down by the guards' bullets. At dusk the militia moved down from the hills with torches and set fire to the tent colony. The next day a telephone lineman going through the ruins counting bodies found a shallow pit beneath a cot. Inside were the charred bodies of two women and eleven children; they had been burned to death. In all, twenty-six people died in what came to be known as the Ludlow Massacre.

After burying their dead in the town of Trinidad, armed miners moved out into the hills, where they began destroying mines, dynamiting mineshafts, and killing mine guards. The governor asked for federal troops to restore order. The army arrived in force and a few months later the strike was broken.[15]

The following year, IWW balladeer and organizer Joe Hill was arrested in Salt Lake City and charged with killing a grocer during a robbery. Although there was no hard evidence against him, Hill's prominence in the IWW and recent union work with local copper miners ensured a vigorous prosecution. The state copper trust, the newspapers, and the police were convinced of his guilt, as was a local Mormon jury. Thousands of telegrams from prominent citizens, foreign ambassadors, the government of Sweden (where Hill was born), even President Wilson, asking Governor William Spry to commute Hill's death sentence went unanswered. In his last note to Bill Haywood, Hill wrote, "Don't waste any time in mourning. Organize." On November 19, Joe Hill was executed by a five-man firing squad in the yard of the Utah State Penitentiary.[16]

Frank Little was an outspoken member of the IWW's general executive board. A one-eyed part Indian with a warrior's courage, he was widely known as the "hobo agitator." In 1916–1917 he was active in leading strikes in Montana and Arizona, including one in Bisbee, Arizona, where the vigilante Loyalty League rounded up twelve hundred miners at gunpoint, put them on open railcars, and shipped them out into the desert. In June 1917, while Little was engaged in that strike, an industrial accident at Montana's Speculator Mine took the lives of 190 men, not an atypical occurrence at a time when a mine owner claimed that it was easier to replace a lost miner than a mine mule. In late July, Little traveled back to Butte, Montana, to help lead a miners' strike against Anaconda Copper. Future mystery writer Dashiell Hammett, working as a young Pinkerton at the time, recalled how an Anaconda Copper official offered him $5,000 to kill Little, an offer he declined.[17] On July 31, 1917, Frank Little got into a shouting match with a group of Anaconda company guards. In the early hours of the next morning, six armed men broke into his hotel room, beat him up, and dragged him in his pajamas to their car, where they tied a rope around him and dragged him three miles to the Milwaukee Railroad trestle. There they lynched him, pinning a note to his body that read "First and last warning." No one was ever arrested for the murder.[18]

Through force of arms, the western mining industry was able to break the militant Western Federation of Miners and, with the help of the federal government, the IWW. Woodrow Wilson's Justice Department used the Wobblies' opposition to World War I as an excuse to raid dozens of their meeting halls throughout the country and put 101 IWW leaders on trial for conspiracy to encourage draft evasion. All 101 were convicted. Fifteen Wobblies, including Big Bill Haywood, were given twenty-year prison sentences. Haywood jumped bail and fled to Russia, where a revolution had broken out. He remained there, a son of the West in exile, until his death in 1928.

Under a determined leadership, the UMW continued to carry on its strikes, win industry concessions, and organize new membership in the eastern coal belt, where miner populations were both more settled and more numerous than in the mining boomtowns of the West. Still, the conflicts were intense and deadly. In West Virginia the army was called out when armed miners and company militias fought in the mountains, and General Billy Mitchell led the first and only domestic air force bombing raid against U.S. citizens, using his biplanes to attack the UMW's positions. With the onset of the Depression, the UMW began a new organizing drive in Appalachia under the leadership of John L. Lewis, another gruff giant of a man who helped unify labor, under the banner of the Congress of Industrial Organizations, the CIO.

With their mineral rights bought out from under them, the mountain folk, hillbillies, and immigrant mine laborers of Appalachia were forced to live in a kind of indentured servitude in and around mining towns built, owned, and operated by the coal companies. When, in 1930, union organizers from Pennsylvania, Indiana, West Virginia, and other UMW strongholds began holding secret meetings in the hill country of Kentucky, the mine owners hired goons and gangsters from Chicago to root them out. In places like "Bloody Harlan" County, coal company death squads carried out a reign of terror that included the kidnapping and murder of suspected union organizers. Victims' bodies were dumped at roadsides and in streambeds as warnings to the miners. But with unemployment in the coalfields skyrocketing, miners, desperate to find some way to feed their families, continued to join the union. Many began carrying .38 revolvers, known as "John L. Lewis peacemakers," for self-defense.

On May 5, 1931, in Evarts, Kentucky, a fight broke out between miners and the coal companies' industrial police. The goons drew their pistols, as did many of the miners, and a shoot-out ensued. One miner and three company guards were killed. Evarts shattered the mining industry's grip of fear and intimidation on the region. Although the violence would continue for years to come, the miners now began to call openly for strike actions and demand collective bargaining agreements. By the end of the decade, they had won recognition of their rights as union workers.

The UMW never admitted to arming or encouraging the coal miners in their violent means of defense. Unlike the WFM or the Wobblies, the

UMW was not looking for a revolution so much as a square deal for its membership, and the union had a keen strategic sense of when to pull back from a fight it couldn't win. Several times during the 1930s, Governor Flem Sampson of Kentucky sent the National Guard into the coalfields, calling coal country "a hotbed of Reds and Communists." Each time, the striking miners hung out American flags in greeting and peacefully sat out the guards' occupation of their communities. As John L. Lewis noted in 1948, when President Truman sent the military into the coal mines to try to force a strike settlement, "You can't dig coal with bayonets."[19]

Unfortunately, by the end of World War II it was possible to dig coal seams with bulldozers and dynamite. Surface mining — or strip-mining, as it came to be known — reduced the mining industry's need for workers while massively expanding the environmental destruction wrought on the coal-, copper-, and gold-producing regions of America. To the miners' risk of cave-ins, explosions, silicosis, and black and brown lung disease could now be added community and regional impacts from river and groundwater pollution, earthen dam breaks, erosion, flooding, soil contamination, and subsidence.

By the 1970s the UMW had joined several other unions, including the United Steel Workers and the Oil, Chemical and Atomic Workers, in rejecting management attempts to form common fronts for what union spokespeople called "environmental blackmail." These included attempts to win industry-wide exemptions from toxic-emission standards, mine-reclamation requirements, and the Clean Air and Clean Water Acts. The blackmail part involved industry claims that obeying these laws would force them to stage massive layoffs and close plants. The UMW became more supportive of their industry, however, as the inherent environmental costs of burning coal became clearer. It came out in opposition to acid-rain controls on coal with high sulfur content during the first Bush (Sr.) administration, and allied with climate-change skeptics and right-wing Republicans in opposing CO_2 reductions during the Clinton administration (coal has the highest carbon content of all fossil fuels).[20]

"We're trying to make this an issue they [Clinton and Gore] have to be concerned about," UMW head Cecil Roberts told me in 1998 after giving joint testimony with coal company officials to a House subcommittee hearing titled "Is the Clinton-Gore Administration Selling Out Americans?"

In the West the hard-rock mining industry has tried to win workers' backing for 1872 mining law "reforms" that would guarantee little or no real change in the Jesse James–era law. But the number of miners involved in these massive public lands operations is relatively small, and hard-rock miners organized by the United Steelworkers have rejected industry overtures. To people who have lived in places like Butte, Montana; Alamosa, Colorado; and Coeur d'Alene, Idaho, mines and mining have always represented quick wealth for a few and deadly trouble for everyone else. As new people move to the West looking for a clean and safe environment in which to raise their kids, locally based opposition to big mining operations has increased. Even some of the old-timers who have historically benefited from these operations, seeing the growth in foreign ownership of the mines, have begun to ask why this multinational industry should continue to get a free ride from Uncle Sam.

I LEAVE THE HOWARD JOHNSON's motor lodge in Elko, Nevada, on a cold winter morning. The dry desert air freezes my hair, still damp from the motel shower, into brittle furrows. KELK radio reports that *Good Morning, America* is sending a camera crew to town next week to cover the big story. Elko has just been named the most livable small town in America by some author who must put a high premium on clean air, open vistas, fast food, easy freeway access, legalized gambling, prostitution, and gold. Lots of gold. Elko is the fifth largest gold-producing area in the world, helping Nevada turn out some six million troy ounces a year, enough for close to thirty thousand golden rooster statues. The second KELK news item is that a ferret has escaped from its owner and there's a $100 reward for the fugitive varmint's recovery.

"Just head up Mount City highway past the Raleys' and keep going forty-four miles," I've been instructed. "Then turn right at the sign for the mine and it's seven miles to the mill site." Within a few minutes I'm past the last outlying suburban ranchettes, alone on the two-lane black-top humping through snow-blown dells and arroyos. The slush and splatter muddy up the windshield on my red box, a rusting 1983 Toyota wagon with four-wheel-drive if needed. What I need now is some window-washer spray, but the plastic lines are frozen up. I pull over to clean off the glass with a handful of snow, a few black and white magpies by the side of the road my only company. I'm a little surprised I'm being allowed to visit a mine on such short notice. When I called Newmont at 7 A.M. they'd said they needed ten days' notice for a press tour, but the Independence Mine is working out.

"We're interested in staying open to the public but we can't really trust reporters who just want to portray us as scarring the land and exploiting the West," Bob Zurga, the company's CEO, explained on the phone from Reno before reluctantly agreeing to let me go up to the mine. "I think one of the major things that will come out over the next year, you're going to see great disappointment in the role of environmental restrictions across the earth," he went on. "You have to protect the earth, but with efficiency. Already we're seeing a 35 percent increase in lumber prices. We're the biggest taxpayer in Elko County. What will happen when we have to cut back because of increased royalties? We're all being hurt by this approach, which takes people out of nature."

I cruise along at a sedate seventy-five miles an hour through vast snowfields that run up against distant ice-dusted mountains framing barren valleys of truly arctic proportions. A passing truck or three-strand barbed-wire fence become the connective tissue of civilization. Somewhere behind me are the Ruby Mountains and an eighty-six-car railroad train running west out of Salt Lake. There's a sterile beauty in the icy sea of sage and scattered stands of windblown aspen that dot the hills. A shaft of sunlight cuts through the low white clouds to illuminate a single jagged, five thousand–foot peak, and I have to smile at the pure grandeur of it.

"Independence Mining Co. FMC Gold. Jerritt Canyon Mine" reads the small sign on the side of the road. I turn onto the private road, heading up into the cloud-obscured Independence mountain range. Ridges of rock jut toward the low white sky as the mill complex, with its three big smokestacks, comes into view. White steam rises into the white clouds, cream on porcelain. Large semis going in the other direction pass me near the tailing ponds that cover several hundred acres in front of the mill. I pull up at the guard post and am directed to the mine office, where I sign a liability release and receive a yellow hard hat and safety glasses. Through the window I can see a flatbed truck pull up to the gate. Its chained-down load consists of a single huge tire for a 150-ton truck. I'm directed down a hallway to the office of Scott Barr, the mine manager.

We shake hands and Barr offers me a seat. He has a smooth, friendly face with narrow gray eyes and a truly impressive gut hanging over his

"Nevada" belt buckle. The buttons on his striped, coffee-stained shirt strain against the pull of the cloth.

He tells me his mill operates like a chemical plant. They have a chlorine-bleaching process for their slurry along with an oxidizing "roasting" process. "Half the mill's operations are roasting, half bleaching," he explains. "We get a little cyanide in our wastewater, but that's kept in our runoff ponds. We haven't had any wildlife mortalities or serious environmental problems since we opened in eighty-one." The big operators like Newmont (the largest gold producer in the United States, mining in the nearby Carlin Mountains) use heap leaching with cyanide, whereby a weak solution of cyanide is sprayed over exposed ore and the gold is processed out of the liquid runoff. "It takes no pretreatment but the recovery is low, about 60 to 70 percent. Our mill uses fine-grain rock, almost like face powder, and we get 80 percent recovery from our feedstock, which has about one part gold per million."

"How much rock do you have to dig for an ounce of gold?"

He does some quick calculating. "We get 0.14 ounces of gold per ton of ore. We process about eight thousand tons of rock a day and produce three to four hundred thousand ounces of gold a year out of the Jerritt Canyon Mine. We employ seven hundred workers. Newmont and Barrick [a Canadian-owned mining company also operating in the Carlin range] produce about ten times that amount."

He shows me a wall map of the area. "Our claims and operations area covers some two hundred square miles, although the area of disturbance is only a few square miles."

"On public lands?"

"Our mining is all taking place on Humboldt National Forest land."

I ask if Independence is a locally owned mine.

"Independence used to belong to Freeport Gold but is now a subsidiary of Minorco, a Luxembourg-based company owned by the Oppenheimer group."

"DeBeers?"

"Right, DeBeers."

I begin to understand why the American Mining Congress is worried about a perception problem in Congress. If the general public realizes that key pillars of South Africa's onetime apartheid system are digging gold for free on U.S. public lands, the little remaining support for the 1872 mining law might erode down to bedrock. Today, non-U.S.

corporations control fifteen of the twenty-five largest gold mines in the United States, most of which operate on public, or patented, land. The Jerritt Canyon Mine produces about $155 million in royalty-free gold for DeBeers every year.[21]

"And the gold goes where?" I ask.

"We ship our gold offshore for the jewelry market—direct export of the dory with some silver impurities still in it—to Europe, Italy, Switzerland. The tax credit on exports favors that."

Barr, a fourth-generation miner whose grandfather worked the Comstock Lode, accepts that the mining law of 1872 will probably be reformed. "A royalty payment would mean we'd become more selective, only mine the higher-grade ores. The impact would probably be felt for two or three years. We're really concerned the eastern power lobbies may not see the 14 percent of mineral production that comes from public lands as that important, even though a lot of it is gold." He pauses. "Frankly, the validity of any mining on public lands is being questioned. That part of multiple use will be difficult to sustain."

Scott Lewis, the environmental supervisor for Jerritt, drives me up to the mine site. He's a tall, youthful-looking man, six-foot-four with reddish hair and a trim mustache, dressed in a fleece-lined winter coat, boots, and jeans. He graduated from Montana State University in range science in 1983 and later worked coal in Colorado and Texas, where he met his wife. We climb the looping haul road, an eighty-foot-wide strip of oily dirt and gravel that is damp from drifting ground fog. Lewis points to the four-foot raised berms along the cliff sides, which the Occupational Safety and Health Administration requires. He tells me about the NEPA (National Environmental Policy Act) requirements the mine has to meet. He says that state concern over mining has also increased since some mining mercury showed up in Carson City's water supply. I ask him if there are any environmentalists in the Elko area.

"There's people here who like to hunt and play. We've got people with mule deer groups who keep an eye on the agencies and on us to make sure we mitigate for mulies."

We pull up in front of a prefab metal building. Inside I'm introduced to Jim Collord, the mine operations superintendent. Collord is also six-foot-four. They grow 'em big in Nevada, I figure, either because of the open space or the nuclear testing. Collord looks to be in his fifties, with a solid build and a noticeable resemblance to actor Richard Crenna, including the weathered face full of finely etched character lines. He has warm brown eyes that are friendly and unchallenging, which one appreciates when meeting a miner half again as large as your standard black bear.

"To me mining is basic. It's creating new wealth out of the ground," he muses, munching his way through a lunch of carrots and salad. "I'm a third-generation gold miner. My grandfather worked central Idaho mine claims, staked the Thunder Mountain claim. I was born in Idaho in the mining town of Stibnine, a boomtown of a thousand people that's now a ghost town. My dad was injured in a logging road accident in forty-nine, so we moved to California, where he worked quicksilver on the Hearst ranch. He got radiation burns watching an A-bomb go off while flying around in a light plane with a Geiger searching for uranium deposits back in the 1950s. Said he could see the blast wave move across the desert floor. I got my master's degree in exploration from the Mackey School of Mines. Since then I've lived in a number of towns, Rawhide, Nevada; Wolf Fang, Idaho; and Paradox, Utah, among other places."

He also has a sixteen-year-old son he named Jerritt, after the mine. "I couldn't recommend Jerritt go into mining. I think the future of mining in the U.S. is pretty bleak," he admits. "I get very depressed sometimes. The excitement of prospecting has been my history, but now we're coming up against a massive foe in environmentalism."

He removes a Sierra Club fundraising letter that he's tacked up on the bulletin board. "I'm a member of The Nature Conservancy, so I get stuff like this in my mail," he says, handing me the letter.

It's an attack on the Wise Use movement, and has that nonpartisan, direct-mail style of three-dot urgency and barely suppressed hysteria common to the fundraising medium. "We must confront the most dangerous challenges in our history" it reads, lest Wise Use "open up our precious wilds so energy companies can drill for oil and gas and dig for minerals ... destroying crucial wetlands ... clear-cutting our few remaining ancient forests ... inviting massive construction in our most beautiful national parks and wild areas. ..."[22]

"The media goes for this kind of garbage," Collord complains. "The general public doesn't understand that on public land you don't just rape and scrape."

Lewis concurs. "They don't know the extent of the permitting process. Our original Environmental Impact Statement cost $2 million."

"I myself am a charter member of People for the West!," Collord continues. "We tried to get an Elko chapter going but it's pretty inactive. The smaller splinter groups tend not to hang together. The mining companies themselves are more involved. The way I see it, Elko is a mining town, and so in a way it doesn't do much good to preach in Elko, you're pretty much preaching to the choir. I mean this is a town where Clinton came in a distant third [in 1992, behind Bush and Perot]. But if you look at the media trends and stuff, I feel like we're fighting a losing battle."

I ask him if anyone else in the mine is active in People for the West! or similar groups. "Not really. Most of these guys driving the trucks here aren't political, but if you tell them, 'Hey, you're going to lose your job if this mining law goes through,' they'll catch on."

We head outside, climbing into the cab of his four-wheel-drive utility vehicle. The cold air is bracing and smells of diesel, dirt, and sage. He pulls out onto the haul road, oil-blackened and as wide as the Trans-Amazon Highway.

"Some people like to look at mountains or rivers," he tells me as I look out over the edge of the mountain. "I find ore pretty unique. Like what you have in these mountains is 34-million-year-old gold formations that came out of ancient hot springs. I hunt for big structures, follow fault lines, and look for sediments and rock outcroppings that indicate where hot spring systems once existed. We take samples. Maybe drill a thousand holes. I find a lot of beauty in ore bodies. They're a rare part of nature." He points out a jasperoid outcrop, a knobby hill to us laypeople. It's an indicator of past flows. "Hot water once moved through these rocks with gold in solution, some kind of chloride solution, within it. Then the carbon in these rocks locked onto the gold, just like in the milling process."

"How's that?" I ask.

"We run cyanide and gold through activated carbon; coconut charcoal does a good job, the husks are reusable. So we'll flush the gold out onto steel wool, then melt the steel wool, then use a chlorine solution to remove it or else heat the carbon off it, roasting it in an oxygen fire."

We drive up toward a high pass as a muddy hundred-ton truck with a ninety-ton load of rock and ore in its shallow, jacked-up bed passes us, heading down the mountain. Behind it a larger yellow truck rumbles into a turnoff to one of the mine's faces. The truck is worth a million dollars and makes Bigfoot look like a standard Chevy. Each of its eight-foot-high tires costs $52,000. The road we're driving on is salted, but the salt washes away with every rain and a new application has to be laid down—for $82,000.

We pass an ore pile almost black with crushed carbonaceous rock mixed with striations of orange-colored arsenic and then cross over a snow-flurried divide. On one side of the mountain, the waters draw down to the Owyhee River, a tributary of the Snake, which wanders eight hundred miles north through Hell's Canyon and beyond. On the west side of the mountain, the water percolates down to the Humboldt River, which flows west to Lovelock and beyond to the outskirts of Reno. The hillside is terraced with past mining cuts. At close to eight thousand feet above sea level, more Caterpillar haul trucks roll past us.

"Mining's a damn tough job, and this mine is probably one of the toughest, with its elevation, its hilliness, its snow, and its mud," Collord reflects, "working through these freeze-and-thaw cycles, 24 hours a day, 360 days a year. You're fighting the weather and these complex little ore bodies. You have to move a lot of rock to get to the ore. This is tough work."

I ask him about the irregularity of the terrace faces. "We move more material when prices are up, less when they drop. You can track price changes in the angle of the mine faces. Here we blast three or four hundred holes per pit. Our ore is mainly gold with trace amounts of silver, arsenic, and mercury, but mostly waste rock attached."

Lewis points to a future cut site across the valley, where a rare stand of aspen, like anorexic dogwoods, bends in the frosty high-country wind on the rolling face of a snow-swept virgin hillside. "Aspen is important," he says. "You have raptors like the goshawk that are indicator species for the aspen; also cavity nesters, woodpeckers."

"There's some neat country here in Nevada," Collord adds. He likes to cross-country ski as often as he can get away from his work. We pass an old waste dump, where tons of "growth medium" soils have been piled up along the roadside for future reclamation work. Collord gets on the radio. "Hey, I think we ran out of muck for Dan's dump back there. Why don't you move that loader to the 7,060 elevation." "Okay, boss, if that's what you want," a voice crackles back from the dash-mounted unit. "I just drove past the 7,750 bench. I'll move it around."

I ask about some broad lines in the exposed rock face running along the mine terraces above us. "Up this pit, you can see that bedding. That's old ocean floor, about 280 million years old," Collord grins.

We pass a big shovel with a blue cab that looks like the prow of an oceangoing tug. "That's a fifteen-yard shovel, a $2 million machine made by Harvish Figer out of Milwaukee [a company Bill Grannell has approached to help fund People for the West!]."

The road begins winding down a steep canyon ravine—or at least that's my initial impression. It takes me a minute to realize this isn't a ravine but an artificial pit. We pull out onto the crater floor three hundred feet below ground level. I climb out of the truck, looking up toward the rim thirty stories above us. Thirty million tons of rock and ore have been moved out of this hole since 1986. That's about three hundred nuclear aircraft carriers in weight. There are wooden stakes off to our left decorated with multicolored plastic flags where new twenty-five-foot-deep blasting holes are being prepared. "We're still chasing that block of ore body," Collord explains. "Mining twenty-foot slices using our computer models to tail it down."

I'm disappointed to find out there's no new blasting going on today. The trick with industrial blasting is to pack your holes with ammonium nitrate fertilizer and diesel oil, a formula long popular with truck-bomb terrorists in Ireland, Colombia, Lebanon, in the Oklahoma City bombing, and in the first World Trade Center attack. You use dynamite as your blast initiator.

We drive over next to a pickup truck where a safety flag man is waiting to watch a mechanized ballet of behemoths. Even from a hundred feet back, I feel like we're in Tonka Toys as the world's largest frontloader, a 1,300-horsepower 994 Caterpillar, takes thirty-five- to forty-ton bites out of an ore pile. The Cat operator sits in a cab twenty feet off the ground, moving his machine's segmented body, on eleven-foot-high tires, in tight radial turns. The machine's radiator block is the size of a garage door. In four railcar-sized scoops, he fills up a 150-ton, mud-splattered, yellow haul truck and is ready for the next. This is as big and rudely basic as man's industrial processes get. These miners eat mountains and shit gold.

"It moves twenty-one yards of muck in a scoop," Collord says proudly. A boxy, mechanized drill hammer sits on the far side of the pit readying another twenty-five-foot grid for blasting. "We'll blast six hundred holes at a time. About four hundred tons is loosened per hole. Once I did an eleven hundred–hole shoot."

"That must have been spectacular," I say, thinking of the five hundred–pound bombs I used to watch turning half-block sections of Managua, Nicaragua, into rubble and of the IRA's orange-flamed nitro-benzine car bombs blasting downtown Belfast. "It doesn't look that spectacular if you do it right," he tells me. "The trick is to shake the rock loose but leave it in place so that afterwards the diggers can come in and muck it out."

I'm relieved to see that the snowcapped peaks around us still dwarf this human work as we climb back up onto the main haul road.

"This is a small hole," Collord says, referring to the entire Jerritt operation. "We move up to 150,000 tons a day. Barrick or Newmont probably move 500,000 tons a day. You go visit a copper pit like they've got in Butte, Montana, you'll see what really big is."

"The hole that ate a town."

"That's right."

The hole that ate a town and is now the world's largest Superfund cleanup site.

I ask him if he's really worried about his company having to pay the same royalties as a coal mine operator or oil company.

"People don't understand that this is a different operation from coal or gas. We don't set the price. The royalty will just shorten the mine's life. People will be out the gate a year earlier. Some of the low-grade ore won't be worth milling. In other words, we wouldn't be maximizing the use of the resource."

As much as I respect Jim Collord and his work, before maximizing this mine's resources for DeBeers of South Africa, I'd rather see the Humboldt National Forest given over to cross-country skiers, deer hunters, and endangered goshawks.

six

Save It for What?

*These "Wise Use" extremists claim that economically you're going to
take their jobs away from them; they're all going to become poor; their
children are going to starve; and it's all because you're a bunch of
fuzzy-headed tree-huggers. ... It's blatant lying in many cases is how
they present things.* —General Norman Schwarzkopf (Ret.),
at a Nature Conservancy Press Conference

*The APA [Adirondack Park Agency] will take all of our private property.
The APA will be a total dictator. Adirondackers will be forced to live in
concentration camps working as slave laborers for the APA.*
—Lieutenant Colonel Calvin Carr (Ret.),
Leader of the Adirondack Solidarity Alliance

A RED-TAILED HAWK rides a warm thermal above the Pemigewasset
River as it bubbles past the green yards and century-old fieldstone
foundations of the small Victorian town of North Woodstock, New
Hampshire. The town has established a postage stamp–sized park
where a strip of white sand and a wide granite bar reach out to a sud-
den drop-off in the river bottom, a natural swimming hole deep enough
for a breathtakingly cold morning plunge or cannonball dive to the
clear rocky bottom. Right now a couple of young boys are keeping
themselves amused chucking rocks into the hole. Beyond the pool-
sized depression, the Pemi, as it is known locally, rushes knee-high
around a thickly wooded island that divides it just above a rumbling set
of rapids that could prove fast thrills for a kayaker or skilled canoeist.
The rushing sound of the crystal white water bridging over glacial boulders also provides the perfect tonic for my tired bones, ensuring a good
night's sleep at a local inn along the river.

While loggers, ranchers, and multinational mining corporations fight for continued economic access to western public lands under the rubric of Wise Use, quietly scenic parts of America east of the Mississippi, including a forty-mile stretch of the Pemigewasset, have become the prime battleground for the Property Rights movement. As rural life has been increasingly altered by the growth of highways, cluster developments, and shopping malls, people have begun to debate how best to preserve areas, such as northern New England, that still manage to maintain their unique mix of stable populations, pastoral landscapes, and intact ecosystems. Competing ideas have included proposals for environmentally oriented state and local land-use planning, federal protections for unique rivers and vital wetlands, maintaining the values and choices of private property owners who have protected these areas in the past, and a combination of all three that can ensure sustainable rural development. For leaders of the Property Rights movement, only the third of these four options is acceptable, a no-compromise defense of landowners' rights to do with their property as they please without any restriction.

The night before arriving at the Pemi, my longtime adventure mate, Nancy, and I had driven south through the Franconia Notch from the north-country town of Lancaster. Before leaving there, Jeff Elliot and his wife had warned us to drive carefully, and not too fast. Over the last six months, there have been a number of car/moose collisions, several fatal to both parties, since three-quarter-ton moose, when challenged, tend to turn broadside to their attackers. This sounded like a fair warning, and more reassuring somehow than the ones running on the nightly news back home, where a spate of armed carjackings had San Francisco Bay Area drivers on edge.

Elliot is a bearded high school teacher and former state Fish and Game biologist. He was dressed in jeans and a "Stop Acid Rain" tee shirt the day he took us to see where his house had once stood.

Just before sunset we parked by the side of a two-lane blacktop road and walked five minutes up a trail lined with wild ferns, painted trillium, and pink moccasin flowers, accompanied by swarms of blood-hungry mosquitoes. In a clearing stood the remains of Elliot's two-story cabin, burned to the ground three years ago. Part of the floor is charred but still intact where his 250-gallon hot water tank ruptured in the flames. A rusting metal stove leans against the remnant of a wall beam amidst a scattering of twisted nails and hooks. The rest of the building is all blackened charcoal timbers tangled up with blackberry bushes and wild grasses and surrounded by a half-crescent of scorched trees.

"I'd gone to visit a lady friend in Worcester, Mass., turning off my propane gas before leaving Friday night," he tells us. "On Wednesday around noon a fellow teacher saw the fire from the heights and called the fire department. She described it as a fireball-type explosion. By the time the fire department got here, there wasn't much they could do. The fire inspector said it was arson."

We climb around the blackened remains. Broken glass bottles, empty beer cans, and cigarette butts suggest that local teens have made the place their hangout. "Look at this," Elliot calls out, leaning down while slapping a mosquito off the back of his neck. I approach, thinking he's found some forgotten keepsake, but what he wants to show us is a cone-shaped morel mushroom growing out of the black ash. "I'd been living here four years and lost everything in the fire," he says, slapping at another mosquito that's alighted on his face. "I wasn't the only one who lost his home," he smiles, and points to where a weasel had lived just outside his front door.

He takes us farther back into the woods, searching for a rare iris he spotted on his last trip out to his property. I offer to pick a Canadian mayflower for Nancy, but she'd prefer more Avon Skin-So-Soft, which we're using as mosquito repellent. Elliot, who's a trained entomologist and freshwater ecologist, shows us a hole in a rotting tree trunk leading to a shallow burrow below. He tells us that there are unexplored ecosystems of shallow caves and burrow networks in the forest floor. We hear a woodpecker knocking nearby. Elliot says there are also flying squirrel, moose, coyote, beaver, and bear in the area. The Highway Department used to dump road-killed moose and deer at the front end of his property, which attracted black bears.

In 1989 he led a campaign against the clear-cutting of New Hampshire's forest domain. "Philosophically I aligned myself with Earth First!" he says. "The natural world has a right to exist regardless of the human condition. It's not that I don't sympathize with women's rights or fighting poverty or whatever. That's just not my main concern. I was brought up here in New Hampshire. What I know and what I'm going to fight to defend is the wilderness—all of it that's still left, all of it, without compromise.

"A state policeman told me an angry logger burned my place down," he continues on our way back to the car, passing the ruins of his former home once more. "He wouldn't tell me what he based his information on." Elliot has his own theory about a local logger who had been an outspoken opponent during the clear-cutting campaign, but admits he'll probably never know for sure who torched his house.

Since that fire, two other anti-logging activists he knows have been burned out by arsonists, Michael Vernon and fellow New Hampshirite Jaimie Sayen. Vernon, a town official in Solon, Maine, woke up with his house on fire and had to dive off a second-floor porch into the snow to escape the flames that eventually gutted his home.[1]

Says Jaimie Sayen, who lives on the edge of a wilderness area north of the White Mountains, "I don't think it's a coincidence that in the last three years Jeff Elliot, Michael Vernon, and myself have all experienced arson. The thing is, I'm not intimidated. I've been involved in this forest stuff for years and I'm not going away. These guys who inspire this stuff, like Don Gerdts in the Adirondacks or Ron Arnold, are not going to last, because they are only negative. They only know what they're *against*. They have no vision. They will have some limited success as demagogues for a while, but the question really is how to swat them off before they do too much damage." Swatting, I find, is a popular metaphor in the northeast forests during mosquito and blackfly season.

Since the late 1980s, when a French holding company put half a million acres of Diamond Match timberland in New York, Vermont, New Hampshire, and Maine on the international real estate market, the region's environmentalists, state governments, and congressional delegations have been trying to develop a land-use plan to protect the northern forests.[2] The increasingly militant Property Rights movement has been attacking the idea of forest protection, calling it an attempt to steal land from its rightful owners.

Having lived in New England for five years, I'm aware that more than 90 percent of the land in this region is privately owned and well maintained by people who take pride in their seasonal enterprises and pastoral landscapes. Like everywhere else, New England has seen population shifts, particularly in southern New Hampshire and Vermont, with people migrating northward from the cities. For the most part, however, the new arrivals have adapted to the region's traditional ways of viewing the world, which include a healthy skepticism toward ostentatious wealth and all levels of government above the town meeting. Respect for private property rights is as natural to a New England Yankee as thrift, patriotism, and the conservation ethic. So New England would seem to be fertile ground in which the Property Rights movement could take root. Of course the devil, as they say, is in the details.

The New Hampshire Landowners Alliance (NHLA), with a core of about twenty activists, has been one of the most high-profile Property Rights groups operating in New England. In 1993 it led a successful campaign to block a "Wild and Scenic River" designation along a forty-mile stretch of the Pemigewasset River, a portion of land that included the North Woodstock/Lincoln area. This designation would have prohibited dams and federal water projects on the Pemi, keeping it protected in its present free-flowing state. However, six out of seven towns along the proposed stretch voted against that designation after NHLA convinced area residents that the 1968 Wild and Scenic Rivers Act was part of a government plan to take control of their property, even though the New Hampshire congressional delegation had tailored the Pemi agreement to exclude any land acquisitions.[3]

NHLA is headed by Cheryl Johnson, a short-haired, bright-eyed native New Hampshirite who runs a computer graphics business out of a small office above the nineteenth-century Mad River Inn in Campton. Dressed casually in jeans and a man's dress shirt, with her NRA bill cap on a nearby shelf, she takes time out from assembling the national Alliance for America newsletter to talk about how she first became politically active.[4]

"For me it started in January of ninety-one, when the Pemi was nominated for state protection," she says. "I was totally apolitical. I'd never read a newspaper. I went to this river-management meeting with about two hundred people. Friends of my husband said they needed support, so that's why we went."

One of her husband's friends (and his employer at the time) was Ed Clark, part owner of Clark's Trading Post, a local tourist attraction, and of several hydroelectric facilities. Ed Clark hoped to erect a dam across a steep gorge on the river at a point called Livermore Falls, the site of a nineteenth-century mill. State river protection would prevent any dams from being built.

Says Johnson, "Our feeling was the rivers were protected, local zoning already protected them enough. But they wanted to establish locally based appointees named by the governor. It turned into a major battle and people got stomped on. The hydro dam didn't go in, even though historically this had been a working site. There had been a grinding mill there for logs going to the paper mill in Lincoln. Ed Clark had planned a detailed historic restoration. He wanted to rebuild the old mill so that it would have attracted tourists. He spent fourteen years and $450,000 working on the project. Now the owner of that land has had to sell it to the state for two to three hundred thousand because if it can't be developed it's just a liability. College kids use the beach there for drinking and jump off the rocks and sometimes kill themselves.

"Anyway, in May of ninety-one, the river got state designation," she continues. "Then, in February of ninety-two, the federal study began. It was the same thing again, only a bigger deal. We didn't want the feds involved. I never intended to be a leader. I wanted to do the group's newsletter, but this guy dropped out and I was left doing more and more of the work. Gradually I started reading the newspaper and watching the news on TV. At first I thought it was just us fighting this designation. Then I realized there was something bigger going on. I went to the Fly-In for Freedom in D.C.,[5] and met all these other property owners and other types like ORV operators and got educated about what the preservationists were trying to do to us. I became real angry seeing how their magazines were all putting out the same propaganda. When I got home I mailed eleven years of environmental magazines back to *National Wildlife.* Then I went to St. Louis for the founding of the Alliance for America. It was my first flight on a commercial airliner. Now I'm secretary of the group. You have to understand this is a real grassroots movement. We have to pass the hat around to finance our work.

"In 1992 to ninety-three we built our [NHLA] membership up to 1,500 and began to educate people," she continues. "We brought in speakers like Don Rupp from the Upper Delaware Valley, Joe Wrabek from the Columbia River Gorge in Oregon, and David Howard [from the Alliance for America]. Personally, I think Don Rupp goes too far. He said if this becomes a scenic river then it's a national park, and in a park you can carry a gun. I think he did more harm than good.

"I've heard [Adirondacks leader] Don Gerdts speak in Vermont, and he can really fire people up. He's very much like Chuck Cushman, with a 'Rent-a-Riot' personality. We didn't bring Chuck in because he wanted $1,500 a day for a weekend presentation."

In its campaign to block the "Wild and Scenic" designation, the NHLA put out flyers and press statements claiming that the federal government wanted to turn the Pemi into a national park and seize people's land. They received editorial support from the *Manchester Union Leader,* the state's largest (and notoriously conservative) newspaper. They also told people that the scenic river designation would decrease their property values, although studies of the more than 150 Wild and Scenic Rivers established to date show that the opposite is far more likely to occur.

"The real problem is not property values declining but gentrification," says Glenn Pontier, editor of the *River Reporter* in New York's Upper Delaware Valley. "Our property values have gone up with the Delaware River designation, and this hurts the old-timers around here. What Chuck Cushman, Don Rupp, and people like that do is prevent real discussion of what's going to happen, so that we now have people having to sell their homes because nobody made the right plans or asked the right questions back when the issue was first debated."

I ask Johnson if she'd been involved back in 1979, when the EPA shut down the old Lincoln Paper Mill. The mill had polluted the Pemi, making the river unsafe for swimming, wading, and fishing and giving the town the derisive nickname "Stinkin' Lincoln."

"No. It was polluted, but you were just used to it. It wasn't anything you really thought about, because it had always been that way," she says.

As we leave she gives us copies of the two most recent Alliance for America newsletters. The cover story in the April 1993 issue is headed "Signing Away America" and begins, "As of April 2, 1992, the United States as we know it no longer exists." The article goes on to explain that by signing the U.N. Covenant on Civil and Political Rights, the U.S. government has betrayed God and the Constitution. The story is reprinted from *New American Magazine,* a publication of the John Birch Society.[6]

NANCY AND I pull off by the side of Route 3 behind a couple of cars with Plymouth State College stickers, cross a railroad track, and scuttle down a steep path on a thickly wooded hillside, sliding through brambles, loose dirt, and tangled branches, before regaining our footing just short of a rusting coil of barbed wire. The Pemi River is fifty yards across

here. Opposite the boulder-strewn bank we stand on is a white sand
beach where two young college women in bathing suits and loose tee
shirts are wading in the cool water. To our left, 130 feet above the river,
is the red, rusting remnant of the Pumpkinseed Bridge, a slender double
bow extending from granite outcroppings on either side of a steep gorge
where the waters narrow. To our right, along the riverbanks, are rolling
emerald-green hills so lush they make you wish you were an ungulate.

After taking in the river view, we climb back up to the railroad tracks
and walk along them a short way to the red brick pumphouse of the old
grinding mill. Moss- and lichen-covered rocks lead down to a second
beach by a cataract of thundering white water, where the gorge has nar-
rowed to no more than twenty-five feet across. Four students, three
guys and a girl, are sitting high up on the beach. One of the lads, pony-
tailed and bare-chested, is playing the guitar, a cigarette dangling from
his lips. We walk out on a granite ledge next to the thundering falls, fast
tons of white water shooting across an exposed staircase of granitic rock.
It sounds like Dolby white noise and is as visually hypnotic as fire.

We return to the car and move on, then make another stop at the
Mill at Loon Mountain, a wood and brick complex of boutique shops
and restaurants that, along with the Lincoln Center Shopping Mall and
the River-Green Condominium/Hotel, have surrounded what's left of
the abandoned paper mill. We climb around inside the original mill's
hollowed-out, red-brick boiler building. Just behind it I find the old effluent canal out to the river, its water still a bright orange color. Inside
the Loon Mountain shopping complex, between a cookie shop and a
bookstore, is a display case of old photos showing the mill in operation
and the spruce logging camps that fed its pulpers before the turn of the
twentieth century. Pictures of steam boilers date from 1915; one shot
of the mill's front parking lot dates from the 1950s.

Peter Gould, who works for Lincoln Mill Associates, the real estate
agency that oversees the mall, has heard that there was conflict over lost
jobs and environmental regulations back in 1979, when the EPA shut
down the mill. "Luckily, the whole town of Lincoln retrofitted from a mill
town to a resort town in a pretty short time," he says. "The Loon Mountain ski area opened in 1966, and so that gave a head start to the effort."

At its peak, the contaminated paper mill employed some five hundred
workers, roughly the same number as are now employed in the shopping
mall, restaurant, and condominium complex alongside the restored river.

On our way out of town we make a final stop at Clark's Trading Post. There's a promotional billboard on the riverbank just before you get there, but the low-slung, brown-shingled cabin that's been stretched a city block long would be a hard place to miss in any case. Inside, the trading post is filled with all sorts of gimcracks: chipmunk postcards, Indian tomahawks, feathered headdresses, leather bullwhips, the Last Supper on a cross section of pine wood, Davy Crockett coonskin caps, jawbreakers, maple-sugar candy dolls, saltwater taffy, costume jewelry. Clark is not around, but his black bears are—nine of them in cement-walled and cement-floored compounds next to the trading post. Behind the pens is a small circular bear stadium used for weekend perform-ances. You can peek through ceramic chutes in the concrete walls or pay to drop food down to the pacing animals, whose black coats appear patchy from mange. Next door to the trading post is Clark's Station, a theme park with miniature train rides and bumper boats. Clark's Trad-ing Post conveys a hint of what a "historically authentic" Livermore Falls dam restoration project might have looked like, including, per-haps, the waterslide and leaping-trout show.

———————

ABOUT SIXTY-FIVE MILES SOUTH of Canada, near the Vermont bor-der, Nancy and I realize we've crossed an undefined boundary and have entered the much-debated Northern Forest. We're looking out across endless miles of low, forested mountains stretching to a blue-tinted hori-zon that is unbroken by visible clear-cuts or any discernible towns of size. Occasionally a small village outlines itself against a hillside, a white New England church steeple pinning it to the landscape like some exotic proof that, given the right opportunity, humans can complement the natural terrain as easily as a herd of deer on a sunlit ridgeline.

We drive into Vermont, where much of the woodland has been cleared to make way for tidy red-barn dairy farms, following directions that take us off the tarmac and onto one of the area's many intercon-necting dirt roads. "Pat Buchanan is right," grins State Senator John McClaughery, a six-foot, blue-eyed, square-jawed, not-quite-handsome politician and conservative philosopher. "There are two cultures at war—an educated elite, who want good government, control of anti-social tendencies, and a smooth-running system, and the other culture, an independent, freedom-loving culture of low-level anarchy resistant to order and authority. We see this battle on gun control, property rights, land-use control. It's the American glory."

After a brief stint in the Reagan White House, McClaughery left Washington and returned to the green fields of Vermont.

"Many of my friends stayed on there in D.C. and got rich," he says. "I chose not to." Looking out the picture window in his multiroom, high-roofed, red pine log cabin five miles up an unpaved country road in Vermont's Northeast Kingdom, it's easy to believe he made the right choice. Beyond his wide wooden porch on the front sixteen acres of his two hundred–acre spread is a field of daisies, purple lilac bushes, a few poplar trees, and a ridgeline view of the green mountains. Anxious for at least one sighting, Nancy asks him if there are any moose in the area.

"I lose constituents to moose every year," he says. "They come through their windshields. They're so high off the ground that when you hit one you end up with two thousand pounds of animal in your lap." He's fought to pass a bill that would allow the shooting of nuisance animals. "It's not a sport to shoot them but the problem is they've become a sacred animal here in Vermont, a symbolic issue for the other side. The moose is our whale!" He shakes his head more perplexed than offended. He accuses the governor, Howard Dean, of being in the pocket of the environmentalists.

"You ran against him in ninety-two?" I ask.

"So they say," he smiles.

Governor Dean beat Republican state senator and Property Rights leader McClaughery three to one, with the latter drawing around 23 percent of the vote.

The Property Rights movement in Vermont has focused on repealing two state laws, Act 250 (passed in 1970 and requiring permits for development) and Act 200 (passed in 1988 and requiring each town to develop its own land-use plan). Supporters of the movement include a mixed bag of farmers from the economically depressed Northeast Kingdom, a Burlington real estate developer, backers of a planned Wal-Mart that's running into popular opposition in the town of Williston,[7] and the management of the Killington ski resort, which hopes to siphon off state-owned river water for snow making. Legal support has been provided by the New England Legal Foundation (NELF), one of twenty-two right-wing public-interest law firms coordinated through the Heritage Foundation. But the movement appears to have peaked early during McClaughery's election campaign. In June of that year, Citizens for Property Rights (CPR), the state's major conservative activist group, held a rally at the Killington ski resort. The hotel's lobby was decorated with twenty effigies hanging from the ceiling with nooses around their necks. Each bore a placard with the name of a liberal state politician or environmental leader, including Howard Dean. After Nadine Bailey, the unemployed logger's wife from Hayfork, California, gave one of her stump speeches, a CPR spokesman introduced his group's favorite candidate, declaring, "There is the scent of a lion in the political arena, and that lion is John McClaughery."[8]

"This movement was not useful for my campaign at all," McClaughery now complains. "I mean, of the 100 to 120 people who showed up at that rally, they all voted for me but none delivered their towns. Citizens for Property Rights is now basically defunct. They had this constant mantra of 'Repeal Act 200,' but no real grasp or desire to develop plans and political strategies. Most of these folks are all heart but sadly unsophisticated. Historically we rally to meet a threat but can't sustain a drive. It's like herding rabbits. The preservationists at VNRC [Vermont Natural Resources Council] by contrast know how to hunker down with defeats and stay the long term.

"It's really two different worldviews at work here between us and the environmentalists," he reiterates. "They don't want the woodchucks [native Vermonters] to be able to buy a home and raise a family. They look down on woodchucks and don't want growth. They think anything that increases comfort or convenience should be banned. It's part of what I call the Green Church, this religious compulsion to make people suffer for our sins against nature. These elitist land planners also dominate the liberal media. Seven of the state's nine daily newspapers are pro-preservationist, one is nondescript—kind of eccentric—and one is pro-growth. That's the *Caledonian Express* here in the Northeast Kingdom."

McClaughery helps to balance what he considers the "liberal bias" of the media by sitting on the editorial board of the Moon-controlled *Washington Times*. He is also active in ALEC, the American Legislative Exchange Council, made up of conservative state officials opposed to environmental (and most other) government regulations. And he cowrote a book titled *The Vermont Papers*, a plan for decentralizing Vermont into a county shire system. Much to his annoyance, the ideas in his book have won a following among some of the state's leftists.

I ask him about some of the right-wing radicals who have attached themselves to the Property Rights movement. "We had a northern forest lands meeting here and the idiot John Birch Society showed up," he recalls, frowning like he's just found a deer tick in his coffee mug. What does he think about militia-style vigilante violence going on in the Adirondacks Park, just across Lake Champlain from Vermont?

"You have to understand the Adirondacks people. Back in 1973 I spoke to eight hundred people in the town of Saranac Lake. They've been so put upon and colonized for so long over there I can see why they'd be driven to extremism."

Two days later we cross the lake in order to investigate the Property Rights movement in the Adirondacks for ourselves. A handful of small sailboats bob at their moorings as we approach the nineteenth-century port hamlet of Essex on the car ferry from Charlotte, Vermont. As far as we can see along the western shore of Lake Champlain run the dense green forests of the Adirondack Mountains—what we in the West would call foothills, actually—a five million–year–old geological dome 160 miles wide and a mile high. From satellite photos you can see water running off this dome in all directions to form the Hudson, Saranac, and a hundred other rivers. The mountains are thick with a profusion of first-, second-, and third-growth oak, maple, beech, spruce and fir, hemlock, yellow birch and white pine, sumac, black cherry, and wild apple. On reflection, these hilly mountains are as quietly breathtaking in their own arboreal way as any bare-rocked, snowcapped mountain crag the Rockies might offer up for our inspection. The Adirondack uplift is contained within a century-old park boundary larger than the state of Vermont, larger in fact than any U.S. park outside Alaska.

It seems odd, then, that one of the most militant Property Rights movements in the United States, one that escalated from protests to punches to vandalism and an organized campaign of terror involving death threats, arson, and gunfire, should be carried out by people who have chosen to call a park their home. But then there are many unusual aspects to the Adirondacks Park scene, not the least of which is its location. Normally when you think of great wildernesses, New York is not the first place that comes to mind. But in 1894, New York State amended its constitution to declare the Adirondack Mountains "forever wild." This followed decades of massive overcutting of the upstate forests. By 1850, New York was producing a fifth of the timber cut in the United

States. The Hudson River was choked with log rafts heading toward the mills at Glens Falls. Along with white pine for lumber, spruce was being milled for paper, hemlock bark used in tanning, and almost anything with roots and branches converted into charcoal for industry.

The Adirondacks timber boom had its price, however. Loggers clear-cut more than two-thirds of the mountains, stripping forest cover and leaving behind only those hardwoods that couldn't float. In addition, game hunters using hounds and fishermen powder-blasting streams for fish decimated the area's wildlife: deer, trout, moose, beaver, cougar, bear, wolf, and bald eagle all but disappeared from the countryside. Sportspeople and hunters began complaining of this destruction of the wilds in the pages of *Forest and Stream* magazine. The logging industry dismissed these early preservationists as "Denudatics," for their opposition to the denuding of the mountains. But the Adirondacks also serve as the watershed for New York City, and by the 1870s the loss of forest cover was causing increased erosion and flooding, which in turn threatened the water quality of the Hudson River and commercial transportation on the Erie Canal. Influential members of the New York Board of Trade and Transportation, including the Vanderbilts, who owned the Erie Canal, soon joined the outdoorsmen of *Forest and Stream* in demanding protection for the Adirondacks. *Harper's Weekly* and other popular magazines ran drawings of vast fields of stumps and raging forest fires set off by the sparks thrown from charcoal-burning lumber trains. The *New York Times* editorialized in favor of making the Adirondacks "the Central Park" of the world. Governor David B. Hill, a quiet conservationist in his own right, began the legislative process that would lead to the establishment and constitutional protection of the park.

Initially, the blue-line park boundary encompassed 2.6 million acres, including private lands that the state planned to buy up. Over time, however, the blue line expanded to almost 6 million acres, of which only 42 percent is today owned by the state. Half the remaining land is owned by park residents, with the rest divided between outside ownership and the forest products industry.

The early years of the park saw the growth of small hamlets and villages sustained by a mixed economy of selective logging, tourism, and health care. The town of Saranac Lake became famous for its sanatorium, established by Dr. Edward Trudeau (great-grandfather of

Doonesbury's Garry Trudeau), and private lodgings with open porches known as "cure porches" where people with tuberculosis came to "take the airs." Among the town's more distinguished visitors were Mark Twain, Robert Louis Stevenson, Margaret Sanger, Albert Einstein, and Somerset Maugham. The nearby town of Lake Placid would also gain fame as the site of the 1932 and 1980 Winter Olympics. Farming inside the blue line was widespread in the early part of the century, as much of the Adirondacks had been reduced to field and pasture. The forest cover didn't begin to fully reestablish itself until the 1930s. Even then it was a new kind of forest, 50 percent softwood to 50 percent hardwood in contrast to the earlier 80:20 mix. As the number of paved roads through the park grew during the 1950s, tourism increased. Still, much of the area remained economically depressed, its local population dependent on seasonal jobs provided by resorts, logging, and wilderness guide work. With the opening of the Interstate 87 "Northway" in the mid-1960s, real estate interest in motels and second-home developments along the shorelines of the area's 2,700 lakes and ponds skyrocketed. Lake George, in the southern part of the park, became one of the first towns overrun with strip developments consisting of motels, marinas, amusement parks, and apartment complexes.

In 1968, worried that there was almost no form of land-use control or zoning inside the blue line to protect the park's wild and natural aspects, Governor Nelson Rockefeller appointed a "commission on the future of the Adirondacks." In 1971, responding to the commission's recommendations, the state legislature established the Adirondack Park Agency (APA) to develop long-range land-use plans for both public and private property in the park. Some local residents of the park hamlets were outraged at the idea of having to follow zoning guidelines established by a state agency (although only 10 percent of the hamlets had set up any zoning of their own). Developer Anthony D'Elia and Saranac businessman Frank Casier were among a number of early home rule advocates who founded the League for Adirondack Citizens Rights, which held town meetings (including the one attended by John McClaughery) and demonstrations demanding the abolition of the APA. In 1976 local state assemblyman Ron Stafford sponsored a bill that would have replaced the APA with a locally elected board. Days before the bill was to be voted on, an arsonist was caught trying to set fire to the newly constructed APA headquarters building in the park town of Ray Brook.

"I'd given a speech in Canton. I think I'd actually told this community group that the troubles were over," recalls the athletically built director of the APA, Bob Glennon, his green eyes sparkling at the recollection. Glennon, a newly hired agency employee at the time, had gone out for beers with his friend and APA colleague Dick Beamish after the 1976 community meeting. "That's why it was two in the morning when I pulled in behind our building to fuel up my state car," he admits, smiling. "When I got out I smelled gas. I went inside and saw these two cans and noticed a guy dressed in black with a black ski mask kind of hunkered down in a corner. I remember being mad and knocking him down. The adrenaline kind of took over. I knocked him down and then kneeled on him and reached for this phone on the desk and called the state troopers. They arrived a few minutes later and arrested him and began reading him his rights off this little card. It was kind of weird. The next day there were bail fund cans in all the local bars," he laughs.

The arsonist was quickly identified as Brian Gale, a Tupper Lake resident. Gale had been paid to torch the building. Who paid him and why have never been established, although there were persistent rumors about a Saranac-based home rule leader. Gale was allowed to plead guilty to a charge of third-degree burglary and sentenced to sixty days in jail. Stafford's proposal to abolish the APA was voted down at the statehouse in Albany.[9]

"This was similar to what we're seeing today: contrived violence timed to influence legislation," claims former APA man Dick Beamish, who went on to work as the Audubon Society's representative in the Adirondacks, before founding a local newspaper.

Things quieted down over the next decade. The park's permanent population grew to some 130,000. Incomes, which had been among the lowest in the state, rose gradually to meet the norm for rural New Yorkers. The park, only a day's drive from seventy million people's homes, began to attract close to ten million visitors a year. They enjoyed a multiuse range of activities, from swimming and waterskiing at lakeside resorts to hiking and canoeing across countless miles of isolated backcountry wilderness. Then the building boom of the late 1980s and 1990s touched off a new round of conflict between those who saw the park as a natural treasure to be preserved and those who felt they had a right to profit from developing their scenic surroundings as they chose. Soon, a thousand new homes a year, including huge lakeshore condominium complexes, were under construction. Ninety thousand acres of prime forest land was put up for auction by land speculators, and by the early 1990s the real estate industry had replaced logging, tourism, and the state payroll as the mainstay of the Adirondacks economy.

Worried for the park's future, then Governor Mario Cuomo established what he called the Commission on the Adirondacks in the Twenty-First Century. He appointed fourteen people, including six park residents, to the commission. One of those Adirondackers was Robert Flacke, a former APA chairman and owner of three motels and nine other businesses in Lake George. Flacke had a falling-out with park environmentalists after they opposed his 1979 plan for a sewage-transfer system that would have shipped Lake George's wastes out of the lake basin and over the hills to the Hudson River, allowing his small city to continue its rapid growth. Even before the commission completed its 245 recommendations,[10] Flacke was leading a campaign to kill any new land-use proposals, particularly one that called for a yearlong construction moratorium while new environmental and lakefront protection standards were being established. In May 1990, weeks ahead of the official findings, Flacke's dissenting report was released to the media. Its release helped to mobilize several militant property rights groups, including the ultra-conservative Citizens Council of the Adirondacks (CCA), led by retired Long Island ad man and failed real estate developer Donald Gerdts, and the Adirondack Solidarity Alliance (ASA), headed by a retired army lieutenant colonel, Calvin Carr.

On May 5, Gerdts and Carr held an anti-commission rally, attended by some two hundred people, in the park hamlet of Elizabethtown. "This is Day One of the Adirondacks rebellion," Gerdts declared.[11] Following the rally, they marched on the office of the Adirondack Council, the park's long-established, eighteen thousand–member mainstream environmental group, best known for its willingness to compromise on almost anything. The protestors, in no mood to compromise with "radical preservationists," painted the council's windows with swastikas. A dozen men led by Gerdts then went to the home of Eric Siy, a council staff member. "They threatened to burn down my house," Siy recalls. "Gerdts said things like, 'I should have dropped you the first time I saw you.' My neighbor, who's a deputy sheriff, finally came over and got them to go away."[12]

Over time other Adirondack Council members would receive similar death threats. Rotten vegetables and skunk oil would also be dumped on the sidewalk in front of their office, bent roofing nails would be left on the street to flatten their tires, and used condoms would be sent to them in the mail. Liquid manure was sprayed on the building shortly before a planned picket by the ASA. "Some good Adirondacker decided to give them some back," Calvin Carr sniffed, grinning, as he arrived on the scene with his picket sign a few hours after the vandals struck.[13]

"My car was vandalized at my home with the fender bashed in," says Adirondack Council administrator Donna Beal, a third-generation park resident whose parents were local schoolteachers. "It sickens me if, because of your beliefs, you're subjected to violent tactics. It just goes against everything this country stands for."

Events quickly escalated that summer, with Gerdts and Carr vying to outdo each other in the realm of the outrageous. They organized a motorcade protest drive to Albany with several hundred cars, slowing down I-87 traffic to a fifteen-mile-an-hour crawl. Gerdts directed the rally by CB radio from an exit ramp while Carr flew overhead radioing his own directions from his personal helicopter.

Next, a group calling themselves the Minuteman Brigade, or Liberators, started sending out threats that they would burn down the state forest reserves if any of the commission's recommendations were carried out. Tee shirts appeared with the slogan "Only Cuomo Can Prevent Forest Fires." Flaming arrows were fired at the APA and Adirondack Council offices, the home of a Department of Environmental Conservation (DEC) police officer, a state police substation, newspaper offices, and other area buildings. Daniel Sage, a Schroon Lake Property Rights activist and vocal defender of the brigade, compared supporters of the Twenty-First Century report to Communists who should "be burned out and executed."[14]

Gerdts faxed a warning memo to Governor Cuomo declaring, "Only your direct and immediate intervention will prevent bloodshed and major property damage."

"This guy comes from Queens. He was probably born on a piece of asphalt. He's now up there telling everybody he's ordained to tell you how to deal with the forests?" the bemused governor commented to a group of upstate reporters.

But by now intimidation was becoming a fact of life in the park. People who wrote letters to local newspapers arguing in favor of the commission report—including Elenore Webb, a Blue Mountain Lake resident in her eighties—received threatening phone calls at home. After making a threatening call to a man whose letter to the *Adirondack Daily Enterprise* he didn't like, Gerdts was charged with harassment. When George Davis, executive director of the governor's commission, tried to give a speech in the park, he was disrupted by dozens of angry hecklers. His state police escorts were so unnerved they had a police car parked outside with its motor running in case Davis was forced to flee.

Meanwhile, Bob Flacke established the Blue Line Council, which, along with other pro-development groups, portrayed itself as a moderate force staking out the middle ground between the "radical preservationists" of the Adirondack Council and the "understandably angry" Property Rights activists, whose violent tactics they refused to condemn.

"Flacke positions himself in the middle by encouraging the crazies," claimed Dick Beamish. "It's a phony strategy but it's had some success."

The Blue Line Council and other park "moderates," together with the New York State Farm Bureau and Ron Stafford (who had become chairman of the state senate's powerful finance committee), were able to pull together a statewide coalition to defeat a 1990 bond act. The bonds would have provided hundreds of millions of dollars' worth of funding for new state land acquisitions inside the park, funding that would eventually become available under Republican governor George Pataki.

In the Adirondack Mountains themselves, a new series of events was heating up, one that would provide at least one good visual for a *60 Minutes* report on Wise Use.

In 1989 the DEC had blocked a mile-long dirt road into a wilderness area and popular picnic site called Crane Pond, converting it into a hiking trail. In June 1990 a group of masked Liberators using a logging crane removed the boulder blocking the road. They labeled the barrier the "boulder of shame," put it on a truck, and drove it down to Albany in a protest caravan. Later, with members of the Mohawk Warrior Society from the Akwesane reservation on the Canadian border, they held a rally and meeting in nearby Schroon Lake. The Liberators, the ASA, and the Warrior Society exchanged pledges of support in their common struggle against the New York State authorities.

"It would have been real scary if the Warrior Society and ASA had formed some kind of serious common front. That could have led to some real bloodshed," says a state police official who had begun monitoring the Property Rights militants around that time. The Warrior Society had been involved in a series of shoot-outs with anti-gambling Mohawk traditionalists who opposed casino operations on the reservation. Members of the Warrior Society were also suspected of involvement—along with gunrunning and cigarette smuggling—in the shooting of a New York State National Guard medevac helicopter that flew over their reservation. The chopper was hit by seven rounds from an AK-47 rifle, which disabled the main rotor and seriously injured a doctor onboard.

After a three-day standoff among DEC police, the ASA, and the Schroon Lake townspeople who demanded the right to drive to Crane Pond, the DEC agreed to leave the road open to motor traffic. Don Gerdts and other activists began passing out leaflets for a Fourth of July victory celebration. The leaflets advised people to "bring your deer rifle in case rabid animals should be in the area."[15]

On September 3 a small group of Earth Firsters and their supporters—including Jeff Elliot and his wife, from New Hampshire—decided to protest the DEC's decision to reopen the wilderness area to vehicle traffic by blocking Crane Pond Road.

"We went there, camped overnight, and next morning a dozen of us stood in the road," Elliot recalls. "By 8 A.M. there were forty to fifty local men and some women drinking and shooting guns nearby. The only state trooper there said, 'It looks like trouble. I'm going to get reinforcements,' and drove off, and that was the last we ever saw of him. Then the locals backed up a pickup and revved the engine like they were going to run us over. We decided it was time to leave, which is when we realized we were being held hostage. They'd blocked the only road out with their cars. Don Gerdts was real nervous about the gunfire. He got up on a pickup and tried to get his people to clear the road so that we could just leave. We were in our cars waiting to get out of there from about 9:30 A.M. to 1 P.M. That's when I left my car to take a leak and saw this TV guy arriving and began to talk to him."

At that point Elliot, the reporter, and his cameraman were approached by Warrensburg town supervisor Maynard Baker, a stocky, sixty-year-old ex-marine with a reputation for getting into bar fights.

"This old-timer comes over and he's screaming about his road, shaking with rage," Elliot recalls. "I tell the TV guy that we think the road should stay open, that it should have access for the disabled and for flying squirrels, raccoons, silkworm moths, and any Homo sapiens willing to walk instead of drive. And the old guy screams, 'You heard them, they're a bunch of homosexuals.' I say, 'Look, whatever your special interest group is …' and that's when, pow, he hits me. I went down and, I admit, kind of hammed it up. I mean, he had a good punch but it didn't connect all that well." Elliot's wife gives him a skeptical look.

Eventually the dramatic video of Baker punching Elliot and then being pulled away by his friends as he shouts, "Go back to wherever you came from but get out of here, out of our lives and our business!" was included in a *60 Minutes* report titled "Clean Air, Clean Water, Dirty Fight," which examined violence against environmental activists and the growth of the Wise Use movement. After its broadcast, Baker told the *Adirondack Daily Enterprise* that he'd been misquoted by Leslie Stahl, who told viewers he had regretted his action. What he'd actually told a researcher for *60 Minutes*, he insisted, was that he was sorry he had had to punch Elliot but that, given the same circumstances, he'd certainly do it again.[16]

On July 8, 1991, shots were fired at an occupied APA truck near the town of AuSable Forks. Three park agency staffers had just finished talking to a property owner about permit requirements for a subdivision. There were a number of people on the scene, including some members of the ASA. As the park agents were backing out of the drive, someone fired about a dozen shots at them. The truck was hit in the right front fender, hubcap, and tire.

"They drove out of there on their flat and called in to the police as soon as they got safely away and could reach a phone," says Lieutenant Pete Person of the State Police Bureau of Criminal Investigation (BCI), whose agents investigated the shooting and other incidents in the park. "We found .22 long rifle shell casings at the base of a tree some distance across the road. There were also some cigarette butts and tire tracks. It looked like someone had been waiting there for some time and a second person had picked him up in an all-terrain vehicle. We'd had some uniformed officers patrolling nearby who were able to interview sixteen people from the scene. We polygraphed five people, and the two we suspected tested untruthful, but we couldn't get a confession and can't use that as evidence. There are two theories at this point: one that they were after the park agency for their own reasons and another is that these two were paid to do this."

In the early morning of November 14, 1991, the Ticonderoga dental office of Dr. Dean Cook, board secretary of the Adirondack Council and an outspoken critic of toxic discharges from a local paper mill, was gutted by fire. Fire inspectors ruled the fire an arson but refused to speculate on whether it was politically motivated. Dr. Cook is certain he was targeted because of his work with the council and his outspoken opposition to discharges from the International Paper Mill in Ticonderoga.

A short time later, Elizabeth McLain, commissioner of environmental conservation for the state of Vermont, went to a public meeting in Ticonderoga to explain her state's concerns over the paper mill's releases of dioxin into Lake Champlain.

"Someone took a gallon of yellow paint and poured it over the roof of my car while I was in that meeting," she says. "I don't even think I was singled out. I think this could have happened to any car parked there with a Vermont plate. I wasn't scared. I was angry that political debate had sunk to this level."

In the fall of 1991 the ASA joined up with the Alliance for America at its founding meeting in St. Louis, Missouri. David Howard, a Property Rights activist from the Adirondack hamlet of Bleeker, became the national group's first president, and Harry McIntosh, from the hamlet of Caroga Lake, became vice president for administration. McIntosh owns the computers that the alliance uses for its database and national networking. The first time I called the national alliance, identifying myself as a reporter, McIntosh immediately started to tell me about an article he'd read in *New American*, the John Birch Society magazine. "It's about this woman who helped prevent the New York schools from teaching homosexuality to schoolchildren. You know what they had in these textbooks for little kids? They teach you about sucking cock in school. That's what was in there." I told him I had a hard time believing that. "Me too. You wouldn't think this sort of thing could go on in America!" he replied indignantly.[17]

Don Gerdts and fellow activist Carole LaGrasse, who'd also attended the St. Louis meeting and Washington, D.C., Fly-In for Freedom, set up a short-lived public-access cable TV show out of Plattsburgh, New

York, partially funded by the John Birch Society. However, LaGrasse complained that the Birch Society was too intellectual, not activist enough.[18]

"Personally, I was shocked when my minister handed me an article on the Adirondacks from the Birch Society magazine," says Adirondack Council administrator Donna Beal. "I didn't know they even still existed."

As the militancy of the Property Rights movement increased, its active support among park residents faded. On June 15, 1992, the state assembly voted 104 to 35 to pass a bill giving the APA control over development on shorelines, on roadsides, and in the park's undeveloped backcountry, the first attempt by the legislature to put into effect any of the Twenty-First Century Commission's recommendations. Ron Stafford promised to kill the bill in the senate. A pro-Stafford rally was organized by the ASA, Bob Flacke's Blue Line Council, and other Property Rights groups from the park with backing from the Adirondacks' paper industry (Flacke sits on the board of Finch, Pruyn & Co., a paper company with 154,000 acres of holdings in the park). Despite weeks of massive publicity, only about two hundred Adirondackers showed up for the rally. They carried professionally printed placards reading "We Support AdiRONdacks STAFFORD."

"There is nothing in this bill but slavery for the Adirondacks," Calvin Carr shouted to the small crowd gathered on the steps of the capitol. "Cuomo," another speaker insisted, "could not be more socialist if he'd been educated in Moscow." After Ron Stafford was introduced, he promised the cheering crowd that "no bill proposing stricter zoning in the Adirondack Park will pass in the Senate."[19]

"The ridiculous thing is there's tougher zoning in suburban Albany than in the Adirondacks," claims John Sheehan, the Adirondack Council's then state lobbyist in Albany.[20]

After listening to the Stafford rally, Sheehan went inside the statehouse to look for a reporter. There he was confronted by ASA member Norbert St. Pierre, of Crown Point, who said, "When we come gunnin', we're gonna come gunnin' for you." Sheehan asked him what he meant. "I mean we're going to shoot you," St. Pierre replied. When Sheehan walked back outside a few minutes later, Calvin Carr came up to him, threw a bottle of orange juice against his chest, and then punched him in the mouth. Much to Carr's surprise, Sheehan punched back. The police arrested Carr, bleeding from his ear, but later released him without filing charges. Sheehan believes Carr's attack on him was calculated to draw attention away from the rally's small turnout.

Two months later, on the night of August 7, APA commissioner Anne LaBastille's attached barns were burned to the ground in an arson fire that also destroyed her Chevy pickup truck, motorboat, riding tractor, and thousands of dollars' worth of tools. A few hours later someone used a hand-carried pump sprayer to do several thousand dollars of damage to the Adirondack Council building, covering its front walls and windows in turquoise latex paint.

Anne LaBastille is a well-known author whose books include *Woodswoman; Women and Wilderness;* and *Mama Poc,* which recounts her long, unsuccessful effort to save the great grebes of Lake Atitlán in Guatemala; and *Beyond Black Bear Lake,* the first popularly written account of the impact of acid rain on the lakes and forests of the Adirondacks and upstate New York.

"I'm a woman alone, so I'm a great target," she says when asked why she thinks she was singled out for attack. "What's happening in the Adirondacks reminds me a lot of the death squad stuff in Central America [where the game warden she worked with was murdered]. Luckily, I was away the night of the arson. Otherwise I might have run out to the barn to save my truck and been blown up with it."

Ten months after her barns were burned, Anne LaBastille retired from the APA commission. "It was primarily for professional reasons. I'm traveling a lot, lecturing, and working on my books. But it was also a high-risk position. If they had caught these people and had them behind bars, I might have reconsidered," she admits.

"Anne became a symbol to these people," says Bob Glennon, the director of the APA, who captured Brian Gale trying to burn down the APA office back in 1976. "They'd point to her as a world conservationist and say she didn't represent the Adirondacks' point of view, meaning theirs. Truth is, we're a much better agency for her having served. I joked to Anne that 'if you want to catch an Adirondacks arsonist you have to do it yourself,'" he grins. "She wasn't amused."

Gordon Davis is the attorney and landlord for the Adirondack Council. His yellow and brown, chalet-like office building sustained $4,500 in damage. "I'm geared for the traditional type of political activity Americans get involved in, where you divide and argue and find agreement, not this South American revolutionary type of violence these other people are practicing," he says. Davis is a large, red-faced Irishman with sharp blue eyes, a flowing crescent of gray-white hair, and a Kennedy-type accent. His law office is on the top floor of his Elizabethtown building. The ground floor is divided between the storefront Adirondack Council offices and the Essex County Industrial Development Agency. Above the council offices hangs a carved wooden plaque of a loon, splattered with the blue-green paint from the attack.

"I was woken up that morning by a guy I knew was a member of the Solidarity Alliance and also happened to be a house painter. He called me at home about 8 A.M. and said, 'Sorry about your office building.' I asked him what he was talking about. He said, 'They painted your building last night' and then offered to clean it up for a fee. I told him to forget it.

"After I found out that they'd also burned Anne LaBastille's barns, I called a press conference in front of my building to condemn the violence. I asked the D.A. to join me, but he said he was otherwise engaged. I called Joe Boone, the county supervisor. He also wouldn't show up. So I went down to Albany to see Cuomo and said, 'Can't you put some of these guys in jail?'"

After Davis's visit, Governor Cuomo ordered the state police to step up their investigations and wrote a pointedly open letter to Ron Stafford suggesting that "the first thing you can do, as the North Country's most prominent leader, is to speak out against these injustices and to let those who are responsible know that their actions will not be tolerated."[21]

"Stafford called me back all bent out of shape," Gordon Davis recalls with a wicked smile. "He's saying, 'You know, I'm against violence,' and I said, 'No, I don't know that, Ron. You haven't condemned this politically oriented violence in public.' He said he certainly would and he did, the night of the next election, three months later. After the results were in and he'd been reelected, he gave a quote to the press condemning the violence."

I ask Davis about rumors that have circulated among county officials of a plan to blow up his office building. "I've heard rumors of such a plan," he says, but won't go into detail. "Look, this violence has affected the whole debate over the future of the Adirondacks. I myself am more circumspect, realizing there are a bunch of crazies out there, so if I'm affected, a blabbermouth like me, then how do you think it affects the average person living up here?"

Although a $10,000 reward was offered for the arrest and conviction of the arsonists and vandals involved in the attacks, no one has come forward with any information. Word among anti-enviro activists was that whoever claimed the money wouldn't live to spend it.

"Most of their activity at the moment is kind of teenage stuff, like spray-painting all the state park signs, which still costs a tremendous amount of money to clean up," says state police investigator Rich Cybeck, who keeps track of the ASA, Liberators, and other Property Rights militants. "We just had $700 to $800 damage to a sign across the road from Dale French's house that's been hit three times before. Sometimes I'll notice a sign that's been graffitied with turquoise paint and figure that person's still active. Their linkups with the national Wise Use groups is kind of interesting when you look at all the problems they've been creating. What I really worry about is that everybody here hunts, and with access to hunting weapons, what's a lot of high school sophomoric stuff now could in a heartbeat turn into my having a homicide case on my hands."

After several tries I'm unable to reach Don Gerdts or Carole LaGrasse. Activists tell me Gerdts has lost credibility and dropped out of the political scene but that Calvin Carr and the ASA remain committed to the cause.

I AGREE TO MEET retired lieutenant colonel Calvin Carr and his aide-de-camp Dale French at Frenchman's Family Dining, in Crown Point just north of Ticonderoga. It's a mounted-fish-and-antlers kind of place, a prefab log cabin diner with wagon-wheel lighting fixtures, half-thawed salads, and hot coffee. Carr, French, and his wife, Jerris, are sitting at a back table drinking their coffees when Nancy and I arrive.

Carr is much as I expected him to be, a little bigger than average, with a long rugged face, hairline mole, battleship-gray eyes, thin lips, and squared-off chin. He's potbellied but with an erect posture. Dale French is red-faced and tubby with thin hair, long sideburns, and a reddish blond mustache that droops slightly below his lips. He's wearing jeans and a too-tight, red, cotton short-sleeved shirt. His wife, Jerris, is rail-thin with shiny black hair and a lined face, dressed in jeans and a pink sleeveless blouse.

Carr tells me he owns a small seven-worker paper factory that produces specialized resin-treated pulp papers, called foils, that are used for institutional furniture, restaurant trays, and dishes.

French says he was a nuclear power plant design engineer but returned home to Crown Point in 1983 because he wanted to be left alone. "Then Mario Cuomo started all this stuff up with his 1990 report."

"I was sweeping up at my warehouse when Dale brought me the preliminary paperwork and I thought it was a joke," Carr recalls. "I said, 'This looks more like a plan for the Ural Mountains than the Adirondack Mountains.'" He gives me an appraising look before launching into an extemporaneous rap on free-market environmentalism. "I don't think there's anything to indicate that some subsequent generation is any more deserving than this generation," he says. "So when people talk about preserving the Adirondacks, preserve it for what? Save it for what? There's no shortage of anything in this country. There are more trees, iron, copper, and oil than ever. There's no validity to saying there's a finite supply of oil. Oil is being produced constantly. All the copper or iron we've taken out of the ground could be recycled. Nothing disappears. People talk about 1 percent of the world's water is fresh water. All the water in the world is potential fresh water. It's a natural system of recycling. There's no scientific basis for what they're doing, so the only rationale must be to take us to utter socialism. The mentality driving the park agency is designed to eliminate people and jobs from this area."

"We're fortunate to have Cal here. It's hard to attract industry to our towns," Jerris says, finishing her coffee.

I ask how living in the park has hurt them personally, trying to get to the origin of their anger.

"Well, like with my factory. If I wanted to expand it, any building over forty feet high [four stories tall] needs an APA permit," Carr complains. "Outside the hamlet it's harder still. I own a two hundred–acre farm. It's producing a third less income than three years ago and government regulation is at fault."

"What do you farm?"

"You can't make money at farming today the way the system is set up. My intention in buying that farm, like any businessman, was to make it a performing asset." French nods his agreement. "But that farm is costing me because I can't sell off a portion of it at a normal market price, even though it's on a road."

"You mean you can't get a permit from the APA?"

"I'm not going to allow the park service to say what I can and can't subdivide on my land. I wouldn't go to them for a permit. The moment you ask them to permit you, you acknowledge their jurisdiction."

"We simply subdivide our land and tell them to go to hell," says French, who now earns his living assembling prefab log homes. "We've got three buildings up the road we did that way and the APA has backed off. The APA won't challenge us. We've rubbed their nose in it."

"The only power the APA has is the same as we citizens, except the attorney general is their lawyer," Carr claims.

I ask how politically effective they think their I-87 highway blockade was, but Carr gives me a tactical response.

"We created a fifty- to sixty-mile traffic jam. I organized the activities from the air. The state police got sent to the wrong exits. They didn't know what was going on."

"Didn't Don Gerdts organize that blockade?"

"Gerdts is very good at self-promotion, very bad at organizing. Dale and myself and Jerris did the primary organizing. Personally, I felt that Gerdts wasn't ethical, that he wasn't in the conflict for patriotic reasons."

He explains that from his helicopter (a Hiller bubbletop that he rents out for commercial seeding contracts) he can see well beyond the houses along the roadsides of the park. "There's no overdevelopment in this park. There's a vast wilderness for fifty miles. So what do they think they're saving? If everybody'd just be honest we could talk to the environmentalists, but their lies and deceptions make it impossible to discuss anything with them. Their grand plan is to control people by locking up resources. The environmental grass roots are shills for the people they think they're fighting. Once the government owns it all, it will all be developed. It is socialism, and what's going to happen in this revolutionary process is the poor slobs doing the footwork will be the first into the meat grinder."

"We know some of them are just dupes, but we have to look at all of them as the enemy because we're at war," French pipes in. "We don't take prisoners. We hammer their hides. If their beliefs impact our lives then it's war, and like Calvin says, 'All's fair in love and war.'"

"So are you a member of the John Birch Society?" I ask Carr.

"No, the John Birch Society was part of a list of groups I swore not to join when I became an officer of the U.S. Army."

I ask him about his career.

"I was ten years in the army, twenty-two in the reserves. I retired as a lieutenant colonel." (A number of his followers have since promoted him to "general" of the Adirondacks campaign.)

Carr was an instructor pilot in Vietnam, flying combat missions with new trainees. Later he worked on developing night-vision flight programs for helicopters with DARPA, the Defense Advanced Research Projects Agency. He was the first to recognize and report on the "exaggeration of performance" phenomenon related to night-vision fighting, the perceptual distortion pilots experience that leads some to crash into mountainsides or plow into the ground thinking they still have time to pull out. He also flew the first Chinooks without mechanical linkages, admitting that relying on fly-by-wire electronics took some getting used to. "As a combat soldier I always look at calculated risk," he says, which seems to invite the question of how he views the use of violence to achieve political ends.

"People have approached me to do things. I've said just keep that thought for use at some future point when it may become necessary," he claims.

"What about all the vandalism to the Adirondack Council office and people's property?"

"Dirty tricks is just the kind of stuff that comes with organized resistance," he shrugs.

"Yeah, so what?" French mumbles before deciding to speak out on behalf of the vandals.

"If those people don't have that outlet, what recourse do they have? The hills are full of angry, ignorant people who might do anything. I told an investigator you may attribute their anger to what we say, but we're not going to compromise the truth of what we're saying. We're educators and informers. We'll tell the truth, that's all."

"Didn't you also punch John Sheehan at a rally in Albany?" I ask Carr.

"John Sheehan and his friends came looking for trouble and they found it. We were having this get-together in support of Ron Stafford and he wasn't welcome there. As I understand it, a fight broke out." He smiles, pleased with himself.

"But then he hit you back?" Nancy says.

He laughs. "Sheehan got a piece of my ear. He's a big guy but he doesn't have much of a punch."

I ask about the park agency shooting.

"Forget it in connection with us," French snaps. He's been through a couple of interviews with the state police and clearly didn't enjoy the experience.

"If we're going to have a civil war, we're not going to put our people in the line of fire," Carr argues. "Three of our people were standing there when the APA vehicle got shot. They were in harm's way."

I ask about other incidents, such as the burning of Anne LaBastille's barns.

"She resigned from the APA because she was terrified after her barn burned, and all I can say is good riddance," French smiles ferally. "I'm not sorry for her. I don't have any sympathy. She deserves everything she got."

"If it wasn't for us there would be a real civil war going on here," Carr claims, implying a level of control, if not restraint, that seems credible. The ASA and the Liberators probably function as a two-tiered political/military organization, like the Sein Fein and the IRA, the kind of setup that someone such as Cal Carr, who brags of being trained in counter–guerilla warfare, would be familiar with.

"I spent most of my adult life affiliated with this government and now I find it so repugnant I can't believe I'm an American. We may need a new form of government to replace what they've given us now," he says, sounding very much like a right-wing revolutionary.

"It's a changed world. We work quietly with computers now," French adds. "With the Alliance for America, we've connected with the grass roots. We've found out about the shrimpers and loggers and others under assault like us, this assault on rural America, and we're going to take a stand. We will not allow our children to be forced into urban cesspools like New York. We may have to become survivalists in the end."[22]

In the meantime, as part of their new approach to organizing, they've begun producing a radio show, *Reality Check*, broadcast on two local stations. They give me a tape of a recent broadcast. Most of the program consists of Rush Limbaugh–inspired banter between Carr and French, with a long send-up of the APA as reported by "Ray Brook Rose" (a woman, probably Jerris, putting on a fake Japanese accent, trying for the Tokyo Rose effect).

"Parents," she wheedles in an exaggerated singsong, "it is your duty to instruct your children in the ways of the earth mother. Teach them that cutting trees is forbidden. Using hairspray, shampoo, soap and all other chemicals is not natural. Tell them to cast off these evil chemicals and soon they will have a new and unique air about them. Children should be trained to alert the chosen ones when they see or hear anyone breaking the laws of [Earth Goddess] Gaia as written in the gospel according to Bob [Glennon]."

Carr and French's major topic of concern is an upcoming conference at the University of Vermont on what they believe are plans for declaring the Adirondacks and Lake Champlain a U.N. biosphere reserve. The symbolic designation for areas where people and nature function in sync had actually been granted in 1989. The conference is something of an academic follow-up.

"We can stop this thing cold if we create sufficient controversy surrounding its creation. And we better do it or one morning you're going to wake up and people with blue helmets are going to be deciding what you do with your life," Carr warns his listeners. "There are treaties in place that allow for the United Nations to enter into a country for the purpose of controlling biosphere reserves."

The June 22, 1993, Biosphere Reserve Conference, which was to have been addressed by Vermont governor Howard Dean, is cancelled at the last minute owing to concerns over possible disruption and vandalism after the ASA announces plans to stage a protest. "We just couldn't afford the $5,000 to $6,000 we would have needed for security—to have people protecting the cars in the parking lots from having their tires slashed, for example," says Rose Paul from the State of Vermont Natural Resources Agency, one of the groups that had planned the meeting.[23]

"The meeting would have gone on if there was no chance of anyone getting hurt. But these guys have a history of carrying concealed weapons into meetings, not of using them but of having pistols on them," adds Carl Reidel, director of the environmental program at the University of Vermont.[24]

OVERLOOKING A three-quarter-mile-long pond is a rustic brown cabin with green-trimmed shutters. Three overturned canoes lie in the shade of a cedar tree down by a short wooden dock. On the cabin's porch, a birdfeeder is attracting a crowd of finches, chickadees, red-breasted nuthatches, and a big blue jay who's bullying the others back from the seed. In the distance a woodpecker is clacking away, searching deadwood for grubs and other tasty insects. At a different time or season, one might catch sight of loons on the pond or great blue herons and sharp-taloned ospreys fishing for their dinner. The Adirondacks are, among other things, a birder's paradise.

Dick Beamish and his wife, Rachel, step out on the cabin porch to greet us. He's a bald, wistful-looking man, with a Caesar comb of silver-brown hair and soft blue-green eyes. She's a thin, healthy blond with classic Nordic features. He's wearing a checked chambray shirt, jeans, and moccasins. She's in stylish but practical sand-colored cottons. Seeing them standing by their cabin by the lake, I'm reminded of an L.L. Bean ad. But the swarming blackflies don't allow us much time for commercial reflection. They wave us inside their screened porch, flapping their hands frantically to discourage the biting flies from following us in.

"They go after the weak. They're really the scum of the earth," Beamish declares a few minutes later, talking not about the blackflies that infest the Adirondacks every June but the militia-type activists who occupy the park year-round.

"Conservationists tend to be too meek and subdued in responding to these pro-development forces," he argues. "We don't like confrontation. We think it's in bad taste. I run into people all the time who like the letters I write to the newspapers and tell me how much they agree with them but don't want to write letters themselves. They're afraid to get into a pissing match with these skunks. So a few hundred people end up setting the agenda for 130,000. This whole Wise Use movement is tiny compared to those who want to preserve our environment, to the eighteen million New Yorkers who value the Adirondacks and could easily swat them down. But instead, this tiny faction has set the terms of the debate these last three years and will continue to do so until we decide to get out there and be as forceful as we have to in order to stand up to them."

———

WE'RE CLIMBING A mud-slick trail up the side of Mount St. Regis. Unlike the well-maintained switchbacks of the West, Adirondack trails are no-nonsense, straight-over-the-top bushwhacker paths through streams and over tangles of root systems, rocks, and boulders. Moving up the mountainside, I startle a six-point buck, who bounds off into the thick vegetation. Small, brown, mottled tree frogs appear underfoot, hopping clear of my sneaker treads just in time. The blackflies are taking a more aggressive stance, willing to sacrifice themselves if they can get a good taste of blood before they die. By the end of the day the back of my neck will look like a terminal case of acne, with some forty swollen, red bite marks.

After two hours of climbing nature's answer to Stairmaster, we reach the scenic payoff. The 2,873-foot Mount St. Regis's granite round top provides a spectacular vista of dark green mountains and island-studded blue lakes stretching out to the horizon below a shifting pattern of cloud shadows. We have a good hundred miles of visibility across the great northern forest dome of the Adirondacks and can see a scattering of small settlements and a high-peak wilderness to our west. This was the western frontier two to three hundred years ago, when white settler culture was new to the continent. This forested land provided game for generations of Mohawk and Algonquin people, beaver pelts for Huguenot fur traders, rich loamy soil for Dutch farmers, and a place of refuge for loyalists displaced by the American Revolution.

From our high vantage point, the summer-green canopy contouring these low rugged mountains and scattered hamlets also bears an uncanny resemblance to a tropical war zone. Cal Carr, the veteran of helicopter warfare in Vietnam, has noted this similarity in his talk of civil war and counterinsurgency. When Carr speaks of flying his helicopter over the Adirondack wilderness and asks, "Save it for what?" you can hear echoes of the American major who, after the 1968 battle of Ben Tre, said, "We had to destroy the town in order to save it." What Lieutenant Colonel Carr and his followers don't seem to realize is that, like the Vietnam War, their war against the wilderness is the kind of venture whereby even if you win, you lose.

seven

Road-kill an Activist

*If the preservationists have their way, this country will be nothing but one
big national park.* —John Hosemann, Chief Economist,
American Farm Bureau Federation

*From the age of the dinosaurs / Cars have run on gasoline /
Where, where have they gone? / Now, it's nothing but flowers /
There was a factory / Now there are mountains and rivers /
You got it, you got it / We caught a rattlesnake /
Now we got something for dinner / We got it, we got it /
There was a shopping mall / Now it's all covered with flowers*
—"(Nothing but) Flowers," Talking Heads

"DAVID, LET ME BE FRANK. That's a LaRouchite magazine you're
holding, but it also happens to be one of the best science magazines
being published in the U.S. today." Dixy Lee Ray, zoologist, former
head of the Atomic Energy Commission (AEC) under Richard Nixon,
and one-term governor of Washington (1977–1981), goes on to explain
how the National Science Foundation, National Academy of Sciences,
American Association for the Advancement of Science, and the rest of
the scientific establishment have fallen victim to the politically correct
dogma of the environmentalists. This is not the case, she continues, for
followers of jailed neo-Nazi Lyndon LaRouche, who publish *21st Century Science & Technology*. "I'm not interested in their politics," says
Ray, "but they're doing some of the best work on cold fusion and other
technologies frozen out by the science establishment. I read their magazine regularly."

As governor of Washington, Dixy Lee Ray named a litter of pigs
after statehouse reporters. Later she had the pigs slaughtered, pack-

aged, and served at a capitol press conference.[1] In the winter of 1993, less than a year before her death at the age of seventy-nine, she remains as feisty as ever. Appropriately shaped like a bomb, with a thick neck and close-to-the-scalp helmet of gray-white hair, Ray is experiencing something of a popular revival, having recently published her second anti-environmentalist book and worked as Rush Limbaugh's radio correspondent during the 1992 Earth Summit in Rio (which she labeled "the flat-earth summit"). She has become the unofficial standard-bearer for an emerging counterscience that attempts to discredit as "environmental hysteria" commonly accepted research on acid rain, pesticides, ozone depletion, fossil fuel–enhanced climate change, toxic waste, radiation, and all other human-originated sources of pollution.

"I find that most of the people I respect work outside the accepted wisdom," says the nation's onetime chief advocate of atomic power. "Because of that, many of them have been unable to get their work published." Although she is unappreciated by the fact-checking, peer-review-based science establishment, the many people who have heard Ray speak at Wise Use conferences around the country consider hers to be the voice of plainspoken scientific enlightenment.

I am at a three-day Environmental Conservation Organization (ECO) conference in Reno, Nevada, where Ray is to speak along with a number of other prominent anti-environmentalists. The ECO conference, which has the feel and fervor of dozens of other anti-enviro conferences that have taken place in recent years, is being held in conjunction with the annual meeting of the Land Improvement Contractors Association (LICA). LICA is a construction industry group involved in water diversion, reclamation, dam building, and other development projects likely to be affected by the wetland permit requirements of the Clean Water Act. In 1990, LICA demonstrated its opposition to these government regulations by establishing ECO. ECO literature explains that the organization seeks to "optimize the balance between environmental protection and economic vitality" by opposing "hastily drawn reactionary legislation that fails to adequately protect our human resources."[2] ECO is operated out of LICA's Maywood, Illinois, office by LICA executive vice president Henry Lamb.

Despite winter storms that threaten to close down the Reno airport and Interstate 80 at Donner Summit, more than a hundred people have arrived for the ECO conference and are being directed to the far end of a hallway off the main casino floor inside the candy-striped, copper-tinted, high-rise Hilton. Some three hundred developers and contractors have also arrived safely at the plush hotel/convention center for their annual meeting. After picking up ECO conference materials and copies of the *New American* and *21st Century Science & Technology* from the stacks on the registration table,[3] I enter a large, carpeted conference room with movable walls where ECO's first session is under way.

"There are market solutions to the environment. My answer is to make the right to pollute a property right and tradeable issue, which is what's beginning to be done on a limited basis. We have to appeal to mainstream environmentalists like ourselves against the lunatic fringe. Pollution permit trading is the way to get them turned our way." John Hosemann, the rotund chief economist for the American Farm Bureau Federation, is speaking to about eighty-five mostly middle-aged and older white people arrayed in several rows of straight-backed chairs.

"The government once encouraged the draining of swamps. Now it calls them wetlands and punishes the farmer who wants to turn them into productive land," he continues.

Since World War II, more than fifty million acres of agricultural land have been converted to urban/suburban use by real estate developers, while another fifty-three million acres of swamp have been converted to agricultural use. This was long considered a reasonable trade-off, but that was before the role of wetlands in groundwater filtration, aquifer purification, flood prevention, and fishery, waterfowl, and wildlife regeneration was fully understood. Given the choice of protecting agricultural land from development or continuing to drain and fill swamps, the Farm Bureau has come out strongly in favor of continued wetlands development.

"The Endangered Species Act is another big problem," Hosemann warns his audience. "It's ruled by biologists and botanists. There's no economic consideration given in its application. The West and South will be hammered the most, because the Northeast killed their animals long ago. So that's where all our national industry and agriculture will have to locate, according to an economist I know. Our national parks will be renamed biosphere reserves, and the only thing left in them will be these small trails where, if we agree to only take so many steps and not wander off or leave anything on the ground, we'll be allowed to look at these endangered animals."

He goes on to talk about the need to form an anti-environmentalist alliance with labor and to describe recent discussions he's had with the Teamsters in Arizona. "I mean, we'll never get [then AFL-CIO director] Lane Kirkland on our side," he admits, "but we can cut away at the AFL's components, like the New Jersey construction unions who came out against this wetlands nonsense when they saw it would mean less building. ... So if you can throw some white gas on the problem and someone else comes along and drops a match, we got something going. Let's get this revolution under way."

During the first break, Clark Collins from the Blue Ribbon Coalition walks up and introduces himself to Hosemann, who says he's never heard of Blue Ribbon. "But I'm open to be educated."

The next speaker is Bill Hazeltine, a retired mosquito-abatement director and chemical company employee who begins his presentation with an attack on Rachel Carson's 1962 book, *Silent Spring*. "Carson should be looked up in the fiction section of the library," he suggests to amused snickers. He goes on to talk about "ethnic groups" in Mississippi who threw rocks at mosquito spray trucks because they thought they were part of a plan to commit genocide against blacks. As a result, he claims, four people died of mosquito-borne encephalitis. He warns of a similar "strange alliance" forming in California between hunters and wildlife advocates who are paying farmers to create wetlands (for ducks and other waterfowl). These will only increase insect nuisances and create new health threats, he asserts, unless fish and game agencies can be convinced to return to their old practice of insecticide spraying in wildlife refuges.

Henry Lamb gives his welcoming speech on behalf of ECO. He's a slim, fastidious, silver-haired gentleman in a red tie, white shirt, and blue suit. He explains how free enterprise capitalism is superior to any other form of capitalism, and then sets up a question-and-answer session for himself, Hazeltine, and Hosemann.

Hazeltine talks about a proposed ban on methyl bromide (an ozone depleter) and explains that because it is used to protect grain in transit, its absence may expose grain supplies to deadly microtoxins.

Rogelio Maduro, associate editor of *21st Century Science & Technology*, stands up to talk from the floor. Rogelio, who has a bachelor of science degree in geology, is the coauthor of *The Holes in the Ozone Scare*, a book published by the LaRouchites that has provided most of the ammunition used by Dixy Lee Ray, Rush Limbaugh, and other science critics who deny that synthetic chemicals are causing atmospheric ozone depletion.[4]

"How many people have died as a result of environmental policies like the banning of DDT?" the LaRouchite asks rhetorically. "I'd say millions, because it was the most effective weapon against malaria. Right now methyl bromide is supposedly being banned for ozone depletion, but I think this is really an attack on refrigeration, because that's what CFCs and methyl bromides are used for: the storage and transportation of food. If you look at the environmentalists' policies, they say they want to reduce world population to 500 million, to between 500 million and 2 billion, and the best way to do that would be to destroy the world food system. That would create mass starvation. That's the way to achieve their aim."

"I'd say about 40 million people have died as a result of this banning of DDT, and I have to agree that if there is a conspiracy attacking food production this is a way of achieving it," Hazeltine agrees. He goes on to suggest that with the reduced use of insecticides, "we're also vulnerable to AIDS, because although mosquitoes have been eliminated as carriers, the stable fly could still become a vector for spreading HIV virus."

"I don't know about any apocalyptic scenarios," says the Farm Bureau's Hosemann. "My prediction is we'll just rot. Our country will just deteriorate into a Third World situation. I know of one analyst who estimates our gross domestic product loses as much as $1 to $2 trillion a year because of regulations, about a third of our total production. We're down to a population that's scientifically illiterate. We'll end up like Argentina, sitting on all these resources and not doing anything with them."

The highlight of the first day's sessions is a talk by James Catron, attorney and activist from Catron County, New Mexico. In 1990, Catron County, a rural district larger than Connecticut but with a population of only 2,600, gave birth to what has come to be known as the counties movement. An amalgam of the Wise Use and ultra-right *posse comitatus* (power of the county) movements, it claims that county commissioners have the right to establish land-use plans that preempt federal authority on federal lands within their borders. Seventy-five percent of Catron County is federally owned land. This includes the Gila National Forest, where most of the county's ranchers graze their cattle.

Their plans and ordinances would make it a criminal offense for federal employees to enforce environmental laws if they are in conflict with county plans.

"The ordinances scared the hell out of us," Mike Gardner, a Forest Service district ranger in Catron, admitted to a reporter a few years later. "I've got small children. It would be tough to tell my kids why I'm being arrested. It was intimidating."[5] As the counties movement grew, the Departments of Agriculture, Interior, and other government agencies felt compelled to remind Catron's and other county sheriffs of the felony provisions of the U.S. code relating to interference with or assault on federal agents.

As legal justification for county movement ordinances, Jim Catron, former Mountain States Legal Foundation attorney Karen Budd, and other Wise Use lawyers cited the National Environmental Policy Act (NEPA), which states that important cultural aspects of national heritage must be preserved in carrying out environmental regulations. These attorneys claim that ranching, mining, and logging represent the "local custom and culture" of rural counties in the West. While their ordinances would almost certainly be overturned in federal court, where the supremacy clause of the Constitution (establishing the primacy of federal law) would come into effect, activists such as Catron and Budd have been careful to avoid court fights, keeping their *posse comitatus* arguments in the political realm. Dozens of counties in the West have now passed anti-environmental ordinances modeled after the original Catron County regulations, often with the aid of the National Federal Lands Conference, a Utah-based clearinghouse for the movement.

Former BLM director Jim Baca (who went on to become mayor of Albuquerque) sees little real legitimacy in the ordinances. "It's pretty simple to understand that if you look at any of the counties that have done this and look at the makeup of their county commissioners, every single one of those members who voted for those ordinances are in one way or another in conflict of interest. They're ranchers, or they're feed store owners, or they're somebody who's been exploiting land, and they just don't want to be knocked off the gravy train. These ordinances are unconstitutional, so we tend to ignore them as rantings and ravings from the county commissions. I think the one thing that they do point out, though, is we need to do a better job of trying to work with the local folks and trying to mediate some of these land disputes out in these rural areas."[6]

Jim Catron is not one of the local folks Jim Baca has in mind when he talks about dialogue and mediation. Dressed in a white windbreaker and white Stetson, Jim Catron has the kind of wiry nervous energy, animated angular jaw, and brown-eyed predatory gaze that remind me of deceased Death Squad leader Roberto D'Aubuisson of El Salvador. "We are not in a struggle with environmentalists but with tyranny. There is no moral difference between Earth First! and Stalin. If the radical environmentalists took power you would not live, you would not be left alive," Catron warns his audience. "The feds were managing us out of existence. So we began reading laws and regulations and found that the law protects our local customs and culture and economic base," he continues. "Our custom is we believe in the value of production. It is our cultural use of the land to mine, timber, hunt, fish, and graze.

"Eighty percent of the people in Catron County have Scots-Irish last names," Catron continues. "The Scots-Irish were a warrior people, at home on the frontier, a warrior race too wild for the civilized East. So they were pushed to the frontier, where they confronted the Indians, who they understood, because they were another warrior people. They'd kill or marry the Indians, made no difference, any way you could pacify them. That's our customs and our culture. When they set up the Forest Reserves in 1890 and said we couldn't cut our trees, we set fire to the forests all across the West until they reconsidered things in light of our needs. Maybe today the feds have more respect for county sheriffs and jails than they do for their own laws. ... But understand, we're working within the law. It's the federal agencies like the Forest Service who are the criminals. They have to go around in body armor with M-16 automatic weapons. They say it's because of drug running, but we know it's the people of Catron County they're afraid of. We're also working with Indian tribes and Hispanic villagers," he claims. "They realize the radical environmentalists' agenda means an end to traditional ways of life. Until now greens have wrapped themselves in the American Indian cloak, but the Indian lived free, the Green Party was founded in Germany on the ideas of Nietzsche, Engels, and Marx."

Northern Arapaho journalist Debra Thunder disagreed in an opinion piece in the *Salt Lake Tribune*. "By describing local custom and culture in purely economic terms, the movement's proponents preclude the West's numerous but poverty-stricken Indian tribes," she wrote. "How, I wonder, can a nation that claimed this sacred and beautiful land in the name of God love the Creator but not the creation? How can a 'culture' survive when its very existence is defined by the consumption of the finite resources that give it identity?"

"The ranchers haven't been here in the American West long enough to establish a set of cultures or customs within the meaning of federal laws that are intended to protect culture," adds Walter Echo-Hawk, a Pawnee attorney with the Native American Rights Fund in Colorado. "Furthermore, the grazing and timbering special interests are being rapidly supplanted by changing American values—environmental and recreational. So it's impossible to say what local culture [in the West] may be, because it's in a period of rapid social change."[7]

Still, Jim Catron remains confident that the conqueror race holds the superior customs and culture. He recommends that I read *Albion Nation* by David Fisher Hacket. "It explains how four of the five peoples who settled America were from the British Isles," he says. I ask him if it isn't true that the Spanish mission padres introduced cattle culture to the Southwest. "The Scots-Irish settled the country and started ranching cattle," he answers sharply. "Hispanics are village people. They liked to stay close to town. They were afraid to ranch. They didn't have the initiative."

Over a year later I get a call from a New Mexico newspaper reporter who tells me Jim Catron vehemently denies making the statements reported in (the first edition of) this book. I bring my tape recorder to the phone and play them back for the reporter. He goes on to write a fairly scathing article on Catron and the counties movement.

At the end of the first day of the conference, Henry Lamb pitches ECO's new direct-access phone net.

"Using it you can send [pre-e-mail] faxes to your congresspeople that will be delivered with only your name and address attached, no organizational ID," he tells the crowd. "You can send twenty faxes for thirty dollars or you can select prewritten messages by phone. A computer in New Jersey will determine who your congressman is if you're not sure and where to send your message if you don't have the address. We have a wide selection of other information on our phone menu, including status reports on wetlands, animal rights, property rights, protests. And you can voice-access them," he smiles, and then demonstrates on the jury-rigged phone/tape setup on the table in front of him. We hear a dial tone and a recorded ECO ID as his call connects. Then he says, "Property rights," and a canned voice begins reporting over a loudspeaker on a New Hampshire Landowners Alliance rally. "We're hoping to develop a state-level ECO information system in the near future," he beams as he hangs up. Sales reps from the company that set up the system privately explain that they've installed similar voice-activated networks for the Democratic Party, the American Foundation for AIDS Research, and the Tropicana Orange Juice Company.[8]

The second day of the conference begins in the LICA exhibit hall with helium-filled balloons and a free buffet of juice, rolls, and muffins. High-heeled chorus girls in skimpy, sequined red bikinis and red feather boas walk among booths promoting laser leveling, grading and robotic excavation systems, Biosol Fertilizer, John Deere construction tractors, and job-site insurance coverage.

ECO's morning session is given over to political strategies. Candace Crandall, a former PR person for the Saudi Arabian Embassy, is representing the Science and Environmental Policy Project (SEPP), a mainstay of the counter-science movement. She says they want scientists to write commentaries for them, but more importantly they want to influence journalists in how they write about environmental science. They're planning a conference with a panel of scientists who are highly skeptical of the "environmental alarmism" that has become so popular. "A very important reporter from a major newspaper I was talking to was very excited about this conference and what we're doing. I'm real optimistic we can bring the press over to our side," she says.

"Was that Keith Schneider?" I ask her, referring to the *New York Times* environmental reporter who's been questioning the cost and benefits of environmental regulation while promoting Wise Use as the "third wave" of environmentalism.

"Yes, isn't he great?" she gushes.

Mike Colburn from the Political Economy Research Center, a think tank in Bozeman, Montana (where future secretary of Interior Gale Norton is a visiting Fellow), explains how the center does academic research on free-market environmentalism. It also tries to influence congressional staffers and national reporters, he explains, by hosting three-day wine-and-dine seminars at the Lone Star Ranch outside Yellowstone National Park.

Kathleen Marquardt, of the anti–animal rights group Putting People First, a stylishly dressed woman with a broad, intelligent face, complains that the Clintons stole her group's name for their presidential campaign slogan, but admits that she was still pleased to see all the furs worn at the inaugural ball. She explains why it is important to understand that animals don't have rights, they have instincts. Animal rights activists, she says, believe that rats and cockroaches are equal to or better than humans, but in truth "they don't care a hoot about the animals. They are just using them to attack humans."

She began fighting the animal rights groups, she recalls, after her daughter came home from public school and said they had had a speaker from PETA (People for the Ethical Treatment of Animals) who called her mother a murderer for hunting. Putting People First, Marquardt asserts, initially represented "average Americans who drink milk and eat meat and benefit from medical lab research ... but quickly expanded from anti–animal rights to combating all environmental extremism because it's all the same." PPF's latest campaign is in defense of Norway's decision to return to commercial whaling. "We support the consumptive use of marine resources, including marine mammals for human benefit," she smiles thinly. "Whales are not these geniuses Greenpeace makes them out to be. Whales are the cows of the sea. Their meat's lean and full of protein. If we ate whale meat we'd be much healthier."

"The difference between an environmentalist and a greedy developer," lectures Michael Greve from another conservative think tank, the Washington-based Center for Individual Rights, "is an environmentalist already has his mountain cabin. Environmentalism is a cause for the wealthy, for the haves against the have-nots." Greve has a clean-cut manicured look about him, speaks with a European accent, and wears a hand-tailored three-piece suit that has to have set him back a fair farthing. "The term *environmentalist* is going the way of *feminist—no* one wants to admit they are one," he claims. "But the environmentalist drivel is still seeping into the national psyche. It's like women who say, 'I'm not a feminist,' but when you try and have a sex or gender discussion with them it's just impossible." Or maybe, I think, it's just him.

After lunch I talk with Gerald Stram, an older farmer from Wisconsin with a gray crewcut and a rough complexion. He owns a 350-acre beef cattle farm that he bought after retiring from the railroad twenty-five years ago. Now he raises seventy-five head of cattle in what's known as a cow/calf operation. "I raise them from erection to resurrection," he jokes. He's attending the conference with his friend Gene Leubker, of Landowners of Wisconsin, a small group the two helped establish.

"The state set up a protected zone along ninety miles of the lower Wisconsin River," Stram explains, "from Baraboo to the mouth of the river, where it feeds into the Mississippi at Prairie du Chien. That restricted our land use because of the view from the river. For twenty-five feet back from the river, I can't cut my own trees. Beyond that I have to get permission for a ways," he explains. "The law went into effect at the end of eighty-nine. Five of us got together and formed our group in ninety. We don't have hit teams like some of those bikers in California,[9] but we were angry enough that if you were DNR [state Department of Natural Resources] you wouldn't get out of your car in our area."

In 1992, 250 members of Landowners staged a protest inside the state capitol rotunda in Madison. "This was to protest their plan to fence off all our creeks and streams to keep the cattle out of them and they would have only paid 75 percent of the cost. If they'd have paid for it all, that would have been another thing. When it came to the governor, he vetoed that law," Stram says proudly. "It showed me we had some political influence. After that fight we got two hundred new members."

"Ask me about my recipes for spotted owls," Kathleen Marquardt jokes, standing behind her display table at the end of the conference's second day. Along with copies of her *Putting People First* newsletter, she has a variety of bumper stickers for sale, including, "Don't Steal. The Government Hates Competition," "Save a Skunk, Roadkill an Activist," and "Save a Pig, Roast an Activist."[10]

Jim Catron is standing nearby talking to Bill Moshofsky from Oregonians in Action, part of the Oregon Lands Coalition.

"The big companies sold us out. They took their $1.6 million loss and closed the mill," Catron complains.

"Simpson is the only one of the majors giving our group money. Mostly we're getting our funds from middle-sized operations," Moshofsky nods sadly.

"I went to this corporate executive for money and he tells me 'I can't 'cause my kids are green and my grandchildren are emerald green,'" someone else complains.

I ask Kent Howard, the seventy-year-old president of the National Federal Lands Conference, which coordinates the counties movement, what he thinks about the John Birch Society trying to link up with the anti-environmentalist cause.

"I read the Birch Society magazine every month. I probably should be a member, because I agree with what they say," he answers. "I never got around to joining, but if you look at how the Council on Foreign Affairs [sic] and the Trilaterals run everything it makes sense. Even Reagan was a member."

Howard, who has mottled, weathered skin, thinning hair, and lively silver-blue eyes, recently retired from a lifetime of ranching.

"My place was up on the Idaho border ninety-six miles from Elko, up on the Snake River way past the Independence mine. One of the last bits of paradise on earth," he states as fact, not opinion. "I raised 1,400 head of cattle on 5,000 deeded acres and 160,000 acres of federal land. Two years ago, at sixty-eight, I got out. The value was just going down with the threat of increased grazing fees and environmentalist attacks on riparian areas. I sold the ranch to the Rocky Mountain Elk Foundation. In some ways I feel like a traitor, because the taxpayers ended up paying for it. After the Elk Foundation bought it from me, they sold the land to the BLM and the Nevada Division of Wildlife."

Leaving the convention hall, I notice Dixy Lee Ray at a back table. It's after five and she wants "a real drink," not the light beer on sale at the LICA snack bar. Dr. Robert Balling from Arizona State University goes off to the casino bar to get her a couple of scotch and sodas.

"When I left the governor's office in eighty-one I wasn't vested [time necessary to collect benefits]," she tells me, explaining her return to activism. "The state requires five years of service for severance, and I only had four. I only had a small pension that I had to augment writing and speaking." Even now, with her book sales approaching 100,000, she can't afford to neglect her paid speaking engagements.

"I try to keep it to four or five a month and don't let them get spread around the country if I can help it. I try to limit my travel. The old bod can't take it anymore."

Balling returns with her drinks and she begins sipping. "I've really enjoyed my retirement years, even if Fox Island isn't the center of the cosmopolitan world," she continues.

Fox Island is a rustic haven in Puget Sound south of Seattle, where Ray lives on a three-acre shorefront farm with her sister, six dogs, a few geese, some chickens, 120 fruit trees, and a beehive to pollinate them. "I let the bees keep their honey as long as they do their job," she says.

The last morning of the ECO conference is given over to counter-science, with slide shows and presentations by Balling, Dr. Fred Singer, and Dr. Hugh Ellsaesser, to be followed later by Ray's keynote presentation.

Balling is director of climatology at Arizona State and the author of *The Heated Debate,* an anti-greenhouse thesis published by the Pacific Research Institute, a conservative think tank based in San Francisco. S. Fred Singer is president of the once-Moon affiliated SEPP and former chief scientist for the Department of Transportation. Hugh Ellsaesser is a meteorologist and guest scientist at California's Lawrence Livermore nuclear laboratory. All three argue that human impacts on the atmosphere and climate are either vastly overrated or, in the case of industrial carbon dioxide buildup, actually beneficial to humans.

"The way to cope with the greenhouse effect is to enjoy it," Ellsaesser suggests, going on to postulate that lower coronary rates since 1950 may be linked to increased CO_2 in the atmosphere. "CO_2 stimulates the biosphere like a fertilizer," he claims. "Unfortunately, scientific literature has a bias. Anything we call pollution is considered morally wrong. Any beneficial effects are filtered out. We are failing to consider the cost versus benefits of CO_2 buildup. We should listen to Ronald Reagan, who says government is part of the problem, not the solution. All these bureaucrats, scientists, and environmentalists gain from disaster scenarios. Only whistle-blowers like me and Bob don't benefit from telling the truth. It takes courage standing up to the preferred wisdom and having to publish wherever you can."

Ray's speech focuses on energy. "Energy is the life blood of industrial western civilization, and environmentalists and greenie radicals hate it," she instructs her listeners. "We're being told we must conserve electricity, when we in fact have an assured and affordable supply of electricity. What is so noble about conserving energy? We know how to use it and produce it and with little impact on our environment." Dick Cheney couldn't have said it better.

Among the list of environmental problems she reviews and finds of no real consequence is the population explosion, which has seen the number of people on the planet more than double since 1950, from 2.5 to over

6 billion. "The population problem is based on present trends continuing into the future, which they never do," she assures her audience. "Population growth goes up and down like global warming. If you looked at the growth rate of racquetball courts in the 1970s and extended it, the whole country would be covered by racquetball courts today."

Less than a year later, on January 3, 1994, Ray dies of a bronchial ailment at her Fox Island home. She was fighting "the greenies" to the end. Three days before her death, she criticized, as alarmist media, reports about secret Cold War radiation experiments conducted on some eight hundred Americans without their knowledge during the 1940s and 1950s. The experiments included injecting patients with plutonium and feeding mentally retarded teenagers, pregnant women, and Washington State prisoners radioactive milk and other tainted substances. "Everybody is exposed to radiation," Ray told the Associated Press just before she passed on. "A little bit more or a little bit less is of no consequence."

Following Ray's presentation to ECO, retired general Richard Lawson, president of the American Coal Association, arrives from Washington, D.C., just in time to give a short but impassioned presentation to the group. He is a large, bushy-browed man with a bulldog visage and dark, slicked-back hair.

"When I was the commander of U.S. forces in Europe, it infuriated me to hear long-haired dirty demonstrators carrying placards and smoking whatever they smoked at night called peace marchers. The troops guarding the wall were the peace marchers. The environmentalists remind me of the same thing, of those people," he declares to a hearty round of applause. "The strangest thing you hear now is that this planet is not for people. We must go back to wigwams and loincloths because that's clean. I wonder if they ever saw what the Sioux nation left behind after they went over the hill. ... There are going to be nine billion people in forty years, and in the real world the issue is how we feed and clothe and house those people or you're going to need more generals than you've ever seen."

"I commend you for being on the front lines of freedom. The efforts of groups like yours are rocking the establishment to its foundations," adds John Fund, an editorial writer for the *Wall Street Journal* and one of the last speakers at the conference. Fund, a sleek, pale-skinned conservative who collaborated on Rush Limbaugh's book *The Way Things Ought to Be*, tells the group that his friend Rush sends them a ditto—

and that Bill Ellen, one of the movement's "political prisoners," sends his solidarity from the Petersburg, Virginia, federal prison. "If we can get Bill's story out we can get the American people to realize that if the bell tolls it will toll for them as well. After our editorials in the *Wall Street Journal* asking President Bush (Sr.) to pardon Bill Ellen [just before Bush left office], the U.S. attorney in Maryland held a press conference to denounce the *Wall Street Journal*, and the law enforcement community closed ranks and said Bill Ellen has to stay in jail. I attribute this to their unwillingness to go after violent criminals. ... They don't want to go after violent criminals but they have to go after somebody, so they go after environmental criminals. I mean, who are these people? Are they really criminals, developers, big business, or your neighbors? I just want to tell you, you have allies you don't realize. The *Wall Street Journal* is very interested in this struggle, because if they get to you they're going to go after investors, and they're going to go after business, and they're going to go after all of us. That's why I say, your struggle is our struggle."

After a big round of applause, Henry Lamb presents the *Wall Street Journal* writer with the first access card for ECO's new telephone information network. He then asks Ocie Mills to stand up in the audience. A burly fellow rises slowly to his feet. "Ocie has completed his twenty-one-month sentence for precisely the same offense that Bill Ellen went to jail for, offending the bureaucrats," Henry announces to another round of applause.

Bill Ellen and Ocie Mills are two of a handful of convicted violators of wetlands-permit provisions of the Clean Water Act whom the Property Rights movement has adopted as martyrs and political prisoners. Bill Ellen served six months for destroying federally protected wetlands while building a series of duck ponds for a private hunting club on the eastern shore of Maryland not far from Peggy Reigle's investment property. According to the *Wall Street Journal*, Ellen met with state and local officials and secured thirty-eight permits for his worksite. He claimed that his conviction was based on an expanded definition of *wetlands* developed for a 1989 federal manual that was applied retroactively to an area he'd filled in 1987. In what the *Wall Street Journal* pointed to as the biggest irony of the case, Ellen actually created forty-five acres of wetlands and enhanced habitat for ducks and geese in developing the preserve.

The U.S. Department of Justice, which prosecuted Ellen's case, countered that the U.S. Army Corps of Engineers issued three cease-and-desist orders between 1987 and 1989 ordering Ellen to stop all construction. Ellen ignored the orders and failed to obtain any federal permits. The department also insists that the wetlands he destroyed in 1987 were core wetlands, which qualified for full protection under federal regulations going back to 1976. Although Ellen created forty-five acres of wetlands, the Justice Department insists that in the process he destroyed eighty-six acres of tidal marshes and forested wetlands, habitat and breeding grounds not only for waterfowl but also for two endangered nongame species, the Delmarva fox squirrel and the American bald eagle.[11]

What the Justice Department, in defending its case, failed to mention, but many wetlands ecologists are quick to point out, is that the Army Corps of Engineers, which reviews wetlands projects, is notoriously lax, routinely approving wetland fill permits. This despite President Bush (Sr.'s) pledge of "no net loss of wetlands." A 1999 report (undisputed by the Corps) found a 40 percent decline in inspections and 80 percent fewer court cases brought against people who destroyed wetlands between 1994 and 1998.

The bearded, white-haired Ocie Mills of Milton, Florida, stands about six-foot-two. He seems friendlier in person than on the cover of the *New American* magazine, where he appears behind black prison bars with his son Carey above a cutline reading "Eco-Villains? No—Just pawns in the federal land-grab scam."[12] Ocie is attending the ECO conference with his wife, a short, pleasant woman with frizzed yellow hair.

"I've been arrested and arrested and re-arrested," he says almost proudly. "In 1976 two DER [Florida Department of Environmental Regulation] agents wanted to come on my property without a warrant. A fight broke out and I made a citizen's arrest, had these two guys laying on the ground, and that was the beginning of my troubles. They came back later and arrested me for assault and brandishing a weapon, which was my .38 revolver.

"Another time they said they wanted to look at a ditch I was clearing out with a backhoe. It was snake-infested and we had five kids."

"We were worried about those snakes," his wife confirms.

Mills goes on. "The DER claimed jurisdiction on the ditch. I went to trial, was found not guilty, and then I sued them. I was awarded damages and settled on appeal for $15,000. That was a six-year battle. Then, up around eighty-seven, eighty-eight, we had a fight over cleaning out another ditch and hauling fill to build a house. This time DER got the EPA and the Corps of Engineers involved. They told me, 'We're bringing in the big boys,' and then declared it a wetland. I ended up on trial with an eighty-six-year-old judge who misdirected the jury. I challenged the judge after the transcripts were changed by the court reporter to cover up the fact that the man was deaf. I defended myself against seven government lawyers and ended up spending two years at Souflee Field penitentiary along with my son."

He suggests I contact the *Pensacola News Journal* if I want details on the case not covered in the *New American*. "They ran some fair coverage for the liberal media," he concedes affably.

I take his lead and call the *News Journal*. I detect a groan coming from the other end of the phone line when I mention Ocie Mills's name. "This is like one of those stories that will never go away, and I've tried to pass it off to the political correspondent and others but they keep passing it back to me," says Ginny Graybiel, the reporter who's been covering the case for the last seven years.[13]

"It's a very confusing case because of the different state and federal charges," she explains. "You could say that the DER were out of control. Ocie probably violated environmental laws, but it's hard to know what to do with him. He's one of these people who will break the rules just to show he doesn't respect them. Meanwhile we have major paper mills polluting the region and the DER has spent millions on this one little case. The first federal judge who was involved was not senile like Ocie makes him out to be. He was just an old-time autocratic judge who was hard of hearing and maybe should have resigned a few years earlier. Ocie was sentenced to twenty-one months in federal prison, which he served, along with his son—largely, I think, because he insisted on representing himself. Then he appealed his conviction. A new Reagan-appointed federal judge upheld his conviction but went on to question whether DER or the feds should be enforcing what he called these 'Alice in Wonderland' environmental regulations. You can't really make too much of this in terms of Pensacola," she adds. "We're basically dealing with two small lots where supposedly he put clean sand on his property. And I'm not that familiar with the wetland laws, but the DER has been considered really lenient towards Champion Paper and their big mill on Eleven Mile Creek, which has been polluting Perdido Bay for years. It makes them a target of suspicion around here when you see how they've gone after this small businessman while being so favorably disposed to a major polluter. As far as Ocie himself, I think he should get a life. He's this obstreperous guy with a little band of followers, fringe-type people, not unlike John Burt, the antiabortion preacher down here in Pensacola [who led a protest during which one of his followers shot and killed Dr. David Gunn]."

Mills and Gene Lilly, a dredge suction miner with a Klondike Pete mustache and gold-nugget ring from Happy Camp, California, get into a discussion on drugs and the temptations they can generate for the average working man in terms of the money that could be earned for one night's transportation work. "Drugs is just an excuse to build prisons," Mills suggests. "If they legalized it that would take the profit out of it."

"Sure, look at the Weaver killing in Idaho," says Lilly, referring to the 1992 shoot-out in the mountains of northern Idaho between white separatist Randy Weaver and federal agents that left three people, including Weaver's wife and son, dead. "That was just an assassination, using drugs and weapons charges as an excuse."

"They killed Scott in California and claimed that was a drug raid too, but he was a property rights activist," Mills claims.

Donald Scott, a reclusive, sixty-one-year-old millionaire rancher in Malibu, California, was killed in a drug raid on October 2, 1992. The raid was carried out by thirty agents from a drug task force led by the L.A. sheriff's department but including the Los Angeles Police Department, Drug Enforcement Agency, National Guard, and National Park Service agents with support from the border patrol. Scott was killed when he came out of his bedroom and aimed a pistol at the armed intruders. The search warrant used in the raid claimed that fifty marijuana plants had been spotted from the air, but none was found on the two hundred–acre spread. A follow-up investigation by the Ventura County district attorney indicated that a sheriff's deputy might have lied in obtaining the warrant, and that the raid itself may have been partly prompted by a desire to seize the $5 million property under federal drug-forfeiture laws.[14] Because the National Park Service participated in the raid and had tried to hold discussions with Scott about incorporating his ranch into the adjoining Santa Monica Mountains Recreation Area, Property Rights activists, including Chuck Cushman, demanded an investigation to determine whether the killing had been inspired by the Park Service. But the L.A. sheriff's department, who led the raid, and the potentially abusive use of drug-forfeiture laws by law enforcement agencies, became the primary focus of subsequent investigations, lawsuits, and media coverage.

Given its industry origins, the ECO conference might have been expected to represent a moderate or centrist position within the anti-enviro movement. Instead it reaffirmed the lack of a political center among the anti-greens and their inability to reach beyond the Far Right in forming core alliances and coalitions. The defining political division within the movement, then, appears not to be between the center and the fringe, but between those who believe they can achieve their goals working through the established political process and those who see intimidation and violence as legitimate tools in their war against the preservationists.

"WE HAVE OUR OWN WAY of doing things. We have a dozen activists and eighty to ninety other people to get things done, as long as we keep them somewhat under control," brags Rick Sieman, leader of the southern California–based Sahara Club, the group Wisconsin farmer Gerald Stram was referring to when he spoke of California biker "hit teams."[15]

By "getting things done" Sieman is referring to threats, occasional assaults (by club members who are said to be armed with "baseball bats and bad attitudes"), and lists in the Sahara Club newsletter and on its computer bulletin board of environmentalists' names, addresses, phone numbers, and license plate numbers. The lists are usually followed with this admonition: "Now you know who they are and where they are. Just do the right thing and let your conscience be your guide."[16]

Dozens of environmentalists throughout the country have reported receiving obscene phone calls, death threats, and "Dear Faggot" letters following Sahara Club's publication of their names and numbers. Sieman admits taking pleasure in causing grief for the "limp-wristed faggots," "queers," "butch bitches," and "ecoterrorists" of the BLM, Sierra Club, Greenpeace, Earth First!, and other perceived enemies of homophobic outlaw dirt bikers.

Sieman and "Phantom Duck" Louis McKey founded the Sahara Club in the fall of 1990 after the BLM shut down the famous Barstowto-Vegas motorcycle race (see Hunter Thompson's *Fear and Loathing in Las Vegas*), which had been drawing as many as three thousand entrants a year and damaging sensitive desert terrain while threatening the endangered desert tortoise. Sieman announced that the newly formed club would stage a protest race, and that he and his supporters would come armed to protect themselves against ecoterrorists.[17] About a hundred people turned out for the Thanksgiving weekend protest, as did a large contingent of law enforcement troopers. Ten people, including Sieman, McKey, and Barry Van Dyke, son of actor Dick Van Dyke, were arrested after some chasing around the desert. Sieman was packing an unloaded .22 revolver. Another rider had a loaded .38.[18]

"Sieman argued that they had to bring guns to defend themselves," BLM law enforcement agent Felicia Probert tells me, "because Earth Firsters might appear disguised as BLM agents, which we found pretty unlikely. I think we might have noticed imposters in our midst and arrested them if we had. We've seen a shift in their focus since that time from opposing the BLM to opposing environmentalists as they became part of the Wise Use movement."

The Sahara Club, along with more mainstream recreational biker and four-wheel-drive clubs, independent miners, and mining companies, became active in a Wise Use campaign to oppose the California Desert Protection bill first proposed by ex-Senator Alan Cranston. Sahara Club protestors disrupted several public hearings where Cranston appeared. During 1992 hearings in Beverly Hills, Sahara Clubbers physically harassed several women from the Sierra Club who were trying to testify. Later, after Senators Dianne Feinstein and Barbara Boxer were elected to office, the Sahara Club newsletter warned its members that the desert plan was alive and being pushed forward by "these ultra-liberal bitches."[19]

The Sahara Club has taken particular delight in going after Earth First!, which it sees as its counterpart on the environmental side. Sieman happily recalls the night an Earth First! spokesman came to speak at an L.A.-area college.

"We showed up with ninety to one hundred members [others put the number at thirty] with black tee shirts under our shirts showing a large muscular arm choking an Earth Firster. We took off our shirts and went up on the stage and took the mike from him and refused to let him speak. Pat Martin, who's a big 275-pounder, got in his face and I had to restrain Pat from getting violent and maybe going to jail. They called in the cops but they couldn't do much. This went on for about an hour. We had a wild time. I was telling the students that this guy was a terrorist. The college president asked us to leave and when I saw that there was no time left, that the time they'd booked the hall for was almost up, I said we'd leave if we got our money back. So we filed out and I had our guys coming back in a side door and collecting the money again. We made $360 profit that night."

A similar event took place in northern California after Earth First! began organizing against the logging of redwoods. Candice Boak, whose husband worked as a logging contractor in Humboldt County, decided to take a stand on behalf of timber. She recalls how Chuck Cushman came to town "and helped us form a group, choose the name Mothers Watch, and so forth." Once Mothers Watch was established, it received support from local timber companies in organizing pro-industry demonstrations and rallies. Mill workers were given days off to attend Yellow Ribbon protests. Boak was invited to the home of John Campbell, Pacific Lumber's president, and they soon became friends. Mothers Watch also videotaped environmental demonstrations and, according to Boak, sent dubs of the tapes to the police and FBI.

In 1990, Mothers Watch and WE CARE, one of the grassroots groups set up by the California Forestry Association, organized a "dirty-tricks" workshop put on by Rick Sieman of the Sahara Club.

"It was just harmless stuff that added some humor to the summer," Boak claims, without elaborating on the content of the workshop.[20] The next day, Tim Haynes, one of her husband's logging employees, was arrested and charged with making a bomb threat after he tossed a box wrapped in duct tape containing a stack of Sahara Club newsletters into the Arcata Action Center, the local environmental storefront, shouting a warning as he ducked out the door.[21]

Siemen claims that he has conducted thirty to thirty-five dirty tricks workshops around the country for "logging groups and logging companies" in the Northwest, hunters in Arkansas, and Wise Use activists in Texas, New Mexico, Illinois, and Pennsylvania.

"I offer eighty to one hundred things you can do to stop the human debris," he says. "We're talking some gray stuff here," he chuckles when asked to cite a few examples. "Say I heard of something I'd never use in one of my workshops," he laughs, indicating that of course he would. "Like, say you put wrong year stickers on the license plates of long-haired filthy doper types. You could whip them off on your computer and with a good color copier on sticky-backed paper you'd give law enforcement a reason to stop them and search them for drugs or weapons or whatever." Other dirty tricks include what are referred to as "pizzas and turds." "Pizzas" are any mail-order merchandise you have delivered in the name of an environmentalist or organization you're targeting. "Turds" are mailings using their return postage to send them heavy and/or offensive objects, ranging from anvils to human and animal feces. Trying to solicit funds in the name of a group such as Earth First! as part of a sting against other environmental groups is a dirty trick that's also called mail fraud and has resulted in at least one postal investigation of the Sahara Club.[22]

"See, if you try and go through the system, you get involved in this convoluted bullshit process," Sieman complains. "I teach people how to go after the person responsible for your grief. Like this Forest Service guy closed down a road that should have stayed open to the public. What's the easiest way to find out where the guy lives? Follow him home. I mean, you can't reason with eco-freaks but you can sure scare them."

Ed Knight recalls a different effort to stop Earth First! in northern California.

"You reach an agreement up front. You don't expect that someone's going to come forward and say, 'Yeah, I paid him to shoot those people.' You understand you're on your own. We were told if we killed any of them there was $40,000 that was there to defend us in court or to help us get away." At sixty-four, Ed Knight looks like a biker version of Santa Claus. A large, white-bearded ex-logger and onetime Galloping Goose turned Hell's Angel, he lives in Willits, California, a wide spot on Route 101 in the logged-out interior of Mendocino County. This is just south of Laytonville, where local Yellow Ribbon activists tried to get the school board to ban Dr. Seuss's *The Lorax* from the elementary school reading list, calling it anti-logging propaganda.

"I've heard everything, from out-and-out murder to torture," Knight says of vigilante plans to counter feared Earth First! monkeywrenching (vandalism of logging equipment) during Redwood Summer protests. "There was a general consensus that anyone caught spiking a tree would be crucified and the tree'd go to town with them attached," he continues, referring to armed meetings that took place in bars and on worksites during the protests. Knight was one of a number of guards who was hired by independent gyppo loggers to set up ambushes in the woods near their equipment, work that differed little from guarding the area's marijuana plantations during harvest season except that the loggers provided better armament. "They gave me this Uzi that was just a beautiful weapon. I'd never handled one of them before," the old biker recalls with a note of wistfulness.[23]

PERIODICALLY, THE MEDIA has associated the anti-enviro movement with political cults as well as violence and intimidation, forcing a scramble among Wise Use and Property Rights activists to distance themselves from some of their less reputable allies. In attempting to avoid being labeled a fringe element, anti-enviro leaders such as Peggy Reigle of Maryland have publicly insisted that any attempt to connect their "grassroots movement" with Birchers, LaRouchites, or Moonies is a preservationist smear.

"Preservationists in our area accused us of being Moonies. That's Ron Arnold and his crowd. We don't have or want anything to do with them," explained Joan Smith of California Women in Timber and the Alliance for America. She then went on to compare the environmental movement to the Chinese communist party.[24]

For first-timers attending anti-enviro events, receiving a flyer about a "government land takeover" emblazoned with a bald eagle perched on a clutch of flags above the John Birch Society logo can prove disconcerting.[25] Founded in 1958 by candy manufacturer Robert Welch, the John Birch Society subscribes to a paranoid conspiracy theory claiming that most of the world's governments are controlled by a small group of "insiders" made up of international bankers, politicians, and atheists (possibly Freemasons) determined to achieve world conquest through the many levers of power they control, including the Council on Foreign Relations, Trilateral Commission, United Nations, and World Bank. Communism, according to Bircher theory, was just one of the insiders' many scams for achieving world domination.

The Birchers reached their zenith of power during the 1960s, organizing precincts during the 1964 Barry Goldwater presidential campaign and later working to counter the civil rights movement. With a hundred thousand secret, selectively chosen members and a string of bookshops, they promoted a number of campaigns to "Impeach [Supreme Court Justice] Earl Warren," "Expose the 'Civil Rights' Fraud," and "Support Your Local Police." The Birch Society also supported J. Edgar Hoover's FBI, sharing information on civil rights and antiwar protestors through freelance spies such as John and Louise Reese, publishers of a private newsletter called *Information Digest*. The Birch Society, using a technique made famous by one of their heroes, Senator Joe McCarthy of Wisconsin, claimed that there were 154 known Communists working for Dr. Martin Luther King to advance the "Negro revolution," a claim that soon became an article of faith among white separatists and racists. The Birch Society also believed the civil rights movement to be part of a "proletarian plot" by the United Auto Workers' Walter Reuther and his "stooge," Bobby Kennedy, who together formed a dangerous "pair of insiders." By the 1970s, Welch had passed the mantle of leadership to a younger generation of paranoids. These included, for a time, Congressman Larry McDonald of Georgia, an old-style, states-rights radical who was convinced that the insiders had gotten to President Gerald Ford. In divorce proceedings filed in Washington, D.C., in the mid-1970s, McDonald's wife pleaded alienation of affection after he told her they could no longer make love until the Communists were driven out of the capital. In a coincidence that no self-respecting Bircher believes was anything less than an insider plot, Larry McDonald was among the 269 people killed when Korean Airlines Flight 007 was shot down by Russian fighter jets after straying over Soviet airspace on September 1, 1983. By 1990 the Birch Society's membership was down to 25,000, mostly older people, despite an attempt to stay contemporary by linking up with the Christian Right and attacking AIDS funding, gay "perversion," and sex education in the schools. In a bid to keep itself afloat, the society restructured its finances and, after thirty-odd years, moved its national headquarters from Belmont, Massachusetts, to Appleton, Wisconsin, Joe McCarthy's hometown. The fall of communism turned out to be an easier adjustment for the Birchers than for many others on the Right, since, according to their worldview, communism was only one of many cloaks worn by the insiders. Among the new disguises they were quick to identify and combat was George Bush Sr.'s "New World Order" and environmentalism. "If it's not stopped, the bandwagon of environmentalism could lead to the scrapping of our nation's form of government and the destruction of our liberty," warned the *New American* in a special issue on the environmental threat.[26]

"GREENPEACE, SHOCK TROOPS for a New Dark Age" was the headline cover story in one of Lyndon LaRouche's publications, *EIR—Executive Intelligence Review.* Other articles included "Fusion Advances Augur Economic Revolution," "Kissinger 'Insane and Morally Dangerous,'" and "The Debt Plans: Only LaRouche's Will Work." The Greenpeace article accused the environmental group's members of being saboteurs for "a green fascist New World Order," "shock troops of the Green Comintern," murderers of seals and kangaroos, and an "irregular warfare force."[27]

This seems funnier than any parody of the Far Right *The Onion* or *The Daily Show* could come up with until one considers that *EIR* is distributed to dozens of corporations, right-wing groups, and intelligence agencies throughout the United States, Europe, and Asia and that the LaRouche organization itself has a history of unpredictable violence and cultlike behavior.

Most Americans who've heard of Lyndon LaRouche remember him as a peculiar third-party presidential candidate who once bought network airtime to expostulate his economic theories during presidential primaries. When two of LaRouche's followers won Democratic nominations in Illinois for lieutenant governor and secretary of state, party gubernatorial candidate Adlai Stevenson III removed himself from the party ticket, saying he couldn't run on the same slate with neo-Nazis.

A 1989 analysis of LaRouche by Political Research Associates, a Cambridge-based think tank that studies right-wing movements, reported that his "paranoid and conspiratorial view of history involving racial bigotry, cultural intolerance and a large dose of anti-Jewish hysteria, and ... LaRouche's idea that his followers will someday evolve into a master race of latter day Platonic 'Golden Souls,' qualifies him as a Neo-Nazi."[28]

Although LaRouche served five years in prison for mail fraud and tax evasion involving $30 million in unpaid campaign loans, his multi-million-dollar business and intelligence network continued to function in his absence. It turned out *EIR, The New Federalist, 21st Century Science*

& *Technology,* and reams of other publications, all asserting that the world is dominated by a secret cabal led by the British oligarchy and its Jewish backers, including "Soviet Agent" Henry Kissinger. His follow- ers also claim that Queen Elizabeth controls the world's drug cartels, that Prince Philip and Prince Bernhard of the Netherlands pull the strings on the environmental movement, and that drugs and envi- ronmentalism are key tools in a plan to bring on a New Dark Age, a descent into madness that only Lyndon LaRouche has the political genius to prevent.

LaRouche's own evolution from Far Left to Far Right to Far Side of the looking glass has included a string of assaults and lawsuits directed on his behalf, accusations of brainwashing and sexual aberrations tak- ing place within his organization, as well as documented ties to armed racists, anti-Semites, government intelligence agencies—even a couple of national security officials in the Reagan White House. Now in his eighties, he was raised in New Hampshire, serving as a noncombatant in World War II. After the war he joined the Trotskyite Socialist Work- ers Party. In the late 1960s he split with the SWP and became the guru of the Labor Caucus of Students for a Democratic Society, until SDS expelled him in 1969. Under the name Lynn Marcus, he then formed the National Caucus of Labor Committees (NCLC) and preached the need for rapid industrialization to build the working class (his belief in the power of industry is one of the few constants in his political evolu- tion; the cover of an issue of *21st Century* promises to "Save the Earth with Technology").[29] In 1973, LaRouche went through a transforma- tion after his wife left him for one of his followers (a man LaRouche later browbeat into confessing he'd been "psychosexually brain- washed" by the CIA, KGB, and Britain's MI 5). Shortly after the breakup, LaRouche decided to establish "hegemony" on the Left, or- dering his followers to attack members of SWP and other leftist groups with baseball bats, chains, and karate nunchucks, sending dozens of people to the hospital. Those who remained loyal to him during "Operation Mop-Up" became the inner core of his increasingly cult- like organization. In 1974, police broke into a New York apartment and arrested six LaRouchites who were holding a woman against her will, attempting to "deprogram" her after she tried to leave the group. LaRouche developed increasingly bizarre theories of sexual impotence, homosexuality, and brainwashing, dividing the world among his followers, their enemies, and the common "sheep and beasts." In the mid-1970s, LaRouche began to establish contacts on the extreme Right, attempting to infiltrate and co-opt the American Conservative Union, Young Americans for Freedom, the John Birch Society, and the KKK. Through Mitchell WerBell, the inventor of the Mac-10 silenced submachine gun, he developed additional contacts with mercenaries and CIA contract agents and decided to go into the intelligence business for himself. He began to publish *EIR* reports on the activities of liberals and leftists. *EIR* got wide dissemination among less discriminating members of the law enforcement and intelligence communities. The LaRouchite reports were liberally sprinkled with outlandish claims— for example, that the antinuclear movement was actually fronting for armed nuclear terrorists and that the Soviet KGB was behind environmental groups including Greenpeace. Reagan advisor and National Security Council senior analyst Dr. Norman Bailey would later tell NBC that the LaRouche network was "one of the best private intelligence services in the world," a claim that inspired snorts of derision among intelligence professionals.

By 1984, LaRouche had aligned his group with the very hard Right, which included Holocaust deniers and the Aryan Nation. Then, in one of his mercurial turns of inspired megalomania, he decided to run for president. His organization was put through what its members called "the cultural revolution."

"We transformed from an intelligence-gathering and -reporting operation to a full-time fund-raising apparatus," testified campaign finance director William Wertz at LaRouche's 1988 tax-evasion trial.[30] Using long-established mind-control techniques, the organization subjected members who failed to meet financial quotas to merciless ridicule and accusations of sexual impotence. Fundraisers were instructed, "If you're talking to a little old lady who says she'll lose her house, get the money. If you're talking to an unemployed worker with kids to feed, forget it—get the money. Most people are immoral anyway." An IRS expert testified that from 1983 to 1986, LaRouche's organization borrowed $33.2 million, of which only $3.2 million, less than 10 percent, was repaid.

On December 19, 1988, an Alexandria, Virginia, jury convicted LaRouche and six of his supporters of conspiracy, mail fraud, and tax evasion. At his sentencing the aging political cult leader claimed that he was a victim of a British intelligence plot, a claim the judge dismissed as "arrant nonsense."

With LaRouche in jail, his followers sought out new areas in which to exert their influence. They went online, placing "press releases" on the Internet accusing Greenpeace of financial mismanagement and terrorism.

In Europe, LaRouche-affiliated groups like Patriots for Germany and the European Labor Party disrupted meetings of Greenpeace, the Greens, and other environmental groups.

In the United States, the LaRouchites' most successful campaign has been the promotion of anti-environmental counterscience through publication of *21st Century Science & Technology*, meetings, seminars, congressional testimony (against the banning of methyl bromide), and their collaboration with the Wise Use and Property Rights movements.

On January 26, 1994, Lyndon LaRouche was released from federal prison having served one-third of his fifteen-year sentence. A decade later his followers remain active.

ON NEW YEAR'S DAY, 1987, the Reverend Sun Myung Moon, self-styled messiah, founder of a multibillion-dollar international business empire, and publisher of Ronald Reagan's favorite newspaper, told his disciples that he desired "the natural subjugation of the American government and population"[31] under what he described as "an automatic theocracy to rule the world."[32]

His longtime chief aide, Colonel Bo Hi Pak, would later tell conservative activist David Finzer, "We are going to make it so that no one can run for office in the United States without our permission."[33]

Back in the 1970s, Moon—or "Father," as his five to ten thousand U.S. followers call him—used his female church adherents to influence male members of Congress and secretly purchased a D.C. bank for the Korean CIA, actions that resulted in the congressional "Koreagate" hearings of 1978. Bo Hi Pak then accused Congressman Donald Fraser, who headed the hearings, of being a Communist.[34]

In 1982, the year Moon performed a mass wedding ceremony for two thousand randomly chosen couples in Madison Square Garden, he also established the *Washington Times*. The right-wing tilt of the *Times* appealed to President Reagan, who said it was the first paper he read in the morning. Several of its columnists, including Pat Buchanan and Bill

Rusher, soon began appearing on national television. The *Washington Times* was part of a billion-dollar U.S. media investment by the church. Although the *Times*, *Insight* magazine, the *World & I*, and several of Moon's video production and publishing houses lost an estimated $300 million in revenue during the 1980s and 1990s, they also brought him tremendous access to conservative sectors of the U.S. establishment. The creation of the *Times* as a kind of right-wing *Pravda*, along with millions of dollars directed to various New Right causes and individuals such as Terry Dolan and Richard Viguerie, won over most of the nation's conservative critics. By the early 1980s they had stopped calling Moon a cult leader and begun speaking of him as a dedicated anti-Communist.

"Look at the facts. Father is not even a citizen of the United States, yet when he goes to Washington, they say, 'You are the number one conservative leader in this country!'" Moon told his disciples in 1988, referring to himself in the third person.[35]

In 1983 the church set up a U.S. chapter of CAUSA, the Confederation of Associations for the Unification of the Societies of the Americas, which quickly became an active player on behalf of Reagan administration policies in Central America. CAUSA worked closely with Lieutenant Colonel (later radio–talk show personality and failed Senate candidate) Oliver North, providing support to the Contras after Congress cut off aid to the Nicaraguan guerillas. CAUSA also gave $50,000 to General Gustavo Alvarez Martinez, the U.S.-backed strongman in Honduras whose internal security forces established that nation's first death squads. But when Bo Hi Pak arrived on the scene and began advising Alvarez on how to set up his own one-man political party, lower-ranking Honduran officers decided things were getting out of hand and staged a coup.[36] CAUSA's U.S. student arm, CARP, the Collegiate Association for the Research of Principles, also worked with the FBI, spying on and disrupting a Central American protest group. At Southern Methodist University and elsewhere, CARP members threw rocks and got into fistfights with speakers from CISPES, the Committee in Solidarity with the People of El Salvador.[37]

In 1987, following a meeting at the Miami Intercontinental Hotel, the church established the American Freedom Coalition of Bo Hi Pak; Robert Grant, the chairman of Christian Voice, a right-wing fundamentalist lobby; Grant's advisor, Gary Jarman, a loyal ex-Moonie and former activist in the American Conservative Union; Moon-funded conservative leader David Finzer; two executives from the *Washington Times;* and the CEO of a Moon-controlled Washington PR firm.[38] Pak and Jarman conceived the AFC as a fifty-state lobby for right-wing causes that would gradually evolve into a pro-Moon third party. Grant would function as the AFC's presidential figurehead. The church got the AFC going with a $5 million loan and a contribution of seventy full-time staffers.[39] The AFC's first successful effort involved the distribution of *Ollie North: Fight for Freedom,* an hourlong video tribute to the indicted Iran-Contra figure, which aired on some one hundred television stations around the country and raised more than $3.2 million for the organization.[40]

Alan Gottlieb, who knew Jarman through the American Conservative Union, agreed to write a fundraising letter for the AFC's North program. He also agreed to hold one of his fundraising seminars for the group, perhaps hoping to snag it as a client (his friend and competitor Richard Viguerie ended up with the direct-mail contract for both the AFC and the *Washington Times).* Gottlieb and Ron Arnold had earlier met with Bo Hi Pak at the *Washington Times* headquarters building in D.C., not to discuss anti-environmental issues, according to Arnold, but to persuade Moon's lieutenant to let them reprint *Washington Times* columns in Gottlieb's syndicated news service.[41] Ron Arnold was also listed as a speaker with CAUSA during this period.

At its launching in 1987, the AFC broke into several task forces, including one on the environment headed by Merrill Sikorski, a former Alaska state assemblyman and advocate of opening up Alaska's Arctic National Wildlife Refuge (ANWR) to oil development. Arnold and Gottlieb invited Sikorski and the AFC to attend and help sponsor the 1988 Wise Use conference in Reno, incorporating the AFC's proposals for ANWR into the Wise Use agenda and acknowledging them in the Wise Use book for providing "additional funds or in-kind services."[42] Following the Reno conference, the AFC held a number of early Wise Use organizing meetings in the Northwest.

"We organized conferences with local groups in Oregon, Washington, and Idaho, where the CDFE was also active," recalls Merrill Sikorski, who quit the AFC several years ago to return to Kenai, Alaska. He now directs an environmental awareness program in the local high schools sponsored by Unocal. "I started getting disenamored with the AFC because of their focus on the Unification Church," he says. "Their involvement with the church was too overriding. ... The AFC also lacked a strong leader, lacked someone like Jerry Falwell."[43]

When I called and asked about AFC's role in the founding of Wise Use, Robert Grant, still the nominal head of the organization, hung up the phone.[44]

The AFC opened its Washington State office in Alan Gottlieb's Liberty Park office building, sharing space there with a number of other right-wing groups, including Accuracy in Media, which also had extensive links with Moon's network.[45] According to documents on file with the state of Washington,[46] Ron Arnold was AFC chapter president from 1989 to 1991, and Gottlieb was an AFC state director in 1989 and 1990. In a February 1989 cover story written by investigative reporter Walter Hatch, the *Seattle Times* identified Gottlieb as one of six key contacts in a Unification Church–affiliated network in the Northwest that included the AFC, CAUSA, and the American Constitution Committee (which fought to secure a presidential pardon for Sun Myung Moon after he was jailed for tax evasion). The article also detailed how the church functioned as a multinational business/political empire and discussed how in Japan a high-ranking church defector and journalist, Yoshikazu Soejima, was repeatedly stabbed in a near-fatal attack while preparing an exposé on the church. The article reported that in the United States the *Chicago Tribune* had been picketed for referring to church members as "Moonies."

"In Washington State, where the Unification Church is building a local network of conservatives, Moon's allies have threatened more than just a protest," the *Seattle Times* added. "Ron Arnold ... of the Center for the Defense of Free Enterprise, said one of the center's activities is filing lawsuits. 'If you wrote something that was a smear against the Unification Church,' Arnold warned, 'you could count on seeing us in court.'"[47]

"Resource-Use Conference Had Links to Moonie Cult," read the headline of the *Vancouver Sun* that July 8.[48] As first the western media and then the environmental media picked up on the story of the Moonie connection to Wise Use, not only CDFE but also the entire Wise Use movement found itself on the defensive.

When Clark Collins, of the Idaho-based Blue Ribbon Coalition, wrote to the Montana AFL-CIO suggesting an alliance, James Murry, the executive secretary, replied, condemning Wise Use's anti-labor

connections in Idaho along with its newly revealed ties to the Unification Church. When Collins wrote back suggesting that Murry respect
other people's freedom of religion, Murry exploded.

"Your knee-jerk defense of the Moonies because of religious freedom
doesn't wash," he wrote. "The Moonies' religious cult practices have
nothing to do with this issue: the question here is the Moonies' political practices and their hidden political agenda. The Moonies' political
actions are a legitimate concern of every citizen who believes that
America's destiny should be controlled by the American voters, not a
Korean cult leader."[49] The Montana AFL-CIO under Murry and his
successor, Don Judge, soon developed into a center of opposition to
Wise Use activity in the West.

"Wise-Use Promoter Denies Church Ties," the *Idaho Falls Post-
Register* reported a few months later. The article quoted Ron Arnold as
saying that Wise Use was not associated with the Unification Church
but would welcome its support. Gary Glenn, executive vice president
of the Idaho Cattle Association, was not happy with that response. He
made it clear that his group would withdraw from Wise Use if the Unification Church became an open member. "The movement has been
weakened by the perception that it might be involved with Moon," he
explained to the *Post-Register*.[50]

Four years and many Moon articles later, Ron Arnold is still threatening to sue, but no longer on behalf of the Unification Church.

"We've sent notices to these environmental groups that unless you
want to contest it in court, watch the rhetoric," he says. "They're saying we consorted with a known felon [Moon served thirteen months
for federal income tax evasion, four and a half more than Alan Got-
tlieb]. They've toned down their rhetoric and now talk about our al-
leged links with Moon. ... Personally I think there's an element of
religious/racial prejudice on the part of these environmentalists. Like,
'Who is this slanty-eyed gook preacher?' They pick anyone way out in
right field and use them against us. It's a smear and we don't like it.
Why would a religious movement from Asia be interested in environmental issues anyway?"[51]

"Forget that religious stuff. I think the Unification Church is a foreign operation that's got entanglements at the grassroots level involving timber exports to Japan and Korea, oil, and other resources," says
Eric Nadler, the reporter on a PBS *Frontline* documentary titled "The

Resurrection of Reverend Moon." "AFC chapters campaigned heavily for continued logging in the Northwest and Alaska. And unlike their previous political work in Central America, here you have them [Moon] involved in an issue without a Communist in sight, and it seems to boil down to a basic economic issue, with foreign economic interests driving their actions."

Tracing the Moon operation back to its origins, as author Dan Junas of Seattle did, helps to explain how foreign economic interests came to dominate the work of the church. The aging Sun Myung Moon first established his Holy Spirit Association for the Unification of World Christianity in 1954 in a shack made of U.S. Army ration boxes on the outskirts of Seoul, South Korea. After the Korean War, several young military officers, including Bo Hi Pak, converted to his cause. By the late 1950s, the Unification Church had begun overseas missionary work, gaining its largest following in Japan. According to Moon's home-brewed theology, Korea is Adam to Japan's Eve. The two nations are destined to join together to form the true nation to which all must bear allegiance when the Second Coming (of a Korean-born messiah) is affirmed.

In the early 1960s, Moon's followers in Japan became politicized, taking to the streets to fight leftist demonstrators opposed to the U.S.-Japan security treaty and rioting on behalf of Japanese businessmen with close ties to the church. The three most influential of these businessmen were convicted war criminals and Japanese ultranationalists: Yoshio Kodama, a Yakuza (Japanese organized crime) leader; Nobusuke Kishi, a former prime minister; and Ryoichi Sasakawa, who controls Japan's $14 billion–a–year speedboat racing industry and once referred to himself as "the world's wealthiest fascist."

Together they helped establish the World Anti-Communist League, of which CAUSA would eventually become an integral part, and also helped bankroll Moon's expansion into the United States. Among Moon's earliest political activities in America were attempts to counter the peace movement with pro–Vietnam War demonstrations coordinated with Young Americans for Freedom (the group in which Alan Gottlieb got his start) and the Nixon White House. While the U.S. media (and many parents of runaway teens) grew concerned about the mind-control techniques being used by the Unification Church to recruit young Moonies, Moon himself was speaking to his followers about what he considered a far more urgent issue. "America has trouble with Japan regarding the devaluation of the dollar and the yen, and also trade," he told his followers in 1971, "but the United States must hold Japan on its side. America must open the way to aid Korea through Japan. ... We have to put an anchor in America not to withdraw from Asia."[52]

Attempting to understand the multibillion-dollar international business empire that Moon has created in the years since he arrived in the United States could give an IRS auditor an aneurysm. In 1990, *U.S. News & World Report* estimated that at least 335 international companies were affiliated with Moon's church, producing everything from heavy weapons to machine guns, computers, clothing, and soft drinks. In the United States, the church has at least 150 companies involved in media, real estate, and commercial fishing, including boats, canneries, processing, wholesaling, distribution, and sixty-five Japanese sushi restaurants.[53] Much of the fish that the church processes in Alaska is sold to Japan, while its media operations seem more oriented toward influence peddling than bottom-line profit taking. Business analysts who have tried to follow the financial dealings of the church say that its U.S. operations lose money and its Korean operations earn only modest profits. Its major profit center is reported to be Japan, home to Moon's largest flock and to Sekai Nippo (*World Daily News*), Japan's answer to the *Washington Times*.

In 1984 a Japan national bar association report found that church-organized, high-pressure sales schemes had bilked consumers out of $165 million.[54] Ex–church members in Japan say the church's mobile sales force was in fact far more effective at raising funds than the bar association reported, but that the real money came from partnerships and investments with Japanese banks and industry. Two officials at Sekai Nippo told the *Washington Post* that at least $800 million in church-controlled money had been transferred from Japan to the United States between 1975 and 1984.

"If they're using substantial amounts of Japanese money, they're not only running a Korean agenda, but they're also serving as political mercenaries for the Japanese, and it should be a matter of great concern," Pat Chote told the makers of the PBS *Frontline* documentary. Chote is the author of *Agents of Influence*, a book that examines Japan's past attempts to shape U.S. policies.

By the 1980s, Japan, a resource-poor nation, had established what many observers described as a neocolonial trade pattern with the United States, selling America finished products such as cars, TVs, and other electronics and in exchange purchasing raw logs, fish, coal, beef, and oil. A Japanese-owned pulp mill in Sitka, Alaska, had been the main beneficiary of below-cost logging in the Tongass National Forest until late 1993, when it closed. Much of the Tongass's unfinished timber had been exported to Japan and South Korea. In 1988, Alan Gottlieb's Free Enterprise Press published *People of the Tongass,* a 360-page defense of below-cost logging in the Tongass National Forest. At the same time, the Mitsubishi Corporation was the main purchaser of raw logs from Weyerhauser, which later found itself losing market share to finished paper products from Japan. The Japanese were also grazing beef cattle on public lands in Montana and remain the main purchasers of Alaskan fish. The Unification Church owns large fish-processing plants in Washington and Alaska that export to Japan and Korea.

When this book first came out the American Enterprise Institute's magazine published a review titled "Green Whine," which reprised this argument as "Mitsubishi ... Moon ... what's the difference? They've all got slanty eyes, right?" going on to claim that I was promoting "Yellow Peril paranoia." Picking up and expanding on this theme, Republican congressman and Property Rights activist Richard Pombo told a Wise Use gathering that I was so racist I'd identified Moon as Japanese. Today Pombo is chairman of the House Resources Committee.

Still, the Moonies' efforts to help get Wise Use off the ground and their ongoing editorial support through the *Washington Times, Insight,* and other Moon-owned publications seem designed to advance the economic cause of Moon's "true nation" of Korea/Japan. If anti-enviros who have worked with the American Freedom Coalition and other Moon-funded groups on the Right failed to understand this, it just goes to show, as Bo Hi Pak told a meeting of the AFC, "what a great sense of humor God has."

eight

Up Against the Law

The law, in its majestic equality, forbids the rich as well as the poor to sleep under bridges, to beg in the streets and to steal bread.
—Anatole France, 1894

The Constitution does not guarantee that land speculators will win their bets. —Pace University Law Professor John Humbach, 1993

ON JULY 23, 1993, the state of Alaska sued the United States for $29 billion. It was the latest volley in an environmental war launched against the country from "Wally's World," which is what local critics called Alaska under the administration of seventy-five-year-old governor Walter Hickel. In 1990, Hickel was elected candidate of the Alaskan Independence Party, with 39 percent of the vote in a three-way race. With decriminalization of marijuana also on the ballot, it wasn't long before bumper stickers appeared reading "Pot Got More Votes Than Hickel." Aside from his desire to get the feds to open up the Arctic National Wildlife Refuge for oil development and his plan to shoot enough wolves to increase the moose and caribou herds, turning the Alaskan plains into a "hunter's paradise," Hickel proposed building major freeways and rail lines into the wilderness, piping Alaska's water south to California, and putting state funds into a feasibility study on the mining of asteroids.

In its suit, filed with the U.S. Claims Court in Washington, D.C., the state of Alaska argued that the establishment of national parks and wilderness areas in Alaska is a breach of contract and a legal "taking" in that it denies the state revenue. According to its 1959 statehood agreement, Alaska is to receive 90 percent of all revenues from oil, mineral, and gas leasing on federal lands, a multibillion-dollar windfall that has given state residents an annual cash bonus in lieu of paying taxes. But many Alaskans still see themselves as a colony of Washington. They resent the extensive system of parks, wildlife refuges, and wilderness areas established by the federal government, which they accuse of trying to turn Alaska into a "museum." The get-rich-quick frontier mentality of Alaska's older, "territorial" generation found legal expression in State Attorney General Charles Cole's complaint that while national parks and wildlife refuges may attract tourists, they should not be kept off-limits to mining and oil drilling. According to Alaska's legal-takings theory, if the United States insists on protecting "Wild and Scenic" tracts such as Denali National Park by excluding extractive industry, it must compensate the state 90 percent of the value of the oil, gas, and minerals it leaves buried in the earth.[1]

Years later another suit was brought in the U.S. Claims Court by Maritrans, Inc., a barge company, claiming that provisions of the Oil Pollution Act of 1990 (inspired by the *Exxon Valdez* oil spill disaster in Alaska) was an unconstitutional taking because it shortened the economic life of their single-hulled oil barges by requiring them to double-hull for safety. The company demanded a billion dollars in compensation.

Although these particular suits failed, they fall within the bounds of a growing school of anti-environmental legal theory that has gained credence over the past decade, part of a broader judicial backlash against environmental law. Where once Supreme Court Justice William O. Douglas argued that parts of nature and its "environmental wonders" are entitled to be represented in court, today Supreme Court Justices Scalia and Thomas insist that any protection of nature that negatively impacts the dollar value of real estate must be financially compensated by the government.

One of the notable changes in the teaching and practice of law over the last thirty years has been the emergence of environmental law as a major current in the legal mainstream. Almost every law school in America now includes a survey course on the subject, and many schools offer specialized instruction and degrees in it. Lawyers familiar with the nuances of environmental law can be found in most government offices and corporate suites, a development that reflects both the rapid growth of protective environmental legislation and the ongoing legal clashes over how these laws are to be interpreted. Environmental advocacy groups have learned to use lawsuits as effective weapons in their battles to prevent the development of wilderness areas or compel government agencies to enforce anti-pollution laws where industry or the government itself has placed communities at risk. Businesses and corporations have had to hire teams of lawyers to interpret the growing and often contradictory environmental rules and regulations promulgated at every level of government. Polluters and other environmental law-breakers have become the target of "green cops" working out of U.S. attorneys' offices, natural resource agencies, and local jurisdictions. Unlike bank robbers and muggers, however, these criminals have responded to their indictments, fines, and convictions not with feigned contrition but by attacking the laws they've been convicted of violating. During the Reagan administration and the first Bush administration, when Congress refused to gut certain key environmental laws unpopular with industry, the executive branch developed what became known as a "train-wreck strategy" to undermine the laws they didn't like. When 213 counties failed to meet a 1982 Clean Air deadline, the Reagan administration proposed enforcing a never-used provision of the law to ban all new construction of homes and offices in those communities, hoping (in vain, it turned out) to provoke an anti–Clean Air Act backlash.[2] Refusal by the EPA, Department of Interior, and other agencies to enforce laws governing toxic cleanup, clean water, wilderness protection, and the Endangered Species Act seemed designed to provoke environmentalist lawsuits, forcing stringent court rulings that left no room for compromise or conciliation. Administration spokespeople and their conservative backers would then point to "judicial gridlock" as proof that environmental laws didn't work.

Almost all sides in the northwest timber wars agree that by using this kind of intentional inaction, the first Bush administration pushed the spotted owl controversy into the courts, which resulted in rapid closure of U.S. national forest lands to logging and left long-term economic and ecology issues unresolved. In 1993 the Clinton administration announced its own "Option Nine" northwest forest plan, which, although disliked by all sides, was nonetheless seen as a step away from use of the courts as a tool of political sabotage by the government.

Under the administration of George Bush Jr. the Justice Department and other government agencies invited lawsuits by industries challenging environmental policies in order to reach out-of-court settlements favorable to those industries. For example, when a timber company won a decision by a judge in Idaho that would have opened vast federally protected roadless areas to logging, John Ashcroft's Justice Department refused to appeal the decision, instead opening discussions on how to implement the wilderness logging scheme. At the same time, the administration took bureaucratic measures to expand on these settlements. One example was a very narrow legal interpretation of the 1964 Wilderness Act by Gale Norton's Department of Interior. Having settled a suit with the state of Utah, agreeing not to designate 2.6 million acres of federal land as wilderness, the DOI went on to announce (on a Friday evening when it was least likely to be picked up by the media) that there would be no new wilderness designations on over 250 million acres of public lands.

Moving beyond the government's ability to create legal train wrecks or promulgate inside deals, some corporations and developers discovered that they could use the law as a tool of intimidation, going after their opponents with what came to be known as SLAPPs—Strategic Lawsuits Against Public Participation.

In West Virginia the DLM Coal Corporation filed a multimillion-dollar libel action against Rick Webb and his small nonprofit environmental group after they requested an EPA hearing on pollution of local rivers by mine runoff and wrote an editorial in their newsletter criticizing strip mining.

In Squaw Valley, California, stunt skier Rick Sylvester was slapped with a $75 million lawsuit for speaking out and writing letters to the editor against a planned development.

In Louisville, Colorado, a developer sued local activist Betty Johnson for unlimited damages after she organized a petition drive for a growth moratorium. According to a survey in Florida, 15 percent of all growth-management advocates in that state have been the target of SLAPP suits.

In Alaska the Shee Atika timber company sued the Sierra Club for $40 million when the Sierra Club took up the cause of Alaskan natives who wanted to keep logging off their traditional hunting grounds.

ACCORDING TO PENELOPE CANAN and George Pring, the two University of Denver professors who first coined the term, SLAPPs are used by corporations and developers to silence public opposition by dragging people into court with spurious suits. The goal is not to win settlements but to intimidate critics and create a "chilling atmosphere" designed to discourage other would-be citizen activists.[3] Of the hundreds of SLAPPs being filed every year, Professor Canan reports, about 60 percent are directed against people and groups protesting unchecked growth and other environmental abuses. "Right now we're seeing a rapid increase of cases involving landfills and toxic waste sites," she says, citing examples in Fort Worth, Texas, and Terre Haute, Indiana.[4]

"As a tactic it's designed to make environmentalists get scared and go away," says Joe Brecher, a private attorney who worked with the Sierra Club Legal Defense Fund (now Earthjustice). "It targets local ad hoc neighborhood groups, people who don't expect to be sued for speaking their mind. I've had a few cases where it's worked, where the clients couldn't stand the heat and got out."[5]

Victor Monia, a SLAPP victim in a suit involving a California citizens' group who had won a one-year moratorium on hillside development, described how, after a developer sued them for $40 million, "people melted away ... people who had been very active just sort of disappeared."[6]

Although 83 percent of SLAPPs are dismissed before they reach trial, they can still cost defendants tens of thousands of dollars in legal expenses and tremendous amounts of personal time and energy.

Rick Sylvester compared the impact of a SLAPP to "having a monster move in with your family." Another SLAPP victim described how "I became so preoccupied by the suit that it changed my whole focus and direction in life. This case was an overhanging cloud. Even though you may prevail, you'll spend a ton of money fighting it. You can win and still lose."

The SLAPP that probably deserves top honors for pure chutzpah was filed not against an environmentalist but against Vietnam veteran and antiwar activist Brian Wilson. Wilson, protesting arms shipments to Central America in 1987, sat down on a railroad track to blockade an ammunition train at the Concord Naval Weapons Station in suburban Concord, California. He expected to be arrested for civil disobedience. Instead he was run over by the train when it failed to slow down and he was unable to scramble out of its way in time. He lost both legs and had part of his skull crushed in. Before he'd even been fitted for artificial legs, he was sued by the military train's engineer, brakeman, and conductor. They claimed he inflicted great emotional stress and trauma on them.

In recent years several SLAPP victims, including Rick Sylvester, the Squaw Valley skier, have fought back with countersuits for civil rights violations and malicious prosecution. As early as 1991, a Missouri woman won an $86.5 million settlement against a waste-incinerator corporation that had sued her for criticizing them.

Despite these "slapp-backs" and legislative efforts in several other states to discourage SLAPPs through early judicial review and recovery of attorneys' fees, many polluters and developers continue to find it easier to use the court system as a weapon of intimidation than to try making their cases with the public. Still, SLAPPs are by nature reactive and involve a certain level of risk in terms of both public relations and the possibility of countersuits against plaintiffs. Today's Property Rights advocates, working through a network of right-wing nonprofit law firms and legislative think tanks, have hit upon a more proactive legal strategy. They are pushing for a radical reinterpretation of the Fifth Amendment "takings" clause that they hope will lead to the effective dismantling of environmental legislation and ultimately to the Holy Grail of conservative wish fulfillment: a rollback of the regulatory state (including unemployment insurance, Social Security, and the like) established during Franklin Delano Roosevelt's New Deal.

Most people are familiar with the First Amendment of the Bill of Rights, which guarantees freedom of speech and assembly, religion, and a free press. They also know about the Second Amendment, which reads, "A well-regulated militia being necessary to the security of a free state, the right of the people to keep and bear arms shall not be infringed." And many people know of the Fifth Amendment—but only that clause heard regularly on TV court dramas and in congressional hearings—which protects a defendant against self-incrimination. However, the Fifth Amendment also states, "No person shall be ... deprived of life, liberty, or property without due process of law; nor shall private property be taken for public use, without just compensation."

Today, when the government condemns private land to build an interstate highway or a Texas ballpark (as was done when George Bush Jr. was part owner of the Texas Rangers), the Fifth Amendment guarantees that the displaced landowner be paid market value for his or her lost property. In 1887, Kansas brewer Peter Mugler argued the first case for a "regulatory taking," claiming that a prohibition law passed in his state meant he had been denied his property rights under the Fifth Amendment, because his brewery had lost its value. The Supreme Court ruled against him, stating that "a government can prevent a property owner from using his property to injure others without having to compensate the owner for the value of the forbidden use." This "nuisance clause" has enabled governments to establish health and safety regulations, labor codes, and environmental protections that limit what an individual owner can do with his or her property without having to pay that owner compensation.

In 1926, in a case titled *Village of Euclid v. Ambler Realty,* the Supreme Court confirmed that zoning ordinances, which establish agreed-upon beneficial land uses for a community, are another form of legitimate government restriction on property that does not constitute a taking.

These precedents, which recognize that democratically determined social values may limit the unrestricted use of private property—so that, for example, a riverfront property owner might not be allowed to dump manure upstream from his or her neighbor's property—would not be seriously challenged for the next sixty years. The institutional forces that would launch this next major challenge began taking shape in the 1970s.

———————

IN 1971 THE U.S. Chamber of Commerce hired attorney and future Supreme Court Justice Lewis Powell to advise it on how to counter environmental and consumer activists. He recommended the formation of a business-sponsored legal center that would not hesitate to "attack the [Ralph] Naders ... and others who openly seek destruction of the system."[7]

In 1973 the Pacific Legal Foundation, the first of a chain of business-sponsored "public interest" law firms, was established in Sacramento, California. According to an early profile in *Barron's* magazine, PLF's founding mission was to "stem the rampage" of environmentalists and welfare advocates. Its earliest cases included the defense of DDT spraying in national forests and legal challenges to Environmental Impact

Reports. The PLF has gone after antinuclear activists, rent-control advocates, affirmative-action programs, and more recently the slow-growth initiative process, arguing in the latter context that "growth can bring about complex and varied land-use problems that must be carefully addressed. But resorting to the ballot box for solutions is not appropriate."[8]

Two years after the inception of the PLF, the National Legal Center for the Public Interest was founded to assist in the creation of additional pro-business nonprofit law firms. Since then at least twenty-two of these "free enterprise" law firms have appeared, including James Watt's Mountain States Legal Foundation (MSLF), the New England Legal Foundation, and the Washington Legal Foundation.[9] Every year the Heritage Foundation holds a conference at which the directors of these firms come together and strategize. Although all the firms share a common conservative free market philosophy, PLF and MSLF have been at the forefront of the anti-environmental movement. MSLF (where Secretary of Interior Gale Norton also got her start) billed itself as the litigation arm of Wise Use.

Free legal services to anti-enviro groups don't come cheaply. The pro-business nonprofits are funded by tens of millions of dollars from right-wing foundations, including Coors, Olin, Scaife and Bradley, and major corporations including Exxon, Ford, Union Carbide, Georgia-Pacific, and Phillips Petroleum.

In 1984 the *Yale Law Journal* dedicated most of an issue to an analysis of the pro-business law firms by Tulane law professor Oliver Houck, who wondered whether they rightfully qualified for 501(c)(3) nonprofit status as "public interest" charities. He examined two IRS requirements: their cases could not be substantially directed to insiders, and they could not be "economically feasible" for the private bar.[10] Houck found that 70 out of 132 cases filed by the PLF were invalid by the terms of the IRS requirements and another 16 were questionable. "In questions bearing upon nuclear power and the regulation of utilities, PLF's ties to the benefited corporations were remarkably close," the report noted.[11]

"In at least twenty-four cases on the docket, the position MSLF was advocating directly benefited corporations represented on its board of directors, clients of firms represented on its board of litigation, or major contributors to MSLF's budget,"[12] noted Houck. The report detailed how the law firms provided insider profits to their sponsors while pursuing causes whose beneficiaries—including oil companies, utilities, and mining corporations—could just as easily have hired private attorneys.

Applying the IRS criteria, Professor Houck found that the work of the pro-business nonprofits "stretches the concepts of charity and public interest practice beyond meaningful definition." The *Yale Law Journal* report produced many raised eyebrows in the legal community but no discernible action by the IRS under President Reagan.

In the early 1980s the Federalist Society, a conservative legal forum, began to establish itself at various law schools around the country as a counter to the left-of-center National Lawyers Guild. "We had all these professors influenced by the New Deal saying everything was supposed to be an improvement since Roosevelt packed the court [*sic*], that property and economic rights were somehow lesser than social rights," recalls Jim Burling, a takings expert working out of the PLF's Sacramento office. "We were being told that Chief Justice Rehnquist's rulings were some kind of reactionary throwback to a retrograde era before FDR. I wasn't aware there was an influential alternative intellectual tradition in conservatism until groups like the Federalist Society got going."[13]

In December 2000, Chief Justice Rehnquist, in what many Democrats considered a "reactionary throwback," helped select George Walker Bush as president in a 5–4 Supreme Court vote that ended a controversial election recount in Florida. Today President Bush's solicitor general, secretary of energy, and secretary of Interior are all leading members of the Federalist Society while his attorney general, John Ashcroft, is a close affiliate. Bush has rejected the tradition (going back to Republican president Dwight Eisenhower) of having the American Bar Association advise on judicial nominees and instead turned to the Federalist Society to help vet them. About half the people he has nominated as federal judges are out of the ranks of the Federalist Society (whose membership includes less than 1 percent of the nation's lawyers).

A stronghold of the Federalist Society in the 1980s was the University of Chicago, also home to Milton Friedman's "Chicago School" of economics and the revisionist "law and economics movement" that looks at the law in terms of economic costs and benefits rather than "abstract" concepts of right and wrong.

While Friedman's free-market economic theories would be the major contribution of this university to the Reagan revolution, Richard Epstein, a professor at the law school, was also destined to play a role with the publication of his 1985 book, *Takings: Private Property and the Power of Eminent Domain*.[14] There he argued that under the Fifth Amendment the government must pay property owners whenever environmental regulations, health and safety rules, or zoning laws limit the value of their property. He went on to suggest that even income taxes could be seen as a form of takings. The same year Epstein's book appeared, President Reagan appointed Loren Smith chief judge of the U.S. Claims Court, a relatively obscure judicial backwater where cases involving government contracts, patents, Indian claims, and federal pay disputes are settled. Smith, a veteran of the Nixon Watergate legal defense team and a Reagan campaign attorney, numbers among his heroes conservative scholars Robert Bork and Richard Epstein.[15]

That Epstein's interpretation of the Fifth Amendment was also being read by higher-ranking officials in Washington is confirmed by Charles Fried, U.S. solicitor general from 1985 to 1989. In his 1991 book, *Order and Law: Arguing the Reagan Revolution*, Fried wrote, "Attorney General [Ed] Meese and his young advisors—many drawn from the ranks of the then fledgling Federalist Society and often devotees of the extreme libertarian views of Chicago Law Professor Richard Epstein— had a specific, aggressive, and, it seemed to me, quite radical project in mind: to use the takings clause of the Fifth Amendment as a severe brake upon federal and state regulation of business and property."[16]

"I'm glad to see Charles nailed it right on the head in seeing where we want to go with this compensation clause," says Nancie Marzulla, president of the Washington, D.C.–based Defenders of Property Rights, which she founded with her husband Roger.[17] In the mid-1980s, Roger Marzulla was assistant attorney general under Ed Meese and Nancie an attorney in the Justice Department's much-criticized civil rights division. Toward the end of the Reagan administration, Roger Marzulla directed Mark Pollot, his special assistant on land and natural resources, to draft Executive Order 12630, which President Reagan signed on March 15, 1988. The presidential order, which followed Epstein's radical theories rather than existing case law, required government agencies to evaluate the private property takings implications of any regulatory actions they conducted.[18]

While the courts had not yet accepted this type of "regulatory takings" argument, they were becoming more open to a politicized, or "activist," approach to the law as Ronald Reagan and George Bush Sr. filled the courts with growing numbers of conservative federal judges—including Supreme Court Justices Antonin Scalia and Clarence Thomas, the most ideological of the "Supremes."

"You always know how Scalia will vote," I was told by a lawyer who has argued in front of the Supreme Court. "You just don't know how he'll justify it in terms of the constitution."

By the 1990s, 60 percent of all federal judges had been appointed during the Reagan/Bush years, including all sixteen judges on the U.S. Claims Court (later renamed the U.S. Court of Federal Claims).[19] During his eight years in office, Bill Clinton appointed some moderate judges (along with at least one conservative) but didn't invest any of his considerable political capital to nominate liberal candidates who might have promoted a more expansive vision of the Constitution like William O. Douglas or Louis Brandeis.

Two things lawyers familiar with the Court of Claims tend to agree on are that it conforms to the conservative "ideological litmus test," which became a standard part of the judicial selection process during the 1980s (and again in 2001–2004), and that its former chief judge Loren Smith, who still sits on the court, puts on a swell magic show. Whether performing for the Federalist Society, the libertarian CATO Institute, or a PLF conference in Seattle, the stocky, cigar-chomping jurist, with his full beard and waxed mustache, seems to relish center stage. He's shocked attorneys with his spring-loaded gavel trick, tied up bureaucrats with fancy rope tricks, and illustrated the bankruptcy of his opposition with a bag that keeps changing colors every time he turns it inside out. "Some people think I'm doing a good job as chief judge," he told a Federalist Society meeting in Washington, D.C., in the early 1990s, pulling a wad of cash out of his pocket. "But my critics think all I've done is this," he smiled before lighting the fake money with a match, holding the blazing flash paper aloft as if it were Lady Liberty's torch.

"His sleight-of-hand isn't limited to parlor games," reported the *Legal Times*. "A few listeners ... concluded that in his takings rulings, Smith is more than capable of pulling questionable interpretations of the law out of his hat or making precedents vanish."[20]

Following the philosophical lead of Professor Epstein (whose next book argued that civil rights legislation is a breach of contract law), Judge Smith has ruled favorably on a surprising number of regulatory takings claims. In *Loveladies Harbor v. United States,* he ruled that denial of a permit to a New Jersey developer seeking to fill tidal wetlands for luxury home sites was a taking, and awarded the company $2.7 million. In *Florida Rock Industries, Inc., v. United States,* he supported the takings claim of a company that wanted to quarry limestone in a wetlands area, awarding it a million dollars after its mining permit request was turned down under the Clean Water Act. And in *Whitney Benefits, Inc., v. United States,* he awarded $150 million to a coal-mining company prevented from mining private lands in the Powder River area of Wyoming. Ironically, one of the strongest advocates for property rights, the National Cattlemen's Association, had favored federal protection of surface (grazing) lands from mine-company abuses.

On July 9, 2003, Smith gained a soulmate when the Senate voted 54–43 to confirm Victor Wolski to a seat on the Court of Federal Claims. Wolski is a veteran of the PLF—a fact disguised in his Justice Department bio, which reads that he worked at "a California based non-profit law foundation that represents clients pro bono"—kind of like Rural Legal Assistance—only for Agribiz. A longtime Property Rights advocate and self-described "libertarian ideologue," he has bragged, "Every single job I've taken since college has been ideologically oriented, trying to further my principles." It would seem a good argument for an applicant to the Republican National Committee. The Senate decided it also qualified him for the bench.

While the Court of Claims property rights cases have mostly been reversed by the U.S. Court of Appeals, the possibility of winning a "regulatory taking" in this court has set off a decade-long flood of property rights litigation, as have a couple of Supreme Court decisions.

In 1986, developer David Lucas bought two lots on a barrier island off the coast of South Carolina for $1 million. In 1988 the state passed the Beachfront Management Act, designed to curb development in ecologically sensitive (and storm-threatened) areas. Lucas, prevented from building on his lots, claimed he'd suffered a total loss on the value of his land and sued for compensation. Lucas won in trial but it was reversed by the state supreme court, which ruled that the state had "legitimate police power" in protecting public safety in the storm zone (Lucas's lots had been at least partially underwater 50 percent of the time since 1949).[21] He and his lawyer then petitioned for a hearing before the U.S. Supreme Court, which was granted during the 1991–1992 court session.

Although the Property Rights movement that rallied to Lucas's cause portrays itself as representing small homeowners confronted by "land-grabbing" government bureaucracies, a review of some of the briefs filed in support of the *Lucas* case suggests who is most likely to bene-fit from court decisions that recognize this type of regulatory taking. Among the sixteen groups filing amicus curiae briefs were the PLF, MSLF, American Farm Bureau Federation, National Cattlemen's Association, National Association of Homebuilders, International Council of Shopping Centers, Land Improvement Contractors Association, American Mining Congress, National Coal Association, National Forest Products Association, and U.S. Chamber of Commerce.

Among the briefs in support of South Carolina's right to regulate beach development were those from the Chesapeake Bay Foundation, Coast Alliance, Audubon Society, U.S. Council of Mayors, Council of State Governments, twenty-six states, Guam, and Puerto Rico.[22]

In a split decision on the last day of the Supreme Court's calendar year (a day on which the Court also had to decide on an anti-abortion challenge to *Roe v. Wade*), the justices filed a five-vote bare majority opinion in favor of Lucas. Antonin Scalia, the Court's leading ideologue, wrote the majority opinion, which argued that since Lucas had suffered a total loss of value, and since building on the island was not prohibited prior to when he purchased his land, the case should be remanded to South Carolina for a financial settlement. In a footnote, Scalia also indicated the Court's willingness to consider future cases involving a partial loss of value due to regulation.

While the *Lucas* finding was too narrow to have much application in other cases, Property Rights advocates were hopeful that the Court's conservative majority would soon agree to expand the definition of regulatory takings to include a partial loss of value. This in turn could open the way to massive compensation claims against the government and the subsequent unraveling of most environmental regulations. However, in June 1993 the Court upheld a lower court ruling in a case known as *Concrete Pipe* that rejected a partial takings claim under the Fifth Amendment. Since then, the Court has refused to review additional takings cases.

Takings also became a hot issue for debate within the country's law schools and legal journals. In 1990, MSLF Property Rights advocate and future Secretary of Interior Gale Norton argued for a major shift in takings jurisprudence in the *Harvard Journal of Law and Public Policy*, suggesting, "we might even go so far as to recognize a homesteading right to pollute or to make noise in an area. This approach would eliminate some of the theoretical problems with defining a nuisance." Over the following years both the Stanford and the University of Vermont law reviews printed symposium and law conference papers on the subject.[23]

"The intellectual impact of *Lucas* is greater than its practical impact," claims John Echeverria, a gray-eyed, casually confident attorney and takings expert at Georgetown University who formerly worked at the Audubon Society. "The question is, is *Lucas* the foundation for rewriting the Fifth Amendment or only an oddity? At this point I'd have to say it's pretty much of an oddity."[24]

Wise Use advocates in the West seem to agree. Says Ron Arnold of the Center for the Defense of Free Enterprise, "I advised the Pacific Legal Foundation not to go with the *Lucas* case, because he's a developer building homes for rich people and won't get much public sympathy. Wayne Hage is different. He's a family man, a cowboy, and a rancher—all these great images. We've been doing his direct-mail fundraising and getting a great rate of return. We've rallied actors to his cause—Hollywood actors like Sam Elliott in Carmel Valley. Michael Martin Murphy, the country-western singer, has done a benefit concert. We've gotten piles of media."

If the *Lucas* case was an oddity, ex-rancher Wayne Hage's takings claim is more frontier theater than jurisprudence, even if it did get argued in front of Judge Loren Smith, with his magical realism approach to the law.

Represented by Mark Pollot, author of Reagan Executive Order 12630, Hage sued the U.S. Forest Service for $28.4 million, claiming that when they reduced the number of cattle he was permitted to graze on his 240,000-acre allotment in the Toiyabe National Forest, they took his property from him. Actually, *permitted* is too polite a term for the running battle Hage and the Forest Service conducted over several years across the desiccated rangelands of southern Nevada. In the summer of 1991, armed Forest Service employees rounded up seventy-three of Hage's cows after he refused to move them from an area they said he'd overgrazed and damaged. Rather than reclaim his cows by paying the cost of the roundup, Hage decided to sell the rest of his two thousand head of cattle, claiming that he could no longer run a profitable enterprise because of Forest Service harassment.[25] He then filed suit, claiming a regulatory taking. Historically, the courts have ruled that a permit to graze, log, or otherwise operate commercially on public lands is a revocable license, like a driver's license, a privilege and not a property right.

Hage argued that the government's restriction of his grazing permits constituted a taking because of the "preexisting" property rights of early white settlers, a claim he expostulates in angry, numbing detail in his book *Storm over Rangeland,* published by CDFE's Free Enterprise Press.[26] Arizona State University law professor Joe Feller, one of the country's top experts on public lands law, uses Hage's book as a teaching tool for his students, letting them write papers dissecting the "legal nonsense" he says it contains.[27]

Hage's battle did gain the eye of at least one sympathetic politician, Idaho three-term congressman (she refused to be referred to as a congresswoman) Helen Chenoweth, a pro–Property Rights, pro-militia opponent of the Endangered Species Act whom he married in 1999. By early 2002 even Judge Loren Smith felt compelled to rule that Hage's grazing allotment did not constitute private property, a hard bit of cud to swallow for Wise Use's poster cowboy.

One of the more imaginative claims in Hage's suit argued that the introduction of elk into Nevada's Toiyabe National Forest constituted a taking, because the wild elk eat grass and drink from watering holes that his cows might otherwise have used. This claim convinced Nevada attorney general Frankie Sue Del Papa, whose state Department of Wildlife had first introduced the elk, to join the suit on the side of the Forest Service. When she hired an attorney from the National Wildlife Federation to represent Nevada, a mini-brouhaha exploded among the state's Wise Use advocates. The cattlemen and Farm Bureau attacked her as a preservationist while she countered that the state had a legitimate interest in preventing rulings favoring "permittees who abuse the land."[28] In a separate case, Wayne Hage was tried and convicted in Las

Vegas on charges of cutting down and removing mature piñon and
juniper trees from the public lands where he'd held his grazing permits,
a felony conviction he appealed.

"You can ask, is ranching a legitimate use of public lands, which is
what this argument is really about, but that's a political, not a legal,
issue," argues John Echeverria. The environmental lawyer recalls reaching a similar conclusion at a conference on property rights he once attended. "When I got there I said, 'The first thing people need to agree
on is what the Fifth Amendment really means,' and this farmer replied
that he didn't care what it meant; if a government regulation hurt his
value he'd oppose it. I think property rights is really part of a broader
focus on rights that's taking place in our society today: people talk
about their right to live, their right to die, their right to privacy. It's not
being balanced with a sense of responsibilities to society. Unless you
act with some sense of responsibility to your neighbors, any possibility of maintaining community is destroyed, and that's what I see happening in America today."

While attempts to redefine the meaning of the Fifth Amendment
through the courts seem to have reached their limit, legislative efforts
continue at both the state and federal levels. In 1990, then Senator Steve
Symms of Idaho sponsored a bill that would have codified into law
Reagan Executive Order 12630, requiring the attorney general to cer-
tify that all government regulations were in compliance with private
property rights as defined by Professor Epstein.

The Symms proposal was originally rejected by the Senate. In 1991,
attached as a rider to the surface-transportation bill, it passed the Senate and was killed in conference with the House. The next year it again
passed the Senate as a rider to a bill proposing that the EPA be raised
to cabinet rank, a bill that failed to go anywhere. Before Symms left the
Senate in 1992, he asked Senate Republican leader (and 1996 Republican presidential candidate) Bob Dole of Kansas to act as sponsor for future takings bills, which Dole agreed to do.

"It's an important issue, private property," explained former Dole
staffer James "Witt" Wittinghill, who oversaw the bill for the senator.[29]
"This legislation says you can't put blinders on and charge ahead denying people use of their property for the environment or any other cause."

The legislation, S. 177, cosponsored on the House side by conservative Democrat Gary Condit of California (who would later lose his seat

following the disappearance/murder of his intern/girlfriend Chandra Levy), didn't appear to be making any progress during the 1993–1994 congressional session. "We'll go ahead with it when we think we have fifty-one votes," Wittinghill smiled coolly, crossing his legs and freeing his black cowboy boots from the pants cuffs of his black, chalk-striped suit. "It won't survive as stand-alone legislation, but we could always add it to an appropriations bill. Senator Dole has long supported cabinet rank for the EPA, provided it went through as a clean bill. So although many people were encouraging us to again add this as a rider, it wouldn't have made sense in terms of the senator's position that this should be a clean bill."

"Dole was going to offer it on the EPA cabinet level proposal but backed off when he saw he didn't have the votes," countered Bill Klinefelter, the legislative director of the AFL-CIO's Industrial Union Department. "If they thought it had any chance of passage they would have pushed it. We successfully beat back this last takings attempt with better education in the Senate. We demonstrated that takings is far broader (in its implications) than it was being portrayed," the pugnacious union man claimed. "It wasn't just about wetlands. It's really aimed at all regulation, and could be used to attack OSHA as easily as environmental regulations. Plus, it would set up its own regime, an antiregulatory bureaucracy."[30]

Klinefelter lobbied the senators as part of an environmental/labor/consumer coalition that included the steelworkers, National Wildlife Federation, and Consumers Union, a progressive convergence that wouldn't be seen again until the anti–World Trade Organization free trade protests of 1999. "We also got letters supporting our position from Attorney General Janet Reno and other members of the Clinton administration. I'd say that for the time being, at the federal level, we've beat this thing down." He smiles firmly.

A series of takings proposals returned to Congress the next year, beginning with the Newt Gingrich–inspired Republican takeover of the House in 1994. In statehouses across America, from New York to California, the number of takings bills also expanded and diversified. Two versions of takings bills have been introduced in most of the states. The first type is the assessment bill, based on the Reagan order requiring state agencies to set up reviews of the regulatory takings implications for virtually all government actions.

234 The War Against the Greens

The more radical type is the compensation bill developed by Mark Pollot for the American Legislative Exchange Council (ALEC) and based on a bill first introduced in Vermont by Republican state senator McLaughery. This version would automatically pay compensation to any property owner whose property value declines 40–50 percent or more as the result of a government rule, regulation, or program.[31]

"The best I know, this is 100 percent grassroots activity by all kinds of people that have property interests," says John J. Rademacher, general counsel for the American Farm Bureau Federation (AFBF), the multibillion-dollar, not-for-profit insurance company and farm-advocacy organization. The AFBF—which lists support of regulatory compensation payments as one of its 168 policy positions, along with opposition to "one world government," U.S. withdrawal from the World Court, abolition of most civil rights legislation, and revision of the Child Labor Act for Agriculture—has been one of the primary forces behind the introduction of statehouse takings bills.[32]

"The Farm Bureau was very active in getting these bills introduced in Arizona and Utah [where they passed]. If you ask most politicians at the state level, they'll tell you that the Farm Bureau is behind them," brags Andy Neal, chief lobbyist (or research analyst, as he prefers to be called) for the California Farm Bureau Federation.[33] *Forbes* magazine also credits "the Farm Bureau's lobbying clout" for whatever success takings bills have had to date. Still, some critics worry that the Farm Bureau's lobbying on this issue may have a long-term negative impact on agriculture.

"'Takings law' to limit the power of government may result in environmental anarchy," warned Drake University Law School professor Neil Hamilton at a Soil and Water Conservation meeting in Kansas City also attended by Farm Bureau president Dean Kleckner. "If the farm community stakes its response to public desires for environmental protection on an extremist position which in essence says, 'If the public wants me to protect the environment on my land then pay me,' ... farmers may risk a political and social backlash which may cause the public and lawmakers to re-examine support [subsidies] for agriculture."[34]

Aside from the Farm Bureau and other anti-wetlands lobbies, such as the Homebuilders Association and International Association of Shopping Centers, takings has become a legislative centerpiece for ALEC, a think tank made up of 2,500 conservative state legislators and long based in the Heritage Foundation building in Washington, D.C.

In 1990, *Detroit News* columnist Warren Brookes warned ALEC's annual convention in Boston that "if the flat-earth environmentalism that now dominates the U.S. Congress and the [first] Bush Administration ... continues to be enacted at its present pace, nothing less than the future of the American dream and freedom itself are on the line."[35]

Since then, ALEC has pushed compensatory takings bills as part of an anti-enviro legislative package along with "no net loss of private property" bills, which would require states establishing new parks to sell off their old parks. ALEC is also lobbying for "greater than" bills, which would prevent states from passing any environmental regulations tougher than already established federal standards.

"ALEC is a little more big business oriented than we are," confesses John Shanahan, environmental analyst with the Heritage Foundation. This is like a Roman Catholic cardinal calling the Orthodox Church "a little more godly." At least 350 corporations contribute a minimum of $5,000 each to work with ALEC and have access to its legislator members. They also provide recreational opportunities for these elected officials. One ALEC convention included a skeet shoot sponsored by the NRA, a golf tournament by R. J. Reynolds, a tennis match by Philip Morris, and a hospitality suite by the Distilled Spirits Council.[36]

By the mid-1990s, four states had passed ALEC and Farm Bureau–sponsored takings bills: Arizona, Delaware, Washington, and Utah. Twenty-nine other states had defeated or failed to act on the bills. With a tight economy and strapped budgets, many states rejected the bills because of their potential cost. In Maryland the state treasurer estimated takings assessments would cost $10,000 for every commercial property studied. The New Mexico Fish and Game Department figured it would need $1.5 million a year to review its own actions. In Utah the Cowboy Caucus was allowed to claim a Property Rights victory, and the governor signed a takings bill only after a "black-widow" provision was added exempting every state agency from having to file reports. Arizona, which passed its takings bill in 1992, delayed implementation after opponents collected more than 71,000 signatures to put it up for a referendum vote in 1994 (in which it was defeated). In Wyoming, a conservative ranching and oil state, a takings bill was defeated after the only witnesses to testify in its favor were lobbyists from the Farm Bureau and Mining Association.

Opposition to takings bills also grew as environmentalists began linking up with organized labor and consumer groups. Both the AFL-CIO and the National Governors Association have adopted policies against takings. "After receiving a call from environmentalists, we called our people in Wyoming to help defeat it out there," says the AFL-CIO's Bill Klinefelter. "This is radical stuff and in some ways almost ridiculous, but it'll be with us for a long time because it's a good organizing tool for the other side," he says. "Takings has become the visible symbol of Wise Use."[37]

"It is important to recognize the property rights movement is laden with individuals and organizations whose larger goal is promoting a conservative political agenda to limit the power of government," adds Drake University's Professor Hamilton. "The 'property rights' debate is not just a question of constitutional law but a clash of political ideology over the direction of national resource protection policy."[38]

"Government does and has done and always will do scores and scores of things that affect people's property positively and negatively. Government can't function without doing that," says Jonathan Lash, an attorney and president of the World Resources Institute. "Everyone agrees that part of the legitimate role of government is to regulate and adjust relationships among members of society who don't have equal power in society, and you can't do that without affecting wealth. So when you build a new school, when you build sewers, when you build roads or fail to build roads, you affect property. If you regulate industrial pollution, you affect someone's property, and if you don't regulate it you affect other people's property. So the simplistic formulation that government is using environmental regulations in a way that deprives people of their property rights simply ignores the full range of what is going on in the world."[39]

For anti-enviro radicals and the many industrial hard-liners who support them, that may sound like so much liberal obfuscation. They know who their enemies are and, with their moral absolutism, believe that if the legal system doesn't meet their needs, they have the right to defend their property by any other means necessary. As Helen Chenoweth-Hage said to a Wise Use rally in 2001, "Well, we're in a war, aren't we folks?"

The Green P.I.

THE PRIVATE INVESTIGATOR stood by the rubble and ash pile in the
wooded clearing eight miles outside of the old resort town of Eureka
Springs, deep in the Ozark Mountains of Arkansas. The dank smell of
charcoal still permeated the humid air a month after the flames had con-
sumed Pat Costner's cedar-shake home of seventeen years. Costner, a
small-framed country woman with dark hair pulled back in a bun, tried
to describe the layout of the three-bedroom house that she'd built herself, now reduced to a cracked cinderblock base surrounded by a grove
of singed walnut trees. A dozen chickens wandered through the ash,
leaving gray claw-prints behind them. The arson team the detective had
hired out of Tennessee had proved its worth. After lifting up the building's collapsed tin roof, which the local fire inspector hadn't bothered
with, they'd discovered the metal fuel can used to torch the building.
But even before locating the can, they had known the fire had been deliberately set. The average house fire will not exceed 500 degrees
Fahrenheit at floor level or 1,800 degrees at ceiling level. But in the left
front corner of Costner's house they'd found melted bedsprings, indicating temperatures exceeding 2,700 degrees F and in the office area the
aluminum bases of two chairs had melted down into a puddle, indicating floor-level heat of at least 1,300 degrees F. These extreme temperatures could only have been generated by a flammable liquid or other

accelerant. The arson investigators collected debris from different parts of the house in four one-gallon cans and sent them to a private forensics lab in Hendersonville, Tennessee, for analysis. Using gas chromatography and mass spectrometry, the lab determined that the debris in two of the cans contained "components identifiable as evaporated gasoline." These samples included ash and charcoal taken from the office/library where Pat Costner, Greenpeace USA's director of toxics research, had kept her critical files, records, and reports.[1]

Reluctantly, Pat approached the private investigator to find out what had come of five days of follow-up interviews in and around town.

"It looks like there was a man asking about you just before Christmas. He returned with another man after New Year's. They were stocky, white guys. People described them as kind of thuggish. A night watchman overheard them talking about having trained at Quantico [a Virginia Marine base that also houses the FBI's training academy]. They wanted to know where you lived but no one at the bar and restaurant where they had dinner would tell them anything." The P.I. paused, waiting. Pat shook her head in bewilderment. Then she said, "I remember someone calling saying they thought it was the FBI asking for me, and I just didn't think anything else about it at the time. I figured they knew where I was if they had anything to ask me."

The P.I. nodded, not surprised. Eureka Springs was the kind of place where people left their doors unlocked when they went out at night and told their kids to be polite to strangers. There was a moment of awkward silence broken only by the monotonous two-note refrain of cicadas and the occasional clucking of Costner's chickens.

"Are you all right?" the investigator asked, squeezing her hand.

"I'm fine, thanks. Just nerves," Pat answered. "I really don't know what I'd have done without your help."

"That's what I'm here for," Sheila O'Donnell replied, her face briefly lighting up with a smile as fresh as a Donegal breeze.

Five-foot-seven and solidly built, with shoulder-length salt-and-pepper hair, broad cheeks, and wide (but not innocent) eyes, Sheila O'Donnell is not your typical private investigator. She's nonviolent, progressive, and lacks a law enforcement background, but this granddaughter of Irish immigrants still has all the hallmarks of a good detective: tenacity, toughness of character, and an unflinching willingness to engage difficult problems head-on. To environmental activists under siege from Maine to south Texas, Sheila has become known as the "Green P.I."

"Right now I'd say about half my cases are environmental," she explains over cappuccino on a warm spring day near her home in Mill Valley, California. "I've got ten cases involving violent attacks on environmentalists. I've talked to activists in twenty-five or thirty similar cases. I turned copies of those cases over to the Center for Investigative Reporting [an award-winning journalism project based in San Francisco] and they've been able to develop another 120 examples and it's continuing to expand. I'm sure the real numbers are well into the hundreds—thousands if you count vandalism, phone threats, and harassing letters. My worry is that there's really no place for people to go when they get a threatening call in the middle of the night or find their dog beheaded on their front steps. I mean they can call me but I'm only one person."

On an *Eye on America* news segment about the problem that aired March 3, 1993, CBS correspondent Eric Hayes reported, "Most of these [cases] are not high-profile environmentalists; they're not out sabotaging industry. They're more likely to work within the system to protect the environment. They're finding, though, that the system can't protect them."[2]

"Right now the FBI won't touch this," says Linda Chase, a staff aide to Congressman George Miller, who was chairman of the House Committee on Natural Resources until the Republicans took control of the House in 1994. "They think ecoterrorism, tree spiking, attacks on logging equipment [and later arsons directed against development projects and SUVs] is a national problem," Chase explains, "but reports of environmentalists being physically attacked they just want to pass on to the local sheriff."[3]

"The FBI has not been even-handed in crime prevention," a congressional source involved in oversight of their budget told me. "The FBI's underlying mind set is that defense of the status quo is not terrorism but challenging it is, so in that light they may see property damage as more serious than attacks on individuals. I think the anti-environmental violence could at least be called criminal activity that the FBI is ignoring."

With neither the FBI nor local law enforcement agencies showing much interest, the investigative effort has fallen to a small group of reporters and activists around the country, along with Private Detective

Sheila O'Donnell. O'Donnell's background, she admits, has given her a cynical view of how much help environmentalists under siege can count on from the people who collect their taxes.

"It's like the early days of the civil rights movement in terms of the escalating violence," she says. "Unfortunately, a number of these incidents come after a long period of threats and intimidation that law enforcement has tended to ignore. There's a definite feeling that the enforcement agencies, particularly the FBI, are not on the side of the activists."

O'Donnell herself was raised in a large Irish Catholic family in the town of Newton, outside of Boston. Her father was a professional gambler who played the horses. Her mother stayed home to take care of a sick older brother, who died of a rare bone disease when O'Donnell was sixteen. A graduate of a private girls' school run by Irish nuns, she had a hard time adjusting to college life, trying several schools before dropping out to take a job as a secretary at McGraw-Hill. At twenty-three, restless and disturbed by all the young men she knew who were going off to a war that didn't make any sense to her, she left her family and moved to Washington, D.C., where she found work with the New Mobilization Committee to End the War in Vietnam. "I was so naive I went to their office in a dress and heels. They told me to go home and change," she recalls with a smile. "They found out I could type and got me a job with a Mobe Committee lawyer. It was a period when the D.C. cops were being very aggressive because there were these almost constant protests going on. There were the big moratoriums, and people took to the streets after the Cambodia invasion, Kent State, the mining of the [Vietnamese] harbors, all these different incidents. In May seventy-one we had over fourteen thousand arrests in the course of a weekend. People would write lawyers' numbers on their arms with ballpoint pens, and I'd be the one answering the phone when they called from jail. The FBI began following us to legal strategy meetings. I'd go into the women's room and see a man's shiny leather shoes and white socks in the next stall."

O'Donnell's transformation from antiwar liberal to legal skeptic came during the trial of Daniel and Philip Berrigan, two Jesuit priest brothers accused of conspiracy to blow up heating ducts under the Capitol and of planning to kidnap Henry Kissinger. "I was amazed that the government could bring these charges against these two antiwar priests without proof," recalls the former parochial school student. "When the government rested their case, so did the defense. The jury went out just long enough to select a foreman, coming back with a not guilty finding. To see the government involved in this kind of misconduct just shocked me."

O'Donnell became active with the leftist National Lawyers Guild, getting work as a paralegal investigator. "The first case where I began to work as an investigator was looking into a right-wing spy operation," she recalls. "There was this woman calling herself Sheila O'Conner, who'd infiltrated the D.C. office of the National Lawyers Guild for the FBI, and she had a boyfriend named John, and I had a boyfriend named John at the time, and naturally people started confusing us. There was some suspicion about this woman, particularly after she borrowed somebody's car and disappeared. I got a call from an investigator with the New York state assembly trying to figure out who these people were. We found out their real names were John and Sheila Louise Reese and they were putting out a newsletter called *Information Digest,* a very unreliable intelligence brief on the Left for corporate and governmental clients, including the John Birch Society. I began tracking their work and found documents tracing him back to the Newark riots of 1967. He'd been mixed up with these riots where over thirty people were killed. Shortly thereafter, a small group of us started a magazine called *Public Eye* to publish research we were developing on John Reese and the Birch Society, Lyndon LaRouche, and other extremists.[4] There were links we were discovering, like the LaRouchites were targeting the anti-nuclear movement, claiming people opposed to the Seabrook Nuclear Power Plant in New Hampshire were terrorists and using *Information Digest* as their source to scare the hell out of the New Hampshire state police. Their talk of nuclear terrorism frightened the cops, and we worried they were likely to overreact and hurt someone."

At about the same time, O'Donnell began doing street work to improve her investigative skills. Her criminal defense cases ranged from medical malpractice to drugs and homicides, but no divorces or child custody disputes. "My ancestors did enough domestic work," she jokes. One case she took on involved a fourteen-year-old busboy accused of the torture-murder of his mother's friend. "His mother and the victim both worked as waitresses at this restaurant/pub, and there was a question if the owner might have offed the woman," O'Donnell recalls. "She had lent him money and then threatened to go to a lawyer when he wouldn't repay it. That night she was tortured and killed by a right-handed assailant, and our young client had lost his right arm in a childhood accident, so we were pretty sure he wasn't the perpetrator." O'Donnell got a job as a waitress at the pub to develop more information on the owner. She found that the other waitresses were both scared and suspicious of the man. When the case finally went to trial, the defense argued that the pub's owner had better cause and opportunity to have committed the murder than the accused boy, winning an acquittal for their client. Shortly thereafter the bartender at O'Donnell's regular hangout began referring to her as "Dickless Tracy."

In 1985, O'Donnell moved to California. "I'd just turned forty, and this journalist from the Bay Area asked me to move in with him, and so I decided to leap without looking and moved to Marin. And while he and I didn't work out, everything else proved worth it." She obtained work with a couple of San Francisco detective agencies, later becoming a one-third partner in Ace Investigations, opening a small office within sight of the municipal pier on the wide crescent beach at Pacifica just south of the city on Route 1.

In 1988, while back in Washington on a civil litigation case, O'Donnell met a couple of people working with Greenpeace. Later they invited her to a camp in Maine, where she held a workshop for their international toxics campaigners, teaching them how to trace documents, conduct interviews, and other investigative techniques. "I was very impressed with these folks," she recalls. "They were young, bright, really high energy, and highly motivated. They loved the earth and knew how to have a good time as well as how to work. Many had come to their activism through their play—surfers who'd seen their beaches polluted or hikers who found clear-cuts where they liked to trek, that sort of thing."

Judi Bari was not that kind of an activist. A former postal union organizer, carpenter, and single mother of two young girls, Bari had always been a tireless political advocate for the disenfranchised. She identified with the plight of working people, including loggers and mill workers, as much as she identified with the redwood forests whose protection became a major cause in her life. Even the folk music she wrote and played with fellow Earth Firster Daryl Cherney had the didactic politics (if not always the lyrical polish) of a Woody Guthrie or a Phil Ochs. Art, she believed, should be socially responsible. In the late

1980s, when Bari began organizing Earth First!'s campaign to save northern California's redwoods, one of the first projects she took on was defending the rights of Georgia-Pacific workers exposed to PCBs during a chemical spill at the Fort Bragg mill. Other Earth First! leaders whose backgrounds were in wilderness protection were uncomfortable with her mixture of worker and feminist politics and radical environmentalism. Still, they chose not to argue with one of their more effective organizers—that is, until she renounced the controversial tactic of tree spiking (pounding nails into trees that can damage saws and potentially hurt loggers). She wanted to focus on nonviolent forms of civil disobedience: people sitting in trees, chaining themselves to mill gates, and blocking logging trucks and bulldozers with their bodies.

Bari was driving in her car with a friend and their children in August 1989 when they were run off the road by a log truck they'd blockaded the day before. She recalled that the truck driver came up to her afterwards, looking shaken and saying, "I didn't know there were children in the car." No charges were brought against the man.[5]

Over the next nine months she worked to organize the Redwood Summer protests, which she hoped to model after the nonviolent Mississippi Summer protests of the 1960s civil rights movement. Bari received a growing number of death threats during this period, including a clipped newspaper photo of herself playing the violin with a rifle's crosshairs superimposed over her face.

On May 23, 1990, Bari and Daryl Cherney headed south to the Bay Area to meet with Redwood Summer supporters. On May 24, after stops in Berkeley and Oakland, they took off again for Santa Cruz, a college town a few hours south of the Bay Area where they hoped to recruit students for their demonstrations. They didn't get far. Just before noon on a busy street in the city of Oakland, a pipe bomb exploded beneath the driver's seat of Bari's 1981 Subaru station wagon, shattering her pelvis and dislocating her spine. Cherney, riding in the passenger seat, suffered facial lacerations and eye damage from flying glass and metal. Within minutes of the explosion, even as firefighters and paramedics were working to save Bari's life and rush the two victims to Highland Hospital, the FBI's domestic terrorism squad, working with the Oakland police, had commandeered the investigation from the Alcohol, Tobacco and Firearms agents on the scene. That night, based on information provided by the FBI, the Oakland police obtained a search warrant, telling a judge that Bari and Cherney were "members of a violent terrorist group involved in the manufacture and placing of explosive devices."[6] Oakland police and FBI agents then raided Seeds of Peace, a seedy collective house in the flats of Berkeley whose young pacifist communards had met the previous night with Bari and Cherney to discuss providing logistical support for the Redwood Summer protests. The raiders were looking for a bomb factory but instead found a portable kitchen, cooking utensils, sacks of brown rice, and a couple of Portasan toilets in the backyard. Nonetheless, the next morning, homicide lieutenant Mike Sims of the Oakland PD held a press conference to announce the arrest of Bari and Cherney for possession and transportation of an explosive device.

"The decision to arrest was based, uh, the placement of the device in the vehicle, the, uh, nature of its construction, physical and other evidence that was, uh, developed by the investigators," the tall, blond cop hesitatingly read his statement in front of dozens of reporters, Mini-cams, and microphones.[7]

"I remember hearing about the bombing and arrests on the radio and thinking, that doesn't sound right. I've never heard of environmental activists getting involved with bombs," recalls Sheila O'Donnell. A short time later she received a phone call from Greenpeace USA executive director Peter Bahouth, asking her to look into the bombing for them. Greenpeace had been the victim of a 1985 terrorist bombing in New Zealand that had sunk their ship, the *Rainbow Warrior,* and cost the life of one of their volunteers, photographer Fernando Pereira. The bombing turned out to be the work of French secret agents bent on preventing the *Rainbow Warrior* from leading protests against France's nuclear weapons testing in the South Pacific. Greenpeace hated terrorism and wanted to know the truth about the Oakland bombing. "If Judi and Daryl were involved they wouldn't support them, but people who knew the two of them were convinced they wouldn't be involved in something like this," O'Donnell recalls.

It was more than a week before Bari was able to stay conscious and pain-free long enough to meet with the private investigator in the intensive care unit of Highland Hospital. An armed police guard stood at her door, although she was in traction and still too weak to have the explosive powder washed out of her matted brown hair. On her second day in the hospital, after extensive surgery and blood loss, the police had moved Bari's bed to the jail ward. Her surgeon, on discovering what they'd done, had it rolled back up to the ICU, instructing the police to keep their hands off his critically injured patient.

Bari recalled the moment of the bomb blast. With a strangely disjointed clarity, she had known instantly that she was the victim of a bomb, that this was a political assassination attempt, and that she might die. Then, as they'd pulled her from the wreckage, the pain had struck in a sickening, overwhelming wave. She had begged the paramedics to give her something for the pain, but they told her they couldn't, that if they did she might die. The pain was so bad, she wanted to die anyway. To give herself a reason to live, she tried to visualize her two daughters, but was unable to conjure up their faces.[8]

O'Donnell and Bari spoke for some time until Bari tired. Impressed with Bari's courage, determination, and even flashes of humor in the face of what was obviously still intense pain, O'Donnell left the hospital committed to working on the case. "You don't want to be gullible, but after a while in this business you develop an instinct for when people are lying to you and when they're telling the truth," she said. "And I had the feeling Judi was honestly frightened that someone was out there who wanted her dead, and not having succeeded might try again, and that the government just wanted to blame it on her."

The government's charges against Bari and Cherney, although widely reported in the media, would prove grossly misdirected. Immediately after the bombing, police told the press that Bari must have known the bomb was in her car because she'd put her guitar case on top of it. But the guitar case was barely damaged. An affidavit filed by Police Sergeant Robert Chenault claimed that an FBI agent at the scene of the explosion told him the bomb was on the floorboard behind the driver's seat. But Bari's surgeon, Peter Slabbaugh, said that the injuries to her pelvic area and buttocks indicated that the force of the blast had come from below, not behind, an impression confirmed by an Oakland fire captain on the scene. When the FBI released the car to the defense team, it didn't take the expertise of the Silicon Valley bomb expert O'Donnell had hired to recognize the obvious. The car's roof was bowed out above the driver's seat. Where the driver's floorboard should have been was a jagged hole (part of the flooring had also been removed by the FBI). The front seat was shredded down to exposed and heat-seared cushion wires, one of which had punctured Bari's colon. The passenger's seat was less severely damaged, and the rear bench seat and floorboard were more or less intact, with only minor shrapnel damage. A fist-sized hole, like that left by a rocket grenade, was punched out of the driver's door panel where one of the screw-on end caps of the pipe bomb had shot off. If the bomb had been better constructed, with the end caps properly sealed, it would have done its intended job, killing both passengers.

After six weeks of claiming that the bomb had been in plain sight behind Bari, the police finally conceded that the bomb was hidden out of sight under her seat. Immediately following that admission, however, they announced that finishing nails taped to the outside of the bomb matched finishing nails found in an FBI raid of Bari's Mendocino home (where she worked as a carpenter). FBI bomb expert David Williams told Oakland police sergeant Michael Sitterud he could testify that the nails found in Bari's house matched the bomb nails to within a batch of 200 to 1,000 nails, a claim quickly leaked to the *Oakland Tribune* and other local media.[9]

On investigating that claim, O'Donnell and her team talked to several highly skeptical nail manufacturers. The manager of one Bay Area nail plant had been visited by the FBI and had told them that finishing nails are basically indistinguishable from one another. He explained that most nails, particularly finishing nails, are now manufactured overseas. The nailpress machines that are used are often of a common type, such as the German-made "Wafios." A wire is fed into the machine where it is cut at a rate of 1,200 to 1,400 nails a minute. The machine stamps the head and shapes the point. The gripper holding the wire leaves marks that can later be matched to that gripper. Gripper dies wear out and have to be replaced every four or five weeks. Cutter dies are machined in the plant and changed every day, meaning that theoretically a finishing nail could be matched to a single day's production on a single machine, one out of a batch of 576,000 to 672,000 nails. Without being able to match the nails more precisely, the government did not have much of a case. On July 17, the Alameda County district attorney decided not to press charges.[10] Several months later, in an interview with a local PBS producer, the FBI admitted that its nail evidence was inconclusive.[11]

"With the FBI, I think they had Earth First! terrorists dancing like sugarplums in their head. I don't know that they ever for a moment asked, 'Are these people victims?'" O'Donnell says.

Her skepticism seems well placed in light of an additional FBI crime-lab analysis of the pipe bomb conducted shortly after the explosion. The bomb consisted of an eleven-inch piece of galvanized pipe attached to a piece of wood paneling and packed with an explosive mixture of potassium chlorate and aluminum powder. Nails were taped to the outside of the pipe to create additional shrapnel. There was a light-switch safety device, a nine-volt Duracell battery to provide an electrical charge, and a cheap Bullseye pocketwatch timer.[12] In addition there was a crude motion-trigger device made up of a ball bearing and two bent wires that would necessarily have been jolted together to complete the bomb circuit, meaning that the car would need to be in motion for the bomb to explode. Bari remembers cutting through Oakland traffic and then hitting her brakes hard just before the explosion.

But the FBI report refers to the ball bearing and wire fragments as "a booby trap device." Experienced IRA bomb makers occasionally would booby-trap time bombs with parallel motion switches in order to kill army bomb technicians who tried to move the bombs. But such booby traps are not likely to be found in crudely built homemade pipe bombs, and not even a suicide bomber would arm a motion-trigger device while driving to his target.

Still, for the FBI to correctly identify the ball bearing and wires as a motion trigger rather than a booby trap would have meant acknowledging that the car's driver, Judi Bari, was the intended target of the bomb—a victim rather than a terrorist.

"If you come to the scene of a crime with your own theory of who's responsible and you refuse to turn that around, you build a house of cards that will come crashing down around you," says O'Donnell.

The FBI and Oakland PD continued to try to build a case against Bari and Cherney, even after the would-be assassin sent a letter to a local newspaper taking credit for the crime. On May 29, five days after the bombing, Mike Geniella, a reporter covering timber issues for the *Santa Rosa Press Democrat*, received a three-page typewritten letter signed "The Lord's Avenger."

"I remember saying to myself, now we've got the real nuts involved," Geniella recalls of his first reading of the letter. He says he put it down for a minute and returned to a story he was working on but suddenly stopped typing to look at it again. "And I thought, God, this letter describes a bomb. And it not only describes a bomb, it describes a second bomb. And then it was that kind of—like when the adrenaline starts pumping."[13]

Written in a rambling manner that mixes hellfire-and-brimstone fundamentalism with an army manual's precision of language, the letter provides detailed descriptions of both the car bomb and a second pipe bomb, which had been left at a Louisiana Pacific lumber mill in Cloverdale, California, two weeks earlier. That bomb had been set on the porch of the mill office next to a five-gallon gas can but failed to penetrate the can and start a fire after one of the bomb's screw-on end caps blew off. After receiving the Lord's Avenger letter from the *Press Democrat,* the FBI quickly keyed in on that case.

"Four or five suits arrived, very high energy. They took the evidence, said they'd be in touch, and that's the last we saw of our bomb," recalls Rich McComber, the Sonoma County sheriff's deputy who'd first investigated the LP incident.[14]

After examining the letter and the LP pipe bomb, the FBI concluded that the Lord's Avenger "either built the two bombs or knew how they were built."

The Avenger claimed that the LP bombing was meant as a provocation to be blamed on Bari. A cardboard sign left near the bomb site read "L.P. Screws Millworkers," an R-rated sentiment not completely in keeping with Bari's occasionally X-rated exhortations. When the LP bombing failed to draw much notice, the Avenger decided to use a more direct method.

"The Lord had shown me that his Work needed no Subtergufe [*sic*] and must be clear and Visible in the eyes of all. I was his Avenger. The demon must be struck down."[15]

The Avenger claimed to have planted the second pipe bomb in Bari's unlocked car while she was meeting with loggers in the Mendocino County town of Willits to try to negotiate a nonviolence agreement for the Redwood Summer protests. He also claimed that the assassination attempt was a response to her pro-abortion activity at a "baby-killing clinic," where he saw "Satan's flames shoot forth from her mouth her eyes and ears."

Bari had organized a counterprotest against a group of Right-to-Life demonstrators at the Ukiah Planned Parenthood Clinic in November 1988, where, to the tune of "Will the Circle Be Unbroken?" she and

Daryl Cherney sang a lusty chorus of "Will the Fetus Be Aborted?" which included these lines:

> Betty Lou, she got pregnant, and was addicted to fifteen drugs,
> She went down to the abortion clinic, and was accosted by
>   right-wing thugs.
> Will the fetus be aborted, bye and bye, lord, bye and bye?
> There's a better world awaiting, in the sky, lord, in the sky.[16]

"We were really outrageous," Bari later admitted. "In retrospect I probably would have done it differently, but because of the way that they were acting, we decided if they were gonna be bullies, we'd show them what their tactics were like."[17]

The Lord's Avenger letter went on to suggest a second reason for the bombing: "All the forests that grow and all the wild creatures within them are a gift to Man that he shall use freely with God's Blessing to build the Kingdom of God on Earth. They shall be never ending because God will provide. ... Judi Bari spread her Poison to tell the Multitude that trees are not God's Gift to Man but that Trees were themselves gods and it was a Sin to cut them. My Spirit ached as her Paganism festered before mine eyes. I felt the Power of the Lord stir within my Heart and I knew I had been Chosen to strike down this Demon."

"If law enforcement had used all their resources from the time of the bombing to track real leads like this letter instead of trying to nail Judi and Daryl, I think we might have been able to catch the bomber early on," Sheila O'Donnell contends.

A 1991 documentary on the bombing that aired on PBS stations KQED in San Francisco and KCET in Los Angeles profiled several possible suspects who were never seriously investigated by the FBI. There was Bill Staley, the six-foot-three ex–Chicago Bears tackle and born-again fundamentalist who led the anti-abortion protests at the Ukiah clinic. On camera he denied a clinic staffer's charge that he'd threatened to rape her and make her have his baby. The documentary also aired an interview with Steve Okerstrom, a logging contractor from Willits who lost a $700,000 Fellerbuncher tree-cutting machine in a fire that he believed had been set by Earth Firsters, even though the state fire marshal ruled it accidental. "I know there wasn't a whole lot of effort put in to checking to see whether it was set," he told producer

Steve Talbot. "I know they spent a whole lot more time trying to figure out what happened to the back end of Judi Bari."

The documentary also examined Irv Sutley, a longtime leftwing activist and gun lover who posed Bari and Cherney with his Uzi assault
rifle for photos they considered and then rejected for the cover of one
of their music tapes, *They Don't Make Hippies Like They Used To*.
Shortly after Sutley's photo session, a print of Bari with the Uzi was
sent to the local police along with an anonymous letter signed "Argus,"
claiming that Earth First! had begun automatic weapons training and
offering to spy on Bari. The Willits police later matched the typing of
the informant's letter to the type used in one of the death threats Bari
had received before the bombing. The documentary reported on Mike
Koepf, a former political ally of Bari's and ex–Green Beret with a history of domestic violence who'd become a harsh critic of hers after she
developed a friendship with his ex-wife. It also profiled Bari's own ex-
husband, Mike Sweeney, who had had financial conflicts with her during their divorce and was also a suspect in an earlier electrically
triggered arson fire at an airport whose expansion he'd opposed.

However, Judi Bari categorically rejected the idea that the bombing was
personally motivated. She insisted that the timber industry was behind the
attempt on her life (although no solid proof of this ever surfaced).

In 1992 she and Daryl Cherney filed a civil suit, charging the FBI and
Oakland police with false arrest and violation of their civil rights. On
May 24, 1993, the third anniversary of the bombing, Bari held a press
conference on the steps of the San Francisco federal building to pass out
photos taken at the time of the bombing by the Oakland police and released to her attorney through the discovery process. The photos show
a large bomb blast hole in the floor of the Subaru directly below where
the front seat had been. "From the very first the FBI and the police
knew exactly where the bomb had been placed and they deliberately
lied and tried to frame us," she charged.

The FBI refused to comment because of the pending suit but did
tell Mike Geniella of the *Press Democrat* that they'd closed the case
for lack of evidence. Although handicapped from the bombing—her
right foot paralyzed; her pelvis, nerves, and coccyx damaged beyond
surgical repair—Bari returned to the political front lines. Among her
proudest accomplishments was the Mendocino Real Wood Co-op that
she helped found with several out-of-work loggers. The co-op produced

value-added wood products from the selective cutting and milling of second-growth trees.

In 1997, at age forty-seven, Bari died of complications from breast cancer. Even after her death the civil rights lawsuit she and Cherney had filed continued to wend its way through the legal system, finally coming to trial in the spring of 2002. On June 11, 2002, a federal jury seated in Oakland, California, awarded Bari's estate and Daryl Cherney $4.4 million in damages, finding six out of seven FBI and Oakland police defendants guilty of violating their civil rights. The Justice Department's lawyers had argued that the FBI's investigation of Judi Bari was "similar" to anti-terrorist investigations carried out in the wake of the 9/11 attacks on the United States. It was a long-shot argument that failed to win any jury sympathy.

"The FBI and Oakland [police] sat up there and lied about their investigation," juror Mary Nunn told the *San Francisco Chronicle* after the trial. "They messed up their investigation, and they had to lie again and again to try to cover up. I'm surprised that they seriously expected anyone to believe them."

Back in 1990, when the government dropped its charges against Bari and Cherney but failed to pursue other leads in the case, Sheila O'Donnell began to worry. She feared law enforcement's attitude would be taken as a signal by anti-enviro militants that terrorist attacks against environmentalists would be tolerated or at least not actively investigated by the authorities. She was relieved when she didn't hear of any new attacks. Then, on March 2, 1991, Pat Costner's home was torched.

"I went to this environmental law conference in Eugene, Oregon, in the early spring of ninety-one," O'Donnell recalls. "A number of people came up to me there and said, 'Did you know Pat Costner's home was burned?' I said, 'Has anybody investigated?' Nobody had. When I got home two days later, more people called me, but still no one had investigated. So I called Pat, even though I barely knew her— I'd just met her briefly at that camp in Maine. She was really devastated. She was blaming herself, saying it might have been the wood stove, which she'd left burning when she went out. It turned out she'd been leaving that stove burning for the past seventeen years. Then she told me she had a major Greenpeace report on hazardous waste incinerators due out in two weeks, and I knew we could have something serious here."

On first meeting Pat Costner, you wouldn't guess she's a fifty-three-year-old scientist with three grown children. About five-foot-six, rail-thin, with round, owl-like glasses and an Arkansas accent as thick as honey butter, she has a country simplicity that could almost be taken for severe until a pixie-like grin lights up her face. The daughter of cotton farmers from the state's northeast delta, Costner divides her time between her home in the rural Ozarks and places like Geneva, Switzerland, where she represented Greenpeace on a working committee of the Basel Convention on the Transnational Movement of Hazardous Waste.

Costner has a master's degree in organic chemistry and was working toward her doctorate in the late 1960s when, following her first divorce, she had to go back to work. "When you're divorced and with a two-year-old to raise, childcare can suddenly become the most traumatic issue in your life," she remembers. She spent several years working for Shell Oil developing methods of labeling catalysts and studying kinetics in the oil-refining process using radionuclides. After her second marriage didn't work out, she found herself with three small children to raise. This time she took work in Colorado as a research chemist for a division of Syntex, synthesizing industrial quantities of organic specialty compounds.

"I was living in Boulder with my three kids and didn't like raising them in an urban environment. I became convinced it wasn't healthy," she says. "So I moved back to Arkansas in 1974 and got a lab going in Blytheville, near where I was born. I was doing wastewater analysis, simple stuff like that, but it supported me and my kids. I bought some land near Eureka Springs and started building a house, settling into a rational and healthy lifestyle. We raised beans and chickens and rabbits. Eureka is an old, turn-of-the-century resort community in the hills famous for its spring-water, but by the time we got there all the springs were contaminated by sewage. We tried to have meetings and figure out how to clean it up. The city and this big engineering firm out of Little Rock were developing a wastewater-treatment plan. Some local people gave me a copy of the plan, and I could see right off it was a pile of dreck, that it wasn't going to provide a solution. So I teamed up with some local people and we presented the EPA with evidence to stop the project and to identify the main sources of pollution, which included the central waste-treatment facility in town. Something like 80 percent of the town's sewer lines were leaking, contaminating not only the springs, but wells and creeks throughout the area."

Costner helped found and became chief scientist for the Eureka-based National Water Center, setting up a new lab in town and later publishing a book on waste-disposal problems called *We All Live Downstream*. In 1987, after her book came out, she went to a meeting in Washington, D.C., of the Citizens' Clearinghouse for Hazardous Wastes, where she met Greenpeace toxics campaign director Dave Rappaport. Following a series of meetings, Rappaport asked her if she'd be interested in taking his job while he was off on sabbatical.

"The kids were getting older and spending their summers with their dad, who lived in Houston," Costner recounts, "and they wanted to spend more time in the big city. So I agreed to live in D.C. and work for Greenpeace for a year while the kids were off with their dad in Texas. After that I stayed on with Greenpeace, working out of my home in Arkansas."

Costner goes on to describe the house that was her home and "lifestyle" for seventeen years. "It kind of grew up around me and the kids," she says, talking about the additions they had built onto a common living room/kitchen area with attached sleeping loft and bedrooms. "We used a lot of recycled materials in building out, and a lot of care. First we added a big greenhouse. The greenhouse glass helped warm the house in the winter. Then, the year before the fire, we added a fourteen-by-thirty-foot office/library for all my files and reference books and also a back porch that looked out onto all these trees. We kept forty chickens, bees, and rabbits. The chickens kind of went wild and roosted in the trees, got to acting more birdlike. I'd just feed them some grain or corn I'd throw out in the yard. The house sat here in an east-west valley, with creeks on two sides at the end of a one-and-a-half-mile gravel road." She pauses, reflecting. "I used to feel so safe and good coming down my little bitty road that just me and my neighbor used. Coming home, this was my little spot of sanity, serenity, and peace."

The winter and early spring of 1991 was not a time of peace and serenity for Pat Costner. She and Greenpeace coauthor Joe Thornton were working overtime to complete a sixty-four-page report on toxic incinerators titled "Playing with Fire," which was due out that May. The ironically named report would examine a network of 1,100 incinerators, kilns, and industrial boilers across the United States that burn more than 7.6 billion pounds of hazardous waste a year. The report was expected to name names and ascribe blame for illegal toxic releases and to identify corporations that targeted poor rural areas for new waste incinerators. The hazardous waste industry and its supporters at the EPA were not looking forward to its publication.[18]

A week before Christmas, Costner went to Oklahoma to meet with Native Americans and speak at a public meeting, where she countered claims of a Nebraska-based firm called Waste Tech that the toxic incinerator it wanted to install on the Kaw tribal reservation would only release carbon dioxide. After listing the toxic materials its stacks might release, she went on to argue that incineration plants were not the answer to hazardous-waste disposal, and that industry had to move toward zero discharge of toxins through new methods of production. A week later the tribal council pulled out of its deal with Waste Tech and the first of the two strangers arrived in Eureka Springs asking where Pat Costner lived.

She was also active in a number of other conflicts, including monitoring a PCB incinerator in El Dorado, Arkansas, and the Vertac Agent Orange plant and Superfund site that was burning dioxin waste in Jacksonville, Arkansas (where local anti-pollution activists were being harassed and receiving death threats). ENSCO, the owner of the El Dorado incinerator, hoped to open a larger regional incinerator in Mobile, Arizona. Costner took a number of trips to Mobile to testify and present data against that proposed facility. The previous May, hundreds of local citizens opposed to ENSCO's incinerator had staged a noisy protest during a public meeting. The police cleared the hall, arresting eighteen people and shooting five of them with Tasers. The detainees were held, handcuffed, at a nearby airfield until the hearing was over. Later it was learned that three of those arrested had been identified from videotapes provided to the Arizona police by the Environmental Protection Agency, which supported ENSCO's toxic incinerator plan.[19] The plan was eventually defeated, one of six multimillion-dollar incinerator projects that were defeated with the help of Pat Costner's expert testimony in the year before her house burned down.

While she was working on the final draft of her Greenpeace report, the EPA made several attempts to secure documents on the Vertac Superfund site from an *Arkansas Gazette* reporter, Bobbi Ridlehoover, who'd been running a series of investigative articles on Vertac, the EPA, and its cleanup contractors. The EPA argued that the sensitive documents, which had been removed from the Agent Orange plant by disgruntled workers, were actually dioxin-tainted hazardous waste. Ridlehoover, with the support of her editors, declined to turn the reports over to the EPA, and the government agency backed down. The former plant operators threatened to use the FBI to recover similar documents from a lawyer representing the workers.[20]

By March 2, 1991, Costner couldn't help but be aware of the rising tensions over the toxics-incineration issue and industry interest in her upcoming report, but she didn't consider that she herself might be under observation.

"I was at home that Saturday night," she recalls. "I had a friend in from D.C. who was doing a piano concert in town, so I left for that at a quarter of eight and couldn't have been gone more than three hours. I remember driving home from the concert and seeing a glow in the mist. By the time I got to my house, it was burned to the ground. I mean it was totally destroyed. The only thing standing was a couple of cedar posts, my stove, some burned-up office equipment, and some two-by-sixes where the back porch had been. It was one of those times you're just fully in the moment. Sheila later asked me where my dogs were, and I remembered the dogs tried to get in the car with me as I headed back to town, which was something they normally wouldn't have done. I went to a local hangout and a friend, Jim, said, 'How are you doing?' and I said, 'I'm doing all right but my house just burned down,' and he thought I was joking. Then some other friends came by and asked, 'Is there anything we can do for you?' and I said, 'You could get me a sleeping bag,' and they actually came back with one. Then I had to get out. I hate being emotional in front of people, and so I went back to my place and there were people there standing around looking at the ruins, which I didn't like at all, and Larry Evans, an old local, asked me where I was going to sleep and I said, 'In my car,' but he wouldn't let me. He made me come over to his place and use the sofa, and I couldn't sleep all night. All I could see in my mind over and over is this box. I'd gathered this box of family pictures and set it in the door between the living room and my office, so I could sort through them, and I could imagine those pictures burning up one by one." She pauses. "The next day I poked around in the ashes and the first thing I found was this ceramic chicken that my daughter ..." She begins to cry. "Hold on, let me get into my tough pragmatic mode. I don't usually talk about this. ... It's just amazing how it can still crush and hurt my heart, all this time later."

After a moment she recomposes herself and goes on. "There wasn't much left to find—an earring, the strings to my Gibson Hummingbird guitar. If they were trying to sabotage our report, they failed. It still came out in May like originally planned. I was working on the final draft when the fire happened but the prior copy was with my coauthor in Seattle. What was lost that could take years to reconstruct was my reference library. This fellow in the D.C. office [of Greenpeace] kept calling me after the fire saying maybe they could recover the inventory or something from my hard drive. He wouldn't listen when I told him my computer was just a lump of plastic and metal, so I finally put it in a box and mailed it to him, and I heard they placed it in the front of the office with a sign attached, 'Back up your hard drive.'

"Within a relatively short time, friends lent me an Airstream trailer and I moved it out on the property on a Sunday afternoon and ran a phone line into it," she continues. "On Monday when I came back from town the phone line was just dangling there and I just looked at it and found the other end in the trailer and it was obvious it had been cut. I went back to town and called Sheila, and she told me to find a safe place to stay, not to go back out to my land. And that really frightened me in a way the arson had not.

"That Thursday the arson team arrived and took pictures, and about fifteen minutes later, after moving the roofing, they called me over and pointed out this square, empty fuel can where the living room had been," she recounts. "They said the arsonists had probably doused the office and then laid a fuel trail to the stove, which would have given them five minutes to get away. I remember I'd been replaying that in my mind—the stove door being open after the fire. The stove had fallen about ten inches when the floor gave way, but it had a latch handle that shouldn't have come open, and all my office file drawers were also opened in the office after the fire, and it just hadn't sunk in at the time."

Costner has built herself a new house where her old one once stood.

"I'd never advise anyone to get burned out and rebuild in the same year," she says. "Sometimes when that new house was going up I'd stop and just hate it 'cause it wasn't my house. I'll be real with you. My son Mason was appalled I was building it there till I explained that you can't build a new old house. I don't have the time to build it over twenty years like I did before."

Years after the fire, Costner continues to carry on her work directing Greenpeace's toxic research program. "I'll assure you it's not bravery or bravado that keeps me going. It's just that this is what I do, and I vacillate between being afraid and insecure and just not accepting it as a reality. But I have to keep functioning the way I feel comfortable. I can't imagine doing anything else. There are very few scientists who aren't obligated to industry and government, and I feel privileged that I get to take what I believe is a really fair and objective view of things from my position."

The closest she comes to bitterness is when she reflects on the official response to the fire.

"The city fire marshal came out the day after the fire and said he didn't see any obvious signs of arson. Later he explained he'd meant he didn't see any arson trail as such. The local sheriff didn't come out the day after the fire when I asked him to. Later, after Sheila and the arson investigators got involved, he said he was impressed that it was a crime and if we found out who did it he'd be there to arrest them.[21] Greenpeace asked the FBI to come in on this and they said it didn't meet their criteria for getting involved. I think Sheila was the only person who actually understood what had happened and the implications of it. She was my strength and stability throughout."

IN APRIL 1992, several attacks were aimed at Diane Wilson, a shrimper protesting expansion of a Taiwanese-owned plastics plant near her home in Seadrift, Texas. In the first attack, on April 9, three shots were fired at her mother-in-law, who lives in a trailer on the same land as Wilson, her husband, and five kids. The next day a helicopter landed near their isolated homestead and someone shot the family dog, hitting it twice. One bullet went through its neck, a second .22 round was removed from its leg. The dog, a young Dalmatian, recovered but died suddenly the following spring from suspected poisoning.

In October 1992 Wilson's shrimp boat, the *SeaBee*, was sabotaged and almost sank beneath her six miles off the Texas coast. Although she works her forty-two-foot boat alone, Wilson has never learned how to swim.

This was not the first time Seadrift had experienced violence linked to social controversy. A little more than a decade earlier, Vietnamese immigrants and Anglo shrimpers clashed over control of fishing grounds on the seafood-rich bays and estuaries of Texas's central Gulf Coast. The Ku Klux Klan became involved, one man was killed, and several homes and boats were burned down before peace was restored. "I always put the blame on no one being willing to get involved in the dispute," says Wilson. "There was no communication between the Vietnamese and the Anglos, and the state and federal agencies refused to deal with the situation in its early stages before it got out of control."

It's a critique that could as easily be applied to incidents of anti-environmental violence and intimidation in the 1990s and early twenty-first century.

"My father and grandfather were fishermen and his father too," says Wilson, who also married a fisherman. "I was brought up on the bay, and I got a dear love for the water and the natural way down here."

It is that love of the rich brown bays and blue Gulf waters of the Texas coast that has turned Diane Wilson, a thin but muscular woman with curly dark hair, almond-shaped eyes, and a friendly, determined manner, into an environmental activist and anti-enviro target. Aside from its protective network of barrier islands, looping bays, and marine-rich estuaries, the Texas coast south of Galveston is home to an extensive network of oil refineries, petrochemical plants, and other industries. In 1989 the Associated Press carried a story on the nation's first toxic release inventory (TRI) for industry. Point Comfort, twenty miles across Lavaca Bay from Seadrift, was rated the nation's worst site for land disposal of toxic waste. The source of the problem was a chemical factory run by the Formosa Plastics Corporation of Taiwan, which was in the early stages of expanding its facility. It was planned as the largest chemical factory expansion in the United States in over a decade.

"When I read that AP story, it made me react. When I know something is wrong I do something," Wilson says. "So what I did, I formed an environmental group. We called ourselves the Calhoun County Resource Watch. Calhoun is part of the tri-county area along with Victoria and Jackson counties. Down here there aren't a lot of people or jobs, and industry is totally infiltrated in the whole power structure so there was an immediate backlash to us. I'm not a socialite. I'd never talked to a banker or a mayor of a town in my life," she says. "Suddenly they're coming up to me on the street saying, 'You're getting involved in something you don't know anything about.' When I tried to have our first meeting in city hall, they wanted me to put it elsewhere. I should be at home with my kids, they told me. All our county and state officials who were invited backed out of the meeting. We had about seventy people at the Seadrift school, since they wouldn't let us meet at city hall. At the second meeting all these chamber of commerce people showed up. There were about fifteen of them. They were so rude and sat apart from everyone else and started asking who the hell was I to run down industry. I finally got so fed up with how rude they were, particularly the head of the chamber of commerce and the mayor of Port Lavaca, I finally told him to shut up. It got wild. When they realized I wasn't coming around, they started saying I was a spy working for the attorney general of Louisiana, or that I was a union organizer, which is the same as saying you're a Communist around here."

Y. C. Wang, Formosa's owner, had earlier established a bidding war between Texas and Louisiana to determine which state would get his plastics factory expansion, with its projected fifteen hundred full-time jobs. After Republican senator Phil Gramm of Texas put together a package of tax breaks and incentives that included a $26 million grant to dredge the harbor and build docks and bulkheads for Formosa at Port Lavaca, Wang finally went with Texas.[22] The factory produced ethylene dichloride (EDC), a toxic substance used in plastics production; polyvinyl chloride (PVC); and bulk plastics. According to *Chemical Week* magazine, Formosa also planned on becoming the major U.S. producer of chlorine once its additional plants got online. The expansion of Formosa, called the "Big Daddy of chemical plants" by the *Houston Press,* was also facilitated by a Texas Air Control Board permit for an annual release of 420,000 pounds of dangerous volatile organic compounds (VOCs).

"Formosa brought fifteen reporters in from Taiwan to show them this new plant they were building, and Y. C. was coming with them and I found out about it and was going to show up," Wilson recalls of her first protest in 1990. "So they put out a notice inside the plant saying no one was to harm me and then sent someone to the fish house where I worked to say if anything happened to me they certainly weren't going to be responsible since they'd put this bulletin up.

"In October of 1990 they had three hundred construction workers demonstrate at the Baher Community Center, where this big event took place, and they were paid an hour overtime to come down there and picket in support of Formosa. So there it was: the most powerful elite in three counties out to meet Y. C. Wang and his people, and me and my ten supporters and three hundred construction workers. And there were also three police cars and six police, which is a big force for around here. People were afraid to be seen with me. This woman from the chamber of commerce told me there'd be trouble there. I think it was totally set up for trouble, but we were extremely peaceful so there wasn't any."

Besides bringing Taiwanese reporters to Texas, Formosa took tri-county politicians on all-expense-paid tours of their facilities in Taiwan. They hired a former area congressman as a consultant (his wife sits on the Texas Air Control Board); contributed to local charities, schools, and a hospital; bought ambulances for the paramedics, a computer system for the sheriff's department, and two vehicles for the Point Comfort Police; and paid for a new deputy for Jackson County. According to the *Texas Observer*, Formosa executives also contributed thousands of dollars to Senator Phil Gramm's reelection campaign.[23]

In 1990 and 1991, Lavaca Bay, already suffering chemical runoff from three area plants—Union Carbide, British Petroleum, and Alcoa (which fishermen blame for mercury dumping)—had a major dolphin die-off that killed more than a hundred of the protected marine mammals. In 1991 the EPA fined Formosa Plastics $3.4 million for contaminating the soil and groundwater in Point Comfort, but at the same time issued a draft "Finding of No Significant Impact" on the bay from Formosa's $1.3 billion expansion plan, which would require pumping millions of gallons of chemically laden discharge into the bay.[24]

"It was an outrage," Wilson says. "I'd read about this guy, Mitch Snyder, this homeless activist getting this shelter by fasting, and that got me going. I'd always liked Gandhi and Cesar Chavez, so I decided to do my first hunger strike, protesting the EPA decision not to ask for an Environmental Impact Report. I stayed on the fast for two weeks and threatened to go to the EPA in Dallas and continue it on their doorstep, and they got someone to talk to me. Six months later they demanded an Environmental Impact Report and Formosa volunteered to do it, saying they wanted to assure the community it was safe."

In early 1991, Formosa also hired a video crew and stenographer to begin recording Diane Wilson's statements at public hearings.[25] At the same time, the Taiwanese Environmental Protection Association invited her to visit Taiwan, where they were leading a campaign against Formosa's local plants that were causing major pollution problems in that nation.

"They flew me over there, and while I was there I met a number of dissidents, both environmentalists and pro-democracy types, some of whom were in hiding in the countryside. Some of the people over there told me the Taiwanese government was putting up the money for Formosa to expand," she says. "So on my return home I went to this county judge to ask him about industry and how these things worked, and he kind of joked to me about meeting with the chamber of commerce and local bankers and all these people who were upset with me, saying, 'Now I've told these fellers no matter how upset you get, you can't kill her.'

"I went on a second hunger strike after they went ahead and built the plant, spent a billion dollars without waiting for the EIR to be completed," she continues, "and I was hearing things about the way the plant was rushed to completion, without a general contractor or anything, and so I fasted for an investigation on the plant's construction problems. And by then I had got an environmental attorney from Houston, Jim Blackburn, and we sued them."

On the thirteenth day of her fast, Wilson and Blackburn negotiated a twenty-four-page agreement with Formosa secured by a handshake between Wilson and Pamela Giblin, Formosa's attorney.

"I'd talked to workers at the plant and added workers' right to organize to our list, so then the OCAW [Oil, Chemical and Atomic Workers] came in and I was smeared as a union organizer," Wilson recalls. "I'd ended my hunger strike but within three or four days Formosa started reneging on the agreement."

Pam Giblin told the *Texas Observer* that the company did not renege because "there never was an agreement." Joe Wyatt, the ex-congressman Formosa had hired as their lobbyist, claimed the deal was just a union ploy anyway and that "we don't just shove the union down our workers' throats."[26] It was around that time that Wilson began receiving threatening phone calls at her home.

In early 1992 the Texas Water Commission gave Formosa a permit allowing them to discharge up to fifteen million gallons of chemical wastewater a day into Lavaca Bay once their factory expansion was completed. The wastewater could include cancer-causing chemicals such as chlorine, benzene, chloroform, ethylene dichloride, and vinyl chloride. The State Health Department announced that as soon as the discharges began, they would close Lavaca Bay to oyster harvesting. Shrimpers figured their industry couldn't be far behind. Wilson began organizing among her fellow shrimpers and went on a third hunger strike, traveling to Dallas with a woman from Greenpeace to seek publicity. While she was gone her home was attacked.

The Wilsons live on twenty acres at the end of a dead-end road in a remote willow-and-brush-forest area of Calhoun County, "way out in the boondocks," as Diane describes it. Her mother-in-law lives in a trailer beside the main house. She was going out to get the mail at 8:30 A.M. on April 9 when three shots were fired and hit the ground around her. She didn't see anyone and wasn't sure what to make of it. The next morning the kids missed their bus and Leslie Wilson, Diane's husband, drove them to school. Leslie had served as a helicopter mechanic in Vietnam and had recently given up on shrimping to run a crew boat that took men to and from the area's offshore oil platforms. This familiarized him with the sounds of Coast Guard helicopters that patrolled the coastline. When he returned home from dropping the kids off at school, his mother came to him and said that the dog had been shot. The dog, covered in blood, had run to her door, and she'd heard a helicopter and seen a man with a gun in the front yard, she told him. He went inside to calm the dog and stop its bleeding when he heard a helicopter hovering somewhere in front of the house. He called the sheriff and told him he thought the helicopter was there to pick up whoever did the shooting. The sheriff was reluctant to send a deputy out until Leslie threatened to shoot at the chopper himself.

More than an hour after he called, a sheriff's deputy arrived and told him that the Coast Guard was flying in the area and that was probably what he'd heard. Leslie insisted it wasn't a Coast Guard helicopter. When he went into the house, the deputy asked his mother if he suffered from post-Vietnam stress syndrome. The deputy also suggested that Diane might get sick from her fast and have to go into the hospital or be institutionalized. When Leslie took the dog to the veterinarian later that day, the vet (whose father worked in the bank where Formosa does all its local business) suggested it had probably been in a dogfight. Only after Leslie insisted that he X-ray the animal did he find and remove the bullet from its leg and identify the second through-and-through neck wound. Around midnight that night the helicopter returned, hovering over the Wilsons' house a second time.

"As soon as my attorney heard about the shooting, he thought it was the federal government 'cause we were suing the EPA and all these other agencies," Diane recalls.

Greenpeace contacted Sheila O'Donnell and she gave Diane a call. O'Donnell suggested that the Wilsons contact the local Coast Guard stations and secure a copy of the police report on the incident. They called all the Coast Guard stations within several hundred miles and discovered that there had been no helicopter overflights anywhere near their home on the morning or evening of April 10. When they received a copy of their "assignment report" from the Calhoun County sheriff's department, there was still no mention of a helicopter.[27]

"Sheila called me a couple of times and gave me some suggestions and sent me some information that was helpful," Diane says. "Thing is, you have to do your own protection down here. The local mayor and justice of the peace all have contracts with the company" (as did her local state senator, who managed Formosa's security company, Triple-D).

Among the materials O'Donnell sent her was a six-page brochure she'd written called "Common Sense Security."[28] "Popular consciousness of environmental issues," states the brochure, "has seen tremendous growth in the past few years. People organizing or speaking out against environmental degradation in this country and abroad are facing an escalating pattern of harassment. Increasing also is the number of arsons, robberies, burglaries, and attacks on environmental activists, especially on women. ..." The brochure goes on to suggest that activists "spend a few minutes to assess your work from a security point of view."

Next are listed fifty-four tips categorized under ten headings. Some of the suggestions under "Office" are: "Keep mailing and donor lists and personal phone books out of sight. Always maintain a duplicate at a different location: update it frequently. ... Keep a camera, loaded with film, handy at all times. ... If you are the last person to leave the office late at night, leave the light on when you depart. Do not advertise your departure."

"Common Sense" reminds recycling-minded activists that looking through their office trash could provide a treasure trove of information for an anti-enviro vigilante. Two of the tips under the heading "Telephone" are: "If you receive threatening calls on your answering machine,

immediately remove and save the tape. ... Keep a pad and pen next to
the telephone. Jot down details of threatening or suspicious calls immediately. Note the time, date and keep a file." Under "Mail" the brochure
suggests, "Get a mail box through the Post Office or a private concern.
Be aware that the United States Post Office will give your street address
to inquirers under certain circumstances. ... If you receive a threatening letter, handle it as little as possible. Put both the letter and the en-
velope in a plastic bag or file folder. Give the original to the police only
if they agree to fingerprint it. Give them a copy otherwise because you
may wish to have your own expert examine it."

Other advice is: "Automobiles—Keep your automobile clean so you
can see if there is an addition or loss. ... Put your literature in the trunk
or in a closed box. ... Keep your car locked at all times. Police—Report
any incidents to the local police and ask for protection if you feel it is war-
ranted. ... Report threats or harassment to your local police. Demand that
they take a report and protect you if that is necessary. Talk to the press and
report the police response as well as the incident(s). ... Report thefts of
materials from your office or home to the police: these are criminal acts."

Among "Common Sense Security" suggestions for countering sur-
veillance are: "Brief your membership on known or suspected surveil-
lance. Be scrupulous with documentation. Do not dismiss complaints as
paranoia without careful investigation. The opposition can and frequently
does have informants join organizations to learn about methods and
strategy. ... Photograph the person(s) following you or have a friend do
so. Use caution. If someone is overtly following you they are trying to
frighten you. Openly photographing them makes them uncomfortable.
If you are covertly being followed, have a friend covertly photograph
them. ... If you are being followed [by car], get the license plate number and state. Try to get a description of the driver and the car as well
as passengers. Notice anything different about the car. ... Debrief yourself immediately after each incident. Write details down: time, date, occasion, incident, characteristics of person(s), impressions, anything odd
about the situation. ... Keep a 'Weirdo' file with detailed notes about
unsettling situations and see if a pattern emerges."

Under "Break-ins," the brochure recommends checking "with
knowledgeable people in your area about alarm systems, dogs, surveil-
lance cameras, motion sensitive lights, deadbolt locks and traditional
security measures to protect against break-ins."

The brochure concludes by stating that "if you feel something is wrong, trust the feeling. Your instincts are usually right. ... None of this advice is intended to frighten but to create an awareness of the problems."

Unfortunately "Common Sense Security" lacks a heading for "Fishing Boats."

"In October of ninety-two I was out on the bay hauling my nets and I noticed the boat was listing," Wilson recalls. "I ran and throwed the hatch up and the water is almost over the engine and it was coming in around the filling box [containing the rotor shaft] and the wires were all gone from the electric pump and so I hand-pumped like crazy for a while and later found some wires and hooked up the pump directly to the battery. The wires had been jerked loose. I couldn't figure how it could have happened, but then it happened again three or four weeks later. The filling box is usually tightened down so there's not enough room for water to be leaking in. Someone had to loosen the filling box and pull the wires on the pump, but the first time it happened, you know, you just have a hard time believing someone would really do something like that intentionally, you kind of deny what's before your eyes. And I don't swim at all, even though I'm a shrimper. And also my radio'd been swiped some time before, so I'm out there five or six miles all alone with no radio and think I could've died if that boat sank."

In April 1993, Wilson heard a police scanner somewhere in the woods near her house. "It's not something you'd hear normally 'cause we're way out here away from everything," she explains. A short time later her dog came into the yard, laid down, and died. "We just buried him. We don't have the money to go have a dog's body tested or anything. We barely have $15 between us. But he was only four years old and recovered from the shooting, so it was pretty suspicious."

Rather than retreat in the face of ongoing harassment and intimidation, Wilson decided to go on another hunger fast that spring, protesting Formosa's chemical wastewater-release permits, which were scheduled to go into effect by the end of September 1993. At thirty days, this was the longest of her fasts; it ended in May after state officials persuaded Formosa to work with an independent commission to find ways to reduce or recycle its wastewater. Wilson, although still a minority voice within her job-poor county, was beginning to pick up support.

"Diane's done a lot more good than she realizes. Formosa's expansion is much more scrutinized because of her," says Charles Spiekerman, regional director of the Texas Air Control Board in Corpus Christi, eighty miles south of Seadrift.[29]

By the winter of 1993–1994, legal suits, opposition from the U.S. Fish and Wildlife Service, and organized protests by the $200 million–a–year shrimping industry had temporarily delayed Formosa's discharge permit.

"Matagorda and Lavaca and Spirit Center and San Antonio bays are all hooked together in about a hundred miles of these waters I grew up on," Wilson says. "The coziness is unreal. Plus, it feeds a lot of families. I take the bay real personal. It needs protecting. It has to last more than just this one generation."

She admits that the campaign of harassment and violence directed against her has taken a toll. "I've been called a prostitute, a lesbian, a racist, a bad mother. My parents, sister, and brother are upset with me. My husband and I are nearly on the verge of getting a divorce, but I will not stop. They will not get that bay."

The same month the Wilsons' dog was shot in 1992, Stephanie McGuire's cousin, Linda Rowland, took McGuire's son to the store while she stayed behind at the fish camp they managed on the Fenholloway River in Florida. The Fenholloway, on the state's northern Gulf Coast, was once considered a fishing and recreational paradise until it was reclassified an "industrial river" in 1947 in order to attract Procter & Gamble's Buckeye pulp mill. The "industrial river" classification allowed companies to dump anything they wanted into a river. With its right to pollute ensured, P&G began operations in 1954. Forty years later the Fenholloway ran as black as oil from fifty million gallons a day of industrial discharge from P&G's Buckeye Mill, which produced more than a thousand tons a day of chlorine-bleached cellulose used in sanitary napkins, tampons, and disposable diapers. Studies conducted by the EPA found dioxin levels in the river close to two thousand times what the agency considers an acceptable level of risk. Cancer rates for the county were unreliable since most people went to Tallahassee or Gainesville for hospitalization, but anecdotal evidence suggested a high rate of cancer for rural Taylor County, where the mill was located. The county also has disproportionately high rates of leukemia and blood and liver disorders, problems associated with dioxin and other chemical exposures. And female fish in the river have developed male character-istics—because of pollution-caused hormonal changes, according to EPA scientists. A number of local wells have been contaminated along with the county's groundwater. The tap water has taken on a yellow-green tint and a foul odor. The local newspaper's response was to praise Procter & Gamble for providing free bottled water to area residents. P&G dominated the local economy to such a degree that residents re-ferred to the plant as "Uncle Buck" and called the awful odor emanat-ing from its six hundred–acre facility "the smell of money."

Wall Street Journal reporter Alecia Swasy, in her book *Soap Opera—The Inside Story of Procter & Gamble*, described the county seat of Perry as "a company town seemingly out of the 1800s. ... Locals com-monly refer to blacks as 'niggers,' and segregation still exists at restau-rants and bars. Some still talk about Dixie 'rising again.' Men joke about using whips to turn women into 'good housewives.' Disputes are often settled with guns."[30]

Ned Mudd, a tough-as-nails environmental lawyer out of Birming-ham, Alabama, recalls a two-day trip he took to Perry to represent local residents, including Stephanie McGuire, in a dioxin suit they brought against P&G. "I told my assistant, 'Next time we come down here we're going to rent a fast car and have two shotguns in the back.' It's that kind of a nasty place. I remember saying, 'Somebody's going to get killed in this town.'"[31]

Local rancher Joy Towles Cummings first got into a dispute with P&G in 1989 over a logging lease on her family land. A former ag-chemical saleswoman who took over the family ranch after her grand-mother became too old to manage it, Cummings quickly began to suspect that the plant's chemical pollution of the river, wells, and local springs was far worse than anybody had suspected. She began getting inside information from plant workers about sinkholes below settling ponds and chemical leaks from unlined dumps as well as illegal dump-ing at the mill itself. By the spring of 1991, she was ready to form a citi-zens' group and take on the company. About the same time, Julie Hauserman, an award-winning journalist with the *Tallahassee Demo-crat*, wrote an investigative series called "Florida's Forgotten River," ex-posing the pollution problems along the Fenholloway. In the wake of those articles, Cumming's group, Help Our Polluted Environment (HOPE), gained its first dozen members, including the outspoken

Linda Rowland, who'd worked at the mill for fifteen years, and her painfully shy cousin, Stephanie McGuire. P&G supporters quickly formed their own Wise Use group called Defenders of Taylor County. Defenders wrote state officials denouncing HOPE as a "pseudo-environmental cult." A short time later the HOPE women began receiving threatening phone calls, including one from a caller saying he'd cut out their tongues if they didn't hush. After that, Cummings began packing a .38 revolver in her purse.

"I carry a gun with me all the time. It's not safe for me not to," she explains. "You're pretty much on your own down here. We don't trust the sheriff. His deputies used to follow us around, and more recently he's been covering up like a cat covers its mess."

After Cummings was invited to appear on a local TV show, the show's host, a Baptist preacher, was taken off the air. According to Alecia Swasy's *Soap Opera*, the station owner told the show's host that callers had threatened to burn down the station after HOPE's founder appeared on his program. A local furniture store owner said he was also threatened with having his store burned down because it advertised on the show.

Linda Rowland and Stephanie McGuire had been receiving threatening phone calls for some time. After Cumming's twenty-three-year-old son died in a car accident, Rowland and McGuire received a call from a man who said, "You know how accidents happen. They can happen to you." Boats at their fish camp had been cut loose and pheasants caged near their house had been poisoned. The women began keeping handguns and shotguns near them at all times. At about five on the afternoon of April 7, after Rowland and McGuire's son Shawn had driven off to the store, McGuire waited for the last fishing boat to return from the Gulf of Mexico two miles down the Fenholloway. She later recalled hearing a boat pull up to the dock and going outside to greet it. That's when she spotted a man dressed in camouflage. He told her he'd shot a cow up the road and wanted the owner's name. Feeling uneasy, she began to head back to the house. Before she got there, two other men in camouflage and masks came out of the woods. One hit her on the head with a rock and tossed it into the river. She fell to the ground, managed to get up again, and hit him in the mouth with all her strength. He reached under his camouflage mask, removed a tooth she'd dislodged, and put it in his pocket. The men then knocked her back to the ground, stomping on her hand; burned her skin with a cigar; and slashed her throat with a razor.

"After they cut my throat they poured water in it from the river and said, 'Now you'll have something to sue about,'" she later recounted to Sheila O'Donnell and another P.I., a former navy SEAL from Alabama who photographed and videotaped her injuries. The unmasked attacker told her, "This is the last face you'll see." Two of the men then raped her. One of her dogs, a terrier named Boo-boo, may have saved her life, attacking one of the men and biting him in the face. He threw the dog in the river and, bleeding from his cheek, retreated to their boat. The other two followed. One of them lifted and aimed a shotgun at McGuire. "Oh, God, they're fixing to shoot me," she thought, but the boat's driver revved the engine so that the shooter lost his balance as they sped off toward the Gulf."[32]

McGuire crawled into her house, called her neighbors, and dialed 911. The neighbors, who lived about five miles up the river, arrived before the medics did and drove her out from the camp to where they met the ambulance. She was taken to a Tallahassee hospital where she was treated for her wounds. At the time she was too embarrassed to admit that she had also been raped.

"I think those guys thought they were beating up Linda [Rowland] 'cause she's the outspoken one and they got the wrong gal," says Cummings. "It's easy to mistake them. They're two great big heavy women. What I think is these guys were not from Taylor County," HOPE's leader continues. "Three Taylor County men would not show up to beat up one ole fat gal. If they were mad they wouldn't rape and beat and threaten her. They might holler and get in a gunfight but they wouldn't do that kind of thing."

Cummings had been reporting earlier cases of harassment to the FBI in Tallahassee, and they had assured her they would come down to Taylor County if something major happened. But after the attack they told her they would only get involved if the local sheriff blew the investigation.

The Taylor County sheriff's investigation, as it turned out, was not a model of forensic efficiency. Following the attack, sheriff's vehicles drove over the crime scene. Deputies who said there was not enough blood on the ground to conform to McGuire's story never entered the blood-splattered house, nor did they interview the neighbors, who

were first on the scene of the crime. When McGuire and Rowland returned to the fish camp the next day, they found a watch McGuire had
lost during the attack that the deputies had overlooked during their
quick search of the scene. Sheriff John Walker soon began suggesting
that her injuries were the result of a lesbian quarrel between the cousins.
McGuire was interviewed about the attack on a *60 Minutes* segment on
Wise Use, and after that, Walker tried to charge her with perjury, but
the state attorney declined to prosecute.

Phone harassment of the two women also continued after the attack.
They moved several times, finally leaving the county. After one move
the calls stopped until Joy Towles Cummings accidentally mentioned
their new phone number during a conversation on her home phone.
Then the calls started up again. The local newspaper also published a
story telling its readers where they had moved. One of the women's
rottweilers was subsequently poisoned with table scraps laced with
antifreeze.

"We've got her [and Linda] in a safe place now," Joy says. "They
don't have the support system I have with my friends and family
around me. No one could get onto my farm without us knowing. I also
don't go anywhere without my guns."

60 Minutes rebroadcast its "Dirty Fight" Wise Use report on June 6,
1993. "It had tremendous impact. There was a flurry of activity in Taylor County following the rebroadcast. The Taylor County Chamber of
Commerce and Procter & Gamble responded more strongly to the second running than even the first time," said state attorney Jerry Blair.[33]
Shortly after the rebroadcast, stories that McGuire was either beaten up
in a bar or by "her girlfriend" were widely circulated on the national
Wise Use/Property Rights network.

The private investigator and former navy SEAL who had interviewed
McGuire and taken pictures of her injuries (and was convinced she was
telling the truth) provided the pictures to the Florida Department of
Law Enforcement. A female agent from FDLE was assigned to the case
but she and McGuire didn't get along.

"It never was a good-faith investigation," claims Sheila O'Donnell,
who spoke with the FDLE agent before the agent first contacted
McGuire. "She told me about how she'd heard Stephanie was a lesbian
and she'd looked at her pictures and seen worse injuries that were
self-inflicted," O'Donnell says. "She didn't know my relation with

Stephanie McGuire, but was still willing to make these inflammatory pre-judgmental statements, saying she was suspicious of McGuire and didn't trust her."

On July 13, the FDLE, Taylor County sheriff's office, and state attorney Jerry Blair issued a report saying that McGuire had suffered real wounds but that they didn't believe her story.

In her book, Alecia Swasy reports that Jerry Blair, an elected official, was pressured by Taylor County officials to bring criminal charges against McGuire and that he had received a number of phone calls, including calls from the chamber of commerce and Dan Simmons, the Buckeye Mill's public affairs manager. "They wanted to vindicate the honor of P&G," a source close to the investigation told her. "It is in the best interest of the community and P&G that the attack didn't happen and she be discredited."

In September 1993 the fish camp where McGuire was attacked, including a trailer, cook shed, and hundred-year-old log house, was burned to the ground. Cummings, a friend of hers, and her friend's father were filming pollution seepage along the riverbank when they saw the smoke. As they drove into the camp, they found Dan Simmons taking photographs of the still-smoking ruins. He appeared nervous as Cummings began questioning him about what had happened and why he was there.

"Dan and I usually joke, but I wasn't in a humorous mood just then," she says. "He kept saying I'd lost my sense of humor, but you could see he was nervous. My friend Sandra was making moves like she might just push him into the river, but I figured if anyone was going to do it it was going to be me. Just the week before he'd announced how the water quality of the river was improving and how it was now safe for fishing and swimming. So when he again said how I'd lost my sense of humor, I just shoved him into the river. We were laughing when he came up sputtering and I said, 'Now who's lost their sense of humor?' It's kind of hard to climb out of that river 'cause the banks are all slick from the oil and chemicals the mill puts out. Sandra's dad's an old guy who's kind of bent over and carries a cane, and he extended it to Dan, who reached out to take a hold of it, and when he did Sandra's dad just pushed him back in with it. That really set us to laughing. I expected the sheriff would come and arrest me that night but he didn't. I figure Dan never admitted it happened 'cause if he did the guys at the mill would probably tease him forever about lettin' some gal push him in the river. Later my Greenpeace friends said I shouldn't have done that because it was violence, but I don't think so. I mean, he's the one who said it was safe for swimming and all. Besides, if we didn't have some fun around here I think we'd just about lose our minds."

I ask Sheila O'Donnell why she thinks so many anti-environmentalist attacks have been directed against women.

"Women are the backbone of the environmental movement, particularly the anti-toxics movement, so that's one reason they're targeted," she says. "But I also think there's something else going on here. Women get targeted and men feel guilty they weren't there to defend them. It's a terror tactic. It raises the fear level, and frightened people are less effective organizers. It has a kind of sub-rosa effect. People don't get involved as readily. But I think it also strengthens those people who choose not to be intimidated."

O'Donnell herself seems unintimidated, even though she's encountered a growing number of cases like those of Judi Bari, Pat Costner, Diane Wilson, and Stephanie McGuire. I ask her why she doesn't carry a weapon when she's investigating this kind of attack.

"I don't want that kind of energy around me," she explains. "I go into situations where people are armed and if I feel uncomfortable I leave. Otherwise I might stay and engage in something I don't want to be a part of. To carry a weapon you have to be convinced that you're willing to take another person's life, because you don't want to wound an armed person, you have to kill him. And I think to carry that gun you really have to be fresh, to be practiced. Cops are fresh because that's what they do with their lives. But I feel that my work is really about supporting life, not taking life."

ten

Bomb Throwers, 1997

*We wonder why we have got the Freemen or the militants. We
wonder why, in fact, we have got unrest in this country. It is because
our government, in fact, has got out of hand and out of line with
the Endangered Species Act.*
>—Representative Don Young (R–Alaska) during debate
>in the House of Representatives, June 19, 1996

*All it would have taken was for him [one of the rangers] to draw a
weapon. Fifty people with sidearms would have drilled him.*
>—Nevada County Commissioner Dick Carver,
>speaking of his confrontation with two Forest Rangers

ELLEN GRAY, DIRECTOR of the Pilchuck Audubon Society in
Everett, Washington, had just finished testifying at a County Council
hearing in favor of a land-use ordinance to protect local streams and
wetlands when a man stood up in front of her with a noose and said,
"This is for you."

"We have a militia of 10,000," another man told her, "and if we can't
beat you at the ballot box we'll beat you with a bullet."[1]

Darryl Lord, the man with the noose, was an elected leader of the
Snohomish County Property Rights Alliance. Another PRA leader,
Don Kehoe, was a featured speaker, along with John Trochmann from
the Militia of Montana at an earlier militia organizing meeting near
Everett. Militia materials were also being distributed during a tour
through the region by Wise Use leader Chuck Cushman. Cushman argued that a proposed binational park between the North Cascades and
two provincial wilderness areas in Canada posed a threat to U.S. sovereignty. Kehoe went on to claim that the park was part of a U.N. plot

to dismember the United States and take over a quarter of Washington State, driving out residents and replacing them with "the world's elite," who would be protected by CIA "electronic fortifications." "We're talking about a conspiracy to create a one-world government, a one-world religion and a one-world economy," Kehoe claimed.[2]

Although they don't agree on everything, militant members of the Wise Use/Property Rights movement and members of America's armed militia movement have increasingly staked out common territory since the 1990s.

"We're seeing incredible crossover of people and materials between Wise Use and the militias from Washington to western Montana, eastern Oregon and northern Idaho," says Eric Ward of the Northwest Coalition Against Malicious Harassment, a Seattle-based human rights organization.[3]

"Sometimes I have a hard time telling where the militia starts and the land-use movement ends," agreed Bellingham, Washington, police chief Don Pierce. Pierce was involved in the July 27, 1996, arrest of several Snohomish County Property Rights advocates, part of a larger militia group charged with possession of pipe bombs, which, according to their indictment, they planned to use in a war against the federal government and the United Nations.[4]

In 2001 the Wise Use group Montanans for Multiple Use and the Militia of Montana began working together to protest wilderness road closures and to organize a joint caravan to eastern Oregon in support of farm irrigators involved in a water dispute on the Klamath River. John Stokes, owner of KGEZ radio in Kallispell, Montana, was and is a major promoter of both Wise Use and "patriot" militia conspiracies, regularly denouncing "Green Nazis" and staging rallies where green swastikas are set afire. In 2002, Dave Burgert, one of his regular guests and supporters, was arrested in an armed standoff with police. The arrest led to the discovery of Project 7, a local militia cell. Law enforcement agents uncovered a cache of weapons, 30,000 rounds of ammunition, and hit lists including personal addresses of local judges and sheriff's deputies.

Montana's conservative Republican governor Judy Martz had earlier planned to appear on Stokes's show but cancelled after he suggested expediting her appearance by sending bomb threats to her office. Secretary of Interior Gale Norton, who received a small coffin from Stokes (symbolizing the death of rural America at the hands of "Green Nazis"), sent her regrets that she'd not be able to appear on his show but congratulated him on his good works. Of course it could be argued that Norton receives many invitations to appear on many radio shows, but it's hard to imagine that any others came with token coffins blaming environmentalists for all the problems of rural America.

Although the militias first surfaced in early 1994, they didn't gain widespread recognition until after the April 19, 1995, bombing of a U.S. federal building in Oklahoma City that killed 168 men, women, and children. The arrest of two suspects, Gulf War veteran Timothy McVeigh and his pal Terry Nichols of Michigan, both affiliated with militia activities and beliefs, raised serious questions about this new force on the far right.

Nichols's brother, James, who was initially held as a material witness, is a member of the Michigan Property Owners Association, founded by Property Rights activist Zeno Budd. Budd was a featured speaker at a militia forum held in Detroit in March 1995. When contacted by reporters after the Oklahoma blast, Budd repeated a conspiracy theory widespread among militia followers that the Oklahoma bombing was actually carried out by the federal government in order to frame the militias and declare martial law.

"They think ecosystems management is part of the New World Order that will overrun the United States," says Jere Payton, a local environmental activist in eastern Washington. She recalls her first contact with the militia in the winter of 1994: "We looked out our window and saw a guy walking down the street of our little mountain village wearing camouflage and carrying a gun. This was right after the Militia of Montana came through and had their organizing meeting. ... Someone heard them talking about how they could randomly take us out. There's a lot of loose talk about killing people in our community. Talk like that makes us worry."5

In the West the militias used Wise Use groups as their primary recruiting ground, arguing for military resistance to the government and its "preservationist" backers, and formation of three- to six-man "Autonomous Leadership Units" that look and act suspiciously like terrorist cells. By early 1995, environmental activists in Washington State, New Mexico, and Montana had reported receiving death threats from people identifying themselves as militiamen.

The County Supremacy movement, the arm of Wise Use that claims county sheriffs have the right to arrest federal land managers who fail to respect the "customs and culture" of logging, mining, and grazing on public lands, became a hotbed for vigilante and militia organizing.

The National Federal Lands Conference (NFLC), at Bountiful, Utah, is the coordinating body for the counties movement. Its advisory board includes Wise Use founder Ron Arnold, Property Rights attorney and former Reagan Justice Department official Mark Pollot, and Nevada rancher Wayne Hage.

The October 1994 issue of the NFLC newsletter ran a cover story titled "Why There Is a Need for the Militia in America." It read in part:

> Our individual freedoms are disappearing faster than baby turtles at a seagull convention. ... Did you know that Sarah Brady, the prime mover and benefactor of the [handgun control] "Brady Bill" said before the Congress, "Our task of creating a socialist America can only succeed when those who will resist us have been totally disarmed." There is a greater risk of being struck by an errant lavender blue asteroid than there is of dying form [*sic*] most EPA-regulated pollutants! Do we really need a militia, and why? Because we have scalawags and rascals and mischievous persons and people open to temptation and flat out liars and thieves in places of power in our federal government.[6]

The rambling declaration went on to provide contact numbers for the Militia of Montana, the Constitutional Militia of Arizona, and the journal of the Idaho-based US Militia Association. Founded by Sam Sherwood, the (later disbanded) US Militia recruited loggers and miners by urging them to resist the "Green Gestapo" and the Endangered Species Act. According to the Associated Press, Sherwood told an Idaho audience to "go up and look your legislators in the face, because some day you may have to blow it off."

Following the Oklahoma bombing and reports in the *The Nation, Time,* and elsewhere linking Wise Use with the militias, Ron Arnold told columnist Alexander Cockburn that he'd resigned from the NFLC three years earlier. Although Cockburn, a self-styled leftist who mixes harsh criticism of "liberals" with periodic endorsement of Far Right causes, took him at his word, Arnold offered no hard evidence (such as a letter of resignation). In fact, the NFLC continued to list Arnold as a board member and used his name in promotional materials through 1996.

As many as fifty counties around the country have now passed County Supremacy ordinances claiming local control over public lands. In the fall of 1994, officials of Catron County, New Mexico, which passed the first of these ordinances, proposed forming their own militia (they'd already called for all heads of household to arm themselves).

"Citizens are getting tired of being tossed around and pushed to the limit by regulations," said Carl Livingston, one of the commissioners. "We want the Forest Service to know we're prepared, even though violence would be a last resort."

Local People for the West! (PFW) activist Skip Price, who wore a .45 to county meetings, warned that if the Forest Service tried to fence off his stream, "They're meeting bullets." Rancher Kit Laney said that if the Forest Service tried to move his cattle off public grazing lands, "There will be a hundred people with guns waiting for them."

After Tim Tibbitts, a federal wildlife biologist, went to Catron County to meet with local ranchers and talk about endangered species protections, a rancher opened his car door and told him, "If you ever come down to Catron County again, we'll blow your fucking head off."

Mike Gardner is the Forest Service district ranger for Catron. In March 1995, his office was defaced with painted hammers and sickles. A native of Oklahoma, Gardner has lived in the small Catron County seat of Reserve with his wife and children since 1988. The local militia meets in the house next door to his. "As far as I'm concerned, they're accomplices to what happened in Oklahoma," he says with a slow steely drawl. "That's what the militias are doing, they're advocating violence and insurrection and they got the result you could expect—babies killed."[7]

The militia movement, the largest armed expression of the Far Right since the Ku Klux Klan, is unified by two primary themes. One is the right to bear arms, the other a conspiratorial view of big government (reinforced by federal misconduct in the 1993 Waco assault in Texas and the FBI killing of white separatist Randy Weaver's wife and son). In the wake of the September 11, 2001, attacks on the World Trade Center and the Pentagon, militia websites were full of stories on how the attacks were carried out not by Al Qaeda, but by the federal government and Mossad, the Israeli secret service. This was the same anti-Semitic conspiracy theory widely reported in Egyptian and other Arab news outlets.

In October 1992, two months after the Weaver shoot-out at Ruby Ridge, Idaho (which also saw the death of a federal agent), 150 veterans of the racist Right gathered in Estes Park, Colorado, to plot strategy. The meeting had been called by Pete Peters, a Christian Identity pastor. Christian Identity is a racist theology that claims Jews are the spawn of Satan, people of color are subhuman "mud people," and white Americans are the true Israelites. Others in attendance included John Trochmann from Montana, former Texas Klansman Louis Beam (who'd helped ignite violence between Anglo and Vietnamese shrimpers in the late 1970s), and Klansman–turned–White Aryan Resistance (WAR) founder Tom Metzger.

At this meeting a decision was made to begin organizing armed groups, not around openly racist politics but rather "patriotic" paranoia. With the end of the Cold War, right-wing fears that had largely focused on communism for more than forty years began to shift to the Right's other traditional "enemies," such as the United Nations and the federal government. Waco and Ruby Ridge would get the ball rolling, but militia membership wouldn't really take off until passage of the Brady Act, a mild gun-control law requiring a seven-day waiting period for purchase of a handgun. The NRA, Alan Gottlieb's two gun organizations, and others on the Right would portray this as the beginning of the end of private gun ownership in America.

That the militias were seen as a hoped-for vehicle for "Aryan revolution" was reflected in proposals put forward by Beam and Metzger for "Autonomous Leadership Units," also known as ⌐eaderless Resistance." Recalling the speed and efficiency with which the FBI had rounded up some thirty members of "The Order" when that Aryan Nations–affiliated hate group went on a robbery, counterfeiting, and murder spree in the 1980s, they proposed that the militias create a culture of resistance in which small guerrilla cells would form to carry out bombings and other terrorist acts without any direct or provable links to militia leadership.

Of course it took more than a conspiratorial group and creative use of shortwave radio, Waco videos, and the Internet to ignite militia mania. The reality is that the majority of Americans are seeing their real wages decline and job security evaporate as the economy of the United States is integrated into a new global economy, dominated by transnational corporations. At the same time, rural America is being particularly hard hit by farm debt and consolidation and liquidation of natural resource industries.

Unfortunately, these economic realities and the fears they evoke aren't reflected in either our celebrity-driven mass media or the political culture of the two-party system. As a result, many people have wrongly come to blame their declining status on job competition from immigrants, minorities, and women in the workplace. In this context, Wise Use, militia, and other right-wing organizers have been able to enter predominantly white, rural communities and offer people easy answers to real but complex problems, providing them with conspiracy theories and scapegoats. In areas where there aren't many "Jewish bankers" or "mud people," environmental activists and federal workers who enforce the nation's environmental laws have become the scapegoats of choice.

"I think the Wise Users really want a confrontation," says National Park Service Law-Enforcement Agent Pat Buccello, who teaches a course on "extremist groups on public lands," for Park Service rangers and employees. "They're merging with Christian Identity and all these other right-wing extremist groups. You see the rhetoric changing, where it is now acceptable for them to say, 'I think you ought to be shot.'"

In southern Nevada on July 4, 1994, the late Nye County commissioner Dick Carver, backed up by an armed posse, chased two Forest Service rangers off a road he was illegally bulldozing through the Toiyabe National Forest. "All it would have taken was for him [one of the rangers] to draw a weapon," Carver later bragged at a Wise Use rally, and "fifty people with sidearms would have drilled him."[8]

The pugnacious cattle rancher and county leader had been a keynote speaker at both Wise Use and Christian Identity events. Catapulted to national prominence by his supporters in the grazing and mining industries, Carver appeared on the cover of *Time* magazine on October 23, 1995, for a story titled "Don't Tread on Me—An Inside Look at the West's Growing Rebellion."

In Kalispell, Montana, where land-use planning has become the target of Wise Use activists, Jess Quinn, an opponent of a building permit program, told a militia meeting, "When the hour strikes, there will be public officials dead in the streets."

In eastern Oregon, Forrest Cameron, the manager of the Malheur National Wildlife Refuge, received death threats after a local rancher was arrested for trespassing his cattle on refuge land. Following a Wise Use rally at which Chuck Cushman displayed the phone numbers and addresses of refuge employees and told a crowd of several hundred that they should be made "pariahs" of the community, Cameron's wife and five children also received telephone death threats.

Wise Use intimidation of federal employees has now reached the point that the Forest Service issues security instructions to its rangers in the field, instructing them to travel in pairs and stay in radio contact. It has also printed a pocket-sized card telling them what to do if they're arrested by the local sheriff. "If you are confronted, detained, or placed in custody by state or local authorities, do not resist ... everything will be done to have you released as quickly as possible," it reads.[9]

One widely reported confrontation grew out of a controversial recovery program for endangered gray wolves that saw fifteen of the predators released in the Idaho wilderness in early 1995. Within days, one of the radio-collared animals was found shot dead next to a partially eaten calf in a field belonging to seventy-four-year-old rancher Eugene Hussey. Under the rules of the recovery program, any wolf found killing livestock could be legally shot. Still, no one stepped forward to claim the kill. Had he done so he would have been hailed as a hero by the local Cattlemen's Association and other opponents of wolf recovery, including Lemhi County sheriff Brett Barsalou. After the two animals' carcasses were sent to the U.S. Fish and Wildlife forensics lab in Ashland, Oregon, the reason for the shooter's reticence became clear.

"Humans cheat, they violate laws, they try to take more than their fair share. It's good old human greed and that's what our laboratory's basically there to fight," explains Ken Goddard, the quick-talking, white-haired ex–narcotics officer who directs the federal lab. Set in the rolling hills of southern Oregon, this modern, single-story facility is unique in the way it applies forensic technologies normally used to capture rapists and murderers to the job of catching poachers involved in the illegal killing of endangered wildlife.[10]

According to a report issued by the lab's veterinary medical examiner, "The calf probably died of causes related to birthing and was dead at the time the wolf scavenged the carcass." The fact that there were no deep bite marks to indicate that the wolf had carried the sixty-six-pound calf from its birthing site to where the two bodies were later recovered strongly suggested that "the calf carcass was picked up and moved ... by persons unknown."

If, as it now appeared, the wolf was baited into a death trap, then the Endangered Species Act had been violated, a felony offense.

In March 1995, three U.S. Fish and Wildlife agents returned to the ranch to search for any shell casings that might still remain on the open killing ground. But before they could do their job, they had to retreat from Gene Hussey's land after Sheriff Brett Barsalou told them to leave the old rancher alone and drove off, with Hussey threatening to "go to plan B." One of Hussey's confederates explained that "plan B" meant the sheriff would be returning with the local militia (a claim the sheriff later denied). The agents, noting they were in a box canyon with only one road out, decided it would be better to live to fight another day and vamoosed. Idaho politicians, including Senator Larry Craig and then Representatives Helen Chenoweth and Mike Crapo, expressed outrage, not at the threat of vigilante violence but at the federal agents' "harassment" of an elderly Idaho landowner (even though on a tape recording made by one of the agents, Gene Hussey can be heard cursing and throwing rocks at them while they try to calm him down).

Senator Craig condemned "the increasing presence of an armed federal entity in the states where you have these [natural] resource agencies," going on to suggest that among westerners, "There has always been a healthy suspicion of the federal agent. Now there is developing a healthy fear, especially if the agent is armed."

His warning echoed Rush Limbaugh's earlier radio suggestion that because of environmental regulations, "The second violent American revolution is just about—I got my fingers about a quarter of an inch apart—is just about that far away. Because these people are sick and tired of a bunch of bureaucrats in Washington driving into town and telling them what they can and can't do with their land."[11]

One reason more people don't entirely discount Wise Use's claims about being persecuted and oppressed by "jackbooted federal thugs" and "nature Nazis" is that their view represents the narrow spout of a conspiratorial funnel with a very wide mouth in the West. At its broadest there is the "War on the West" myth (embraced by many western politicians and small-business men) that sees the western states as a colony of eastern capital. This myth, unsupported by any serious economic historian, finds expression in a new "States' Rights" movement.

Like its predecessor in the segregationist South, it hopes to reclaim the power of the states to overturn progressive policies that reflect a broader national consensus (in this case, protection of America's natural heritage on public lands).

A staffer for then Senator (now Governor) Frank Murkowski of Alaska brags, "I helped plan 'War on the West' rallies where we drew several thousand hunters, ORV types, and industries united against a general foe—the federal government personified by [Al] Gore and [Clinton Secretary of Interior Bruce] Babbitt."[12]

Former Texas pest-exterminator (and now House Majority Leader) Tom DeLay spent much of the 1990s railing against the "Jackbooted EPA Gestapo" and identifying the Endangered Species Act as the second greatest "threat" facing his constituents (after "illegal aliens" but presumably ahead of drugs, terrorism, and political corruption).

In New Mexico, Governor Gary Johnson held public meetings following the Oklahoma City bombing with militia and Catron County leaders, while refusing to meet with local environmentalists concerned about their violent tactics. He claimed that the militias were there to help in times of emergency. Asked if he endorsed the County Supremacy theories of the Catron County Commissioners, his spokesman explained, "He's pro states' rights."[13]

Toward the end of the 1996 presidential campaign, candidate Bob Dole also spoke about the federal government's War on the West during appearances in Idaho and Utah. But an editorial in Utah's largest paper, the *Salt Lake Tribune*, blasted the ex-senator for embracing "the Whine of the West."

Unfortunately, when politicians and opinion makers tolerate and promote anti-government paranoia, they also encourage the fringe politics that inevitably go along with it.

The first bomb exploded on Halloween morning, 1993. Days earlier, fifteen western senators had successfully filibustered against a grazing reform bill that would gradually raise grazing fees from $1.86 to $3.45 per AUM (Animal Unit Month—how the government charges for grazing one cow and one calf per month on the West's public lands). The federal Bureau of Land Management's rate is well below what most western states charge their permit holders and about a fifth the rate charged for private grazing lands. (By 1996 the BLM's rate had actually fallen to $1.35 per AUM.) While the Cattlemen's Association argues

that private lands are better-quality range, most ranchers admit that, if
not a "below-cost subsidy," their federal grazing permits are at least a
better-than-average deal, which is why there are so many cattle over-
grazing public lands today. Even the military, another big landholder in
the West, charges more than three times what the BLM charges for letting ranchers graze on its property.

During the 1993 filibuster, Senator Alan Simpson of Wyoming, after
making the predictable condemnation of Washington's War on the
West, warned that increased grazing fees would destroy the western
way of life and "do those old cowboys in."

Not everyone was buying that argument, however. An editorial in
the Wichita, Kansas, *Eagle* took then Republican leader Bob Dole to
task for siding with the ranchers. "Western grazing areas are public
lands. They belong to all Americans," the *Eagle* declared. "The American people deserve fair compensation for the use of their property. It's
sad that Dole wants to continue subsidizing western ranchers when
Kansas has one of the nation's most efficient and productive livestock
industries—an industry that does not get government support."[14]

In a *New York Times* article titled "Wingtip 'Cowboys' in Last Stand
to Hold on to Low Grazing Fees," reporter Tim Egan pointed out that
the top 10 percent of grazing permit holders control half the public
grazing lands. Numbered among this elite were the Metropolitan Life
Insurance Company, the Mormon Church, the Japanese-owned
Zenchiku Corporation, computer titans Bill Hewlett and the late David
Packard, and various oil and mining companies.[15]

At around 12:45 A.M. October 31, the range war escalated dramatically when someone tossed a leather satchel containing a powerful explosive device onto the roof of the BLM building in Reno, Nevada. The
bomb blew a three-foot hole in the flat roof, causing $100,000 worth of
damage to the building and six office workstations below. The explosion could be heard from five miles away. Witnesses reported seeing a
black Honda with an American flag attached and a pickup truck speed-
ing from the scene just after the blast. The FBI and ATF were called in
to investigate.

A short time later, Jim Baca, head of the BLM, received a letter at his
office in Washington, D.C., warning, "If you think Reno was something, you haven't seen nothing yet." It was postmarked North Platte,
Nebraska, and signed the "Tom Horn Society." Tom Horn was a late

nineteenth-century "regulator," a gunman hired by western livestock interests to kill rustlers and scare off settlers.

"I wanted to go out to Reno after the bombing to show the flag," says Baca, "but people in the [Clinton] administration wouldn't let me. They didn't want to make a big issue out of it." Baca, the strongest voice for grazing reform in the U.S. Department of the Interior, was forced to resign a few months later (he went on to become mayor of Albuquerque).

Seventeen months after the Reno explosion, on March 30, 1995, around 7:30 P.M., someone placed a pipe bomb under the windowsill of the U.S. Forest Service office in Carson City, Nevada, just south of Reno. It shattered the window and destroyed a desk, computer, wallboard, and some pictures that District Ranger Guy Pence's kids had drawn for him. "If I'd been in there I would have been killed," says Pence, a twenty-five-year Forest Service veteran whose district covers the Toiyabe and Humboldt National Forests. A short time later the phone rang in the office of Pence's boss, National Forest Supervisor Jim Nelson (the man who had rounded up Wayne Hage's cattle). "You're next," a man said and hung up.

Nye County's Dick Carver, who'd been an outspoken opponent of Nelson and Pence's management of national forest land, claimed the bombing "was an inside job." From his Battle Ground, Washington, farm five hundred miles away, Chuck Cushman suggested that environmentalists planted the bomb.

Four months later, on August 4, just before 10 P.M., a bomb blew up Pence's Dodge van and part of his wood-frame suburban ranch house. Although he was on a horseback trip through the national forest with his eleven-year-old daughter Sitka at the time, his wife, Linda, and their two other daughters—Morgan, thirteen, and Colter, fifteen—were at home. Linda and Morgan were sitting on the couch in the family room about to watch a tape of *Little Women* when Morgan heard footsteps in the gravel driveway. Linda began to open the door but suddenly thought better of it, closing and bolting it instead. Just then the timer on the stove went off. They went into the kitchen to check on some vegetables that were boiling. A moment later the bomb exploded, demolishing the family van, a concrete parking slab, and partially caving in the side of their garage and house, shattering windows and sending shards of glass and sheetrock, like flying shrapnel, into the couch they'd just vacated.

A few days later a shaken but determined Guy Pence held a press conference. "I am angry that someone would apparently go after my family to try to get to me," he said. "I am sad that someone would express hostility against the work I do in such a personal, cowardly way. My family and I are going to go on with our lives. I am back at work."

But a short time later the Forest Service announced Pence's transfer to Boise, Idaho. "My initial reaction was, 'Absolutely not.' I didn't like the message that would send," he tells me. "As far as my wife and I were concerned, we were willing to buy more sandbags and shotgun shells and dig in."

The Forest Service quickly made it clear to the lanky, sun-weathered ranger that it wasn't a question of choice; either he was moving or looking for a new job. In that light he began to consider the advantages of the move. "I couldn't say what threat I might represent to my employees," he explains. "What if one of them were killed riding in a car with me or otherwise targeted in my place? I couldn't take that responsibility on their behalf."

He is careful not to blame Wise Use activists for the unsolved bombings, although he laughs at Chuck Cushman's suggestion that environmentalists did it. "I've always been proud of my relationship with conservation folks. I'd be real surprised if one of my enviro friends was involved. My contests do not come from that side."

During his twelve years on the Toiyabe, Pence had canceled three large grazing permits and removed hundreds of cows from the range in order to reduce their impacts on vegetation, streambeds, and riverbanks. The Toiyabe, which runs for ninety-six miles along the eastern front of the Sierras between California and Nevada, is now considered a showcase for ecological recovery, supporting a wide variety of wildlife including black bear, eagles, deer, elk, and trout.

Conservation writer Ted Williams described a trail ride he took with Pence along the East Fork of the Carson River: "Every four or five hundred yards we dismounted, and Pence showed me photos of the trampled stream banks taken before the Forest Service had kicked off all the cows. ... The river was still in rough shape, but willow, aspen, and alder were anchoring broken banks, and wildlife forage like bluegrass and Indian rice were pushing out unpalatable cheat grass and iris. Chunky Lahontan cutthroats ghosted through clear, deep pools."[16]

"We've certainly over time taken a lot of what I would call positive action with term grazing permits, positive in the sense of impact on rangeland ecosystems," Pence explains. Among the positive actions he's taken over the years was denial of a grazing permit to Dick Carver and refusal to give Carver's friend Bob Wilson permission to build a mining road (the road that Carver eventually bulldozed with his Fourth of July vigilantes).

"Let me assure you that nobody within our circle would have done anything that stupid," Carver declared after Pence's home was bombed. "I just hope the sheriff's office nabs someone real quick and hangs them from the nearest tree."

While careful in his wording, Guy Pence makes it clear he doesn't think the elected government of the United States should be letting terrorists determine where or how federal employees do their job. Asked about national resource politics, he recalls how at the beginning of the first Clinton administration, "there was a tremendous gut hope at the field level that change would come. ... But if you want to manage a sustainable ecosystem," he adds, "you can't wait for a note from Washington. You just have to go out there and do it yourself."[17]

"PLUS ÇA CHANGE, *plus c'est la meme chose*," says National Audubon Society consultant Brock Evans.

"Excuse me?" I respond.

"The more the change, the more the same thing," he says, quoting Alphonse Karr. "I see this as a hundred-years war in which we all play our part."

Evans is on his way to Grants Pass, Oregon, to get arrested with several hundred other demonstrators protesting a timber sale that's taking place under a salvage logging plan President Bill Clinton has signed into law.

The Clinton administration, during its first term, established a weak record on the environment. Its failures were partly offset after 1994 by the president's willingness to veto some of the more onerous attempts of the 104th Congress to roll back thirty years of bipartisan environmental legislation. Still, much of the enthusiasm of the anti-enviro backlash in the 104th could be traced to a key concession and strategic error Clinton made in his earliest days in office. In March 1993, just two months after being sworn in, Clinton gave up on a billion dollars of deficit-reducing revenues after western politicians, led by Democratic senator Max Baucus of Montana, objected to a budget plan to increase fees for public land's holy trinity: logging, mining, and grazing.

"We drove the stake on that one," says an aide to Baucus. "We were in negotiations with the White House and we were prepared to compromise, but twelve hours after we delivered our demands he just capitulated. We were very surprised. We came to the table in good faith thinking we'd address these issues, and he just gave up and walked away."

"That was the first string that unraveled the ball. When they saw him cave in on mining and grazing they knew it was open season," says Jeff Petrich, Democratic counsel to the House Resources Committee.

Willing to invest his political capital and make trade-offs to advance programs around free trade, deficit reduction, and health care, Clinton proved unwilling to take similar risks for the environment during most of his years in office. Only in his last six months did he initiate a number of major wilderness protection initiatives, establishing a "Green" legacy that, in the wake of his impeachment, may owe a lot to Monica Lewinsky, the legacy he didn't want to be remembered for.

On the eve of Earth Day 1993, Clinton announced his intention to sign an international treaty on climate change that George Bush Sr. had initially refused to support at the 1992 Earth Summit in Rio. During his speech in the U.S. Botanical Gardens, Clinton committed the United States "to reducing our emissions of greenhouse gases to their 1990 levels by the year 2000."

The administration's original plan to cut carbon dioxide and other greenhouse gases included a deficit-reducing energy tax and increased gasoline taxes of up to twenty-five cents a gallon. But a computer-driven "grassroots" letter and phone-in campaign orchestrated by the National Association of Manufacturers, along with an oil-funded push by PR giant Burson-Marsteller, helped undermine the plan.[18] The administration abandoned the energy tax in the Senate after House Democrats faced the wrath of industry in order to pass it through their chamber. Relations between the White House and congressional Democrats soured quickly after that. A distrustful Congress now voted to keep the gas tax below five cents, guaranteeing that with the lowest fuel pricing in the developed world, alternative energy sources would remain noncompetitive throughout the Clinton years.

There was also talk of imposing new tougher fuel-efficiency standards for automobiles, but instead President Clinton held a Rose Garden ceremony with the CEOs of Ford, GM, and Chrysler to announce
a government-industry program to create an eighty-miles-per-gallon
"green car" sometime in the future. Clinton promised that the program
would usher in "a new car-crazy chapter" in American history. After
spending seven years and a billion dollars of taxpayers' money (and
making impressive technological progress), the auto industry abandoned the plan when Texas oilman George W. Bush became president.
A few years later, Bush announced plans to work with the auto industry on the creation of a hydrogen-powered "car of the future."

When in the fall of 1993 the Clinton administration announced its
final Climate Change Action Plan to reduce greenhouse emissions, it
turned out to be a voluntary effort based on some redirected federal
dollars and the goodwill of industry. An economist with Environmental Defense, a moderate group that generally favors "market-based" solutions to pollution, compared the regulation-free Clinton plan to
tightrope-walking without a safety net.

In September 1995, the U.N.'s Intergovernmental Panel on Climate
Change (IPCC), made up of more than two thousand of the world's
leading climate scientists, issued a startling report concluding that the
earth is entering or may already have entered a period of climatic insta-
bility likely to cause widespread economic, social, and environmental
dislocation over the next century. Increased emission of industrial
greenhouse gases, the report stated, could lead to regional droughts,
superhurricanes, the spread of new and more dangerous tropical diseases, and rising sea levels that could inundate island nations and heavily populated coastal plains.

A few months later the administration admitted that its Climate
Change plan was off-track, and that the United States was not going to
meet its goal of stabilizing output at 1990 levels by the year 2000.
Britain and other signatories to the climate treaty expressed grave concern that if the United States failed to meet its stated goal, it would be
seen as a green light for China, India, and other developing nations to
continue to exploit their coal and other fossil fuel reserves. After some
continued hesitation, the administration finally committed itself to a
targeted reduction of CO_2 and other greenhouse gases during climate
talks held in Geneva in the summer of 1996. But what those targets

might be and how they'd be enforced on a global basis seemed unlikely to be resolved before the new century (at which point the next Bush administration would simply abandon the treaty process).

If disturbed by Clinton's failure of leadership, the world community was completely perplexed when a Wise Use Astroturf campaign forced the United States to withdraw from a second global agreement. In 1994 the Senate refused to ratify a biodiversity treaty signed by the United States and seventy-eight other nations because of a report put together by Rogelio Maduro. He was the Lyndon LaRouche follower who told the ECO (Environmental Conservation Organization) conference in Reno that banning ozone-depleting chemicals was part of a Green plot to depopulate the world.

Approved by negotiators appointed by the first President Bush and signed by President Clinton, the Biodiversity Treaty — aimed at protecting the world's endangered plants and animals — seemed assured of bipartisan support until the Farm Bureau got in touch with Senator Dole's office. The Farm Bureau voiced strong opposition to the treaty based on its belief that it would undermine U.S. sovereignty while giving equal rights to people, animals, and insects. The bureau based these claims not on a direct reading of the fairly innocuous treaty language, but on a report distributed by the American Sheep Industry Association. This report was written by Maduro (a version of an article he'd published in the LaRouchite magazine *Executive Intelligence Review*) and had gotten wide play on the Wise Use network. Aware that the report was spurious but unwilling to buck agricultural interests whose support they hoped to mobilize in the upcoming 1994 off-year elections, Dole and his supporters chose to kill the treaty.[19]

Although President Clinton's party held a majority in the 103rd Congress, a coalition of free-market Republicans and resource-industry Democrats managed to kill off almost all environmental reform legislation proposed during that period. The California Desert Protection Act, which established two new national parks and a national preserve in Death Valley, Joshua Tree, and the Mojave Desert, would be the only major victory in the 103rd, and even that barely passed, following a barrage of Wise Use, NRA, and mining industry attacks. In what could only be described as an act of spite, the 104th Congress would vote to cut Park Service funding for the Mojave Preserve to one dollar a year.

Typical of this congressional backlash was a February 2, 1994, House vote to prevent elevation of the EPA to cabinet rank unless there was a debate on property rights. A number of House members, such as Democrat Billy Tauzin of Louisiana (who would later switch parties), insisted the EPA's regulations were hurting the economy.

Clinton EPA administrator Carol Browner wasn't buying that argument. "If you go back to the origin of workplace standards in this country," she responded, "to that history, when it was first proposed that you couldn't use children in the workplace or that people couldn't be required to work sixteen-hour days, what did the business community say? 'Oh, we won't make it, we won't be competitive, you can't do this to us.' Well, we seem to have survived just fine and in fact we're a better world for that and hopefully that is where we will find ourselves when it comes to environmental protections."[20]

That kind of rhetoric, along with the perception of Vice President Al Gore as a committed environmentalist, convinced the public that the Clinton administration must be doing right by the earth, successfully advancing a Green agenda. For the most part the major national environmental groups failed to suggest otherwise.

Increasingly centralized and committed to lobbying Washington, they mistakenly saw themselves as serious players in the Beltway power game. After twelve years of bucking the system under Presidents Reagan and Bush, they could now pick up the phone and get through to agency officials who had worked on their staffs or sat on their boards just a short time earlier. They even got to share their thoughts with cabinet members and corporate CEOs on the President's Council on Sustainable Development (PCSD). The PCSD was Al Gore's bully pulpit designed to highlight and help plan linkages between environmental protection and economic growth.

Here, leaders of the Sierra Club, The Nature Conservancy, the National Wildlife Federation, Environmental Defense, and the Natural Resources Defense Council shared a quarterly roundtable with the NAACP; AFL-CIO; the vice president of the United States; secretaries of Commerce, Agriculture, and Interior; the EPA; and CEOs of various Fortune 500 companies including Chevron, Dow Chemical, Georgia-Pacific, and Browning-Ferris.

"We put a lot of our money into educating policy makers," I was told by a staffer for one of the foundations funding the enviros' D.C.

outreach efforts. The key problem with that approach is that policy makers (namely, politicians) tend to be hardwired to more basic drives than eco-enlightenment. As the late-sixties firebrand Saul Alinsky used to say, power in America responds to two poles, money and people. And in Washington, where money is the name of the game, the industrial lobbies have, according to author Mark Dowie, established a rough but consistent math—for every green PAC dollar that comes into town they'll see it and match it by at least ten.[21]

The media, ever attuned to signs of bloodletting but hearing little criticism of the administration from the established Green camp, began to respond instead to the industry-amplified protest sounds of disaffected ranchers, wetlands developers, and Wise Use organizers. Without fact-checking their sources, reporters (including a few free-market ideologues like ABC's John Stossel) began reporting that widespread anger with government overregulation was turning the public against environmental protection.

While the public would soon prove these pundits wrong, there was no question that by the fall of 1994, Wise Use/Property Rights ideology had been incorporated into the belief system of large numbers of conservative Republicans and Rush Limbaugh "Ditto-heads." Right-wing politicians certainly found it easier to claim that their anti-Green votes were a response to a Populist uprising among their constituents than that they were a bow to the wishes of their major PAC contributors in the oil, timber, and mining industries.

"There's a reason Wise Use's political power outweighs their actual numbers and that is their political contributions to politicians in the West," claims ex–BLM director Jim Baca. "If you're a governor in Wyoming, you will listen to the Cattle Growers Association. It doesn't matter about anything else. You do what they tell you."[22]

Unlike the Christian Coalition and the NRA, which turned out legions of campaigners for the Republican revolution of 1994, the Wise Use/Property Rights network contributed few troops (it had few to contribute). Nonetheless, a number of candidates ran hard on Wise Use and Property Rights themes including ex–pest exterminator (and future House Majority Leader) Tom DeLay of Texas; rancher's son, Realtor, and Property Rights organizer Richard Pombo in California; David McIntosh of Indiana (who had previously directed Dan Quayle's Council on Competitiveness); and Helen Chenoweth in Idaho.

Chenoweth, a fifty-seven-year-old grandmother, would gain some media renown for her close ties to the John Birch Society, militia groups, and Wise Use ("When I started helping her raise money, not many people took her seriously," Chuck Cushman proudly confided). During her campaign, she held a series of "Endangered Salmon Barbecue" fund-raisers and gave a stump speech (first heard at a Wise Use Leadership Conference in Reno) about the "spiritual warfare" between environmentalists and real Americans. A tape of this speech would later become available for purchase from the Militia of Montana. After the election, the congressman (as she insisted on being called) accused the U.S. Fish and Wildlife Service of using black helicopters to intimidate ranchers, black helicopters being the mythical vehicle of choice for the U.N.'s invasion forces. Despite the widespread appearance of bumper stickers reading "Can Helen not Salmon," Chenoweth managed to hang on to her seat until 2000.

Following the 1994 Republican victory, newly named House Speaker Newt Gingrich proclaimed that the 19 percent of the electorate who had voted for his party represented "a national mandate" for "revolution" based on his ten-point Contract with America, the ideological centerpiece of his plan to downsize government. Although a Property Rights takings proposal was hidden in the Contract's ambiguously titled Job Creation and Wage Enhancement Act, enviros were quick to point out that the word environment did not appear anywhere in the document.

Nonetheless, the new majority in the House and Senate, working in intimate liaison with corporate lobbyists, quickly began to rewrite the nation's Green laws while cutting funding to the EPA, the Department of the Interior, and other agencies (making sure that environmental programs took the biggest budget hits).

In the House, Tom DeLay led the fight for "regulatory reform" of Superfund, pesticide controls, and other anti-pollution laws, while Don Young of Alaska fought to open up America's vast public lands to what he calls "energy, hydro, fiber, and minerals." "We create parks and refuges and wilderness areas, but they create no dollars for the American worker," he claims. "Mining creates jobs, trees create jobs, farming creates jobs, and American factories create jobs."[23]

Young, who has described environmentalists as a "waffle-stomping, Harvard-graduating, intellectual bunch of idiots," replaced George

Miller of California as chairman of the House Natural Resources Committee (as mentioned before, one of the first things he did was drop the word *natural*). As a leader of the backlash in Congress, Young bragged that, regardless of their opinions, environmentalists "are going to have to compromise. ... If not, I'm just going to ram it down their throats."

House Resources Committee Democratic counsel Jeff Petrich got a taste of what that might mean when he accompanied a Republican delegation to Alaska in August 1995. There he was beaten up in a Ketchikan hotel restaurant by a man who, a few minutes earlier, had been talking with Lloyd Jones, one of Young's top aides. "I was sitting with a member from the Tongass [National Forest] Conservation Society when this guy interrupts, yelling how I can't insult Don Young and shouting obscenities, 'You asshole, you shithead,'" Petrich recalls. "I called him a name back and he started pummeling me." Along with a black eye and cuts, Petrich suffered nerve damage to his face. Local police refused to arrest his assailant and later threatened to charge him instead. "I very much sympathize with how civil rights people in the South must have felt, with the local sheriffs down there," Petrich says.[24]

A short time after taking over as Resources Committee chair, Young introduced the Young/Pombo Bill. This was an attempt to rewrite the Endangered Species Act in a way that would get rid of habitat protection for endangered plants and animals, limit the number of species that could be listed, and make the government pay for any protections that reduced property values. California's newest celebrity-politician, Sonny Bono of Palm Springs (who would later die in a skiing accident), suggested an easier solution for endangered species: "Give them all a designated area and then blow it up."

The Endangered Species Act (ESA), passed with broad bipartisan support and signed into law by President Nixon in 1973, has, over more than three decades, proved successful in saving close to two hundred species from extinction, including the American bald eagle, alligator, and gray whale. Still, as wilderness habitat has shrunk or been ruined by development, logging, mining, and other extractive industries, the number of U.S. plant and animal species listed as threatened has risen to nearly one thousand. This can be explained in part by the fact that the law doesn't kick in until a species is already close to collapse. Since 1968, the United States has lost 75 percent of its songbirds. An estimated one-third of Atlantic and Gulf Coast dolphins have been killed in die-offs linked to water contamination, while other creatures like the manatee and Florida panther seem fated to disappear from the earth in the near future. As the chances of encountering a large predator in the American wilds decrease, the chances of being victimized by a predatory member of our urbanized culture seem to increase. According to Harvard biologist Edward O. Wilson, human-caused species extinctions, mostly due to loss of habitat, are now advancing at ten thousand times the natural rate.[25]

The one species that seems in no danger of extinction is the red herring. The debate over rewriting the Endangered Species Act quickly became a case study in trying to legislate by anecdote, replete with stories of how the law favored rodents, insects, and lizards over people and their property. But on closer examination, many of these Wise Use–supplied "ESA horror stories" turned out to be apocryphal.

In October 1993 a wildfire swept through Riverside County, California, burning twenty-five thousand acres and destroying twenty-nine homes. Some time later, ABC "reporter" John Stossel aired a 20/20 segment on how ESA protection for the brushy habitat of Stephens kangaroo rats prevented owners from "disking" firebreaks around their homes, resulting in the tragic loss of their property. It was a great TV story, an example of government regulation gone mad, with strong visuals thrown in. Unfortunately, the spoilsports at the General Accounting Office conducted a four-month investigation that found it to be untrue. After interviewing homeowners, fire officials, and others who described hundred-foot walls of flames jumping highways and irrigation canals, it was determined that whether or not people cleared brush around their houses had no effect on the destructive path of the wind-driven inferno.

Ten years later, in 2003, Stossel was still running spurious 20/20 reports on endangered species, this time reprising a fully investigated and discredited claim (first made in the *Washington Times*) that federal and state biologists had "planted evidence" that endangered wild lynx cats were living in a forest they wanted to protect.

On February 20, 1994, state and federal agents raided the Bakersfield, California, fields of Taiwanese businessman/farmer Tang Ming-Lin, seized his tractor, and charged him with three violations of the ESA, including the killing of kangaroo rats his farm manager had run over. "When a man's tractor is taken away and he faces jail for killing a rat, that's when we feel the law has gone awry," said Bob Devereux, an

organizer of local protests that followed the raid. Ming-Lin's case quickly
became a cause celebre among Property Rights advocates, ranging from
Rush Limbaugh to the California Farm Bureau to pro-business, nonprofit law firms like the Pacific Legal Foundation, which called Ming-
Lin's attorney to offer free legal support.

State and federal agents (who later dropped criminal charges) claimed
Ming-Lin had been repeatedly warned that he was illegally tilling protected habitat and needed to apply for an "incidental take" permit, but
he continued plowing. However, his lawyer suggested the Tenneco Land
Company might be the real rat. Ming-Lin sued Tenneco, claiming that
when he purchased his 723 acres of saline scrubland for $1.5 million,
they failed to inform him it was also critical habitat for three endangered
species: the kangaroo rat, the leopard lizard, and the San Joaquin kit fox,
all of which had been driven out of surrounding irrigated fields.

A year later, during one of California's worst storm seasons in memory, then Governor Pete Wilson showed up near the flooding Pajaro
River on the central coast. Here he told some forty farmers that as part
of his emergency relief effort he was suspending the state Endangered
Species Act and calling on President Clinton to suspend the federal act
in the state.

"Essentially, what we want to do is common sense, to allow you to
recover," Wilson told the angry farmers, many of whom were blaming
"salamander-kissing" environmentalists for their flooded fields. They
claimed that state protection of the three-inch-long Santa Cruz long-
toed salamander had prevented the clearing of trees, snags, sandbars,
and debris, which had caused the river to overflow its banks. "We know
the Pajaro was sacrificed for tree huggers and environmentalists,"
strawberry grower Clint Miller claimed.

The only problem was that there were no salamanders on the Pajaro.
In 1989, state Fish and Game biologists had conducted a study on the
river but hadn't found any salamanders. A number of state permits had
since been granted for clearing the river, but local counties had failed to
take action until March 11, when the river burst a levee, flooding thousands of acres and forcing the evacuation of three thousand mostly poor
Hispanic farmworkers.

The Army Corps of Engineers determined that given the amount
of rainfall, even clearing the river wouldn't have prevented the flooding. Yet the tale of the obstructionist lizard became the centerpiece of

numerous media stories that went out that day and part of the mythology of the Wise Use backlash.

The chances of maintaining healthy wolf and grizzly bear habitat in the lower forty-eight states remain bleak as the large roadless areas they need for survival have shrunk to about 1 percent of their historic range. Still, predators without PACs remain an easy target for western politicians like Utah's Orrin Hatch, who complained on the floor of the Senate that under the Endangered Species Act, "a man was fined $4,000 for not letting a grizzly bear kill him."

That man, Montana sheep rancher John Schuler, shot a two-year-old bear after it repeatedly raided his sheep corral. The Montana Department of Fish and Game had offered to finance installation of an electric fence or even to shoot the "problem bear" if it continued its raids (they'd captured and relocated it once before). During its fourth and final raid, Schuler went outside and shot the young bear himself. The next morning he found it lying wounded near his house and finished it off. In court Schuler claimed he shot the bear in self-defense, an argument the judge didn't buy. Two environmental groups have since paid to have an electric fence installed around Schuler's corral.

In an unrelated case, rancher Richard Christy complained to an anti-ESA Wise Use rally in Ronan, Montana, that he'd been fined $3,000 for shooting a bear he said attacked his sheep. "Shoot, shovel, and shut up!" the crowd chanted back (in other words, kill the animal, bury it, and don't tell anyone).

Since the 1989 court order that halted logging on old-growth national forests where spotted owls breed and feed, the northwest timber industry and Wise Use groups have argued that not only do owls cost jobs, but they're also prolific breeders that don't need old-growth trees to reproduce. Industry sources have reported sighting owls mating in second-growth tree farms, in logging slash, in mulberry bushes, even atop a Kmart shopping mall in southern Oregon.

In the midst of these stories the National Academy of Sciences released a report identifying the Endangered Species Act as a critically important tool for preserving biological diversity. The report suggested the law's provisions for protecting wildlife habitat needed to be strengthened, not weakened.

"Opponents of the law use all these phony anecdotes as a crutch because the science community won't support their arguments," claims Jim

Jontz, one of the early directors of the (pro-ESA) Endangered Species Coalition. As is often the case, several similarly named groups were established by opponents of the law, including the industry-backed Endangered Species Act Reform Coalition and Wise Use's Grassroots ESA Coalition. Says Jontz, the former Indiana congressman targeted by Wise Use, "In the big picture most people understand this Endangered Species Act is the best law we have to protect the ecosystems we all depend on."

Just to make sure that point got across, ESA supporters put out their own anecdotal stories (with contact names and numbers attached for skeptical reporters). These included a profile of the Eagle Days festival in Sauk-Prairie, Wisconsin, which draws twenty-five thousand tourists every winter to watch bald eagles roost (and contributes to the local economy), and the story of Linda Peko, whose ovarian cancer was cured by taxol, an extract from the bark of the endangered Pacific yew tree. They figured that if it got down to trading media spin, America's feathered symbol and a cure for cancer beat jumping rats, invisible lizards, and sluttish owls.

ROOM H-137 IS LOCATED just off a narrow, tourist-clogged hallway in the Capitol, not far from the rotunda. Along one wall are life-size bronze statues of various states' heroes, including Hawaii's Father Damian and Utah's Philo T. Farnsworth, "The Father of Television." Inside the blue and white squiggle–carpeted meeting room, folding chairs and tables have been formed into a square for a House-Senate conference. An outer ring of chairs is rapidly filling with staffers, oil lobbyists, and reporters. Among the first politicians to seat themselves are George Miller and Don Young.

At 6-foot-4 and 250 pounds, with brilliant white hair and a bristle mustache, Miller is an imposing figure. Clinton Secretary of the Interior Bruce Babbitt described Don Young as an Alpha wolf, but when Miller scans the room with his calculating gray eyes, there's no question that this pack has more than one dominant male. Miller has been given a 93 rating by the League of Conservation Voters, while Young received a zero (on the other hand, the American Conservative Union rates Young at 100 and Miller at zero). Young, twelve years older than Miller and almost as large (he claims to be the same height), still has brown hair, although his beard has gone gray and white.

Young, who is presiding over today's meeting, is wearing a dark suit, paisley tie, and what looks like a red .22-caliber round as a lapel pin. "It's actually a miniature shotgun shell," the lifetime NRA member will later tell me, "to signify I'm a bird shooter. I shoot doves and quails and all those good things."[26]

As props go it's a rather tame one for the outspoken Alaskan. In the past, Young has waved his buck knife on the House floor at a congressman from New York whose advocacy of Alaskan wilderness he didn't approve of (he also cried when large sections of his state were set aside as parks and wilderness areas). Later he brandished an "ooskik," an eighteen-inch walrus penis bone, at Mollie Beattie, the late director of the U.S. Fish and Wildlife Service, when she testified in front of his committee against the sale of uncarved bone and ivory by Alaskan natives.

Miller tends not to use props. When he loses his temper, his sharp rhetoric and intimidating physical presence more than serve his purpose. He received a lot of media attention in August 1995 when, on the House floor, he went after a "lobbyist reform" bill sponsored by Tom DeLay. The bill, aimed at nonprofit organizations, would cut government grants to any group that practiced "political advocacy" (while ignoring for-profit government contractors). When DeLay called it a "glorious day" for reform and another Republican denounced the "perverse" nature of environmental and other nonprofit groups, Miller decided he'd had enough. He charged that what was perverse was "to equate the fat-cat lobbyists sitting in their offices and the office of the gentleman from Texas [DeLay] ... writing the Regulatory Reform Act and gutting the Clean Water Act and to equate that to people in the Red Cross and equating that with people who are helping citizens who are dying of cancer. ... The gentleman from Texas says this is a glorious day. It is a glorious day. If you are a fascist, it is a glorious day."

Today's conference is over granting a half-billion-dollar "royalty holiday" to oil companies doing deepwater drilling in the Gulf of Mexico. This is an idea promoted by soon-to-retire Democratic senator J. Bennett Johnston of Louisiana—he'll go on to lobby on behalf of energy companies—with the support of Republican senator Frank Murkowski of Alaska. It's being pushed as a rider to a bill that will allow the export of Alaskan crude to Asia.

Miller claims that granting the royalty holiday "is like throwing rose petals after the parade has gone by." Industry has already developed the deepwater technology it needs for this drilling, he argues, and, "the oil executives can make some serious money and don't need this larding on." He turns toward Young. "Over a hundred members of your party voted against this. Why are we giving taxpayer money to these people who have no need for it?"

Young turns to Johnston. "Very frankly, Senator, I'm not happy to have this rider on the bill," he says before going on to vote for it, along with a majority of the House-Senate conferees.

"Let's remember we fought a war a few years ago over one thing and that was oil," Frank Murkowski explains to a small gaggle of reporters after the meeting adjourns.

"We fought the [first] Gulf War over oil?" I ask.

"I didn't say that," he shoots back.

Murkowski, Don Young, and Ted Stevens (Alaska's other senator) are also promoting legislation to open up the Arctic National Wildlife Refuge to oil drilling, arguing that we need to expand domestic production (even if only to sell it to Japan). Murkowski and Young also want to transfer jurisdiction over the largest intact rain forest in North America, the nineteen-million-acre Tongass National Forest, to the state of Alaska (which will be more supportive of logging). To promote expanded logging in the Tongass, local timber companies have created a new Wise Use group called CARE, Concerned Alaskans for Resources and the Environment. Chuck Cushman is hired to help organize it. A short time later, local environmentalists begin reporting death threats and harassment.

"The *New York Times* and the *Washington Post* are very reluctant to give the other side of this issue," Murkowski complains, blaming the media for faltering Republican initiatives on the environment. "We find in our own newspapers in Anchorage and Fairbanks we've got these national chains from around the country. ... McClatchy has a major investment in Alaska but I don't see it [drilling in the wildlife refuge] being promoted in their Sacramento paper, and that's distressing to us and we're going to meet the owners and publishers and point this out, because we think charity begins at home."

For the millionaire senator (and future Alaska governor who will name his daughter to complete his Senate term) charity certainly does begin at home. While pushing a law that the Tongass be managed to guarantee 2,400 timber jobs (an idea the Anchorage *Daily News* compares to a "Communist-style economic mandate"), Murkowski also maintains over a million-dollar investment in the First Bank of Ketchikan in the heart of Tongass timber country. The bank's president blames "continued uncertainty in the forest products industry" for a 44 percent drop in profits. At the same time, Murkowski is forced to divest himself of a $30,000 investment in Louisiana Pacific (LP operates the main sawmill in the Tongass), dismissing that sum as "no big deal." In the past, he kept his money in a blind trust administered by Jim Clark, a lobbyist for the Alaska Loggers Association. His chief forestry advisor, Mark Rey, is the former vice president of the American Forest Products Association (and future assistant secretary of agriculture overseeing the U.S. Forest Service under George Bush Jr.).

Don Young's political instincts are more visceral than mercenary, as can be seen by a visit to his office, which resembles nothing so much as a Fairbanks taxidermy shop. The first thing one can't help but notice is the eleven-foot grizzly bear skin behind his desk (which blocks his view of the capitol). There's a skinned wolf on another wall, as well as the mounted heads and racks of half a dozen ungulates and various other trophy animals he's shot. Along with several antique rifles and his famous ooskik, there are pictures of Young with former presidents Nixon, Ford, Reagan, and Bush, and with Spiro Agnew and James Watt.

Beside a huge map of Alaska stands a waist-high segment of the Alaska pipeline presented to Young by the Alyeska pipeline company (which once hired Wackenhut security to spy on its critics and planned a covert operation against George Miller).

Of course, Young may believe turnaround is fair play. In the past he has charged that the federal government is "infiltrated by preservationists" pushing "the socialist agenda to make sure that Big Brother, big government controls all and everything."

"I challenge you to show me when the preservationists ever supported anything," he asks me rhetorically. "Show me where they supported a hydro site, any drilling or any mining or any cutting or any type of natural resource activity. They believe man shouldn't be around, period. We, according to their interpretation, are a cancer upon the earth."

Would he include George Miller among the preservationists?

"He's more pragmatic but he also sings that song because that's his district. His district buys that stuff. They live in what I call the little ivory house of non-reality. I know. I used to live in California."

Young was born in Meridian, California, where he first read and was inspired by socialist author Jack London's novel *Call of the Wild*. In 1959, after graduating from Chico State and serving a short stint in the army, he headed north to the new state of Alaska. He settled in Fort Yukon, north of the Arctic Circle, where he married a Native Alaskan, taught school, worked as a tugboat captain, and became a dedicated hunter and trapper, killing two moose a year to fill his larder. Like many newcomers, Young believed that with Alaska's seemingly unlimited natural resources a man's fortunes were limited only by his imagination. In 1966 he was elected to the Juneau statehouse, where he first met and made friends with the oil and gas men and timber operators who were bringing new wealth and revenue to his state, and who would become his future campaign supporters.

In 1972 he was tapped by local Republicans to run against Alaska's freshman congressman, Nick Begich. During the campaign, a small plane carrying Begich and House Majority Leader Hale Boggs disappeared between Anchorage and Juneau. The presumably dead Begich went on to win an overwhelming victory. Although the body was never recovered, a new election was called in 1973, which Young won by two thousand votes. Since then, he has gone on to win a series of victories in a statewide congressional district two and a half times the size of Texas but with just over half a million people (fewer than George Miller's seventh district in the San Francisco Bay Area). Young's politics have been as bare-boned and boisterous as the state's interior bush towns, which are the base of his support. In one tight race in 1988, Young accused his opponent of receiving "laundered money" from environmental groups. His opponent later sued him for slander (they settled out of court).

Young's style has, on occasion, gotten him in trouble back home. Invited to a Fairbanks high school in 1995 to explain the Contract with America, he spoke of how money from the National Endowment for the Arts was funding "offensive" photographs. A student asked him what sort of things he meant. "Butt-fucking," he replied. Later he told the press he was just trying to educate the kids, to treat them like adults. But a seventeen-year-old Fairbanks junior wasn't impressed. "He's supposed to be setting an example," she said.

George Miller's private office, with its spectacular view of the capitol, looks like a grad student's dorm room. His walls are covered with posters

of Martin Luther King, Lech Walesa, and Ted Kennedy, as well as Bruce
Springsteen and the Rolling Stones. A 1980s protest poster reads "No
Vietnam War in Central America," another targets offshore oil drilling
(Miller was a leader of congressional opposition to Reagan administration policy in Central America and attempts to expand oil leasing off the
coast of California). Behind Miller's large, cluttered desk sits a battered
roller chair that once belonged to one of his political mentors, San Francisco congressman and liberal firebrand Phil Burton—the man responsible for establishing more parks and protected wilderness areas than any
other politician in U.S. history, including Teddy Roosevelt.

Although one colleague describes Miller and Young's relationship as
"just this side of violence," both men insist they personally get along.

"This Congress is a closed society so you cannot make enemies out
of everybody you disagree with," Miller explains. "With Don, what
you see is what you get. ... He believes in no role for the federal government in providing stewardship of the lands, believes they're there
for people to do whatever they want with them. I believe the public
lands and resources are a great treasure of this country, for all the people of this country."

I ask him if, in his heart, watching the environmental initiative in
Washington shift to Don Young and others on the political Right hasn't
discouraged him.

"When I played football, I played center on offense and middle linebacker on defense, and they're two entirely different games," he replies
with a predator's grin. "Now in my mind I'm back to playing middle
linebacker, which means if it moves, hit it."

"As we all know, the environmentalist lobby and their extremist
friends in the eco-terrorist underworld have been working overtime to
define Republicans and their agenda as anti-environment," reported an
internal memo from the House Republican Conference in October
1995. The memo went on to suggest that members try to draw more
positive media attention by planting trees on Arbor Day, joining the
board of the local zoo, adopting a bike trail, or establishing a "Teddy
Roosevelt Conservation Award" in their district. "The time to act is
now," it said, "before your opponents can label your efforts, 'craven,
election year gimmicks.'"

Craven or not, passing seedlings out to the voters failed to alter the
public impression that Congress was slashing away at thirty years of

environmental progress faster than a fellerbuncher through green timber. That feeling would contribute to the loss of a number of Republican seats in the 1996 elections and a dramatic narrowing of their majority on the Hill.

During the 104th Congress's early days, Tom DeLay and former Dan Quayle aide David McIntosh shepherded a "regulatory reform" bill through their chamber, while Bob Dole attempted but failed to get a similar bill through the Senate. Regulatory reform was designed to slow down (some say cripple) the regulatory process by establishing a twenty-six-step risk-assessment and cost-benefit analysis as the basis for making all environmental policy (kind of an anti-bureaucracy bureaucracy).

Among other laws to get a major rewrite in the 104th was the Clean Water Act. HR 961—labeled "the Dirty Water Act" by President Clinton—introduced by Representative Bud Shuster of Pennsylvania (who, along with DeLay, referred to the EPA as "the Gestapo"). HR 961 aimed to eliminate the EPA's water quality monitoring program, to make the Great Lakes cleanup of toxic pollution "voluntary," to revise the definition of a wetland so that up to 80 percent of protected areas would be eliminated, and to exempt sewage discharges into the ocean from existing clean-water standards. The write-up of the bill was carried out at a series of industry task force meetings coordinated by Charles W. Ingram of the U.S. Chamber of Commerce.

The Chamber's headquarters is a huge, stone-columned building directly across the street from Lafayette Park and the White House, with a first-floor formal dining room that looks out on the park's homeless residents. I sign in in the foyer below a large emblem with a logo reading "The Spirit of Enterprise," above a fierce-looking bald eagle, which makes me wonder if the Chamber has taken a position on the Endangered Species Act. I walk down a marble hallway past the Anheuser-Busch briefing center and RJ Reynolds–Nabisco Conference Room to get to the elevators. In a fifth-floor warren of partitioned offices I meet Charlie Ingram, a pleasant chubby fellow with thinning hair, pale blue eyes, and a bright multicolored tie that doesn't match his blue-and-white-striped shirt.

"Clean Water got a lot of attention because it was the first legislation after the Contract," he explains. "The environmentalists felt left out and started attacking the process. ... They're still living in the past, using the same arguments of the 1970s that aren't valid today."

I suggest that because the law has already managed to clean up more than a third of America's lakes and rivers, perhaps it's not broken and therefore doesn't need to be fixed.

"The Clean Water Act has worked well and is well understood," he agrees in perfect spin mode, "but to make further progress we need new approaches and tools—which are standards and regulations based on good science, risk assessment, and cost-benefit analysis. We just want regulations that are fair, efficient, and cost-effective." (Corporate backers of the bill found it cost-effective to donate over $15 million in PAC money during the previous election cycle.)[27]

Republican attempts to move legislation perceived as anti-environmental soon bogged down, however, as the depth and breadth of popular opposition to their plans became apparent. A Frank Luntz poll conducted for Speaker Newt Gingrich found the public preferring "more environmental protection" over "cutting regulations" by two to one, while Republican pollster Richard Wirthlin found "72% of those polled say the environment is so important it should be protected 'regardless of cost.'" After conducting a poll for an industry group, Republican Linda DiVall declared, "Our party is out of sync with mainstream American opinion [on the environment]." Among her findings is that voters, by more than two to one, had more confidence in Democrats than Republicans to protect the environment. "Most disturbing is that 55% of all Republicans do not trust their party when it comes to protecting the environment," she added.[28]

"Right now we've handed the Democrats an issue, we've given it to them on a silver platter, and they are just smiling and salivating about the opportunities it presents," Sherwood "Sherry" Boehlert tells me in his spacious, well-appointed office in the House's labyrinthine Rayburn building. An upstate New York Republican with the bland good looks and manner of a small-town banker who knows his customers by name, Boehlert doesn't appear to be a troublemaker. Still, fellow Republican congressman Richard Pombo of California has labeled him "divisive and destructive."

Boehlert led a small band of moderate (mostly eastern) Republicans in rebellion against their party's Wise Use policies in the 104th Congress. One of only two Republicans to vote against the regulatory reform provisions of the Contract with America, he mobilized thirty-four Republicans to vote against Shuster's Dirty Water bill four months later.

By July 1995, Boehlert had mobilized fifty Republicans to vote against seventeen anti-enviro EPA riders on the VA-HUD appropriations bill. The first vote, on a Friday, was 212–206 in Boehlert's favor. "It was the first time there was a major loss to the party in that Congress," he says with a note of reformist pride. On Monday his initiative failed in a 210–210 tie, "but after intense pressure and lobbying not one single Republican who voted with me defected."

Representative Martin Hoke of Ohio did go AWOL, however, skipping the vote to attend a Gingrich fundraiser in his hometown of Cleveland. A short time later, the activist group Citizen Action flew a banner over a packed Cleveland Indians game reading "Where was Hoke? At a fund-raiser." Hoke was excoriated in the pages of the Cleveland *Plain Dealer,* and the local business paper ran an editorial cartoon of him inner-tubing with Gingrich in a Lake Erie filled with dead fish, garbage bags, and hypodermic needles. Portrayed as a Gingrich "parrot" in subsequent campaign ads, Hoke went down to defeat in the 1996 elections at the hands of a pro-environment Democrat.

Other politicians seen as bad on the environment also felt the heat back home, including Senator Larry Pressler of South Dakota, who lost his reelection bid after being labeled one of America's "Dirty Dozen" by the League of Conservation Voters (and lashing back by labeling his critics "environmental extremists"). In two other Senate races, John Kerry of Massachusetts and Robert Torricelli of New Jersey helped assure themselves of narrow victories by blasting their opponents as anti-environmental. In an interesting turnabout in Colorado (where 23 percent of voters rated the environment as their number-one issue), Republican congressman Wayne Allard, despite his own poor record, won his Senate race by airing ads labeling his Democratic opponent a lawyer-lobbyist for corporate polluters. Victories like these suggested that the environment might play best as a negative campaign tool in which you tar (or oil-slick) your opponent as a Wise User.

The environment, once a forgotten issue on the political back burner, was transformed by the 104th Congress into one of the bellwether issues of the next presidential election campaign. One of the most powerful symbols of the partial government shutdowns that Newt Gingrich was blamed for during his 1995–1996 budget fight with the Clinton White House was locked national park gates. In an attempt to deflect criticism, Gingrich set up a special task force on the environment, naming Boehlert and Richard Pombo as cochairs, kind of like asking a mongoose and a cobra to find consensus.

Meanwhile, the Clinton administration began flying the green banner it had stuck in the back of its closet several years earlier. "I think the environment will loom very large on the campaign agenda," Clinton's campaign strategist and pollster Dick Morris explained to me months before his affair with a high-priced call girl forced him to resign (but increased the size of a book advance he'd been negotiating).[29]

Lest anyone mistake Morris for a Greenpeacer with a toe fetish, among the previous candidates he'd championed was Mississippi's Republican senator Trent Lott. Before he became Senate majority leader in 1996, Lott introduced legislation to muzzle TRI, the Toxic Release Inventory, which informs the public which and how much of 650 toxic chemicals factories are releasing into their communities.

Soon President Clinton's campaign speeches began to include references to Republican threats to "Medicare, education, and the environment." He vetoed bills that would have opened up the Arctic National Wildlife Refuge to oil drilling and cut funding to the EPA. On the campaign trail, Vice President Gore slammed Republicans for their ties to "extremist anti-environmental groups financed by large polluters."

In his 1996 State of the Union address, his acceptance speech at the Democratic National Convention, and again in his election night victory speech in Little Rock, Clinton emphasized environmentalism far more than he had in the past. Vice President Al Gore rhapsodized about "an America where the water is safe and the air is clean, whose national parks continue to thrive and delight our families, whose toxic waste sites are cleaned up, and whose urban brown fields become alive again and green with promise for all our people."

Still, until its final months, the administration did little to link its 1996 election rhetoric to its public policies. In 1995, Clinton had actually signed off on a "Salvage Logging" rider to a budget bill hated by the environmental community. He had first vetoed it (after the White House received some fifty thousand messages of protest), and then signed it after administration officials negotiated minor changes in the language with House Republicans behind the backs of still-angry House Democrats. While Secretary of Interior Bruce Babbitt had argued against allowing salvage logging, Chief of Staff Leon Panetta thought it might be worth a few western votes.

The rider, which in the name of "forest health" and fire prevention overrode all other laws (including the Endangered Species Act and the Forest Management Act), required that 4.5 billion feet of public timber be sold off within eighteen months. The first court-ordered lease sale took place in Warner Creek, Oregon, the site of an arson fire that may have been set specifically to encourage salvage logging.

In the wake of Clinton's flip-flop on the salvage rider, a number of environmental lobbyists staged a "21-chainsaw salute" to Clinton in Lafayette Park across from the White House. Local activists around the country held protests and took out critical ads. Several thousand forest advocates also were arrested in civil disobedience protests at the sites of new salvage logging operations. The rider finally expired in December 1996, but not before reckless clear-cutting was blamed for massive flooding, property damage, and several deaths in Oregon and Idaho. Of course, since the "salvage" cuts focused on large, commercially valuable trees that tend to be more fire-resistant, rather than highly combustible undergrowth, the fire risk to America's forests continued to grow.

"We're not counting on the president's love of the environment to carry us through," said Jim Jontz. "His response to these issues will be based on politics and we can win the political fight. It's not a question of convincing the public they're with us, but of organizing at the grassroots."

The Endangered Species Coalition was one of several groups that helped bring together many of the same political forces that were crucial to winning Clean Air, Clean Water, and other keystone environmental laws in the 1970s. These included recreational hunters and commercial fishermen, major religious groups (even an Evangelical Environmental Network that declared the ESA "Noah's Act"), public health advocates, students, local businesspeople, and organized labor.

"Dire circumstances draw us together," says Bill Klinefelter of the Industrial Union Division of the AFL-CIO. "On pollution and OSHA and stuff there's common issues, clean air, clean water, Superfund. The big timber companies did an effective job of environmental blackmail on labor for a while. But this new Republican group that's taken over solidifies our desire to have allies in the environmental movement."

Wise Use's failure to make or keep friends in labor was demonstrated on September 15, 1996, when five thousand environmental activists gathered at the Pacific Lumber mill in Carlotta, California, for a rally, march, and civil disobedience. They were there to protest plans to log the Headwaters redwood grove. Over 3,500 acres in size, with some trees growing thirty-five stories high, the grove, located within a larger sixty thousand–acre forest along the upper reaches of Salmon Creek in Humboldt County, was first identified by Earth First! backcountry hikers before their 1990 Redwood Summer protests.

At the rally outside the Carlotta mill, Judi Bari, still suffering physical disabilities from the bomb attack of six years earlier (and now confronting news of her inoperable cancer), called for a stop to the liquidation of the forest and for a program to reemploy timber workers in forest restoration. Unlike the Fort Bragg demonstration of 1990, this one had no mob of threatening counterdemonstrators. In the nearby city of Eureka, the Wise Use group Women in Timber worked hard to mobilize a truck-and-car parade of some 250 vehicles, about one-fifth the size (and militancy) of their 1990 rally. Meanwhile, close to a thousand environmental protestors, including Bari and singers Bonnie Raitt and Don Henley, marched to a Pacific Lumber logging road where they submitted to arrest and were led off for booking by police, several of whom expressed their sympathy. Sympathy for the protest was also expressed by a number of community people, PL workers and their families who were fed up with the resource-liquidation practices of Charles Hurwitz, the corporate raider from Texas who had seized PL in a hostile takeover ten years earlier. Since then, Hurwitz had more than doubled the rate of harvest in order to pay off the junk bonds he'd used to force the sale. With the once-family-owned company now facing the prospect of mill closures and layoffs due to overcutting, fewer timber workers were showing an inclination to defend their absentee boss. Two days before the enviros' protest, Pacific Lumber announced a moratorium on the salvage logging it had planned to begin the day after the rally. Clinton administration officials, anxious for environmental victories in California before the 1996 election, were deep into negotiations with Hurwitz to trade Headwaters for government properties of equal value.

In a similar agreement on August 13, 1996, the Canadian owners of the Crown Butte New World gold mine on the border of Yellowstone National Park agreed to abandon their massive mining operation in exchange for $65 million worth of government land elsewhere. President Clinton said the deal meant Yellowstone was more precious than gold, although a *New York Times* editorial suggested that what it really meant was that the 1872 Mining Law had better be reformed before some other mining operator threatened another national treasure in order to extort a similar ransom.

In the final weeks of the 1996 campaign, Clinton again moved to shore up his support among environmentalists by declaring 1.7 million acres of southern Utah's Red Rock wilderness a national monument. This set off a hue and cry from Utah's conservative congressional delegation, who accused the president of staging yet another "federal land-grab."

Still, throughout the West the resource wars that had once incorporated union and nonunion labor into the ranks of the anti-environmental movement had begun giving way to negotiations, bargaining, and community planning that brought together timber workers, fishermen, environmentalists, local businesspeople, students, and seniors in search of common ground.

"The fact is, we're seeing more coalitions being formed between ranchers and environmentalists, and commercial fishermen and environmentalists, and small mill owners and environmentalists. Those coalitions are forming much faster than the Wise Use movement [did]," says Congressman George Miller. "Because people understand, if we can make this resource sustainable I can stay in business, but if I just turn it over to the big guys and they mow it down, I'm out of business. If they pollute this river I don't have a commercial fishery anymore. If the wetlands aren't restored and there's no shrimp, then I can't fish in the Gulf of Mexico. So these connections are being made at a much faster rate than this backlash."

Without much national coordination, an upsurge of Green political organizing began taking shape around the country. In the Midwest, an environmental labor network first established to fight NAFTA has been mobilizing against the environmental rollback. In Washington, Wisconsin, Connecticut, and Louisiana, statewide Green PACs formed (even as campaign finance reform became a near-universal topic of discussion among frustrated enviros). Previously apolitical groups like the Oregon Natural Resources Council began to grow political action wings. In the 1996 campaign, major environmental groups like the Sierra Club and League of Conservation Voters also invested more money, volunteers, and media resources than in any previous political effort. Even with mixed results this was a significant advance from a strategy of "educating policy makers."

The inability of developers and anti-enviros to mobilize a large constituency for Property Rights was also growing clearer.

On November 8, 1994, Arizona voters shot down Proposition 300, a state takings law, by 60 percent to 40 percent. The lopsided win was made sweeter for local enviros by the fact that Proposition 300's backers, including local developers, the National Association of Realtors, the Cattlemen's Association, and the mining industry, outspent them two to one. While environmental advocates linked up with sportsmen, students, and neighborhood groups in a door-to-door canvassing campaign, Proposition 300's supporters focused on major media buys for their TV and radio ads, which portrayed mom-and-pop property owners being abused by callous government bureaucrats. Their one attempt at a big Property Rights Rally drew some ninety supporters.

After Washington's state legislature passed a similar Property Rights bill in January 1995, environmentalists organized a petition campaign leading to a ballot initiative. On November 7, Referendum 48 (the Private Property Regulatory Fairness Act) was defeated 60 percent to 40 percent. In an alignment of forces similar to Arizona's, enviros, neighborhood groups, churches, and organized labor decisively beat building industry groups, Realtors, and the state's timber companies. Still, like a bad penny, takings initiatives continued to periodically show up on state ballots.

For those Wise Use members who had opted out of mainstream politics to pursue militia fantasies of fighting a U.N. takeover, there were heavy ironies that few of them seemed willing to examine. While declaring their desire to fight to the death against the New World Order, they were unashamedly advancing the interests of public lands corporations (including many foreign-owned companies) that have long rejected the concept of national sovereignty when it comes to making money. On one occasion the manager of the largest public grazing permit holder in Montana, the Japanese-owned Selkirk cattle ranch, banned local members of the Montana Wildlife Federation from hunting on ranch lands because, he claimed, they were "destroying our Western lifestyle." If they had a beef with that, they could take it up with his bosses on the other side of the Pacific. The New World Order, to the degree that it exists, has less to do with the U.N. and biodiversity treaties than it does with corporate power. Today, more than fifty of the world's top one hundred economic powers are not even nation-states, but instead transnational corporations.

Western resource industries also have some moral responsibility for spreading extremism in America. Since Wise Use's founding in 1988, representatives of the timber industry, the Cattlemen's Beef Association, the American Mining Congress, the Coal Association, and others have staged and shared Wise Use platforms, conferences, and strategies with County Supremacists, LaRouchites, Moonies, John Birchers, anti-Indian activists, and their paramilitary militia friends. And while they may have felt they were controlling the agenda, by legitimizing and lending credibility to the Far Right these industries helped create and expand political space for the violent enemies of democracy.

To date, the Wise Use/Property Rights backlash has been a bracing if dangerous reminder to environmentalists that power concedes nothing without a demand and that no social movement, be it ethnic, civil, or environmental, can rest on its past laurels.

Of course, only in the cynical argot of Washington, where "perception is reality," could a corporate-sponsored backlash successfully sell itself as a Populist movement. Despite an intimidating combination of local thugs and national phone/fax/e-mail guerrillas, the anti-enviros lack the broad middle, either ideologically or in terms of real numbers, that is one of the defining elements of authentic social movements. If the anti-enviros' links to the Farm Bureau, Heritage Foundation, NRA, logging companies, Japanese ORV manufacturers, and a Korean billionaire who thinks he's God prove anything, it's that large industrial lobbies and transnational corporations have learned how to play the grassroots game.

If Wise Use's attempt to sponsor a "holy war against the new pagans" of environmental protection is fully exposed to the public—the right-wing terrorism and vigilante violence, personal profiteering, political sabotage, dirty tricks, and disinformation—the public's reaction ought to force the transnational corporations into abandoning Wise Use.

But similar backlashes will almost as certainly follow, whether they be linked to population and immigration, loss of biodiversity, chemical impacts on human biology, or climate change. For example, as the scientific certainty of global warming and its potentially devastating impacts increase, the need for a rapid transition away from fossil fuels to renewable energy sources can be expected to lead to major social dislocations. As Al Gore once noted, oil and gas are the sinews of industrial society. For the average person in the early years of the twenty-first century to conceive of a world without petroleum-based fuels takes a leap of imagination or a careful reading of history. In the mid-nineteenth century, before the CO_2 content of our atmosphere had increased by a third, most industrialists would have found the idea of a world without whale oil ludicrous. Whale oil, after all, was the lubricant that kept the machine age humming and brought light to the finest homes and streets. Whaling was a major engine of American commerce in the 1850s playing much the same role the railroads would in the post–Civil War period. By 1857, for example, the town of New Bedford, Massachusetts, employed some ten thousand men working on 329 whaling ships. No one gave serious consideration to finding alternatives to melted blubber or thought about what might happen if leviathan were ever to disappear from the great oceans of the world.

Today's mighty leviathans go by names like Exxon/Mobil and Chevron, Texaco, British Petroleum, Halliburton, Alyeska, and Shell. They reside off the coasts of Santa Barbara, Mexico, and Iraq; on jungle platforms in Papua New Guinea; on heated pipes above the frozen tundra of Alaska and Siberia; and in Washington, D.C. They soak the grounds of Ecuador, Colombia, and Nigeria, sometimes with the blood of patriots who resist their predations. In Nigeria, Shell Oil was implicated in the arming and financing of the former military dictatorship that executed environmental activist Ken Saro-Wiwa and eight of his colleagues. The wasteful flaring-off of natural gas from Shell's Nigerian oil fields over the last forty years is believed to account for about 1 percent of the world's industrial greenhouse emissions. In the late 1990s, British Petroleum (now marketed as "Beyond Petroleum") signed a $60 million agreement with Colombia's army to create a battalion of troops to protect their pipelines from sabotage—this despite a Colombian supreme court ruling against the private hiring of military personnel. "These soldiers are BP's mercenaries. Who do they owe allegiance to— BP or the Colombian state?" wondered Eduardo Gamarra, a political science professor.[30]

To envision the next environmental backlash supported not by U.S. public lands industries but by the global energy sector, the most powerful industrial combine in human history, is not a calming thought. In a worst-case scenario, this backlash will be even more violent, sophisticated, and stealthy than what we're experiencing today, using elements of propaganda, political corruption, and corporate hit squads to try to deny the social and biological consequences of industry's ecologically destructive practices. But there's also a best-case scenario. As environmental awareness moves from an issue to a societal ethic, U.S. citizens, their government, and a business community newly sensitized to the demands of its customers and employees could begin a process of dialogue, of education and planning aimed at creating a clean, healthy, and sustainable future.

Unfortunately the early years of the twenty-first century have not proved particularly calming. Between Saudi-based mass terror, the growing footprint of fossil fuel–driven climate change, and the new Bush administration in Washington, the environmental backlash seems to have once again struck oil.

eleven

Wise Use in the White House, 2000–2004

We have in many ways reached the limits of what we can do through government regulation and mandates.
                        —Secretary of Interior Gale Norton, 2003

Twenty years later it sounds like they've just dusted off the old work.
                                    —James Watt, 2001

WE WALK DOWN a stream-cut canyon to McClure Beach on Point Reyes National Seashore, a jutting peninsula of woods, meadows, marsh, and dairy farms forty-five minutes north of San Francisco's Golden Gate. On its land side the peninsula is home to tule elk, egrets, blue herons, osprey, golden eagles, bobcats, and a few mountain lions; on its ocean side live sea lions, seals, sharks, and whales.

Here by the wild shore, the wind is whipping sand into ghostly sheets of ankle-stinging silicate. Any thoughts of getting in the water are vanquished by a combination of factors. First there are the cold, closed-out, cobalt-blue breakers showing hollow, aquamarine faces just before they smash onto nearshore rocks and sea stacks, sending spray thirty feet into the air. Then there are the three turkey vultures feeding down the beach. As Nancy and I approach, they reluctantly flap away from their carrion feast. We see it's the remains of a sea lion, its upper body freshly pecked at. The lower half of the torso is missing, the jagged scoop of meat suggesting the work of a white shark. As Nancy begins photographing the half-eaten pinniped, I'm reminded of an Edward Abbey quote: "If there's not something bigger and meaner than you are out there it's not really a wilderness." Nearby Tomales Point is one of the world's premier concentration points for great white sharks and their prey.

In the 1960s there were plans for massive upscale housing developments here on Point Reyes peninsula, expansion of scenic two-lane Highway 1 into an eight-lane freeway, and construction of a nuclear power plant on Bodega Bay, just to the north, where twenty-three gray whales recently returned to summer.

It was only through the organized protest and participation of tens of thousands of dedicated conservationists and the work of progressive politicians like the late congressman Phil Burton that these urban/industrial schemes were rejected and the Point Reyes National Seashore established in their place.

Many of today's great wilderness places can be traced to an earlier progressive politician, Republican president Teddy Roosevelt, who protected vast tracts of America's landscape, establishing national parks, forests, and wildlife refuges from California to the Florida Keys.

But when President George W. Bush visits national parks to promote logging in the name of "forest health," or claims that dams help salmon, or refers to environmentalists as "Green Green Lima Beans,"[1] it seems unlikely he's engaged in any deep thinking about his environmental legacy. Still, as a politician he knows he has to appear at least somewhat interested in environmental protection, which is why in 2003 his political advisor, Karl Rove, claimed Bush was following in Teddy Roosevelt's environmentalist tradition.[2] That would be the same Teddy Roosevelt who condemned "the land grabbers and great special interests" of the coal, timber, and oil cartels, and insisted that "the rights of the public to the nation's natural resources outweigh private rights."

The conservative base of the Republican Party tends to view George W. Bush not as a Teddy Roosevelt (despite his "unilateralist" foreign policy) and certainly not as his father's son, but rather as the reincarnation of their hero Ronald Reagan.

A closer reading of history suggests he's more like Warren G. Harding, however. It's not just that Harding was an affable, not terribly bright politician chosen for office by "fifteen men in a smoke filled room," or that his campaign slogan, "Back to normalcy," reflected his tendency to mangle the English language (he'd meant to say "normality").

Harding became the 1920 Republican standard-bearer after the front-runners deadlocked at an oil-dominated party convention in Chicago.

He won the backing of big business based on his pledge to cut the tax rate for the top brackets. As president, Harding fulfilled this pledge, even though Americans making below $66,000 saw no tax-relief. He also filled his cabinet with a combination of old cronies and top industry officials. Muckraker H. L. Mencken described his cabinet as "three highly intelligent men of self-interest, six jackasses and one common crook."

Harding, who took a hands-off approach to managing the presidency, named one of the nation's richest men, aluminum magnate Andrew Mellon, his secretary of the Treasury. George W. named Paul O'Neill, the multimillionaire chairman of Alcoa aluminum, his first secretary of the Treasury.

Harding named his friend and campaign fundraiser, Harry Daugherty, attorney general. Bush named his friend and campaign fundraiser, Texas oilman Don Evans, secretary of commerce.

Harding appointed the defeated and destitute Senator Albert Fall of New Mexico secretary of Interior. Bush appointed John Ashcroft attorney general after Ashcroft lost his Senate seat to a dead man. "I felt like I fell down a sewer and came up with a roast beef sandwich," Ashcroft later admitted.

Before being appointed secretary of Interior, Albert Fall had called for the abolition of the Department of Interior. Before being appointed secretary of energy, Spencer Abraham had called for the abolition of the Department of Energy.

Albert Fall, like Bush's secretary of Interior Gale Norton, was a westerner and an outspoken critic of conservationists. He believed that public lands would prove most productive if given over to industry, while she has argued for increased private energy development on public lands.

In 1921, Secretary of Interior Fall secretly leased the navy's Teapot Dome oil reserve in Wyoming in exchange for a $200,000 bribe. Told that something was amiss, Harding responded, "If Albert Fall isn't an honest man, I'm not fit to be President of the United States." Questioned about White House political strategist Karl Rove's meeting with a company seeking federal favors while still holding stock in that company, Bush replied, "My level of confidence with Karl Rove has never been higher."

The Teapot Dome scandal shocked the nation, ending with Albert Fall's imprisonment despite his insistence that he'd sold off the oil reserves for reasons of "national security." Additional scandals soon rocked the Harding presidency, with investigations continuing well past his death in 1923.[3]

The Bush White House also faced potential scandals over its energy and environmental policies during his first eight months in office. That all changed with the September 11, 2001, terrorist attacks on America. After that national trauma, "homeland security" became a major focus of concern, while the administration's "war on terror" effectively diverted national attention from its war on the environment.

Still, President Bush and many of his top advisors come out of the ranks of the oil, energy, timber, and mining industries that Teddy Roosevelt condemned as "the great special interests." Others, like Secretary of Interior Gale Norton and Secretary of Agriculture Ann Veneman, are veterans of the Wise Use movement these industries helped create and nourish in the 1990s and whose radical agenda has now become White House policy.

"I wish we could take credit for that but we can't," admits Wise Use founder Ron Arnold. "Dick Cheney sits on my Board of Directors but we're not pen pals. Sometimes you just put something out there long enough and it gets picked up, despite what you do."

"It's really Marxian," Arnold, former consultant to the pesticide industry and official biographer of James Watt, continues. "If you look at the economic base and social superstructure, we [Wise Use] are the employees not the management. Corporations are not our friends." (He thinks they've sold out to the environmentalists.) Arnold goes on to claim that George Bush Jr. is likable because "he's less corporate" than his dad.[4]

Actually Bush, his dad, his vice president, his secretary of commerce, and his national security advisor are all petroleum industry alumnae. Condoleezza Rice even had an oil tanker named after her. Chevron changed its name after she was appointed to the White House.[5]

The story of the energy industry's dollar-fueled ascent to the White House is full of drama, both high and low. There is also no lack of Oedipal irony, not the least of which is that the Wise Use movement, which has helped define George W.'s environmental agenda, is in large measure the product of western conservatives' loathing for his father.

"He [Bush Sr.] had big shoes to fill [Reagan's] and the truth is we had no access, so we were pissed," recalls Ron Arnold.

"Not greatly enamoured of him" is how Grant Gerber, Arnold's early competitor on the anti-enviro Right, remembers it. Today Gerber is involved in the Elko, Nevada–based Jarbidge Shovel Brigade, a Wise Use cowboy posse that illegally reopened a Forest Service road closed to protect an endangered species of bull trout. This bit of fed-bashing didn't prevent the new Bush administration from naming Demar Dahl, president of the Shovel Brigade, to a Department of Interior advisory panel on land use.

Certainly George W. identifies himself with the rugged cowboy image that Wise Use has learned to cultivate and market. When President Putin of Russia came to visit Bush at his 1,600-acre hobby ranch in Crawford, Texas, in 2001, he was excited about the prospect of riding horses with America's commander in chief. But he soon learned that, unlike Ronald Reagan, George W. doesn't actually ride horses. He prefers to drive around his ranch in a white Ford F-150 pickup (Putin got to ride shotgun). Bush also enjoys "clearing brush" with a chainsaw. His ranch work, along with Dick Cheney's hunting and fishing, may be what the president means when he speaks of his "appreciation of America's nature."

If the personal is political, then Midland, Texas, where Bush spent his formative years, could be thought of as his introduction to nature, a Lone Star Eden much like Yellowstone National Park if you took away Yellowstone's bears, wolves, trees, mountains, lakes, rivers, and geysers. Midland is of course a flat, once-dusty (since paved) Texas oil town closer to gushers than to geysers.

Although George W., unlike his father, failed to make any money in oil, he did work in the industry in the years before he stopped drinking and found Jesus (and either providentially or through insider trading made $848,000 selling off his oil stock just before his former company went bankrupt). It was also Texas oil money that helped win him elected office as governor of that state and later helped fund his campaign for president of the United States.

During Bush's tenure as governor, the EPA reported, Texas had the dirtiest air in America (Houston being the smoggiest city); it also ranked Texas forty-seventh of the states in terms of water quality and also seventh in release of toxic chemicals onto the land.

Following a series of closed-door meetings with corporate leaders, Bush responded by proposing a voluntary pollution reduction plan.

After heavy lobbying by industry, the statehouse passed the plan. After Bush moved on to Washington, the state legislature reversed course, dumping his voluntary program and passing mandatory pollution-control laws.

Still, during the 2000 presidential campaign, Bush was not strongly challenged on his environmental record by his opponent, Vice President Al Gore. Although Gore was perceived to be an ardent environmentalist, he chose not to run on that issue (or any other, it seemed, that might overly excite his Democratic Party base).

Government scientists, for example, had determined that removal of four marginally productive dams on the Snake River in eastern Washington would be the most effective way to restore salmon runs on both the Columbia and Snake Rivers. In the election campaign, Bush, playing to the rural agricultural vote, stated his firm opposition to breaching the dams (a commitment he would repeat four years later), while Gore, waffling like a spent fish, promised to hold a northwest "salmon summit" after he was elected.

Gore reduced his odds for winning the state of Florida when he refused to come out against a large commercial airport to be located between the Everglades and Key Biscayne National Parks. Florida environmentalists were furious and consequently did little campaigning on his behalf.

George Bush also managed to surprise observers when late in the campaign he appeared to outflank Gore on one of his major environmental issues, climate change. In September 2000, Bush pledged to reduce emissions of four pollutants including carbon dioxide, the greenhouse gas generated by the burning of fossil fuels. It seemed an odd pledge for someone so identified with the fossil fuel industry. The oil and gas industry had by then contributed $33 million to the 2000 election cycle, with 80 percent of that going to the Republican cause. The mining, chemical, and timber industries threw in another $21 million for the GOP.[6]

Bush went on to assume office in January 2001 after losing the popular vote by half a million but winning the Supreme Court vote. His lawyers persuaded the Court, in a 5–4 decision, to overrule Florida's supreme court and close down the monthlong "Florida recount," thus giving Bush an electoral victory. Issues of election bias (the candidate's brother was also governor of Florida, and the chief vote counter, one of his campaign cochairs) made this the most contentious presidential vote in living memory, as did the denial of voting access to large numbers of African Americans.[7]

In his classic study of modern media, *Deciding What's News*, sociology professor Herb Gans wrote that the American media share common values, including maintaining social order and strong national leadership. This would explain why television field producers kept cutting away from dramatic images of tens of thousands of demonstrators lining the inaugural parade route carrying picket signs and banners reading "Hail to the Thief" and "Illegitimate." Clearly such images, while having real news value in terms of the public's right to know, would not have helped restore faith in the established order.

Within weeks of Bush taking office California began to experience energy shortages and blackouts, the result of deregulation of their energy market, which made them vulnerable to supply manipulations by Enron and other out-of-state companies. It was only after the feds—reluctantly—capped wholesale energy prices that the shortages went away. Deregulation and long-distance energy trading of electricity across a dilapidated power grid would also contribute to the massive northeast power blackout of August 2003. FirstEnergy, the nation's fifth largest utility, which set off the cascading power failure, had a long history of neglect, including a shutdown of its nuclear power plant and a major air pollution conviction days before the blackout. Still, it managed to remain well plugged in to Washington, contributing over $640,000 to the Republican Party in 2000.

In early 2001, Bush claimed the country was facing an energy supply crisis and established a White House task force under Vice President Dick Cheney to formulate an oil production plan. The task force was filled with "Bush Pioneers," industry folks like Enron CEO (and Bush family friend) Ken Lay, who'd raised over $100,000 in individual contributions for Bush's election campaign. FirstEnergy CEO Anthony Alexander was another "Pioneer," who met with Cheney to discuss energy policy. In 2004 the Bush reelection campaign supplemented the Pioneers with "Rangers" obliged to raise at least $250,000 each as part of a plan to build a $200 million war chest.

Although the vice president's office denied the General Accounting Office, the investigative arm of Congress, access to task force records or even a list of who participated, one corporate figure known to be behind the administration's energy plan was Cheney himself. In 1999, as CEO of Halliburton, an oil supply company, he'd been a member of the Petroleum Council, an advisory group to the Department of Energy. That year they issued a report calling for the opening of the Arctic National Wildlife Refuge and wilderness areas of the West to fossil fuel development, proposals incorporated into the White House plan.[8]

The first point of the twenty-five-point Wise Use Agenda also calls for opening up the refuge to oil drilling. This is followed by proposals to log the Tongass National Forest of Alaska (which the Bush administration allowed on December 23, 2003), and all other old-growth trees on public lands (with a flip suggestion that replacing "decadent" old trees with carbon dioxide–absorbing young tree farms will reduce global warming). The agenda also calls for gutting the Endangered Species Act, opening seventy million acres of wilderness to commercial development and motorized recreation and giving management of national parks over to private firms "with expertise in people moving such as Walt Disney."

It's worth remembering that when the Wise Use Agenda was issued in 1988, it was seen as an extractive industry wet dream, one that the first Bush White House would never have openly embraced. However, returning to our Oedipal theme, while the father raised taxes, the son carried out the most extensive tax cuts in U.S. history. While the father chased Saddam Hussein out of Kuwait, the son invaded Saddam's Iraq. While the father was distrusted by the hard Right of his party, the son is seen as one of their own. And while the first Bush was rated as having a mixed record on the environment, the same cannot be said for his son.

In his 2004 State of the Union address, President Bush failed to mention the environment. In his 2003 State of the Union address, he called for investing in hydrogen-powered cars. After initial reluctance the administration also implemented Clinton-era proposals to reduce both arsenic in drinking water and air pollution from diesel trucks. And it ordered General Electric to clean up PCB contaminants in the Hudson River.

Reporting on what the Bush administration has done for the environment not only makes for a succinct paragraph but also avoids the tedious listing process required for invoking the ways in which the White House is rolling back a generation of environmental laws and opening public lands to development.

The Washington press corps, ever willing to sacrifice in-depth investigative reporting for a pithy bit of punditry, liked to portray Bush's first EPA administrator, former New Jersey governor Christie Todd Whitman, as the administration's token environmentalist. This refers to her mistaken assumption early on that the president would stick to his campaign pledge to reduce global warming CO_2 emissions. In fact, within two months of taking office the president reneged on that pledge, some of his defenders arguing that he hadn't understood what he was saying. He also withdrew the United States from the Kyoto Accord on Climate Change, signed by more than 160 nations.

Part of the credit for these reversals had to go to Myron Ebell, Chuck Cushman's former Wise Use lobbyist in D.C. who had moved on to the Competitive Enterprise Institute. From here he coordinated climate backlash campaigns, bombarding the White House with calls, faxes, and e-mails from industry and the Right.

In the face of firm scientific consensus that human-enhanced climate change constitutes a clear and present danger, the president insisted there was still an "incomplete state of scientific knowledge of the causes of, and solutions to, global climate change."[9] In arguing this he quoted discredited statistics from the Greening Earth Society, a front group created by the coal-powered Western Fuels Association that argues for the benefits of global warming. He then ordered the prestigious National Academies of Science to review the state of the science. Like dozens of previous assessments, their report concluded that human activities were "causing surface air temperature and subsurface ocean temperatures to rise."

In 2002 the EPA issued a similar report identifying how the United States will experience dramatic changes in the coming decades resulting from climate change, including water shortages, extreme weather events, and infestations of disease-bearing insects (mosquito-borne dengue fever and West Nile virus being two examples).

"I read the report put out by the bureaucracy," Bush then told reporters at a press conference, assuring them he remained skeptical about the whole business. His spokesman, Ari Fleischer, later admitted that the president hadn't actually "read" the report, but had been briefed on it.

One of the conclusions of the EPA's perhaps ironically named Climate Action Report is that global warming will contribute to an increase in U.S. air pollution.

Still, by the time Whitman left the EPA in June 2003, pollution enforcement at the agency had dropped 40 percent. With little for the enforcement agents to do, the Inspector General was soon investigating charges that Whitman misused them for her personal security detail. Agents paid $100,000 a year accompanied her not only on business trips but on vacations, to social functions, and to fundraising events. They were even directed, while driving "the Governor" around, to be on the lookout for Borders bookstores, which she liked to browse in.[10] "We were all thrilled when she left," an EPA enforcement attorney told me shortly after her departure. "We were cheering."

By then the IG was also looking into charges that the EPA misled the public by overstating the purity of the nation's drinking water. Those claims appeared in an upbeat "report card" on the state of the environment that also (under pressure from the White House) had altered its description of climate change, dropping all reference to its impact on "human health and the environment."[11]

Whitman also backed away from clean air standards she'd endorsed as governor of New Jersey, instead touting a White House "Clear Skies" initiative of market trading in airborne pollutants such as nitrous oxide and mercury. If approved by Congress, Clear Skies would do less to clean up the air than preexisting programs that the administration had gutted.

One of those programs, called New Source Review, required thousands of older coal-fired power plants, oil refineries, and industrial plants to install new "smoke-stack scrubbers" when they expanded production. In late 2003 the EPA announced they would no longer be required to install anti-pollution devices. Voluntary action would be sufficient. The EPA next announced it would drop legal investigations of ten utility companies who (like FirstEnergy) had previously violated the program. Though the air would be dirtier, industry would save billions.[12]

Whitman was replaced by states' rights champion Governor Mike Leavitt of Utah, a self-described "moderate" who favors the "devolution of federal power" to the states. Leavitt's first major initiative as head of EPA was to propose mercury emitted from coal-fired power plants, although a known neurotoxin, be removed from the most stringent regulations under the Clean Air Act. Earlier he and the Bush administration had settled a lawsuit in a sweetheart deal that opened 2.6 million acres of Utah wilderness to mining, oil, and gas development.

Taking a page from the state of Utah, the Bureau of Land Management later directed its staff to investigate ways to expedite coal, oil, and gas development on over 250 million acres of public lands.

While Christie Whitman proved herself a loyal trooper (going on CBS's *David Letterman* to praise Bush's "environmental accomplishments" before stepping down), it's Secretary of Interior Gale Norton who remains the president's point woman in promoting "common-sense solutions to environmental policy" that function as a pretext for pillage.

When George W. Bush stood in front of a giant sequoia in California in May 2001 and spoke of "A New Environmentalism for the Twenty-first Century" that would "protect the claims of nature while also protecting the legal rights of property owners," Norton was by his side nodding approvingly.[13] In August 2003 she was again by his side as he toured the West burnishing his environmental image with talk of "protecting healthy forests" and "caring for National Parks." A Wise Use veteran, Norton helped Bush through his environmental tutorial as a presidential candidate, providing the intellectual arguments that deregulation, devolution, and free markets are the best way to achieve environmental goals.

Two decades after Ronald Reagan's secretary of Interior, James Watt, used these arguments to push for the privatization and industrialization of federal lands, pledging to "mine more, drill more, cut more timber," his agenda was again government policy. "Twenty years later it sounds like they've just dusted off the old work," confirms the now-retired Watt.[14]

Today Gale Norton argues that opening the Arctic Refuge to drilling will provide the equivalent of eighty years of Iraqi oil imports (pre-invasion). She's also pursuing energy development, logging for "forest health" and motorized recreation on public lands, mountaintop removal for coal mining in Appalachia, and captive breeding of endangered species in lieu of habitat protection. She's reversed a plan that would have banned snowmobiles from Yellowstone and Grand Teton National Parks and promoted a plan to "outsource" national park jobs to private firms.

There was a brief moment, in the earliest days of the Bush administration, when it appeared that the White House would balance its thirst for oil with a nod toward wilderness protection by naming John Turner secretary of Interior. Former head of the Fish and Wildlife Service under Bush Sr., Turner is also a Wyoming fly-fishing buddy of Dick Cheney's. He comes from the moderate clipped wing of the Republican Party that sees conserving nature as part of the conservative tradition.

But before Turner's name could be put forward, the White House was flooded with angry faxes and e-mails organized by Chuck Cushman, now of the American Land Rights Association (neé Inholders). Cushman still maintains an action list of thousands of Property Rights, mining industry, and Cattlemen's Beef Association members. He warned his listserv that "Turner's long-standing relationships with the Rockefeller family foundation and their financing of the environmental left" would lead to a green takeover of the Department of Interior by "Land-Grabber Turner."

Backstopped by his Washington lobbyist, Mike Hardiman, at the American Conservative Union, Cushman and the Wise Use fringe were able to do what they do best, sabotaging a potentially eco-friendly initiative—in this case by scaring the Bush White House into thinking it might lose some of its core constituents on the hard Right.

"They caved. They blinked. Cheney's probably angry at us but who cares," says Ron Arnold. "Norton is a friend."

And a good one at that. Norton got her start as a staff attorney (later lead attorney) for James Watt's Mountain States Legal Foundation (MSLF), which billed itself as the "litigation arm of Wise Use." She was also on the advisory board of Nancie Marzulla's Defenders of Property Rights.

As a California lawyer, Secretary of Agriculture Ann Veneman also had her Wise Use connections, representing the SAMS (Sierra Nevada Access, Multiple-Use and Stewardship) Coalition made up of timber companies, off-road vehicle associations, and other Wise Use activists opposed to a Department of Agriculture conservation plan for the Sierra Nevada.[15] The Sierra Nevadas are the sequoia, glacial lake, and granite-studded mountains that John Muir referred to as the "range of light," Ansel Adams photographed in black and white, Dave Brower often climbed atop, and George W. used for a photo op.

Veneman's chief of staff, Dale Moore, is a former chief lobbyist for the Cattlemen's Beef Association, a linch-pin of Wise Use, while her spokeswoman used to direct the Cattlemen's public relations operations. Her undersecretary for natural resources and environment, overseeing the U.S. Forest Service, is Mark Rey. Rey is the former Forest and Paper Association vice president who authored Congress's 1995 salvage rider (to a budget bill) that suspended environmental laws in order to accelerate clear-cut logging in the Pacific Northwest. Almost a decade later,

Rey and his bosses are promoting a similar "Forest Health Initiative,"
that President Bush promised would "restore the health of forest
ecosystems" by "cutting through bureaucratic red tape" to reduce public comments, court appeals, and environmental impact statements. It
would also allow commercial logging companies to clear underbrush on
national forest lands in order to reduce the risk of catastrophic fires, and
compensate them by letting them log (or "treat") fire-resistant stands of
healthy old-growth and second-growth trees. There's a certain Wise Use
logic at work here, of course: no forests, no forest fires. On December 3,
2003, President Bush signed "Healthy Forests" into law.

Still, while Wise Use advocates are thriving inside the Washington
beltway, their troops on the ground have thinned noticeably. In January 2001, People for the USA!, formerly People for the West!, the
largest of the backlash outfits, closed its doors.

"It's quite a challenge to bring together a large group when you are
essentially opposing something that is wildly popular," PFUSA director Jeff Harris wrote in the organization's newsletter. "Americans have
embraced the environmental ethic: it is part of our value system like
motherhood and apple pie."

PFUSA also found it increasingly difficult to raise money from the
gold-, silver-, and lead-mining industries that had been major sources
of their past support. The mining industry now had more direct access
to power through people like Assistant Secretary of Interior Steven
Griles, a longtime mining lobbyist.

Former PFUSA staffer, now Wyoming Petroleum Association vice
president, Dru Bower, blamed the organization's decline on environmental protections on public lands that he believes have driven industries onto private lands. "Why would they want to fund us if they have
no interest in that fight?" he asks.[16]

After the organization shut down, a number of dissident members
decided to claim the name and merge with Frontiers of Freedom, an
ultraconservative states rights group founded by former Wyoming senator Malcolm Wallop (they also list Vice President Dick Cheney on
their board of directors).

"Growth is not where it's at for Wise Use," Ron Arnold now ration-
alizes. "We grew for a few years at the beginning but we have too many
conflicting goals and aims, so now I tell people form your own communities of interest."

With less time needed for organizing, Arnold has been promoting himself as a media expert on "ecoterrorism" (and who could question his understanding of the political uses of arson and terror?). In late 2003, Arnold was also retained as a consultant for a University of Arkansas study on terrorism, funded by John Ashcroft's Department of Justice.

I attended a journalism conference in Portland, Oregon, where Bill Pickell of the Washington Contract Loggers Association explained why he lumped the Sierra Club together with the arson-prone Earth Liberation Front. "As a boy I hunted skunks with my dad," he said, "and if it smells like a skunk and looks like a skunk, it's probably a skunk."

This raised a legitimate question in my mind: "Who the hell hunts skunks?" It seems that some Wise Use "communities of interest" have changed little over the years.

"It's the worst thing that ever happened to me in the woods, having a man with a gun pointed at my chest with his finger on the trigger calling me an environmentalist and saying I'm stealing his forest and he's not going to take it anymore. It was a terrible, sickening feeling," recalls Lamar Marshall, an ex-trapper and founder of Wild Alabama, a forest protection group in northeastern Alabama.

That confrontation occurred more than a decade ago in 1992 when Marshall was the subject of threats and accusations from a local Wise Use group called EAGLE (Alabamians: Guardians of our Land and Environment [sic]). That November he and two friends were taking pictures in the Bankhead National Forest when a drunken hunter held them at gunpoint and began ranting about environmentalists locking up the forest. The rifle-toting hunter was with a teenage boy carrying a twelve-gauge shotgun who appeared terrified by the situation. The hunter wanted to lead them to an abandoned well, but they refused to go. Marshall and one of his friends were carrying concealed handguns (a number of environmentalists in Alabama still travel armed for self-defense).

"My friend Darryl had squatted down on the ground about twenty feet behind me and had his pistol down by his side. Later he said if the boy had cocked that shotgun he figured there'd be a firefight and that would sure spoil his day. I said if there'd been a firefight it would have spoiled my life," Marshall says.

After about twenty minutes the gunman, still ranting, handed the boy his rifle to hold as he tried to squat down. When he fell over backwards the enviros took off at a run. They got his license plate number and gave it to the police. The authorities questioned the man before releasing him, saying they didn't consider him dangerous. Five months later he killed himself with a high-powered rifle.

In 2000 and 2003, Marshall was again the target of Wise Use accusations and death threats. In 2000, he, Wild Alabama, and other environmentalists campaigned to get President Clinton to give the Bankhead National Forest national monument status. PFUSA claimed this was part of a plot to establish a U.N. biosphere reserve in the forest, bring in U.N. forces, confiscate peoples' lands, and drive them into the cities. Marshall began receiving death threats; shots were fired outside his home; and, after one Wise Use meeting, a man came by his trading post threatening to shoot him and burn the place down. After that he had to hire armed guards to protect his business.

"Some people are saying they're going to burn Marshall's store and lynch him. I don't think people are serious. They're just angry," explained Myra Ball Bryant, a local Wise Use organizer.

In June 2003, a new group, the Alliance for Citizens Rights (with ties to the John Birch Society and ECO, the developer-created Environmental Conservation Organization), held a meeting of several hundred people in Double Springs, Alabama. They passed out materials reading, "There is a movement afoot, a stirring of patriots who want to reverse this trend toward oppressive government and socialism. But we need soldiers."

Their speakers identified a new U.S. Forest Service plan to reduce logging and restore native hardwoods and longleaf pines to the Bankhead as part of a government conspiracy dating back to the 1992 U.N. Earth Summit in Rio. The plot involved driving rural folks into big cities ("Human Habitation Centers") while giving the majority of the land over to wolves, wildcats, and the United Nations. Again, Marshall and Wild Alabama were targeted as a major threat to people's freedom and property.

"I've been demonized, boycotted, had people going around saying they're gonna kill me. They go on about a government conspiracy," says Marshall. "I think there's a corporate conspiracy to use these folks in order to keep public lands open to any kind of resource exploitation."[17]

Of course not all Wise Use veterans need to mobilize angry citizens to effect public lands policy. Some already run public lands policy.

As attorney general of Colorado, Gale Norton argued against the Endangered Species Act and for the proposition that government should pay financial compensation whenever environmental laws limit a developer's real or potential profits. She also argued for a major shift in takings jurisprudence. "We might even go so far as to recognize a homesteading right to pollute or to make noise in an area," she wrote in the *Harvard Journal of Law and Public Policy*, later recanting her "right to pollute" phrase during her Senate confirmation hearing.

In 1998, Norton became cochair of the Coalition of Republican Environmental Advocates. Newt Gingrich was the keynote speaker at its founding banquet. "The Al Gore, left-wing model of the environment is a centralized, bureaucratic, litigious, adversarial, non-economic, anti-technology model," he said, feeding her guests plenty of red meat. Dedicated to "free-market environmentalism," CREA included auto, coal, mining, and developer lobbyists. Traditional Republican environmentalists like the late Senator John Chafee of Rhode Island and Sherry Bohlert of New York refused to have anything to do with it.[18]

In 1999, now working as a lawyer representing the lead industry, Norton became part of the team advising presidential candidate Bush on developing a conservative "environmentalism for the 21st century." Among those working with her was David Koch of Koch Industries, which in 2000 paid a $35 million fine for oil pollution in six states, as well as Lynn Scarlett from the libertarian Reason Foundation of Los Angeles. Scarlett was also a senior fellow at Montana's Foundation for Research on Economics and the Environment (FREE), which lived up to its acronym by holding a series of all-expenses-paid Property Rights "seminars" for federal judges at a Montana dude ranch.[19]

Norton also spent time as a fellow at the Political Economy Research Center (PERC), Montana's other Property Rights think tank.

David Koch is a major funder of both FREE and PERC. With his family's $23 billion fossil-fuel fortune Koch also bankrolls a hornet's nest of D.C.-based free-market think tanks, including the Heritage Foundation, the Cato Institute, the Competitive Enterprise Institute (CEI), and Citizens for a Sound Economy (CSE), which support the "new environmentalism" of deregulation.[20]

"The last three decades is what I call the old environmentalism," Lynn Scarlett explains to me at a meeting on science and the environment at the Ronald Reagan building in Washington, D.C. She is now

Gale Norton's assistant secretary for policy, and since Norton likes to keep a low profile, Scarlett, slim, well coiffed, and always smiling, has become her front woman with the public.

"The old environmentalism tended to rely on the 4Ps—Prescription, telling you how you're supposed to do things; Process, a focus on the permit you need to 'pass go'; Punishment, as a way to motivate action; and a Piecemeal approach, to air, land, and water," Scarlett explains. "We're not getting rid of regulation, but shifting the emphasis, extending a hand to work with landowners. We think real sustainability has to be about what we call Cooperative Conservation, about engaging people."[21]

The Department of Interior is certainly packed with people previously engaged in the employ of industry.

Norton's deputy secretary, Steve Griles, is a former coal, oil, and gas lobbyist and veteran of James Watt's Department of Interior. Despite signing agreements that he would not meet with his former clients, he repeatedly did, to discuss new rules that allow the dumping of mountaintop removal coal-mining waste in Appalachian rivers, a massive coal-bed methane drilling project in Wyoming, and offshore drilling on the West Coast. This has led to an investigation by the department's Inspector General. Also under conflict-of-interest investigations are Norton's top lawyer (a former Cattlemen's Beef Association official who lobbied for cheap grazing fees on Department of Interior lands) and her director of the Bureau of Land Management (a former Utah official under Governor Mike Leavitt). Not presently under investigation is Norton's special assistant on Alaska, the former head of Arctic Power, a state-funded Wise Use group dedicated to drilling the wildlife refuge, and her assistant secretary for water and science, a former mining lawyer and MSLF and Defenders of Property Rights alumnus who has fought for the abolition of the Endangered Species Act.[22]

With these bunkmates, even Norton's collaborative rhetoric, beaver-like smile, and chipper attempts at outreach (including a letter to actor/environmentalist Robert Redford in which she pitched their shared love of zoo-bred condors) haven't been enough to prevent additional scandals from bubbling up like Texas crude.

Ironically her biggest controversy is an inherited one: the century-old accounting mess at the Bureau of Indian Affairs. American Indians claim the federal government has squandered billions in oil, gas, and timber royalties from their lands and are suing to reclaim the money.

A scandal that has also angered California Indian tribes involves the death of some 35,000 spawning salmon on the lower Klamath River in 2002, attributed to low-water flows after the U.S. Bureau of Reclamation diverted water north to Oregon farmers.

In the spring of 2001 thousands of alfalfa, hay, and potato farmers marched through the streets of Klamath Falls, Oregon, and illegally opened canal headgates to protest a federal decision cutting their irrigation water in order to guarantee protection for endangered sucker-fish and coho salmon.

Like the snail darter and spotted owl before it, the suckerfish, considered sacred by the Klamath Indians, quickly became the poster animal for anti–Endangered Species Act pundits, from talk radio's Rush Limbaugh to editorial writers at the *Wall Street Journal* to the "fair and balanced" folks at Fox News. What few of these conservative critics promoting "suckerfish sandwiches" were willing to acknowledge was that the water crisis was precipitated by the worst drought to hit the Northwest in over a century, a drought that, like the region's forty-six shrinking glaciers, is likely linked to fossil fuel–fired climate change.

"Nineteen ninety-four was the last substantial rain we had," Ryan Kliewer, a young fourth-generation farmer who marched in the 2001 protests, told me. Winter rains in 2002–2003 finally relieved the drought.

After the 2001 protests, Norton's Bureau of Reclamation reversed course, slashing the river flow and returning much of the water to the irrigators, even though a report from a team of federal scientists warned that it would place the coho salmon in serious jeopardy (along with the commercial fishermen and Indian tribes who depend on them). Yet on March 29, 2002, Gale Norton, Secretary of Agriculture Ann Veneman, and Oregon Republican senator Gordon Smith were in attendance at a ceremony where the headgates were reopened to return water to the farmers. Six months later, California congressman Mike Thompson and a group of downriver protestors including Yurok Indians dumped five hundred pounds of dead, rotting Klamath salmon on the front steps of the Department of the Interior, accusing Norton of a massive cover-up.[23]

Still, like "Owls vs. Jobs" during the timber wars, "Farmers vs. Fish" had become the dominant motif in media coverage of the Klamath protests, despite a U.S. Geological Survey report that showed keeping the water in the river would generate thirty times more economic benefit from increased commercial and recreational fishing and other river uses (mainly in California).[24]

Among the Wise Use factions who rallied to the Klamath fight were the Farm Bureau, Pacific Legal Foundation, Frontiers of Freedom, American Land Rights Association, Jarbidge Shovel Brigade, and former congressman Helen Chenoweth-Hage, who told the irrigators, "We're now in a war."

"We are determined that in Klamath we win," added Grant Gerber of the Shovel Brigade.

"The Klamath Basin water war ... represents a subtle coming-of-age for the so-called wise-use movement," reported the *Seattle Times*, going on to suggest that the movement had become more media-savvy, less physically threatening, and more politically astute.

But much like the "Yellowstone Vision" battle a decade earlier in which Wise Use protests provided a "populist" cover for White House manipulation of the process by Chief of Staff John Sununu, the Klamath water war would prove more a political conspiracy than a model of citizen action.

On July 30, 2003, the *Wall Street Journal* reported that Karl Rove had attended a meeting of fifty top Department of Interior managers where he talked about the Klamath, telling them the administration sided with agricultural interests. He gave them a PowerPoint presentation on Republican polling results and reminded them of the need to "support our base." Neil McCaleb, assistant Interior secretary at the time (early 2002), recalled the "chilling effect" of Rove's remarks. Rove had just returned from Oregon where he and the president had appeared with Senator Smith who was facing a reelection challenge. "We'll do everything we can to make sure water is available for those who farm," the president pledged. In 2000, Bush had lost Oregon by a few percentage points, and Rove thought it was winnable in 2004. Klamath farmers were in the eastern "red" (Republican) part of the state, while downriver, California Indian tribes and commercial fishermen were all "blue" (Democratic). And of course fish don't vote.

In the summer of 2003, with endangered suckerfish now showing up dead in the river, the Bureau of Reclamation warned Klamath farmers it might have to again curtail their irrigation allotments. Local Republican congressman Greg Walden made a series of angry phone calls, beginning with Karl Rove. Within hours the water curtailment idea was dropped.[25]

"The Bush Administration needs to understand that federal agencies like the Interior Department are not a division of the Republican National Committee and at their disposal to give out political favors," complained Senator John Kerry of Massachusetts, a Democratic presidential contender for 2004.

The Klamath war wasn't the first time Secretary of Interior Gale Norton has been accused of ignoring or suppressing government scientists. In the fall of 2001 she had to explain why, in a letter to the Senate Committee on Energy and Natural Resources, she'd altered scientific data. She had made it appear that oil operations in the Arctic National Wildlife Refuge would not harm hundreds of thousands of migratory caribou when her own Fish and Wildlife Service had provided her with data suggesting they would.

"We did make a mistake. We will take steps to clarify and correct that," she told reporters in explaining one of numerous discrepancies.

She also concluded that drilling the Arctic wouldn't violate an international treaty that protects polar bears. The Fish and Wildlife Service, which has twice issued reports stating that drilling poses a threat to the bears, was directed "to correct these inconsistencies" (with Norton's position).

President Bush also signed off on an Army Corps of Engineers proposal that made it easier for developers and mining companies to dredge and fill America's wetlands through a "general permitting" process that is rarely if ever challenged. Again, Norton failed to forward comments from her Fish and Wildlife Service to the Corps, even though the Fish and Wildlife Service had written that the proposed policy change would result in "tremendous destruction of aquatic and terrestrial habitat."[26]

Norton's top aides are now actively monitoring career staffers to ensure that scientific assessments don't conflict with their pro-business political goals. As a result, morale among Interior field scientists is said to be falling faster than a wing-shot condor.

Today, the largest on-the-ground constituency organized to open up parks and wilderness areas to roads and development is no longer Wise Use loggers and resource industry employees, but suburban owners of motorized dirt bikes, ATVs, snowmobiles, and personal watercraft. While millions of Americans are having a love affair with fast, loud, off-road vehicles, their owners are creating major user conflicts with tens of millions of other outdoor recreationists who enter wilderness areas believing they've left the noise and pollution of the freeway behind.

Air pollution from winter snowmobilers and harassment of buffalo and other wildlife became so bad in Yellowstone National Park that the Park Service decided to phase out the activity by the winter of 2002. But Norton's Department of Interior—in response to a suit from the International Snowmobile Manufacturer's Association—announced it would reassess the rule-making process, despite 360,000 e-mails and letters, 80 percent of which supported banning the machines.[27]

"I think the national environment groups have turned on recreation with a vengeance now that they've driven the commodity users off the [public] lands," argues Bill Horn, Washington counsel for the Snowmobile Manufacturers. "Our conversations with the Secretary [of Interior Norton] show her greater appreciation of public recreation on public lands. We need these places for everyone's enjoyment not just to have these scientists go in there and create biospheres under glass."[28]

In November 2002 the Bush administration proposed a cap of 1,100 snowmobiles a day, up from the present average of 815, arguing that a new generation of machines will be quieter and less polluting. At the same time the Park Service concluded an internal report (not made public) that found banning the machines was the best way to protect the park's air quality and wildlife and the health of visitors and employees.[29]

The next big push in Interior was the privatization of thousands of National Park Service jobs, including the entire corps of park scientists. The government-wide "competitive sourcing" initiative promoted by President Bush and his Office of Management and Budget targets as many as 850,000 jobs in the largely unionized federal workforce to be replaced by private contractors. The plan was to include up to 11,524 out of 16,470 Park Service jobs.

Fran Mainella, director of the Park Service, sent an e-mail to her employees at the beginning of 2003. In it she assured them that while 70 percent of their jobs were being studied to see if they were "inherently governmental" functions, "70% has never been used as a measuring stick for privatizing National Park Service jobs." Under the initiative, 15 percent of Park Service jobs were to be outsourced by 2004, which, according to Lynn Scarlett, would "help tap professional tools with better delivery of services to the public, and new skills and technologies and discipline."[30]

"The plan is designed to meet ideologically set goals and will rip apart the fabric of the agency," countered Jeff Ruch, executive director of Public Employees for Environmental Responsibility, a Washington-based whistle-blower organization that represents a number of Park Service workers. Ruch claimed that replacing park scientists would lead to "private consulting firms telling the Park Service what it wants to hear in order to get their contracts renewed."[31]

With the Department of Interior also promoting recreational user fees, corporate sponsorship of park activities, and partnerships for bio-prospecting in the parks, one can start to imagine Smokey Bear recast as ComCast Bear, Arches National Park as Golden Arches National Park, and hip ads promoting Yellowstone-washed jeans. Certainly the Wise Use vision of park management given over to private firms "with expertise in people moving such as Walt Disney" seems consistent with Gale Norton's vision.

Despite her early portrayal by environmentalists as "James Watt in a skirt," Norton has shown far more political acumen than the man who once bragged of a commission on which he had a black, a woman, "two Jews and a cripple."

"She makes Watt look like the one wearing a skirt," Jeff Ruch suggests with a grin. Though not the most gender-sensitive way of putting it, I get his point. Rather than openly attack environmental laws and wilderness protections, Norton has used the regulatory process to ease up on industry, and the administrative process to crack down on agency professionals who disagree with her.

Other administration guardians of industries' interests are ex–Dan Quayle aide and one-term senator Spencer Abraham at the Department of Energy, never-say-yes budget bureaucrat John Graham in the Office of Management and Budget, and former oil and chemical lawyer James Connaughton who now chairs the White House Council on Environmental Quality.

While mischief is being done, Congress has failed to act out its traditional role as watchdog of the executive branch. Instead White House energy projects moved into high gear after the 2002 elections that gave the Senate majority back to the Republican Party while maintaining their control of the house.

In the Senate the Environment and Public Works Committee slipped from the hands of Jim Jeffords of Vermont (League of Conservation

Voters rating 77 percent) into the grip of Jim Inhofe of Oklahoma (LCV rating 5 percent). Inhofe's major 2002 campaign contributor, not surprisingly, was the oil and gas industry. Outraged by the suggestion that oil and gas could also be contributing to climate change, he delivered a speech arguing that there is "compelling evidence that catastrophic global warming is a hoax."

He had a theory as to why some of his favorite Wise Use scientists were no longer being treated with due deference by the press. "Certainly, members of the media would rather level personal attacks on scientists who question 'accepted' global warming theories than engage in science," he claimed. "So you have two groups at work here, the environmental extremists doling out the lies and the money to politicians, and the liberal media that nest with them."[32]

In light of the growing power of conservative media monopolies like Rupert Murdoch's News Corp. and Clear Channel radio, the senator's comment reminded me of the old joke that asks, "What's the difference between a Republican politician complaining about the liberal media and a basket full of puppies? Eventually the puppies stop whining."

Among the "radical environmentalists" promoting the "global warming hoax" that Senator Inhofe says is designed for the purpose of "energy suppression" is the U.S. Navy.

In the spring of 2001 the Office of Naval Research (ONR), the oceanographer of the navy, and the (civilian) Arctic Research Commission held a two-day symposium on "Naval Operations in an Ice-free Arctic." ONR believes Arctic summer sea-lanes could be open by 2015 because of rapid melting of the ice cap attributed to global warming. In the summer of 2002 the Bering Sea was essentially ice-free for the first time in recorded history.

A declassified version of the symposium report suggests that disappearing ice could mean loss of hiding places for missile submarines, an altered acoustic environment, and increased threats from international criminal and terrorist elements as an ice-free Arctic becomes a major shipping route. The report calls for increased cooperation with Canada and Russia in patrolling polar waters and building fleets of specially adapted cold-water surface warships to operate there.[33]

Another climate impact is being felt by energy companies searching for oil in the Arctic, specifically on Alaska's north slope. Under state rules they can use their heavy exploration equipment only when the fragile tundra is frozen a foot thick with half a foot of snow on top of it.

In the 1970s the tundra met these conditions two hundred days a year. But according to Alaskan scientists, global warming—caused in part by the burning of oil—has now shrunk this cold season to just over one hundred days a year. The Energy Department has responded with a grant to study how much disturbance the tundra can withstand and if there are ways for the oil companies to work on tundra when it's not frozen.

In light of rapidly mounting state costs from global warming, the Alaska congressional delegation has begun to change their thinking on climate. Still, many in their party have not. One climate skeptic who continues to attack "the doom-and-gloom scare tactics of radical environmentalists" is Property Rights activist and chairman of the House Resources Committee Richard Pombo. Pombo has also argued that the Endangered Species Act needs to be replaced, and tried to get proposed exemptions for the Pentagon extended to all government agencies.

In 2002, CSE gave Pombo its Jefferson Award for "supporting limited government and more freedom." CSE was founded by libertarian oil heir David Koch and is cochaired by former House majority leader Dick ("the hammer") Armey and former (Bush Sr.) White House counsel C. Boyden Gray. Gray's father, tobacco heir and Truman presidential advisor Gordon Gray, may have best summed up free-market environmental philosophy when he said, "Money has a way of talking that transcends mere words."

Oddly, the environment played little direct role in the 2002 elections, during which many Democratic candidates opted to run on a "small vision" issue: prescription drug reform for elderly voters.

At the same time, several Republican candidates, notably Wayne Allard of Colorado (LCV rating 8 percent) and Norm Coleman of Minnesota claimed they were committed environmentalists. In New Hampshire, Senator John Sununu (the son) called for tougher restrictions on air pollutants while backing away from Democrats' attempts to link him to the president's Clear Skies Initiative.[34]

Having failed to gain any seats under the moderate Democratic Leadership Council (dubbed "Republican Lite" by party traditionalists) the postelection minority leadership in the House of Representatives shifted from Richard Gephardt to Nancy Pelosi of California.

Pelosi is a protégée of the late progressive San Francisco politician and environmental hero Phil Burton.

With the president's popularity beginning to decline because of a weak economy and the occupation troubles in Iraq, both Democrats and Republicans began to examine the so-called wedge issues that could impact the 2004 election. Polling showed that environmental protection was the one area where the public gave Democrats a two-to-one advantage over Republicans.

"The environment is probably the single issue on which Republicans in general—and President Bush in particular—are most vulnerable," agreed Republican pollster Frank Luntz. In a 2002 memo to party leaders, he offered proposals strikingly similar to those in the 1995 "Plant a tree on arbor day" House conference memo. Luntz encouraged party members to change not their policies but their rhetoric, warning that "when our environmental policies are explained ineffectively, not only do we risk losing the swing vote, but our suburban female base could abandon us as well."

Among his recommendations are the following:

> "Assure your audience that you are committed to 'preserving and protecting' the environment but 'that it can be done more wisely.'"
> "A compelling story, even if factually inaccurate, can be more emotionally compelling than a dry recitation of the truth."
> "Do not attack the principles behind existing legislation. Focus instead on the way it is enforced or carried out, and use rhetorical questions."
> "Stress that you are seeking 'a fair balance' between the environment and the economy."
> "Give citizens the idea that progress is being frustrated by over-reaching government. If there must be regulation, Americans are most comfortable with local oversight."

On the climate debate he suggests that "should the public come to believe that the scientific issues are settled, their views about global warming will change accordingly. Therefore, you need to continue to make the lack of scientific certainty a primary issue."

He also endorsed some standard Republican litanies about "sound science," "federal bureaucrats," and "common sense solutions" while

giving the dominant fringe permission to continue to go after "environmental extremists," using Ralph Nader and Greenpeace as his examples.[35]

At a certain level, Wise Use's major contribution to politics has been
its self-conscious distortion of language, the adaptation of Green-
sounding names as industry camouflage: the National Wetlands Coalition, the Environmental Conservation Organization, Concerned
Alaskans for Resources and the Environment, and the Greening Earth
Society. Today anti-environmental legislation goes by names like
"Healthy Forests" and "Clear Skies" while a combination of industry
lobbyists and true believers argue that the same unfettered markets that
gave us choking smog and burning rivers in the past have transformed
into the "new environmentalism" of the future.

I recently read a government energy report that talked of "the sustainable use of non-renewable resources," and attended a Boston conference where I met consultants who help developers deal with
"environmentally challenged sites." What they mean by "environmentally challenged" is wild places containing rare and endangered species
or legally protected wetlands.

Early in the Bush-Cheney administration the vice president argued
that though conservation might be a "personal virtue," it is not "a sufficient basis for a sound, comprehensive energy policy" (which of
course no one had argued that conservation alone was).

The White House energy plan did offer a billion dollars to develop
renewable power sources, but only if the money came from revenues
generated by drilling the Arctic National Wildlife Refuge. That
sounded like a gleeful spin on the Wise Use agenda, more red meat for
the political base.

By 2004, Secretary of Energy Spencer Abraham was promoting development of hydrogen fuel-cell technology. But again the administration
plan differed markedly from a plan being promoted by the European
Union. While the Europeans envision hydrogen fuel-cell storage systems
built on renewable energy sources like wind and solar, the Bush plan calls
for the hydrogen to be generated by nuclear and coal-fired power plants.
The difference of course is whether you see hydrogen fuel cells as part of
a necessary transition strategy out of a carbon-based economy or merely
as a neat new technology for charging up your SUV.

In the immediate wake of 9/11 the American public had appeared
ready to make sacrifices and embrace change as they reconsidered their

obligations as citizens of a democracy. Instead the president went on TV and suggested they go shopping.

While a few politicians like Senator John Kerry of Massachusetts and media outlets like *USA Today* argued it was time to move beyond oil and the corrupt terror regimes that pump it, major environmental organizations scrambled to avoid any negative references to the commander in chief. Partly as a result of this timidity, the critical mass needed to mobilize the public failed to materialize.

Seeing themselves as hard-headed pragmatists, George Bush, Dick Cheney, and their neo-conservative friends Don Rumsfeld, Richard Pearle, and Paul Wolfowitz believe we really don't need to eliminate our dependence on fossil fuels from repressive and unstable regimes like Saudi Arabia and Venezuela. Rather we need "unilateral" policies to secure and supplement these supplies, even if that means the military occupation of Iraq and industrialization of America's last wild lands and waters.

In the face of growing scientific consensus that human-caused climate change is real and under way and will result in up to a 10 degree F warming and two- to three-foot sea-level rise by the end of this century, the administration continues to follow the Wise Use path of denial and denigration. They insist that creating incentives to reduce greenhouse pollution (as Europe has done) will severely damage the U.S. economy. You can almost hear the whaling barons of the nineteenth century arguing that the end of whaling will mark the end of mechanization as industry's whale-oil lubricated machines grind to a halt.

Of course the introduction of rock oil or petroleum actually expanded the U.S. economy, just as the introduction of renewable energy technologies is likely to lead to a global expansion of entrepreneurial innovation, competition, and enterprise.

Just before the turn of the twenty-first century, I visited a couple of deep-drilling oil rigs far out in the Gulf of Mexico. It was a loud, thrilling experience watching the platforms' roughnecks and roustabouts pulling energy from far below the earth and the deep blue sea. It was the kind of heroic but dated scene you might have encountered had you boarded one of the last wooden whaling ships at the turn of the twentieth century.

Unfortunately, by favoring their own outmoded petroleum industry, George Bush and Dick Cheney may be undermining America's competitive position in the world.

Today European energy companies like Shell and BP are investing billions in new energy technologies. Shell believes that solar and other renewables will constitute a third of all new energy production by 2050, while BP's CEO thinks that year will see 50 percent of global energy demand met by noncarbon renewables.[36]

Even if there are short-term costs and dislocations associated with a rapid energy transition, every decade of delay is certain to increase those costs. A recent U.N. "CEO Briefing" prepared by Munich Re, a major European reinsurance company, estimates that worldwide insurance losses from severe weather linked to climate change are now running at $150 billion a year and will soon double.[37]

I've seen and reported on dramatic climate impacts already taking place, from the Antarctic Peninsula to the coral reefs of Florida, Fiji, and Australia. As climate change alters and damages unique habitats and the species that depend on them, it becomes ever more important that we conserve and protect what's left, and that we fully value the economic, social, and spiritual worth of our last wild places.

A wetland that's not filled in for a shopping center or damaged by water diversions can, for example, recharge a local aquifer in times of drought. It can provide habitat for wildlife and recreation, act as a nursery for marine fisheries, filter pollution, and inspire diverse human cultures ranging from the Cajun of Louisiana to the "Swamp Arabs" of southern Iraq.

What boomers, Wise Users, and Bush's fund raising Rangers fail to understand is that saving wilderness, whole and undivided, is really about saving ourselves. Only a radical reorganization of the way we see ourselves and our role in the natural world can help turn this backlash around.

We need to begin a rapid transition from oil and gas to sun, wind, tides, geothermal, and hydrogen energy.

We need to revitalize our urban centers and our sense of community while protecting agricultural lands and greenbelts. Even onetime Property Rights strongholds like Boise, Idaho, are now recognizing this by voting for growth limits and open-space protections.

We need to strengthen the Endangered Species Act to protect our fellow creatures long before they reach a critical state and to ensure we maintain the full diversity and promise of life on our blue-marble planet.

We need to establish global standards for the environment, labor, and human rights at least as strong as those for global trade and banking. Although it's no guarantee in and of itself, democratic change can inspire (and be inspired by) ecological movements in places ranging from Poland to Korea and from Bolivia to Mexico and Chile.

Ironically, it's the undermining of democracy in America by a lobbying and election finance system indistinguishable from brown-bag bribery that now poses the greatest environmental threat to our future. We live in a time when too many politicians and business leaders no longer fear being caught in a conflict of interest because they've moved beyond a sense of shame.

Henry David Thoreau once wrote, "Heaven is under our feet as well as over our heads. We need the tonic of wilderness." As a dedicated diver and bodysurfer, I would add only that heaven is also under our flippers. Whenever the forces of heedless industrial sprawl seem overwhelming, a hike around Point Reyes or a bodysurfing session in the wild waters off northern California refreshes my spirit. It's an ice-cold tonic. All I have to do is imagine the noise, traffic, and congestion that aren't there thanks to the efforts of all those dedicated citizens who came before.

After my life's love passed away at the age of forty-three, I returned to one of our favorite beaches to remember her. It was a gusty day, feisty like Nancy, with the winds whipping the sand and frothing the cold translucent waves. Nature gives us a measure of solace and a sense of being a part of something larger, even when large parts of our own soul have torn away. Wilderness lands and waters, from New Jersey's damaged Meadowlands to Alaska's rugged coastal plains, can revive us and endure with us, but only if we choose to stay engaged in the increasingly politicized struggle necessary to protect them.

Between backlash anger and despair that says, "Take what you can get while you can get it," and the faith that we can still leave our kids and future generations a good life in a good land lie only the understanding, the heart, and the will of the American people. It's a thin reed of hope, but it's worked so far.

Notes

Introduction: First Encounters, 1990

1. For additional coverage of the opposing rallies see *San Francisco Examiner*, "Loggers, Activists Square Off" (July 22, 1990): 1; *Santa Rosa Press Democrat* (July 22, 1990): 1.
2. Judi Bari, "The Palco Papers," *Anderson Valley Advertiser* (March 27, 1991): 1. Also a copy of the Pacific Lumber interoffice memo dated April 18, 1990, which reads in part, "Enclosed is a *Press Democrat* article on the environmentalists' internal split over Mississippi Summer. Also enclosed is a flyer with the Earth First! logo, however, as Daryl's name is misspelled, we are not to [*sic*] sure who put it out."
3. Ron Arnold interview with author, February 5, 1993.
4. A. L. Rawe with Rick Field, "Interview with a 'Wise' Guy," *Common Ground of Puget Sound* (Fall 1992): 1.
5. Chuck Cushman interview with author, March 12, 1993.
6. Keith Schneider, "Environment Gets a Flurry of Final Acts," *New York Times* (January 16, 1993): 1, 9.
7. Ed Knight interview with author and documentary producer Steve Talbot, February 11, 1991. Ed Knight interview with author, July 22, 1993.
8. Pat Costner interview with author, September 8, 1993.
9. From interview broadcast on the syndicated television show *Inside Edition*, February 5, 1993.
10. As told to private investigator Sheila O'Donnell. Also reported on *60 Minutes*, September 20, 1992, and by Alecia Swasy, in *Soap Opera: The Inside Story of Procter & Gamble* (New York: Times Books, 1993), p. 222.
11. Sam Hitt interview with author, December 7, 1993.
12. Andy Kerr interview with author, April 20, 1993.
13. Lois Gibbs interview with author, June 25, 1993.

One: Masters and Possessors of Nature

1. Philip Shabecoff, *A Fierce Green Fire* (New York: Farrar, Straus and Giroux, 1993), p. 9.
2. Tom Hayden, *The Love of Possession Is a Disease with Them* (Chicago: Holt, Rinehart and Winston, 1972), pp. 99–100.
3. Ibid., p. 105.
4. Jeremy Rifkin, *Beyond Beef* (New York: Dutton, 1992), p. 78.
5. Quoted by Ed Quillen in "Who Will Coordinate and Inspire the West?" *High Country News* (May 3, 1993): 13.
6. Mike Weiss, "Firetrail—Are Loggers Behind the Rash of Fires in the West?" *Mother Jones* (March/April 1993): 50.
7. Theodore Roosevelt, *Autobiography*, centennial ed., edited and with an introduction by Wayne Andrews (New York: Charles Scribner's Sons, 1958).

8. Jon Krakauer, "Brown Fellas," *Outside* (December 1991): 69.

9. Robert A. Logan with Wendy Gibbons and Stacy Kingsbury, *Environmental Issues for the Nineties: A Handbook for Journalists* (Washington, D.C.: Environmental Reporting Forum, 1992), pp. 179–81.

10. Michael P. Cohen, *The History of the Sierra Club 1892–1970* (San Francisco: Sierra Club Books, 1988), pp. 311–22.

11. David Brower interview with author, March 9, 1993.

12. Shabecoff, *A Fierce Green Fire*, p. 155.

13. David J. Garrow, *Bearing the Cross: Martin Luther King, Jr., and the Southern Christian Leadership Conference* (New York: William Morrow, 1986), p. 553.

14. David Day, *The Environmental Wars* (New York: Ballantine, 1989), pp. 287–90, and other sources.

15. Bernard De Voto, *The Easy Chair* (Boston: Houghton Mifflin, 1955), p. 234.

Two: Rebels and Reaganites

1. "Last Round-Up for the Old West," *The Economist* (March 6, 1993): 16, 23.

2. Bernard Shanks, *This Land Is Your Land* (San Francisco: Sierra Club Books, 1984), p. 266.

3. Ben Santarris, "Landowners Get Sharp Call," *Bellingham Herald* (May 22, 1992): 1.

4. Deane Rhodes interview with author, April 28, 1993.

5. Lou Cannon, *President Reagan: The Role of a Lifetime* (New York: Simon and Schuster, 1991), pp. 86, 531.

6. Shabecoff, *A Fierce Green Fire*, p. 208.

7. Report by the Comptroller General of the United States, *Deficiencies in the Department of the Interior: OIG Investigation of the Powder River Basin Coal Lease Sale* (Washington, D.C.: U.S. General Accounting Office, June 11, 1984), p. 9.

8. Cannon, *President Reagan*, p. 428.

9. Shabecoff, *A Fierce Green Fire*, p. 211.

10. Jonathan Lash, Katherine Gillman, and David Sheridan, *A Season of Spoils* (New York: Pantheon, 1984), p. 67.

11. "The 'Terrible 20' Regulations," *Washington Post* (August 4, 1981).

12. Alan Gottlieb interview with author, March 16, 1993.

13. Trent Clarke, speech to (anti-enviro) Environmental Conservation Organization (ECO) conference, February 20, 1993.

14. Grant Gerber interview with author, May 7, 1993.

15. Ron Arnold interview with author, March 15, 1993.

16. Alan M. Gottlieb, ed., *The Wise Use Agenda* (Bellevue, Wash.: Free Enterprise Press, 1989), pp. 5–18.

17. Quoted by Richard Stapleton in "On the Western Front," *National Parks* (January/February 1993): 34.

18. Chuck Cushman speech to (anti-enviro) Alliance for Environment and Resources conference, January 29, 1993.

19. Based on the official report: Subcommittee on Civil Service of the Committee on Post Office and Civil Service, U.S. House of Representatives, *Interference*

in Environmental Programs by Political Appointees: The Improper Treatment of a Senior Executive Service Official (Washington, D.C.: U.S. Government Printing Office, July 1993). Also based on a December 30, 1992, draft report bearing this disclaimer: "This report has not been officially approved by the Committee or Subcommittee and, therefore, may not necessarily reflect the views of all its members."

20. Clark Collins speech to ECO conference, February 19, 1993.
21. Information from a ten-page unpublished article written by Collins titled "Expanded Version of an Article That Appeared in the January 1992 Issue of *Blue Ribbon* (this is the un-edited version)—National Recreational Trails Fund Act Chronology." It reads in part, "Received a grant from the Honda Motor Corporation that coupled with our other funding and membership revenue, enabled the Coalition to hire me as their full time executive director."
22. Clark Collins interview with author, February 19, 1993.
23. The Captain Mossback character was introduced in *The Mighty Mutandes*, vol. 18 of Ninja Turtle Comics, distributed by Creators Syndicate.
24. Joan Smith interview with author, March 10, 1993.
25. "Friday's Forest Summit: What's at Stake—4,600 Owls vs. 31,100 Jobs," *USA Today* (April 1, 1993): 1.

Three: The Forest for the Trees, 1993
1. Carl Deal, *The Greenpeace Guide to Anti-Environmental Organizations* (Berkeley, Calif.: Odonian Press, 1993), p. 74.
2. Bill Grannell interview with author, February 15, 1993. Also Dave Mazza, "God, Land and Politics, the Wise Use and Christian Right Connection in 1992 Oregon Politics" (Portland, Oreg.: Western States Center and Montana AFL-CIO), pp. 4–6.
3. Typical is the report in the OLC's March 26, 1993, *Network News* that "hundreds of businesses are closing their doors April 2 so employees can be part of history-in-the-making" (an OLC rally at the Portland Timber Summit). The *Albany Democrat-Herald* (Saturday, April 3) reported that Willamette Industries had provided buses to the previous day's rally for two hundred of its Albany, Oregon, employees.
4. This is part of a package of anti-enviro legislation being pushed nationwide by the Washington-based American Legislative Exchange Council (ALEC).
5. Patrick Renshaw, *The Wobblies* (New York: Doubleday, 1967), pp. 163–67, one of several history books that recount the story of Wesley Everest's death.
6. Kathie Durbin and Paul Koberstein, "Forests in Distress," Special Report, *Oregonian* (October 15, 1990), 28 p.
7. During the April 1993 Forest Summit, Vice President Al Gore hinted that the export tax incentive might be eliminated for raw logs.
8. Jan TenBruggencate, "Persis Corp. Gift Preserves Forest Lands in Oregon," *Honolulu Advertiser* (December 28, 1992).
9. The original September 1989 broadcast of the Audubon Special, "Ancient Forests: Rage over Trees," was the target of an OLC/timber industry boycott.

10. Foster Church and Cathy Kiyomura, "Timber Families Stage Rally at Waterfront," *Oregonian* (April 4, 1993): A18.

Four: Grass Roots for Sale
1. Bill Grannell interview with author, February 15, 1993.
2. Chuck Cushman interview with author, March 12, 1993.
3. Grant Gerber interview with author, January 26, 1993.
4. Ron Arnold interview with author, March 15, 1993.
5. Jay Hair, *National Wildlife* (October/November 1992): 30.
6. Congressman George Miller interview with author, June 22, 1993.
7. *Land Rights Letter* (June 1992): 1, 5. Also Ron Arnold and Alan Gottlieb, *Trashing the Economy* (Bellevue, Wash.: Free Enterprise Press, 1993), p. 19.
8. Keith Schneider, "When the Bad Guy Is Seen as the One in the Green Hat," *New York Times* (February 16, 1992): E2.
9. Richard Miniter, "Out to Change the Law of the Land," *Insight* (May 2, 1993).
10. Ron Arnold interview with author, March 15, 1993.
11. According to IRS nonprofit returns, in 1991, Blue Ribbon had a total revenue of $138,309.44, CDFE had $55,583.18, WIRF had $144,296, and the Western States Public Lands Coalition (which runs People for the West!) had $627,135.
12. Kathy Kvarda interview with author at AER meeting, January 29, 1993.
13. Katherine Bouma, "Forestry Commission Met Illegally," *Montgomery Advertiser* (November 15, 1992): 1. Also "State Funds Aided Stewards" (December 1); "Forestry Involved with 2nd Group" (March 28, 1993), and additional reports.
14. Alan Crawford, *Thunder on the Right* (New York: Pantheon, 1980), p. 50.
15. Internal Revenue Service, Form 990, Second Amendment Foundation, 1991.
16. Crawford, *Thunder on the Right,* p. 68.
17. Alan Gottlieb interview with author, March 16, 1993.
18. Court documents copied at Federal Records Center, Seattle, Washington: U.S. Attorney Indictment/Gottlieb; Judgment & Commitment/Gottlieb; and Factual Basis for Plea of Guilty/Gottlieb. Also Peter Lewis, "Tax Case Against Fundraiser Political, Lawyer Hints," *Seattle Times* (January 14, 1984): A8.
19. As quoted by Josh Sugarmann in *National Rifle Association—Money, Firepower and Fear* (Washington, D.C.: National Press Book, 1992), pp. 131–33.
20. Krakauer, "Brown Fellas," p. 69.
21. Ron Arnold, "What's Ahead for Weed Control," Center for the Defense of Free Enterprise speech, delivered to 1981 Washington State Weed Control Association.
22. Ron Arnold, speech to Atlantic Vegetation Management Association, Halifax, Nova Scotia, October 23, 1984.
23. Arnold's advice to Canadian timber giant MacMillan Bloedel, as reported in *Share Groups in British Columbia,* Canadian Library of Parliament report (Ottawa, Ont.: December 10, 1991), tracing the establishment of the Wise Use–like Share movement in Canada and the role Arnold played in establishing it.
24. Marked Exhibit 3 in the deposition of Ron Arnold, April 12, 1988, in U.S. District Court, District of Oregon, *Carol van Strum et al. v. John C. Lawn et al.*

25. Quoted in Canadian Library of Parliament report, p. 17.
26. Arnold and Gottlieb, *Trashing the Economy,* p. 179.
27. Canadian Library of Parliament report, executive summary.
28. Richard Cockle, "Cattle-Grazing Advocates Picket Environmentalists' Conference," *Oregonian* (April 27, 1992).
29. Notices of Default, Sonoma, California, May 21, 1987; May 17, 1989; and other court documents.
30. John McClaughery interview with author, June 9, 1993.
31. Jill Hamburg, "The Lone Ranger," *California Magazine* (November 1990): 90.
32. *The River Reporter* (July 31, 1986): 1, 19.
33. Richard M. Stapleton, "On the Western Front," *National Parks* (January/February 1993): 31–36.
34. Copy of letter, various articles, including Glen Martin, "The 'Killer Mosquitoes' Deception," *San Francisco Chronicle* (November 11, 1991).
35. Loretta Callahan, "The High Priest of Property Rights," *Columbian* (May 17, 1992): 1. The *Columbian* has continued to report on Cushman's local activities, even after he led the first-ever protest demonstration in front of the newspaper's building.
36. Ibid., A10.
37. Court filings and Daniel Defoe interview with author, August 1, 1993.
38. Loretta Callahan, "Deputies Seize Cushman's Antiques," *Columbian* (October 17, 1993).
39. Jim Baca interview with author, July 21, 1993.
40. Larry Campbell interview with author, March 11, 1993.
41. Dick Springer interview with author, March 11, 1993.
42. Joan Laatz, "Protection Sought for Trout in Umpqua," *Oregonian* (April 2, 1993): A25.
43. Memo from Mineral Policy Center, May 2, 1991.
44. IRS Form 990S, Western States Public Lands Coalition, 1991, 1990.
45. The poll was commissioned by the American Mining Congress.
46. Questa's PFW chairperson, Ed Cordova, is identified as MolyCorp's security chief in *Workbook of the Southwest Research and Information Center* (Spring 1992): 13. In earlier interviews with *Audubon* magazine and CNN, he had identified himself as a miner.
47. John R. Luoma, "Eco-Backlash," *Wildlife Conservation* (November/December 1992): 34.

Five: The Golden Rooster

1. "The Story of the Nugget's Gold Rooster," informational brochure, John Ascuaga's Nugget Hotel.
2. General Accounting Office, *Federal Land Management, The Mining Law of 1872 Needs Revision* (Washington, D.C.: U.S. Government Printing Office, March 1989).
3. Michael Satchell, "The New Gold Rush," *U.S. News & World Report* (October 28, 1991): 44–53.

4. Bob Langsencamp interview with author, April 8, 1993.

5. Kit Miniclier, "Mine's Toxic Leaks Render River Lifeless," *Denver Post* (November 11, 1992): 1, 7. Also *Post* articles from November 20; December 8, 22, 24, and 29; and "The Mine That Killed a River" (January 1993), editorial.

6. Elliot Lord, *Comstock, Mining and Miners* (Berkeley, Calif.: Howell North, 1959).

7. Dave Barry, *Dave Barry Slept Here* (New York: Random House, 1989), pp. 103–4.

8. Louis Adamic, *Dynamite* (New York: Chelsea House, 1968), pp. 9–21.

9. Richard Hofstaedter and Michael Wallace, *American Violence* (New York: Random House, 1970), pp. 147–51.

10. Adamic, *Dynamite*, p. 140.

11. Ibid., pp. 134–42.

12. Ibid., pp. 157–65. Also Renshaw, *The Wobblies*, pp. 21–41.

13. Adamic, *Dynamite*, pp. 152–53.

14. Ibid., pp. 143–56.

15. Hofstaedter and Wallace, *American Violence*, pp. 160–64. Also Howard Zinn, *A People's History of the United States* (New York: HarperPerennial, 1990), pp. 346–49.

16. Renshaw, *The Wobblies*, pp. 144–60.

17. William F. Nolan, *Hammett—A Life at the Edge* (New York: Congdon & Weed, 1983), pp. 13–14.

18. Renshaw, *The Wobblies*, pp. 160–63.

19. Harry M. Caudill, *Night Comes to the Cumberlands* (Boston: Little, Brown, 1962), pp. 188–205.

20. David Helvarg, "While the World Burns," *Penthouse* magazine (November 1998): 24–26, 31, 66, 129.

21. Michael Satchell, "The New Gold Rush," *U.S. News & World Report* (October 28, 1991): 46.

22. The six-page fundraising letter concludes, "Don't let the 'wise use' enemies of the environment win! Defend your planet by becoming a Sierra Club member today—and receive our special Sierra Club canvas grocery bag FREE with your membership!"

Six: Save It for What?

1. Vernon was one of several victims of anti-enviro attacks featured on the syndicated television program *Inside Edition*, March 3, 1993.

2. Northern Forest Lands Council, "Northern Forest Lands Overview" (Concord, Mass.: NFLC, 1992), a six-page summary and chronology of the region's forest issues beginning with the Diamond Match sale. The council was established by Congress with the participation of the governments of Maine, New Hampshire, Vermont, and New York.

3. The most detailed survey of Wise Use/Property Rights activity in New England through 1992 is a twenty-page report issued by the Massachusetts-based Political Research Associates. William Kevin Burke, "The Scent of Opportunity" (Cambridge, Mass.: Political Research Associates, December 12, 1992).

4. Johnson is also secretary of the Alliance for America.

5. The Fly-In was sponsored by the Oregon Lands Coalition in September 1991.

6. Alliance for America, "Signing Away America," *Alliance News* (April 1993): 1–2.

7. As the last state without a Wal-Mart, Vermont's local opposition has received widespread press coverage, including Nancie L. Katz, "Vermont—The Last 'Sprawl-Mart' Holdout," *San Francisco Examiner/Chronicle* (August 29, 1993): Sunday Punch, p. 4.

8. Burke, "The Scent of Opportunity," 6.

9. There are a number of books on Adirondacks history and other related topics, such as Roderick Nash's *Wilderness and the American Mind,* that devote some pages to the subject. For a concise, broad-ranging review, see *Adirondack Park Centennial* magazine (1992, 62p.), published by the *Adirondack Daily Enterprise.*

10. The Commission on the Adirondacks in the Twenty-First Century, *The Adirondack Park in the Twenty-First Century* (State of New York, April 1990), 96p.

11. Larry Maxwell, "Protestors Confront Council," *Post Star* (April 13, 1990): 1. Descriptions and quotes from protest events from 1990 to 1992 that are not attributed come from forty-two articles printed during that time in four area newspapers: *Glens Falls Post Star, Plattsburgh Press Republican, Elizabeth Valley News,* and *Adirondack Daily Enterprise* (in Saranac Lake).

12. Eric Siy interview with author, June 1, 1993, and news report.

13. Larry Maxwell, "Adirondack Solidarity Celebrates 1 Year's Fight," *Post Star* (April 24, 1991): 1.

14. Lohr McKinstry, "Liberators Protesting with Arrows, Bulldozers," *Plattsburgh Press Republican* (June 16, 1990): 1.

15. Condemned in a *Plattsburgh Press Republican* editorial, "Bring Your Deer Rifle?" (June 24, 1990): C8. Gerdts's inflammatory leaflets may have marked the beginning of the end of his effectiveness as a political leader in the park.

16. Mathew Russell, "'60 Minutes' Footage of Crane Pond Fight Draws Criticism," *Adirondack Daily Enterprise* (September 22, 1992): 1/6.

17. Harry McIntosh interview with author, April 23, 1993.

18. Jeff Jones, "Getting Wise," *Appalachia Bulletin* (March 1992): 29–31. Also tape of a local public-access television talk show with Birch Society credits.

19. Will Nixon, "Fear and Loathing in the Adirondacks," *E* magazine (September/October 1992): 28–35. Also Robert Worth, "Adirondack Battleground: The Struggle over Property Rights in New York State," a report prepared for a college writing course.

20. John Sheehan interview with author, May 5, 1993.

21. From a copy of the two-page "Dear Ron" (Stafford) letter dated August 25, 1992, in which Governor Cuomo outlines the "harassment, intimidation and even life-threatening acts of violence" that culminated in the burning of LaBastille's barns and spray-painting of Gordon Davis's office building. It is signed "Sincerely, Mario Cuomo."

22. The Solidarity Alliance joined the Alliance for America at its founding in St. Louis, November 8–10, 1991.

23. Rose Paul interview with author, August 25, 1993.

24. Carl Reidel interview with author, August 26, 1993.

Seven: Road-kill an Activist

1. Laura Parker, "The Island of Dixy Lee Ray," *Seattle Post-Intelligencer* (August 10, 1986): F1.

2. From an ECO brochure.

3. *21st Century Science & Technology* (Winter 1992) and *The New American* (February 8, 1993).

4. Gary Taubes, "The Ozone Backlash," *Science* (June 11, 1993): 1580–83.

5. Florence Williams, "Sagebrush Rebellion 11," *High Country News* (February 24, 1992): 1.

6. Jim Baca interview with author, July 21, 1993.

7. Debra Thunder, "Cowboys Ain't Indians: Buffalo Ain't Cows," *High Country News* (May 31, 1993): 16.

8. TelSpec, Telecommunications Specialists, Inc., of Burnsville, Minnesota, set up the ECO phone system.

9. The reference is to the Sahara Club, a group of southern California dirt bikers who have carried out a campaign of disruption, harassment, and violence directed against environmentalists, elected officials, and the Bureau of Land Management.

10. Other favorite anti-enviro bumper stickers are "Earth Firsters! America's Favorite Speed Bumps," "Hungry and Out of Work?—Eat an Environmentalist," and "Spotted Owl Tastes Just Like Fried Chicken!"

11. "The Rest of the Story: The Bill Ellen Horror Story," submitted to U.S. government interagency working group on wetlands by the National Wildlife Federation, 2p. Also *Wall Street Journal* (November 18, 1992, and January 15, 1993), editorial pages.

12. *The New American* (February 8, 1993): 21–26.

13. Graybiel provided a sampling of thirty articles on Mills and his case that have run in the *Pensacola News Journal* from 1989 to 1993.

14. The source on this case was twenty-two articles and editorials in the *Los Angeles Times* (October 3, 1992–April 21, 1993).

15. Rick Sieman interview with author, May 12, 1993.

16. *Sahara Club Newsletter*, #3 (undated): 2. Other encouragements have included "Here's a partial list of actions, names and numbers that honest (and daring) citizens could have some fun with," and "Hit List! Make copies of this list and pass them around to friends. ... Good hunting!"

17. Susan Sullivan, "Angry Offroaders Say They'll Pack Guns to Defend Rights," *Press-Enterprise,* Riverside, Calif. (November 17, 1990).

18. Susan Sullivan, "Ten Arrested as Bikers, Rangers Square Off," *Press-Enterprise* (November 25, 1990). Also law enforcement sources and BLM agent interview with author, May 17, 1993.

19. *Sahara Club Newsletter* (February 19, 1993): 5.

20. Candice Boak interview with author and producer Steve Talbot, December 13, 1990.

21. According to the Arcata Police Department and Steve Talbot.

22. Law enforcement and environmental sources, numerous interviews with author, May 1993.

23. Ed Knight interviews with author and producer Steve Talbot, February 11 and 12, 1991, and with author, July 22, 1993.

24. Joan Smith interview with author, January 29, 1993.

25. "Land Takeover Threatens NY, VT, NH, and ME!" flyer issued by the John Birch Society. Copy provided by Political Research Associates.

26. Sources on the John Birch Society include Chip Berlet, "Trashing the Birchers: Secrets of the Paranoid Right," *Boston Phoenix* (July 14–20, 1989): 10; Andrea Estes, "Birch Society Claims Gains," *Boston Herald* (May 28, 1991): 1–24; and Robert L. Rose, "Will Communists Take Over in 2002? Ask a John Bircher," *Wall Street Journal* (October 2, 1991): 1.

27. "Greenpeace, Shock Troops for a New Dark Age," *EIR—Executive Intelligence Review* (April 21, 1989): 24–31.

28. Chip Berlet and Joel Bellman, "Lyndon LaRouche—Fascism Wrapped in an American Flag," pamphlet (Cambridge, Mass.: Political Research Associates, February 7, 1989), 15p.

29. "Environmental Hoaxes Kill—Save the Earth with Technology," cover and special reports, *21st Century Science and Technology* (Fall 1992): 11–27.

30. "The Limits of Propaganda: Lyndon LaRouche Goes to Jail," *Special Edition* (May 1989): 1.

31. John Judis, "Rev. Moon's Rising Political Influence," *U.S. News & World Report* (March 27, 1989): 27–31.

32. Daniel Junas, "Rising Moon: The Unification Church's Japan Connection," Working Paper #5 (Seattle, Wash.: Institute for Global Security Studies, 1989).

33. Judis, "Rev. Moon's Rising Political Influence," 27.

34. "The Resurrection of Reverend Moon," PBS *Frontline* documentary, January 21, 1992.

35. Walter Hatch, "Mainstream Moon," *Seattle Times* (February 13, 1989): 1.

36. Ibid., and the author's own reporting from Honduras.

37. Ross Gelbspan, "The 'New' FBI," *Covert Action* (Winter 1989): 15–16.

38. Edmond Jacoby, "The Mooning of Ralph David Abernathy," *Regardie's* (May 1989): 85–94.

39. Judis, "Rev. Moon's Rising Political Influence."

40. "The Resurrection of Reverend Moon."

41. Ron Arnold interview with author, April 22, 1993.

42. *The Wise Use Agenda* (Bellevue, Wash.: Free Enterprise Press, 1989), p. xv.

43. Merrill Sikorski interview with author, April 23, 1993.

44. This short phone conversation took place on June 17, 1993.

45. Carl Deal, *The Greenpeace Guide to Anti-Environmental Organizations* (Berkeley, Calif.: Odonian Press, 1993), pp. 24–25.

46. American Freedom Coalition of Washington filings with the Office of the Secretary of State, Corporations Division, Olympia, Washington, 1988–1992.

47. Hatch, "Mainstream Moon."

48. Mark Hume, "Resource-Use Conference Had Links to Moonie Cult," *Vancouver Sun* (July 8, 1989): A6.

49. Copies of these letters were provided to the author by the Montana AFL-CIO.

50. Chuck Malloy, "Wise-Use Promoter Denies Church Ties," *Idaho Falls Post Register* (October 8, 1989): 1–3.

51. Ron Arnold interview with author, March 15, 1993.

52. Junas, "Rising Moon," 25.

53. A second source of information on Moon's holdings in the United States is Alan Green and Larry Zilliox Jr., "Fishing for Respectability," *Washington City Paper* (June 11, 1993): 1.

54. Frank Greve, "Moon Church Gives Millions to New Right," *San Jose Mercury News* (December 21, 1987): 1A, back page.

Eight: Up Against the Law

1. "Alaska Accuses U.S. of 'Taking' Park Lands," reprinted from the *New York Times* in the *San Francisco Chronicle* (July 24, 1993): A6; also documents provided to the author by Alaska Attorney General Charles Cole.

2. Steven Hayward, "California Should Call the EPA's Smog Bluff," *Orange County Register* (May 5, 1993): op-ed page.

3. Julia Rubin, "Intimidation Lawsuits Chill Public Activism," Associated Press (February 4, 1990); "SLAPPing the Opposition," *Newsweek* (March 5, 1990); Eve Pell, *E* magazine (November/December 1991); and other materials supplied by the Political Litigation Project, University of Denver College of Law.

4. Penelope Canan interview with author, April 29, 1992.

5. Joe Brecher interview with author, April 29, 1992.

6. Quoted in Edward W. McBride Jr., "The Empire State Strikes Back: New York's Legislative Response to Lawsuits," *Vermont Law Review* (Spring 1993): 931.

7. *Justice for Sale: Shortchanging the Public Interest for Private Gain* (Washington, D.C.: Alliance for Justice, 1993), pp. 10–11.

8. "PLF Argues Against Ballot Box Land Use Planning," *Pacific Legal Foundation* (Fall 1992): 7.

9. List of "Public Interest Law Firms" dated August 4, 1992, provided by Pacific Legal Foundation.

10. Oliver A. Houck, "With Charity for All," *Yale Law Journal* (July 1984): 1419–1563.

11. Ibid., pp. 1465–66.

12. Ibid., p. 1481.

13. Jim Burling interview with author, May 18, 1993.

14. Richard A. Epstein, *Takings: Private Property and the Power of Eminent Domain* (Cambridge, Mass.: Harvard University Press, 1985).

15. W. John Moore, "Just Compensation," *National Journal* (June 13, 1992): 1404–7.

16. Charles Fried, *Order and Law: Arguing the Reagan Revolution—A Firsthand Account* (New York: Simon and Schuster, 1991), p. 183.

17. Nancy Marzulla speech to ECO conference, Reno, Nevada, February 19, 1993.

18. Executive Order 12630, issued by President Reagan on March 15, 1988, and published in the *Federal Register,* vol. 53, no. 53 (March 18, 1988): 8859–62.

19. Presidents Reagan and Bush appointed twelve of the Court's judges; President Reagan renominated the other four in 1982.

20. Tom Castleton, "Chief Judge Smith Puts Property Rights up Front," *Legal Times* (August 17, 1992): 1–16, 17.

21. *Lucas* trial transcript, supra note 44 at 113 as reported by Richard J. Lazarus, "Putting the Correct 'Spin' on *Lucas,*" *Stanford Law Review* (May 1993): 1422.

22. Amicus curiae briefs in support of petitioner and of respondent as listed in notes 65 and 66 in article by Glenn P. Sugameli, "Takings Issues in Light of *Lucas v. South Carolina Coastal Council,*" *Virginia Environmental Law Journal* (1993): 439, 453 nn.

23. *Stanford Law Review* (May 1993). Also *Vermont Law Review* (Spring 1993).

24. John Echeverria interview with author, June 22, 1993.

25. Tom Kenworthy, "Nevada Cowboy Irate over Discouraging Words on the Range," *Washington Post* (February 16, 1993). Also "Last Round-Up for the Old West," *The Economist* (March 6–12, 1993), and other news reports.

26. Wayne Hage, *Storm over Rangeland* (Bellevue, Wash.: Free Enterprise Press, 1989).

27. Ted Williams, "Taking Back the Range," *Audubon* (January/February 1993): 31.

28. Jon Christensen, "Nevada Sides with Environmentalists Against Rancher," *High Country News* (July 13, 1992): 5.

29. James Wittinghill interview with author, June 23, 1993.

30. Bill Klinefelter interview with author, June 24, 1993.

31. Marianne Lavelle, "The 'Property Rights' Revolt," *National Law Journal* (May 10, 1993): 1, 34.

32. American Farm Bureau Federation, "Farm Bureau Policies for 1993," brochure.

33. Andy Neal interview with author, May 18, 1993.

34. Neil D. Hamilton, "The Next Generation of U.S. Agricultural Conservation Policy," speech delivered at the Soil and Water Conservation conference, March 16, 1993, Kansas City, Missouri.

35. American Legislative Exchange Council, "The Attack of the Killer Watermelons: Flat Earth Science & Zero Risk," *The State Factor* (February 1991). This issue of the council's newsletter consisted of the text of Warren Brookes's speech at the council's 1990 annual meeting. "Watermelon" refers to the anti-enviro claim that environmentalists are Communists: "green on the outside, red on the inside."

36. Larry D. Hatfield and Dexter Waugh, "Conservative Think Tank Targets States," *San Francisco Examiner* (May 25, 1992): 1, 12.

37. Bill Klinefelter interview with author, June 24, 1993.

38. Hamilton, "The Next Generation of U.S. Agricultural Conservation Policy."

39. Jonathan Lash interview with author, July 26, 1993.

Nine: The Green P.I.

1. Copies of Investigative Services Companies' "Fire Scene Examination" report and AK Analytical's "Laboratory Report."
2. *CBS Evening News*, March 3, 1993.
3. Linda Chase interview with author, April 22, 1993.
4. For more on John Reese, see Chip Berlet, "The Hunt for Red Menace," *Covert Action* (Winter 1989): 3–9. Also Ross Gelbspan, "The 'New' FBI," *Covert Action* (Winter 1989): 11–16.
5. Most of the information regarding Judi Bari's case not directly attributed to Sheila O'Donnell comes from interviews with Bari and other subjects, news reports, and other materials collected during a six-month investigation by the author and producer Steve Talbot for "Who Bombed Judi Bari?", a PBS documentary broadcast on KQED, San Francisco, May 24, 1991.
6. From the police department's Affidavit for Search Warrant.
7. "Who Bombed Judi Bari?"
8. As later recalled by Judi Bari in an interview with author and Steve Talbot, February 12, 1991.
9. From the police department's Affidavit for Search Warrant.
10. Nail evidence was also examined in "Who Bombed Judi Bari?"
11. Assistant Special Agent in Charge Edward Appel interview with author and Steve Talbot, May 7, 1991.
12. From the FBI Crime Lab report.
13. "Who Bombed Judi Bari?"
14. Rich McComber interview with author and Steve Talbot, December 10, 1990.
15. From copy of original "Lord's Avenger" letter.
16. Complete lyrics can be found in Susan Zakin, *Coyotes and Town Dogs* (New York: Viking, 1993), pp. 373–74.
17. "Who Bombed Judi Bari?"
18. Pat Costner and Joe Thornton, *Playing with Fire* (Washington, D.C.: Greenpeace USA, 1991).
19. Chip Berlet, "Taking off the Gloves," *Greenpeace* (September/October 1990): 18–19.
20. Bowman Cox, "Reporter Rejects EPA Protection, Keeps Documents," *SEJ Journal* (Winter 1992): 12.
21. Copies of Incident/Offense reports from Carroll County Sheriff's Department and Eureka Fire Marshal.
22. Kate McConnico, "Raw Deals in Point Comfort," *Texas Observer* (September 18, 1992): 16–17.
23. Ibid., p. 17.
24. Sam Howe Verhovek, "Shrimpers Feel at Bay over Plant Expansion," *New York Times* (June 20, 1993): 16.
25. Roy Bragg, "Throng of Opposition Envelops Activist," *Houston Chronicle* (March 3, 1991): D1.
26. *Texas Observer* (September 18, 1992): 17.

27. Copy of Calhoun County Sheriff's Department half-page assignment report on the incident.
28. Sheila O'Donnell, "Common Sense Security," brochure for Ace Investigations, November 3, 1992.
29. Charles Spiekerman interview with author, January 15, 1993.
30. Swasy, who spent several weeks in Taylor County, has a chapter in her book called "Fear on the Fenholloway," which documents and recounts the pollution and violence that occurred along the river. Alicia Swasy, *Soap Opera — The Inside Story of Procter & Gamble* (New York: Random House, 1993), pp. 206–34.
31. Ned Mudd interview with author, October 6, 1993.
32. As recounted in Swasy, *Soap Opera;* and told to Sheila O'Donnell.
33. Jerry Blair interview with author, October 22, 1993.

Ten: Bomb Throwers, 1997

1. Ellen Gray, *Seattle Times* (November 15, 1994); interview with author, February 1995.
2. Eric Pryne, *Seattle Times* (October 19, 1994): 1, 20. Scott Brennan, *Bellingham Herald* (November 13, 1994): 1, 2.
3. Eric Ward interview with author, April 22, 1995.
4. "FBI Nabs Eight On Gun Charges," Associated Press (July 29, 1996). Author interview with Chief Pierce, early August 1996.
5. Jere Payton interview with author, April 22, 1995.
6. Jim Faulkner, *Federal Lands Update* (October 1994): 1, 2, 3, 4, 6.
7. Mike Gardner interview with author, April 22, 1995.
8. Jon Christensen, "County Commissioner Courts Bloodshed," *High Country News* (April 3, 1995): 12.
9. A copy of the instructional card, signed by Forest Service Chief Jack Ward Thomas, was provided to me by PEER, Public Employees for Environmental Responsibility.
10. Interview and author visit to Wildlife Lab, April 20, 1994.
11. As reported by Adam Gopnik, *The New Yorker* (May 8, 1995): 8.
12. Background interview with Murkowski staffer, September 27, 1995.
13. Keith Easthouse, *Santa Fe New Mexican* (May 11, 1995), B1, 5.
14. Editorial, Wichita *Eagle* (October 25, 1993).
15. Tim Egan, "Wingtip 'Cowboys' in Last Stand to Hold on to Low Grazing," *New York Times* (October 29, 1993): 1.
16. Ted Williams, "Defense of the Realm," *Sierra* (January/February 1996): 34.
17. Guy Pence interview with author, January 22, 1996.
18. Joel Brinkley, "Cultivating the Grass Roots to Reap Legislative Benefits," *New York Times* (November 1, 1993): 1, A14. Also Ross Gelbspan, "The Heat," *Harper's* (December 1995).
19. The first (and possibly only) mainstream reporter to cover this was the *Chicago Tribune's* Jon Margolis, in an article titled "Odd Trio Could Kill Nature Pact" (September 30, 1994).

20. Carol Browner interview with author, October 28, 1993.
21. Mark Dowie, *Losing Ground: American Environmentalism at the Close of the Twentieth Century* (Cambridge, Mass.: MIT Press, 1995), p. 85.
22. Jim Baca interview with author, February 15, 1994.
23. *Congressional Record* (October 26, 1993): H8465.
24. Jeff Petrich interview with author, October 1, 1995, and media and police reports.
25. Edward O. Wilson, speech to the Society of Environmental Journalists, Massachusetts Institute of Technology, October 28, 1995.
26. Don Young interview with author, October 11, 1995.
27. Charles Ingram interview with author, October 4, 1995.
28. American Public Opinion Deregulation, Luntz Research and Strategic Services; "Environment Update," *The Wirthlin Report*, August 1995; "The Superfund Reform Coalition—The Political Tides," American Viewpoint, Inc., December 12, 1995.
29. Dick Morris interview with author, October 3, 1995.
30. Diana Jean Schemo, "Oil Companies Buy an Army to Tame Columbia's Rebels," *New York Times* (August 22, 1996).

Eleven: Wise Use in the White House, 2000–2004

1. David Frum, *The Right Man: The Suprise Presidency of George W. Bush*, Lexus-Nexus confirmation.
2. Katharine Q. Seelye, "Environment Fits in Political Strategy," *New York Times* (February 1, 2003).
3. David Helvarg, "Bush Is No Reagan: He's a Harding," Alternet, July 17, 2001. A good deal of the Harding history I found in Nathan Miller's *Stealing from America*, Paragon House edition, 1992.
4. Ron Arnold interview with author, May 20, 2001.
5. Howard Fineman and Michael Isikoff, *Newsweek* (May 14, 2001): 20.
6. The Center for Responsive Politics collects and compiles campaign funding data from the FEC and publishes it on its website, www.Opensecrets.Org.
7. A good recounting of the 2000 election fiasco can be found in Jeffrey Toobin, *Too Close to Call* (New York: Random House, 2001).
8. Geoffrey Mohan, "Bush Oil, Gas Bid Skirts Key Issues," *Los Angeles Times* (August 12, 2001): A1, A25.
9. Douglas Jehl with Andrew C. Revkin, "Bush, in Reversal, Won't Seek Cut in Emissions of Carbon Dioxide," *New York Times* (March 14, 2001): A1, A16.
10. The decline in enforcement and use of enforcement agents for her private security detail was first reported by PEER, Public Employees for Environmental Responsibility, on April 28 and 29, 2003, using Executive Office of U.S. Attorneys figures (for prosecution rates) and interviews and surveys of agents.
11. Guy Gugliotta, "IG Investigates Whether EPA Misled Public on Water Quality," *Washington Post* (August 6, 2003): A15; Andrew C. Revkin with Katharine Q. Seelye, "Report by the E.P.A. Leaves out Data on Climate Change," *New York Times* (June 19, 2003).

12. Katharine Q. Seelye, "E.P.A. Exempts Old Plants from Using Anti-Pollution Devices," *New York Times* (August 27, 2003), and multiple other news reports.

13. Mike Allen, "Bush Pushes Local Control of Conservation Matters," *Washington Post* (May 31, 2001): A2.

14. Mike Soraghan, "Watt Applauds Bush Energy Strategy," *Denver Post* (May 16, 2001).

15. Michael Grunwald, "USDA Chief Worries Sierra Plan's Backers," *Washington Post* (February 15, 2001): A1, A10.

16. Heidi Walters, "People for the USA! Disbands," *High Country News* (December 18, 2000).

17. First of several interviews with Lamar Marshall, October 7, 1993. Later interview with Lamar Marshall, August 14, 2003. Also local press reports of Wise Use materials and videotape of ACR meeting in Double Springs, Alabama.

18. David Helvarg, "Green as a Hundred Grand," *Sports Afield* (October 1998): 16–18.

19. Ruth Marcus, "Issue Groups Fund Seminars for Judges," *Washington Post* (April 9, 1998): A1, A12–13.

20. Curtis Moore, "Money Talks, but Often Hides Its Sources," *SEJ Journal* (Fall, 2000): 1, 25–27.

21. Lynn Scarlett interview with author, January 30, 2003.

22. Katharine Q. Seelye, "Bush Picks Industry Insiders to Fill Environmental Posts," *New York Times* (May 12, 2001): A1, A12; John Mintz and Eric Pianin, "Symbol of a Shift at Interior," *Washington Post* (May 16, 2001): A-21 R; Jeffrey Smith, "Ethics Probe Opened on Interior Dept. Lawyer," *Washington Post* (August 15, 2003): A7; and multiple other stories.

23. Multiple sources, including "Klamath Fish Kill Blamed on Low Water Flows," *Eureka Times-Standard* (January 5, 2003); U.S. Department of Interior News Release, "Secretary to Order Water Release to Klamath Farmers," July 24, 2001; Andrew Revkin, "Study Discounts Halting Irrigation to Protect Fish," *New York Times* (February 5, 2002): A16. Ryan Kliewer and other farmers interview with author, May 21, 2001.

24. "Administration Suppresses Economic Report Slamming Klamath Policy," Faultline.org, January 29, 2003.

25. Tom Hamburger, "Oregon Water Saga Illuminates Rove's Methods with Agencies," *Wall Street Journal* (July 30, 2003).

26. David Helvarg, "Bush's Other War," *The Nation* (February 11, 2002).

27. Various reports, including "Snowmobiles to Stay in Yellowstone," *National Parks* (September/October 2002).

28. Bill Horn interview with author, July 3, 2002.

29. Katharine Q. Seelye, "Report Concludes Snowmobile Ban Is Best for Parks," *New York Times* (January 31, 2003).

30. Julie Cart, "70% of Jobs in Park Service Marked Ripe for Privatizing," *Los Angeles Times* (January 26, 2003), and other reports. Copy of Fran Mainella e-mail to NPS employees. Lynn Scarlett interview with author, January 30, 2003.

31. Jeff Ruch interview with author, February 5, 2003.

32. "Inhofe Delivers Major Speech on the Science of Climate Change," July 28, 2003, Press Release, Inhofe.senate.gov.

33. U.S. Navy, "Naval Operations in an Ice-free Arctic," symposium, April 17–18, 2001, Final Report.

34. David Helvarg, "There Is No Silver Lining," *The Nation* (December 9, 2002).

35. Excerpt from leaked 2002 "Straight Talk" memo from Frank Luntz to GOP, pp. 131–143, which cover the environment.

36. Jeremy Rifkin, *The Hydrogen Economy* (New York: Penguin Putnam, 2002), p. 189.

37. UNEP (United Nations Environmental Program), Press Release, UNEP Division of Communications and Public Information, October 29, 2002.

Bibliography

Adamic, Louis. *Dynamite*. New York: Chelsea House, 1968.

Arnold, Andrea. *Fear of Food*. Bellevue, Wash.: Free Enterprise Press, 1990.

Arnold, Ron. *Ecology Wars*. Bellevue, Wash.: Free Enterprise Press, 1987.

Arnold, Ron, and Alan Gottlieb. *Trashing the Economy*. Bellevue, Wash.: Free Enterprise Press, 1993.

Barry, Dave. *Dave Barry Slept Here*. New York: Random House, 1989.

Berger, Samuel R. *Dollar Harvest*. The Plains, Va.: AAM Publications, 1986.

Birnbaum, Jeffrey A. *The Lobbyists*. New York: Times Books, 1992.

Brown, Lester R., Christopher Flavin, and Hal Kane. *Vital Signs, 1992*. New York: Norton, 1992.

Burnette, Robert, and John Koster. *The Road to Wounded Knee*. New York: Bantam Books, 1974

Cannon, Lou. *President Reagan: The Role of a Lifetime*. New York: Simon & Schuster, 1991.

Carson, Rachel. *Silent Spring*. Greenwich, Conn.: Fawcett, 1962.

Caudill, Harry M. *Night Comes to the Cumberlands*. Boston: Little, Brown, 1962.

Chase, Alston. *Playing God in Yellowstone*. San Diego: Harcourt Brace Jovanovich, 1987.

Cohen, Michael P. *The History of the Sierra Club 1892–1970*. San Francisco: Sierra Club Books, 1988.

Committee on Interior and Insular Affairs, U.S. House of Representatives. *Alyeska Pipeline Service Company Covert Operation*. Washington, D.C.: U.S. Government Printing Office, 1992.

Crawford, Alan. *Thunder on the Right*. New York: Pantheon, 1980.

Dary, David A. *The Buffalo Book*. Chicago: Swallow Press, 1974.

Davidson, Osha Gray. *Under Fire: The NRA and the Battle for Gun Control*. New York: Holt, 1993.

Day, David. *The Environmental Wars*. New York: Ballantine, 1989.

Deal, Carl. *The Greenpeace Guide to Anti-Environmental Organizations*. Berkeley, Calif.: Odonian Press, 1993.

De Voto, Bernard. *The Easy Chair*. Boston: Houghton Mifflin, 1955.

Editors, Time-Life Books. *This Fabulous Century: 1920–1930*. New York: TimeLife, 1969.

Ellis, Edward. *Lives of the Presidents*. Chicago: Flanagan, 1913.

Environmental and Energy Study Conference. *1993 Briefing Book on Environmental and Energy Legislation*. Washington, D.C.: Environmental and Energy Study Institute, 1993.

Freidel, Frank, and Alan Brinkley. *America in the Twentieth Century*. New York: McGraw-Hill, 1982.

Frohnmayer, John. *Leaving Town Alive: Confessions of an Arts Warrior*. Boston: Houghton Mifflin, 1993.

Gans, Herbert J. *Deciding What's News.* New York: Random House, 1980.

Gore, Albert, Jr. *Earth in the Balance.* New York: Penguin, 1992.

Gottlieb, Alan M. *Gun Rights Fact Book.* Bellevue, Wash.: Merril Press, 1988.

Gottlieb, Alan M., editor. *The Wise Use Agenda.* Bellevue, Wash.: Free Enterprise Press, 1989.

Hage, Wayne. *Storm over Rangelands.* Bellevue, Wash.: Free Enterprise Press, 1989.

Hayden, Tom. *The Love of Possession Is a Disease with Them.* Chicago: Holt, Rinehart and Winston, 1972.

Hertsgaard, Mark. *On Bended Knee.* New York: Farrar, Straus and Giroux, 1988.

Hofstadter, Richard, and Michael Wallace. *American Violence.* New York: Random House, 1970.

Karnow, Stanley. *Vietnam: A History.* New York: Viking, 1983.

Katsiaficas, George. *The Imagination of the New Left.* Boston: South End Press, 1987.

Kerner, Otto, chairman. *Report of the National Advisory Commission on Civil Disorders: The Kerner Report.* New York: Bantam Books, 1968.

Kessler, Ronald. *The FBI.* New York: Simon & Schuster, 1993.

Kohn, Howard. *The Last Farmer: An American Memoir.* New York: Harper & Row, 1988.

LaBastille, Anne. *Women and Wilderness.* San Francisco: Sierra Club Books, 1980.

Lash, Jonathan, Katherine Gillman, and David Sheridan. *A Season of Spoils.* New York: Pantheon, 1984.

Lien, Carsten. *Olympic Battleground.* San Francisco: Sierra Club Books, 1991.

Limbaugh, Rush. *The Way Things Ought to Be.* New York: Simon & Schuster, 1992.

Logan, Robert A., with Wendy Gibbons and Stacy Kingsbury. *Environmental Issues for the Nineties: A Handbook for Journalists.* Washington, D.C.: Environmental Reporting Forum, 1992.

Lord, Eliot. *Comstock: Mining and Miners.* Berkeley, Calif.: Howell-North, 1959.

Makower, Joel. *The E Factor.* New York: Random House, 1993.

Manes, Christopher. *Green Rage.* Boston: Little, Brown, 1990.

McPhee, John. *Encounters with the Archdruid.* New York: Farrar, Straus and Giroux, 1971.

Miller, Nathan. *Stealing from America.* New York: Paragon House, 1992.

———. *Theodore Roosevelt: A Life.* New York: Morrow, 1992.

Millett, Richard. *Guardians of the Dynasty.* Maryknoll, N.Y.: Orbis Books, 1977.

Mitchell, John G., editor, with Constance L. Stallings. *Ecotactics: The Sierra Club Handbook for Environmental Activists,* Pocket Books Edition. New York: Simon & Schuster, 1970.

Nash, Roderick. *Wilderness and the American Mind.* New Haven, Conn.: Yale University Press, 1967.

Oelschlager, Max, editor. *The Wilderness Condition.* San Francisco: Sierra Club Books, 1992.

Ray, Dixy Lee, with Lou Guzzo. *Trashing the Planet.* New York: Harper Perennial, 1990.

Renshaw, Patrick. *The Wobblies.* Garden City, N.Y.: Doubleday, 1968.

Rifkin, Jeremy. *Beyond Beef.* New York: Dutton, 1992.

Roosevelt, Theodore. *The Works of Theodore Roosevelt.* New York: Scribner's, 1926.

Scarce, Rik. *Eco-Warriors.* Chicago: The Noble Press, 1990.

Shabecoff, Phillip. A *Fierce Green Fire.* New York: Farrar, Straus and Giroux, 1993.

Shanks, Bernard. *This Land Is Your Land.* San Francisco: Sierra Club Books, 1984.

Sheehan, Neil. A *Bright Shining Lie.* New York: Random House, 1988.

Shenton, James P. *History of the United States to 1865.* Garden City, N.Y.: Doubleday, 1963.

Slotkin, Richard. *The Final Frontier: The Myth of the Frontier in the Age of Industrialization, 1800–1890.* New York: Atheneum, 1985.

——. *Gunfighter Nation: The Myth of the Frontier in Twentieth-Century America.* New York: Atheneum, 1992.

Soderberg, K. A., and Jackie DuRette. *People of the Tongass.* Bellevue, Wash.: Free Enterprise Press, 1988.

Strategic Analysis & Fifty State Review. *The Wise Use Movement.* Washington, D.C.: The Wilderness Society, 1993.

Subcommittee on Civil Service of the Committee on Post Office and Civil Service, U.S. House of Representatives. *Interference in Environmental Programs by Political Appointees: The Improper Treatment of a Senior Executive Service Official.* Washington, D.C.: U.S. Government Printing Office, 1993.

Sugarmann, John. *National Rifle Association: Money, Firepower and Fear.* Washington, D.C.: National Press, 1992.

Swasy, Alicia. *Soap Opera—The Inside Story of Procter and Gamble.* New York: Random House, 1993.

Tebbel, John. *The Compact History of the Indian Wars.* New York: Tower Books, 1966.

Turner, Frederick. *Rediscovering America: John Muir in His Time and Ours.* San Francisco: Sierra Club Books, 1985.

Turner, William. *Hoover's FBI.* New York: Dell, 1970.

Vanderwerth, W.C., compiler. *Indian Oratory.* New York: Ballantine, 1971.

Van Strum, Carol. A *Bitter Fog: Herbicides and Human Rights.* San Francisco: Sierra Club Books, 1983.

Walls, David. *The Activist's Almanac.* New York: Simon & Schuster, 1993.

Wasserman, Harvey. *Wasserman's History of the United States.* New York: Harper and Row, 1972.

Wilkinson, Charles F., *Crossing the Next Meridian.* Washington, D.C.: Island Press, 1992.

Woodward, Bob. *Veil: The Secret Wars of the CIA, 1981–1987.* New York: Pocket Books, 1987.

Zakin, Susan. *Coyotes and Town Dogs.* New York: Penguin, 1993.

Zinn, Howard. A *People's History of the United States.* New York: Harper Perennial, 1990.

Index